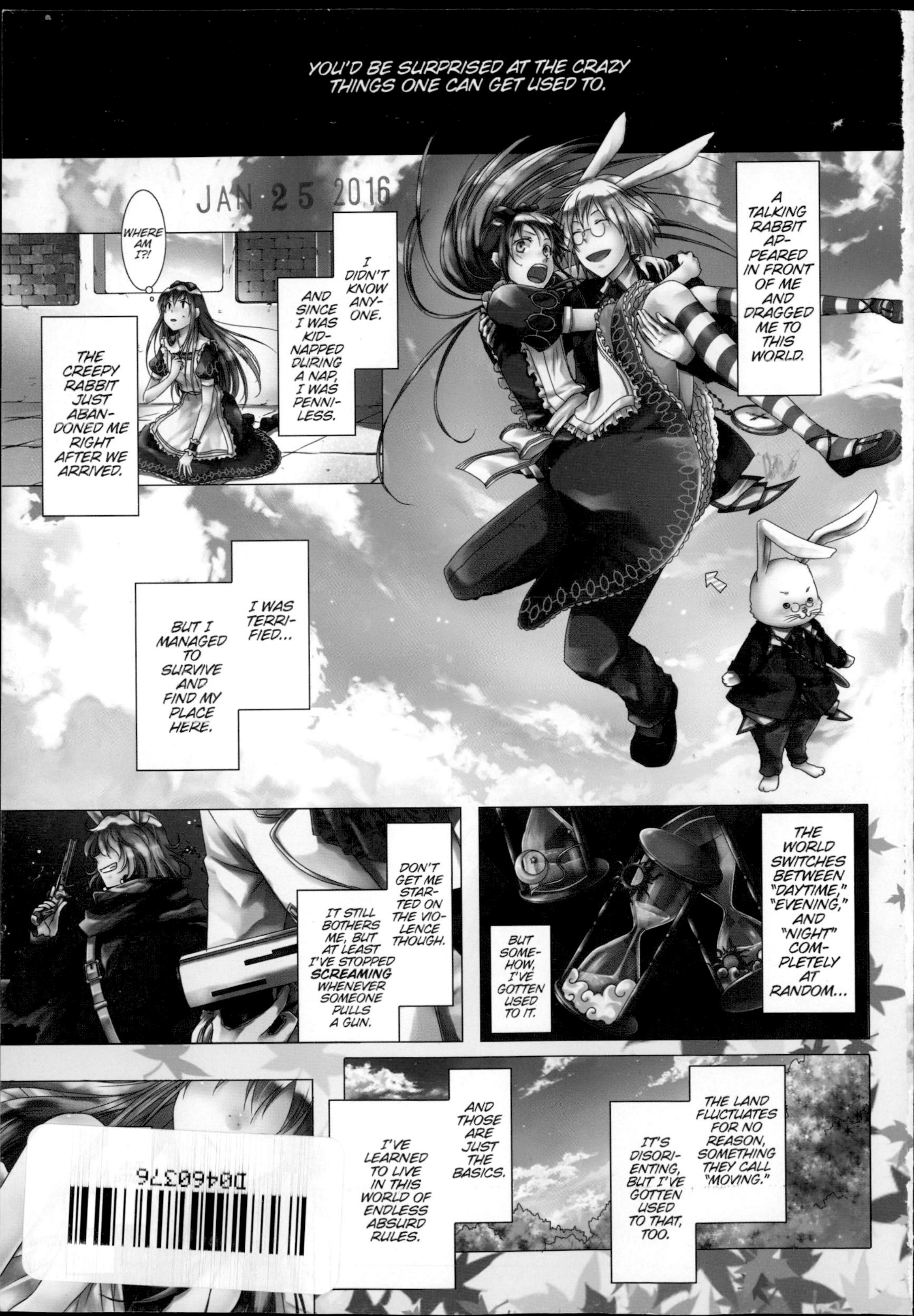

YOU'D BE SURPRISED AT THE CRAZY THINGS ONE CAN GET USED TO.
A TALKING RABBIT APPEARED IN FRONT OF ME AND DRAGGED ME TO THIS WORLD.
I DIDN'T KNOW ANYONE.
AND SINCE I WAS KIDNAPPED DURING A NAP, I WAS PENNILESS.
WHERE AM I?!
THE CREEPY RABBIT JUST ABANDONED ME RIGHT AFTER WE ARRIVED.
I WAS TERRIFIED...
BUT I MANAGED TO SURVIVE AND FIND MY PLACE HERE.
THE WORLD SWITCHES BETWEEN "DAYTIME," "EVENING," AND "NIGHT" COMPLETELY AT RANDOM...
BUT SOMEHOW, I'VE GOTTEN USED TO IT.
DON'T GET ME STARTED ON THE VIOLENCE THOUGH.
IT STILL BOTHERS ME, BUT AT LEAST I'VE STOPPED **SCREAMING** WHENEVER SOMEONE PULLS A GUN.
THE LAND FLUCTUATES FOR NO REASON, SOMETHING THEY CALL "MOVING."
IT'S DISORIENTING, BUT I'VE GOTTEN USED TO THAT, TOO.
AND THOSE ARE JUST THE BASICS.
I'VE LEARNED TO LIVE IN THIS WORLD OF ENDLESS ABSURD RULES.

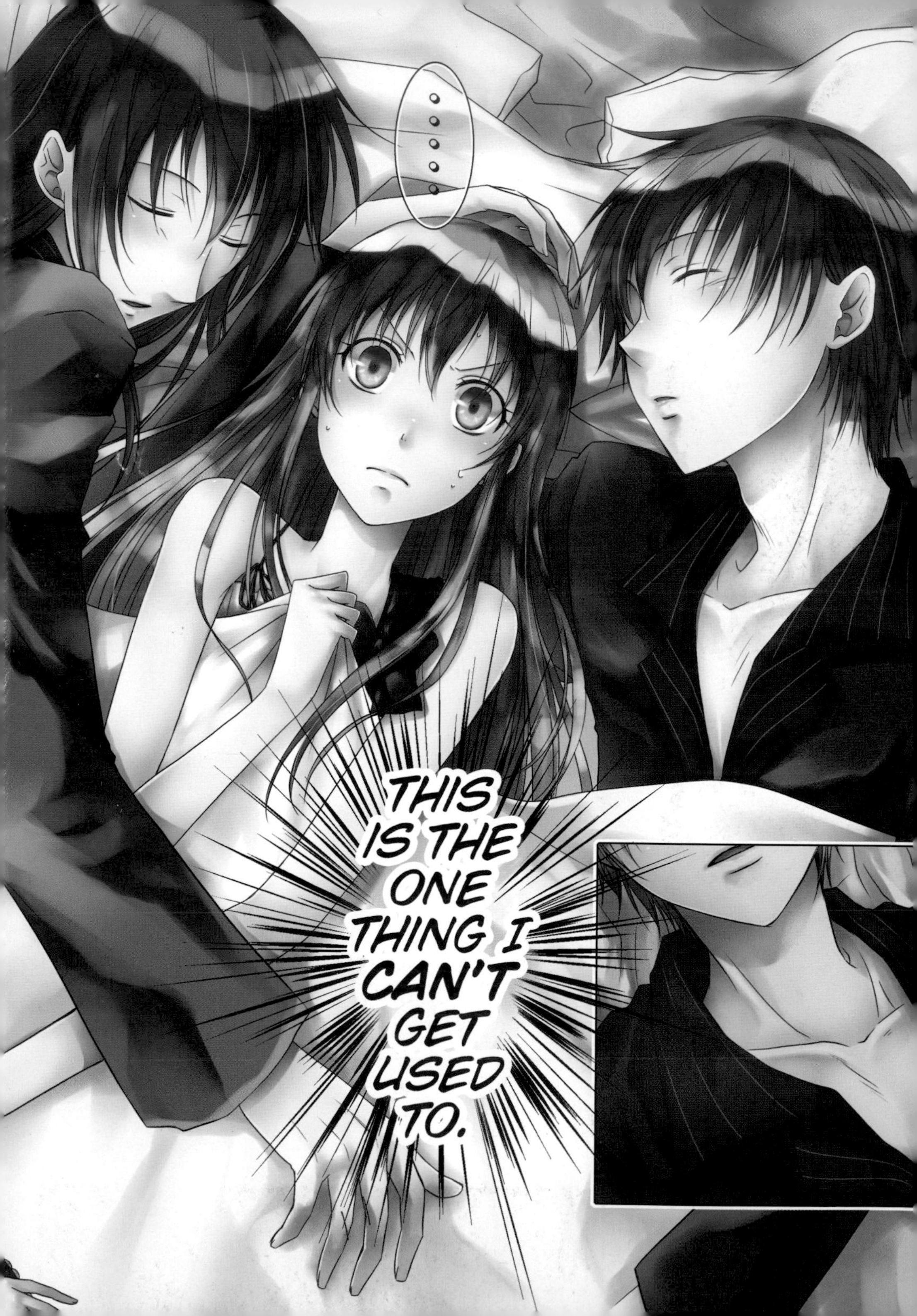
.....
THIS IS THE ONE THING I CAN'T GET USED TO.

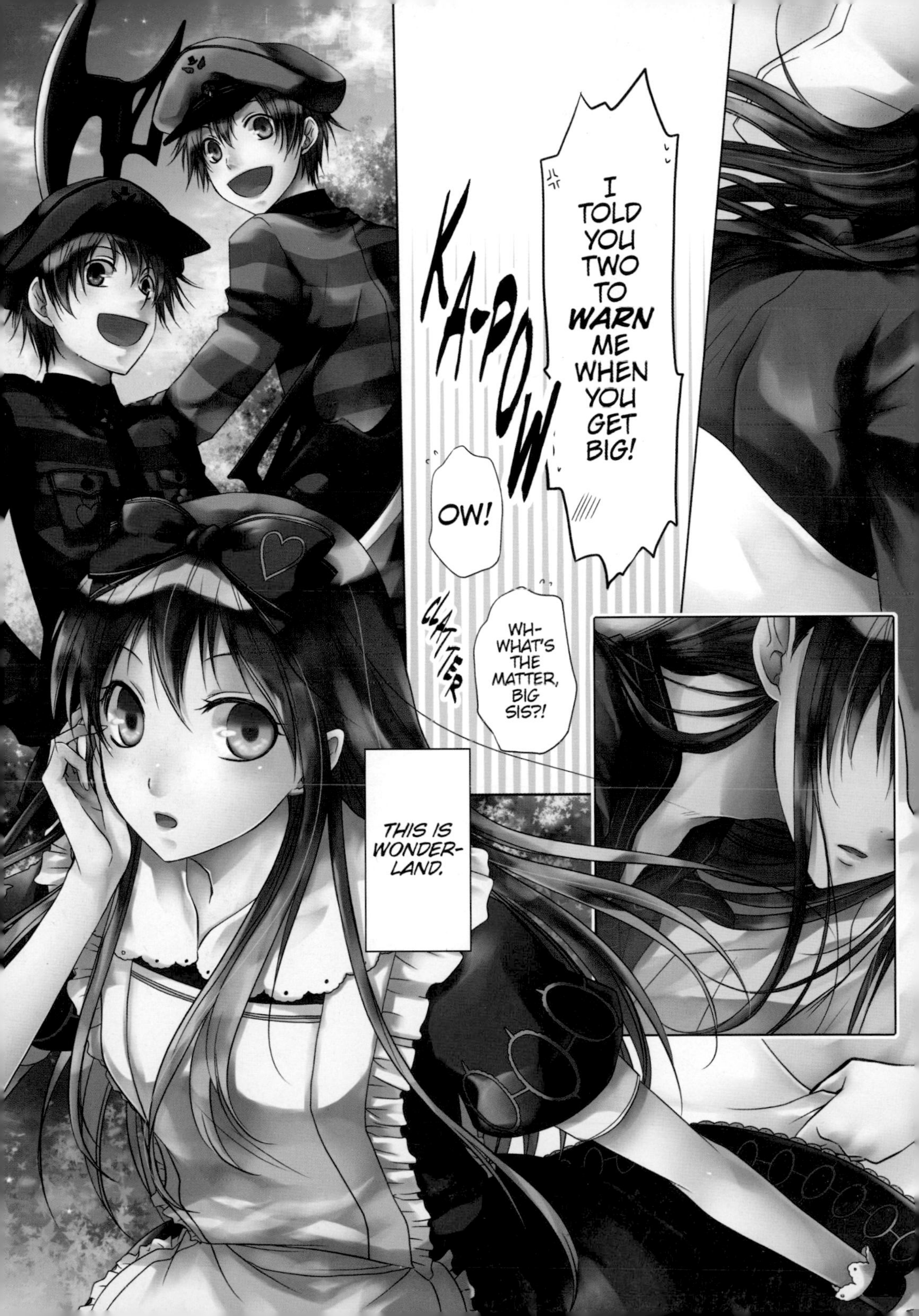
I TOLD YOU TWO TO WARN ME WHEN YOU GET BIG!
KA-POW
OW!
WH-WHAT'S THE MATTER, BIG SIS?!
CLATTER
THIS IS WONDERLAND.

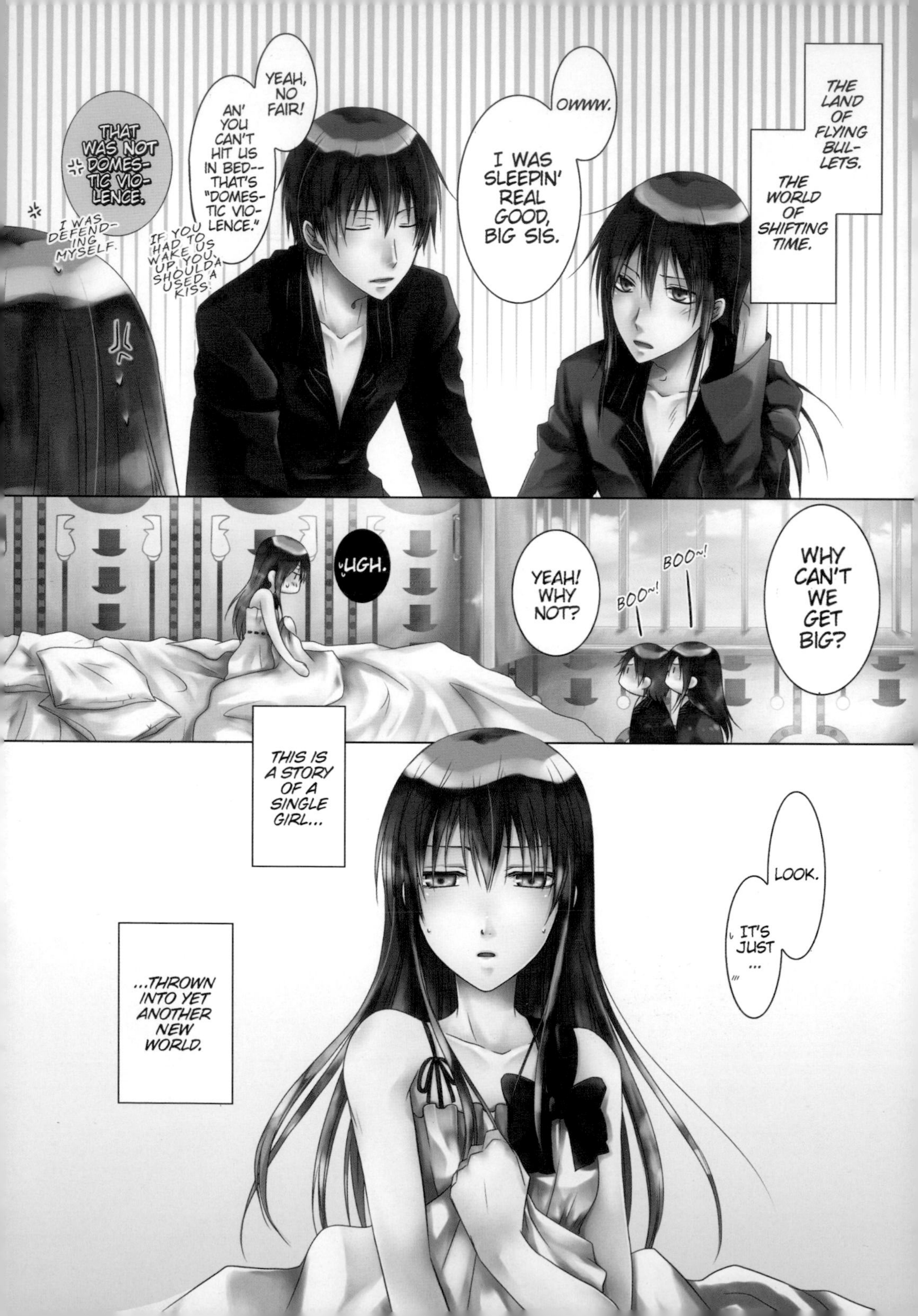
THE LAND OF FLYING BULLETS.
THE WORLD OF SHIFTING TIME.
OWWW.
I WAS SLEEPIN' REAL GOOD, BIG SIS.
YEAH, NO FAIR!
AN' YOU CAN'T HIT US IN BED--THAT'S "DOMESTIC VIOLENCE."
IF YOU HAD TO WAKE US UP, YOU SHOULDA USED A KISS.
THAT WAS NOT DOMESTIC VIOLENCE.
I WAS DEFENDING MYSELF.
WHY CAN'T WE GET BIG?
BOO~!
BOO~!
YEAH! WHY NOT?
UGH.
LOOK.
IT'S JUST...
THIS IS A STORY OF A SINGLE GIRL...
...THROWN INTO YET ANOTHER NEW WORLD.

Alice in the Country of Clover
~Bloody Twins~

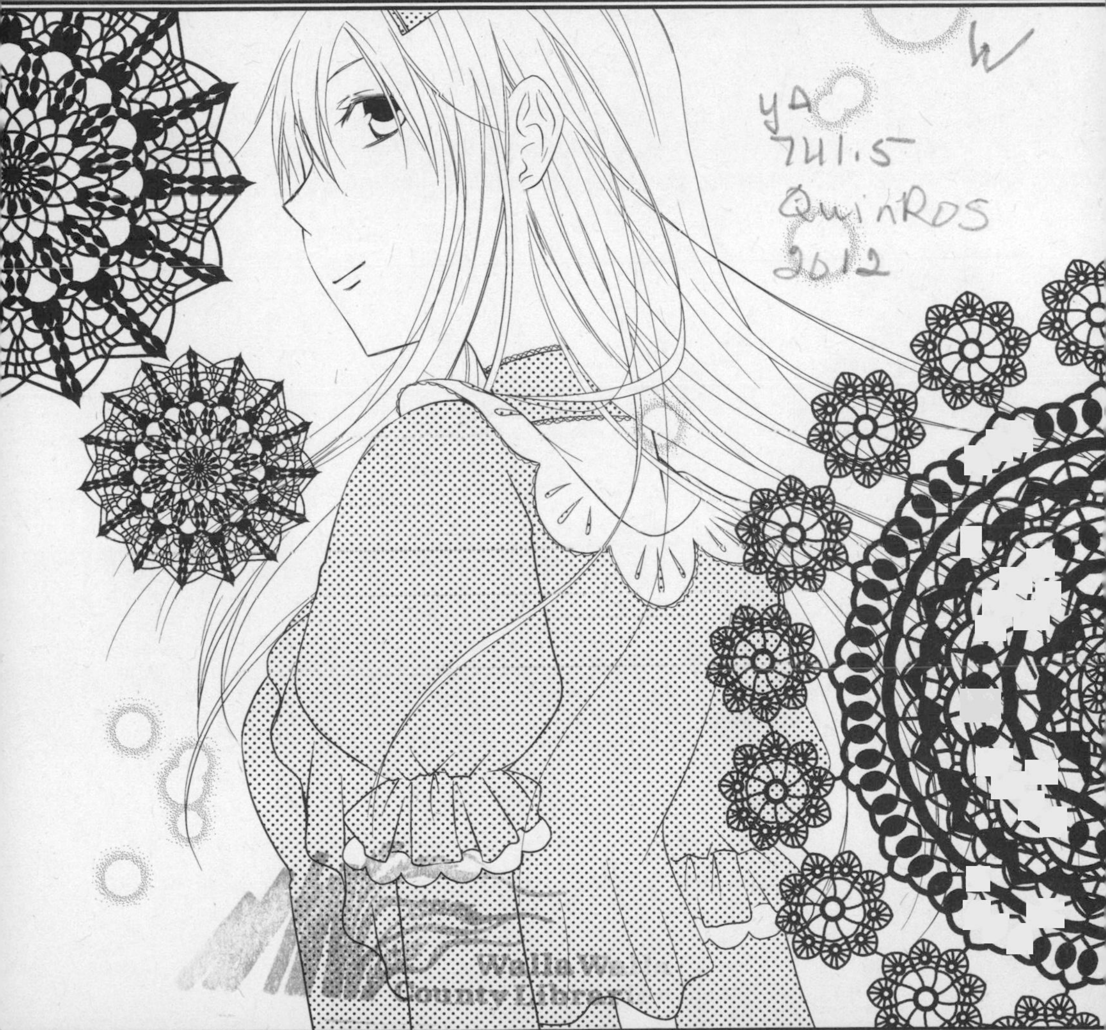

Mamenosuke Fujimaru
藤丸 豆ノ介

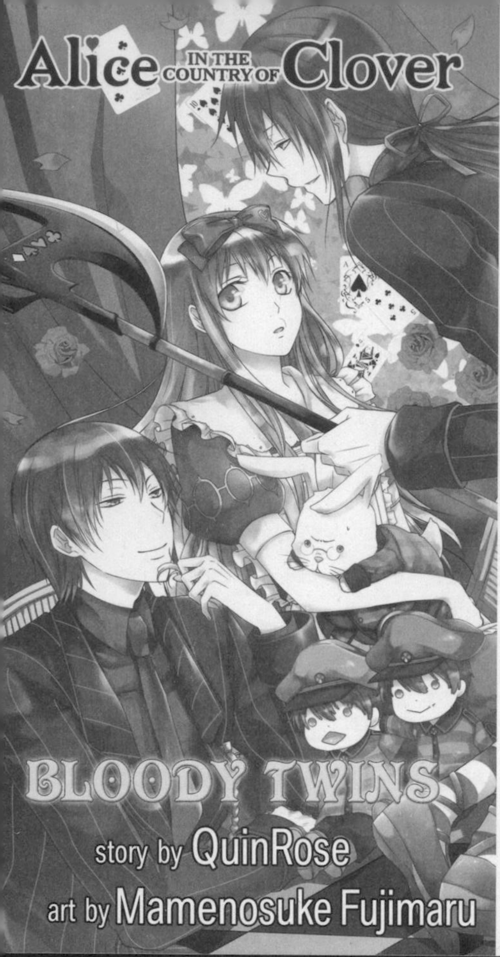
Alice IN THE COUNTRY OF Clover
BLOODY TWINS
story by QuinRose
art by Mamenosuke Fujimaru

STAFF CREDITS

translation Angela Liu
adaptation Lianne Sentar
lettering Roland Amago
layout Bambi Eloriaga-Amago
cover design Nicky Lim
copy editor Shanti Whitesides
editor Adam Arnold

publisher Jason DeAngelis
Seven Seas Entertainment

ALICE IN THE COUNTRY OF CLOVER: BLOODY TWINS

First published in Japan in 2009 by ICHIJINSHA Inc., Tokyo.
English translation rights arranged with ICHIJINSHA Inc., Tokyo, Japan.

ISBN: 978-1-935934-90-5

Printed in Canada

First Printing: June 2012

10 9 8 7

Seven Seas

READING DIRECTIONS

This book reads from *right to left*, Japanese style. If this is your first time reading manga, you start reading from the top right panel on each page and take it from there. If you get lost, just follow the numbered diagram here. It may seem backwards at first, but you'll get the hang of it! Have fun!!

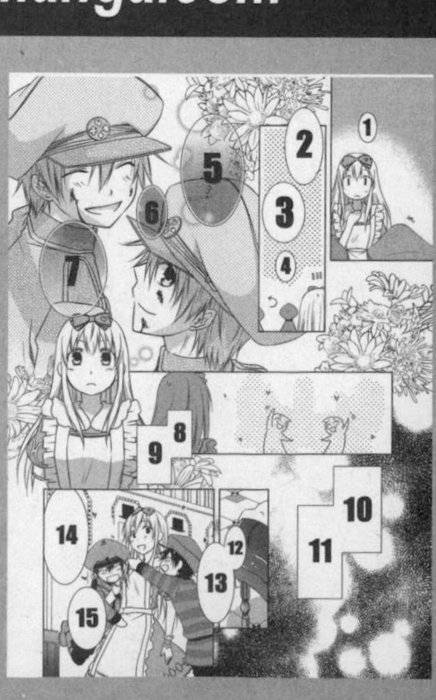
1
2
3
4
5
6
7
8
9
10
11
12
13
14
15

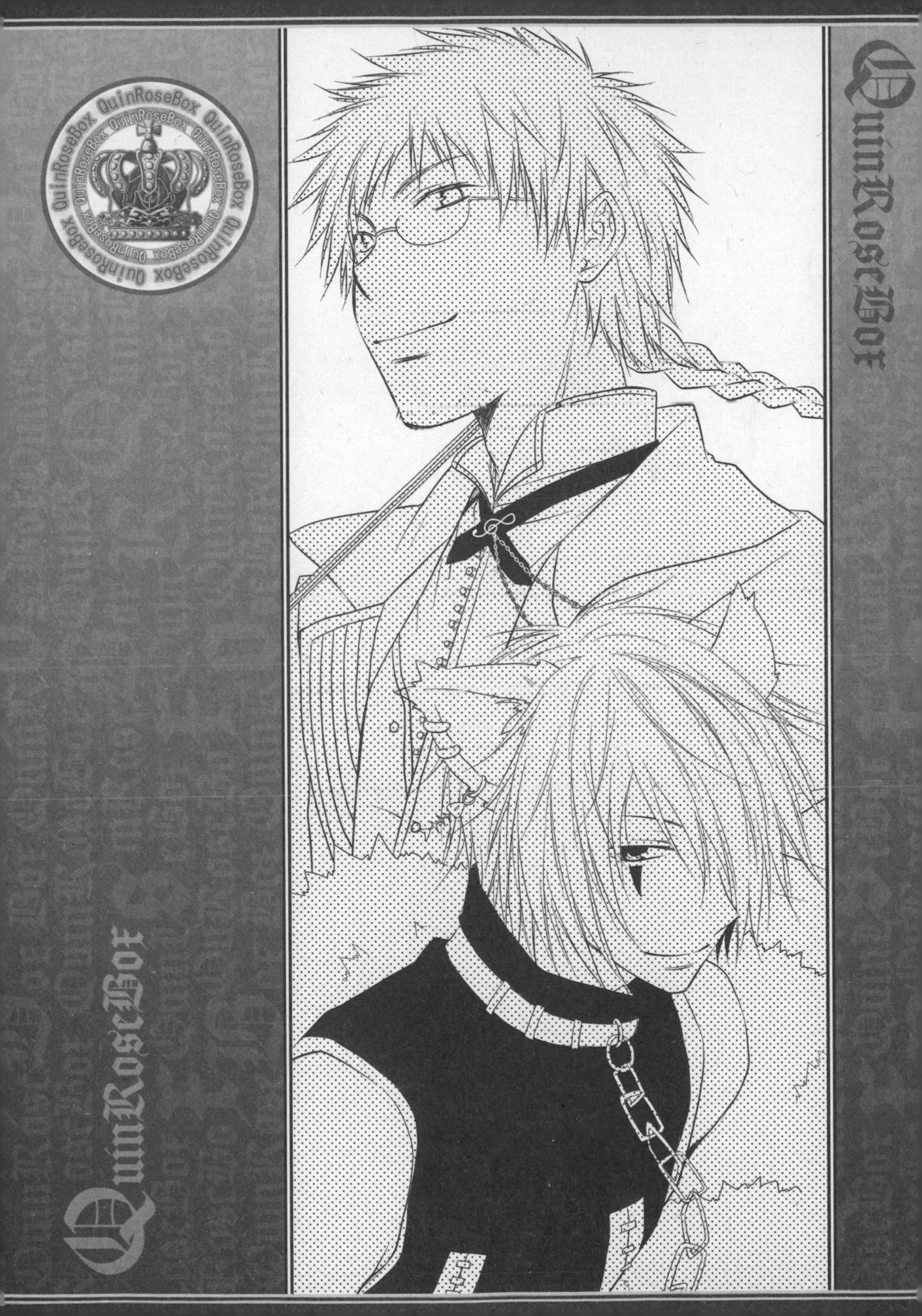
QuinRoseBox
QuinRoseBox
QuinRoseBox

Alice in the Country of Hearts

ハートの国の
アリス

~Wonderful Wonder World~

- STORY -

This is a love adventure game based on *Alice in Wonderland* that develops into a completely different storyline.

The main character is far from a romantic. In fact, she's especially sick of love relationships.

She's pulled (against her will) into the dangerous Country of Hearts, where only the buildings and groceries are peaceful. The Hatters are a mafia family and even the employees of the Amusement Park carry weapons.

The leaders of the inhabitants are constantly trying to kill each other. Many of the skirmishes are the result of territory grabs by three major powers trying to control more land: the Hatter, the Queen of Hearts, and Gowland.

After drinking some strange medicine (again, against her will), the main character is unable to return to her world. She quickly decides that she's trapped in a dream and allows herself to enjoy(?) the extraordinary experience she's been thrown into.

What territory will she stay with and who will she interact with to get herself home?
And will this girl, so jaded about love, fall into a relationship she doesn't expect?

Alice in Country of Hearts
Character Information

Elliot March
VA: Tsuguo Mogami

The No. 2 of the Hatter Family and Blood's right-hand man, Elliot is an ex-criminal and an escaped convict. Very short-tempered, he used to be a "very bad guy" who shot before asking questions. After partnering up with Blood, he rounded out and changed to a "slightly bad guy" who thinks for about three seconds before shooting. In his mind, this is a vast improvement.

Blood Dupre
VA: Katsuyuki Konishi

The dangerous leader of the crime syndicate known as the Hatter Family. Since he enjoys plotting more than working directly, he controls everything from the shadows. He's incredibly smart, but due to his temperamental moods and his desire to keep things "interesting," he often digs his own grave in his secret plans.

Alice Liddell
VA: Rie Kugimiya

She grew up to be a responsible young woman after losing her mother early, but Alice still carries a complex toward her older sister. She respects her older sister very much, but is frustrated about always being compared to her. Since her first love fell for her older sister, she has no confidence in herself when it comes to romance.

Vivaldi
VA: Yuuko Kaida

Ruthless and cruel, the Queen of Hearts is an arrogant beauty with a wild temper. She's enemies with the Hatter and Gowland. Impatient at heart, Vivaldi takes her fury out on everyone around her including her subordinates, whom she considers pawns. Anyone **not** working for her doesn't even register as existing.

Tweedle Dum
VA: Jun Fukuyama

The second "Bloody Twin" and a dead ringer for his brother—in both appearance and personality. As they often change places, it's uncertain which one is the older twin.

Tweedle Dee
VA: Jun Fukuyama

Gatekeeper of the Hatter territory, and one of the dark, sneaky twins. They sometimes show an innocent side, but they usually have a malicious agenda. Also known as the "Bloody Twins" due to their unsavory activities.

Ace
VA: Daisuke Hirakawa

The knight of Hearts and the ex-subordinate of Vivaldi. He's left the castle and is currently wandering. He's a very unlucky and unfortunate man, yet remains strangely positive, thus he tends to plow forward and make mistakes that only worsen his situation. He's one of the few friends of the clockmaker, Julius.

Julius Monrey
VA: Takehito Koyasu

The clockmaker, a gloomy machine expert who easily falls into depression. He lives in the Clock Tower and doesn't get out much. He always thinks of everything in the most negative way and tends to distrust people, but he gets along with Ace. He had some part in the imprisonment of the March Hare, Elliot, and is thus the target of Elliot's hatred.

Peter White
VA: Kouki Miyata

Don't be fooled by the cute ears—Peter is the dangerous guide who dragged Alice to Wonderland in the first place. He claims to always be worried about the time, despite having a strange grasp on it. Rumors say his heart is as black as his hair is white.

Nightmare
VA: Tomokazu Sugita

A sickly nightmare. He appears in Alice's dream, sometimes to guide her—and other times, to **misguide** her.

Mary Gowland
VA: Kenyuu Horiuchi

The owner of the Amusement Park. He hides his hated first name, Mary, but pretty much everyone already knows it. His full name is a play on words that sounds like "Merry Go Round" when said quickly. If his musical talent was given a numerical value, it would be closer to negatives than zero.

Boris Airay
VA: Noriaki Sugiyama

A riddle-loving cat with his signature smirk. He sometimes gives hints to his riddles, but the hints usually just cause more confusion. He also has a tendency to pose questions and never answer them.

The World of "Alice"

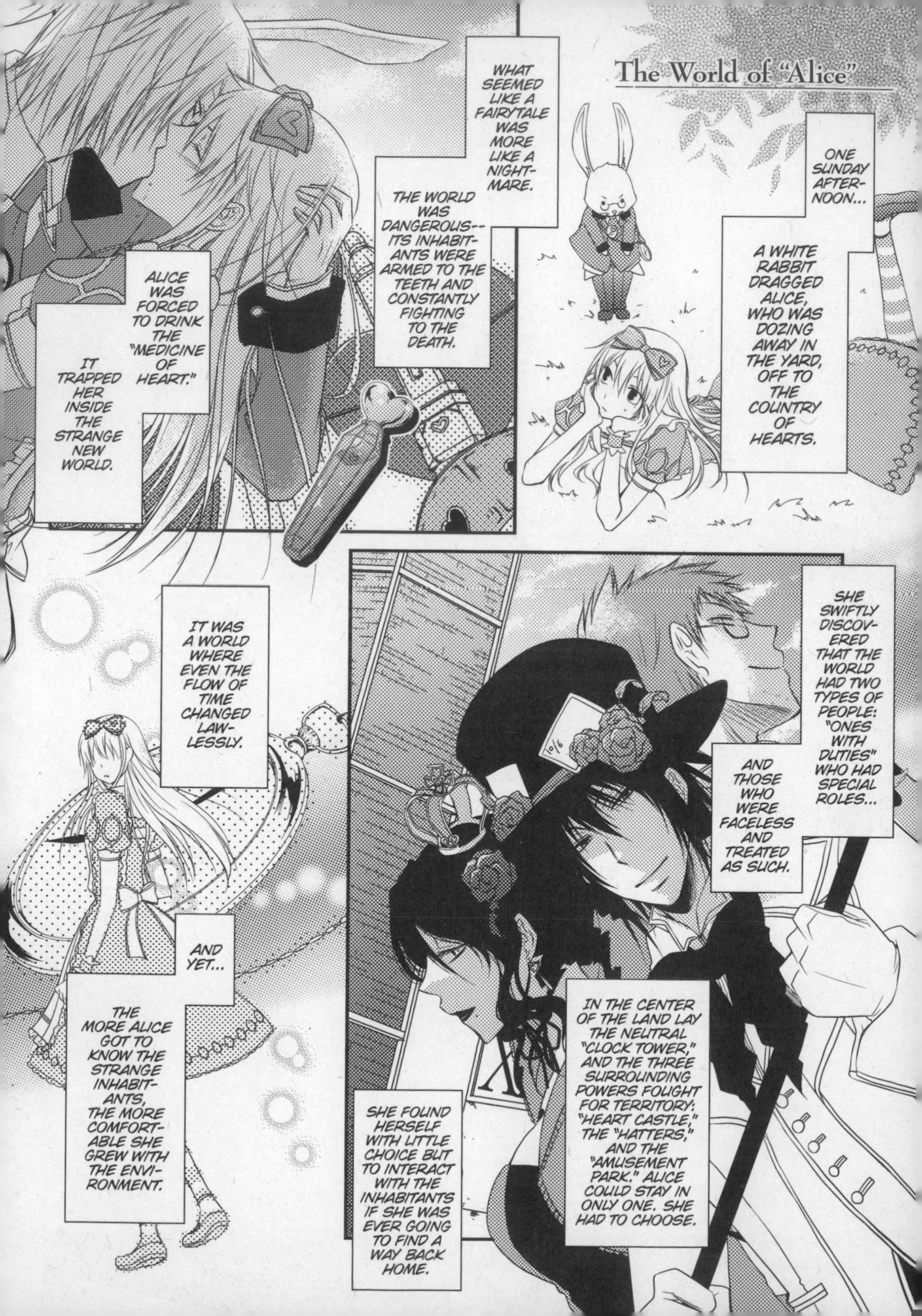
ONE SUNDAY AFTERNOON...
A WHITE RABBIT DRAGGED ALICE, WHO WAS DOZING AWAY IN THE YARD, OFF TO THE COUNTRY OF HEARTS.
WHAT SEEMED LIKE A FAIRYTALE WAS MORE LIKE A NIGHTMARE.
THE WORLD WAS DANGEROUS--ITS INHABITANTS WERE ARMED TO THE TEETH AND CONSTANTLY FIGHTING TO THE DEATH.
ALICE WAS FORCED TO DRINK THE "MEDICINE OF HEART."
IT TRAPPED HER INSIDE THE STRANGE NEW WORLD.
SHE SWIFTLY DISCOVERED THAT THE WORLD HAD TWO TYPES OF PEOPLE: "ONES WITH DUTIES" WHO HAD SPECIAL ROLES...
AND THOSE WHO WERE FACELESS AND TREATED AS SUCH.
IN THE CENTER OF THE LAND LAY THE NEUTRAL "CLOCK TOWER," AND THE THREE SURROUNDING POWERS FOUGHT FOR TERRITORY: "HEART CASTLE," THE "HATTERS," AND THE "AMUSEMENT PARK." ALICE COULD STAY IN ONLY ONE. SHE HAD TO CHOOSE.
SHE FOUND HERSELF WITH LITTLE CHOICE BUT TO INTERACT WITH THE INHABITANTS IF SHE WAS EVER GOING TO FIND A WAY BACK HOME.
IT WAS A WORLD WHERE EVEN THE FLOW OF TIME CHANGED LAWLESSLY.
AND YET...
THE MORE ALICE GOT TO KNOW THE STRANGE INHABITANTS, THE MORE COMFORTABLE SHE GREW WITH THE ENVIRONMENT.

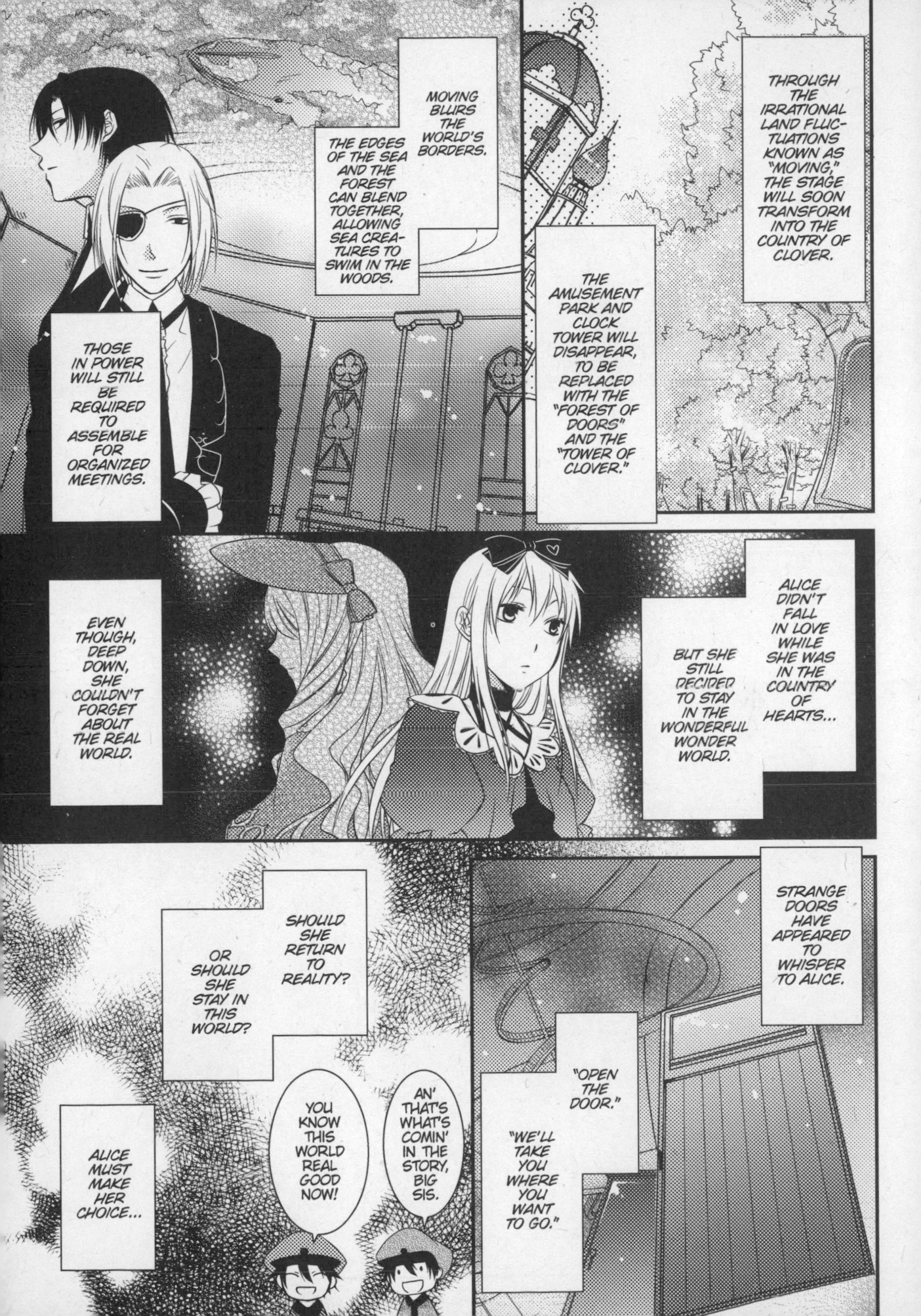
THROUGH THE IRRATIONAL LAND FLUCTUATIONS KNOWN AS "MOVING," THE STAGE WILL SOON TRANSFORM INTO THE COUNTRY OF CLOVER.
THE AMUSEMENT PARK AND CLOCK TOWER WILL DISAPPEAR, TO BE REPLACED WITH THE "FOREST OF DOORS" AND THE "TOWER OF CLOVER."
MOVING BLURS THE WORLD'S BORDERS.
THE EDGES OF THE SEA AND THE FOREST CAN BLEND TOGETHER, ALLOWING SEA CREATURES TO SWIM IN THE WOODS.
THOSE IN POWER WILL STILL BE REQUIRED TO ASSEMBLE FOR ORGANIZED MEETINGS.
ALICE DIDN'T FALL IN LOVE WHILE SHE WAS IN THE COUNTRY OF HEARTS...
BUT SHE STILL DECIDED TO STAY IN THE WONDERFUL WONDER WORLD.
EVEN THOUGH, DEEP DOWN, SHE COULDN'T FORGET ABOUT THE REAL WORLD.
STRANGE DOORS HAVE APPEARED TO WHISPER TO ALICE.
"OPEN THE DOOR."
"WE'LL TAKE YOU WHERE YOU WANT TO GO."
SHOULD SHE RETURN TO REALITY?
OR SHOULD SHE STAY IN THIS WORLD?
AN' THAT'S WHAT'S COMIN' IN THE STORY, BIG SIS.
YOU KNOW THIS WORLD REAL GOOD NOW!
ALICE MUST MAKE HER CHOICE...

Alice in the Country of Clover
クローバーの国の
アリス
~Wonderful Wonder World~

- STORY -

In *Alice in the Country of Clover*, the game starts with Alice having not fallen in love, but still deciding to stay in Wonderland.

She's acquainted with all the characters from the previous game, *Alice in the Country of Hearts*.

Since love would now start from a place of friendship rather than passion with a new stranger, she can experience a different type of romance from that in the previous game. Her dynamic with the characters is different through this friendship—characters can't always be forceful with her, and in many ways it's more comfortable to grow intimate. The relationships *between* the Ones With Duties have also become more of a factor.

In this game, the story focuses on the mafia. Alice attends the suited meetings (forcefully) and gets involved in various gunfights (forcefully), among other things.

Land fluctuations, sea creatures in the forest, and whispering doors—it's a game more fantastic and more eerie than the first.

Will our everywoman Alice be able to have a romantic relationship in a world devoid of common sense?

Alice in the Country of Clover
Character Information

Elliot March
VA: Tsuguo Mogami

Blood's right-hand man has a criminal past... and a temperamental present. But he's not as bad as he used to be, so that's something. Joining Blood has been good(?) for him.

Blood Dupre
VA: Katsuyuki Konishi

The head of the mafia Hatter Family, Blood is a cunning yet moody puppet-master. Alice now has the pleasure of having him for a landlord.

Alice Liddell
VA: Rie Kugimiya

A normal girl with a bit of a chip on her shoulder. Deciding to stay in the Wonderland she was carried to, she's adapted to her strange new lifestyle.

Vivaldi
VA: Yuuko Kaida

The beautiful Queen of Hearts has an unrivaled temper—which is really saying something in Wonderland. Although a picture-perfect Mad Queen, she cares for Alice as if Alice were her little sister...or a very interesting plaything.

Tweedle Dum
VA: Jun Fukuyama

The second "Bloody Twin" is equally cute and equally scary. In *Clover*, Dum can also turn into an adult.

Tweedle Dee
VA: Jun Fukuyama

One of the "Bloody Twin" gatekeepers of the Hatter territory, Dee can be cute when he's not being terrifying. In *Clover*, he sometimes turns into an adult.

Boris Airay
VA: Noriaki Sugiyama

This riddle-loving cat has a signature smirk—and in *Clover*, a new toy. One of his favorite pastimes is giving the Sleepy Mouse a hard time.

Ace
VA: Daisuke Hirakawa

The unlucky knight of Hearts was a former subordinate of Vivaldi and is perpetually lost. Even though he's depressed to be separated from his friend and boss Julius, he stays positive and tries to overcome it with a smile. He seems like a classic nice guy... or is he?

Peter White
VA: Kouki Miyata

The Prime Minister of Heart Castle—who has rabbit ears growing out of his head—invited (kidnapped) Alice to Wonderland. He loves Alice and hates everything else. His cruel, irrational actions are disturbing, but he acts like a completely different person (rabbit?) when in the throes of his love for Alice.

Gray Ringmarc
VA: Kazuya Nakai

Nightmare's subordinate in *Clover*. He used to have strong social ambition and considered assassinating Nightmare... but since Nightmare was such a useless boss, Gray couldn't help but feel sorry for him and ended up a dedicated assistant. He's a sound thinker with a strong work ethic. He's also highly skilled with his blades, rivaling even Ace.

Nightmare Gottschalk
VA: Tomokazu Sugita

A sickly nightmare who hates the hospital and needles. He has the power to read people's thoughts and enter dreams. Even though he likes to shut himself away in dreams, Gray drags him out to sulk from time to time. He technically holds a high position and has many subordinates, but since he can't even take care of his own health, he leaves most things to Gray.

Pierce Villiers
VA: Souichirou Hoshi

New to *Clover*, Pierce is an insomniac mouse who drinks too much coffee. He loves Nightmare (who can help him sleep) and hates Boris (who terrifies him). He dislikes Blood and Vivaldi for discarding coffee in favor of tea. He likes Elliot and Peter well enough, since rabbits aren't natural predators of mice.

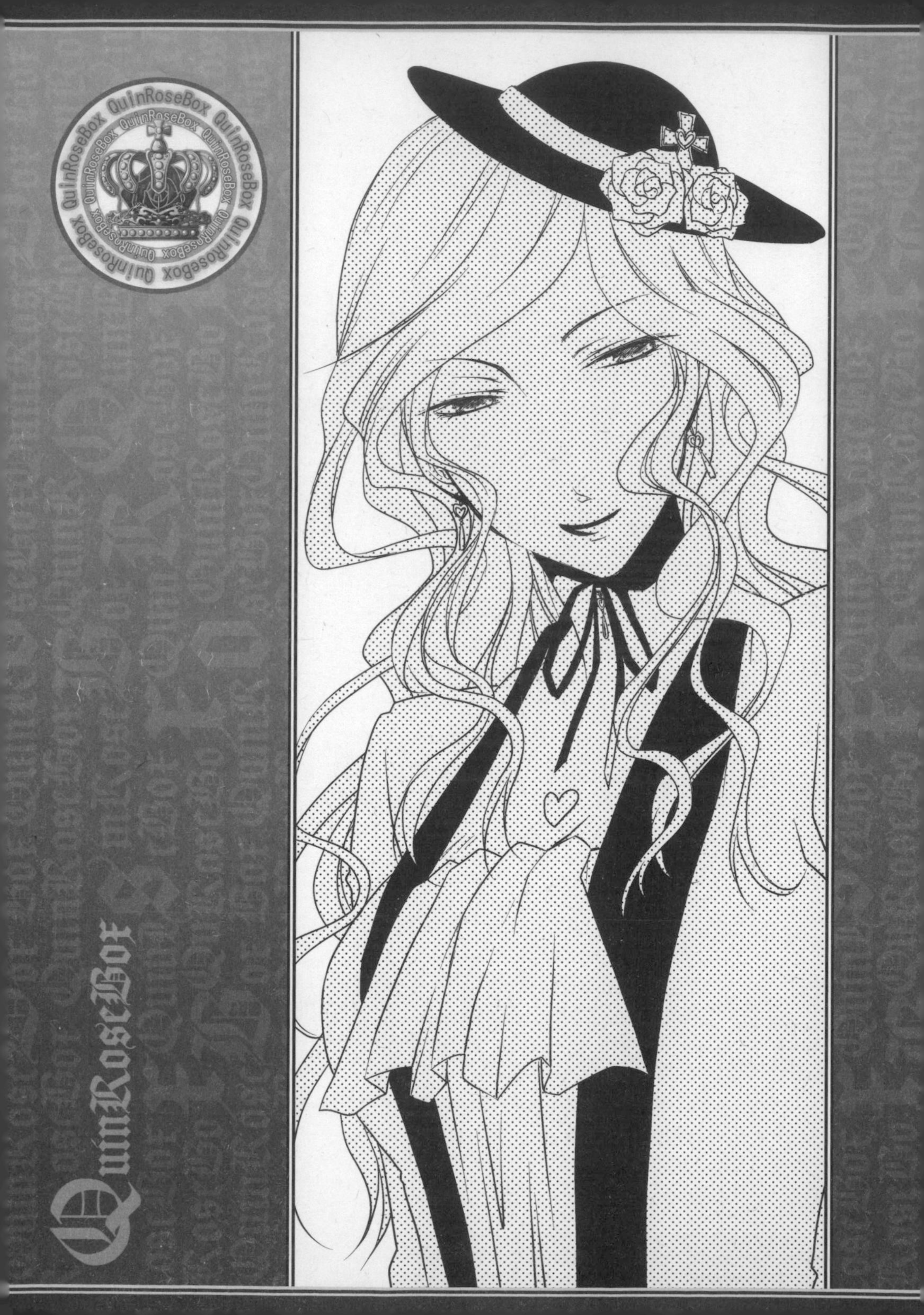
QuinRoseBox

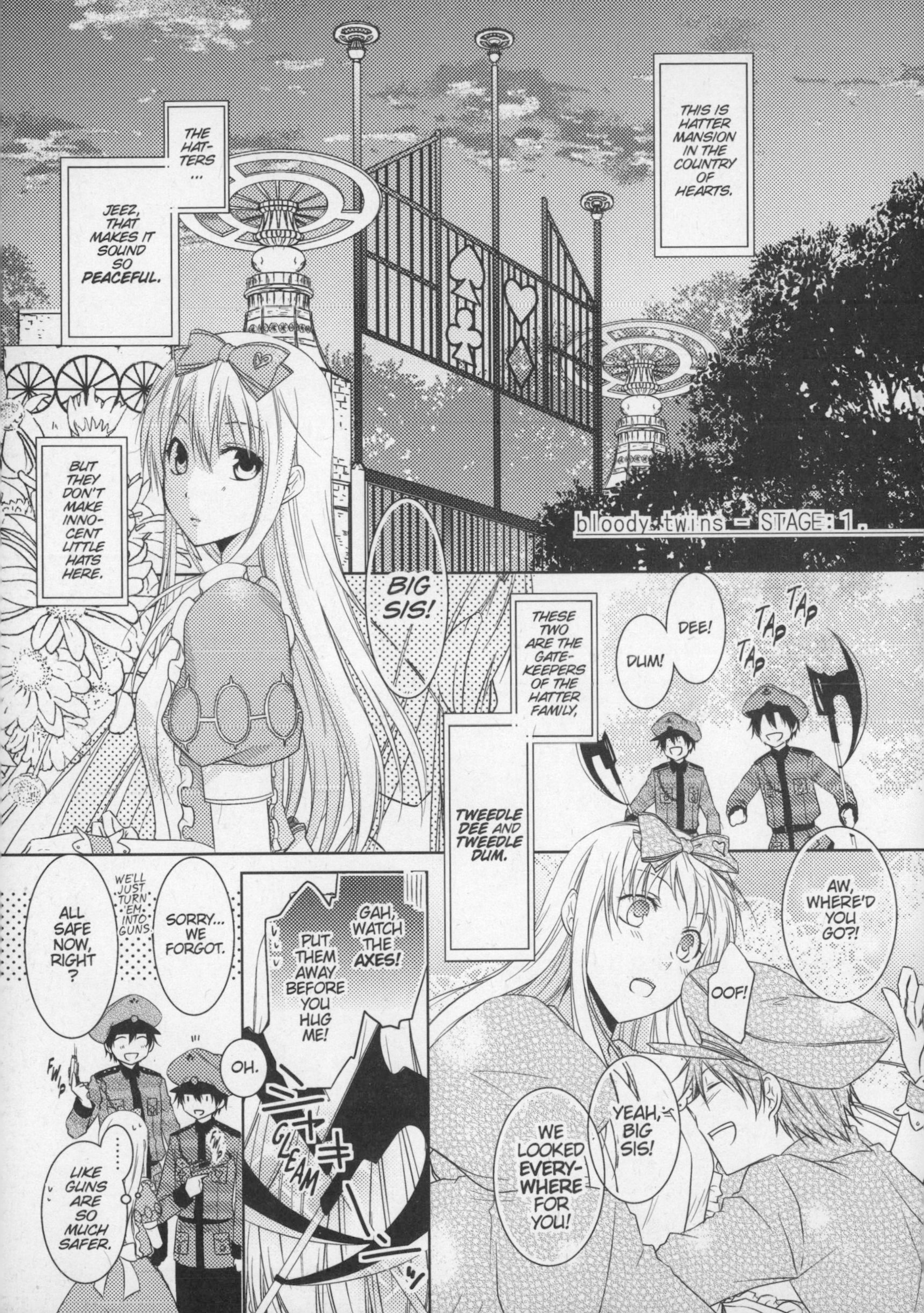
THIS IS HATTER MANSION IN THE COUNTRY OF HEARTS.
THE HATTERS...
JEEZ, THAT MAKES IT SOUND SO PEACEFUL.
BUT THEY DON'T MAKE INNOCENT LITTLE HATS HERE.
bloody twins - STAGE:1.
BIG SIS!
TAP TAP TAP
DEE!
DUM!
THESE TWO ARE THE GATEKEEPERS OF THE HATTER FAMILY,
TWEEDLE DEE AND TWEEDLE DUM.
AW, WHERE'D YOU GO?!
OOF!
YEAH, BIG SIS!
WE LOOKED EVERYWHERE FOR YOU!
GAH, WATCH THE AXES!
PUT THEM AWAY BEFORE YOU HUG ME!
OH.
GLEAM
SORRY... WE FORGOT.
WE'LL JUST TURN 'EM INTO GUNS.
ALL SAFE NOW, RIGHT?
FWIP
......
LIKE GUNS ARE SO MUCH SAFER.

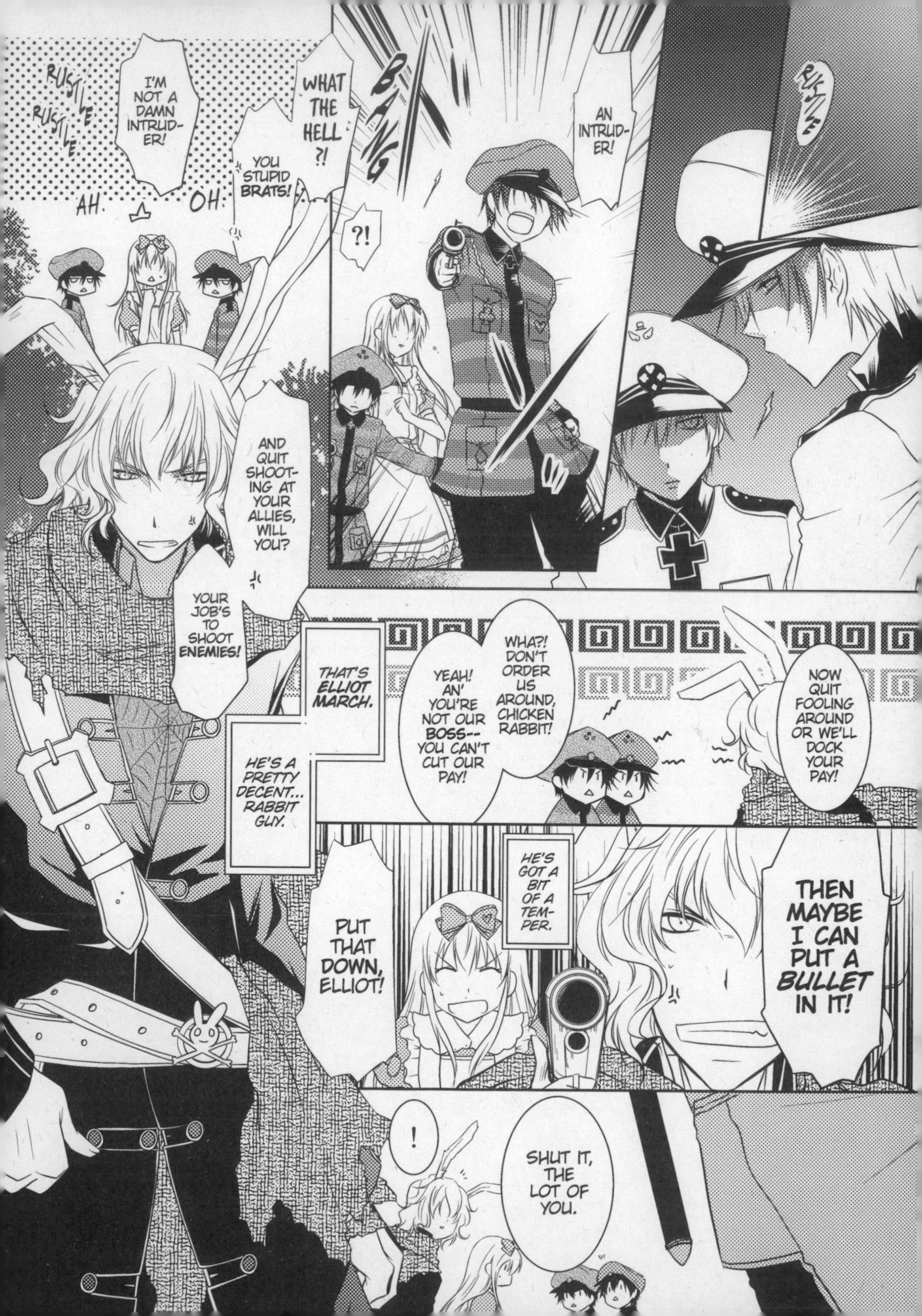
RUSTLE
AN INTRUDER!
BANG
WHAT THE HELL?!
?!
I'M NOT A DAMN INTRUDER!
RUSTLE RUSTLE
YOU STUPID BRATS!
OH.
AH.
AND QUIT SHOOTING AT YOUR ALLIES, WILL YOU?
YOUR JOB'S TO SHOOT ENEMIES!
THAT'S ELLIOT MARCH.
HE'S A PRETTY DECENT... RABBIT GUY.
NOW QUIT FOOLING AROUND OR WE'LL DOCK YOUR PAY!
WHA?! DON'T ORDER US AROUND, CHICKEN RABBIT!
YEAH! AN' YOU'RE NOT OUR BOSS-- YOU CAN'T CUT OUR PAY!
THEN MAYBE I CAN PUT A BULLET IN IT!
HE'S GOT A BIT OF A TEMPER.
PUT THAT DOWN, ELLIOT!
SHUT IT, THE LOT OF YOU.
!

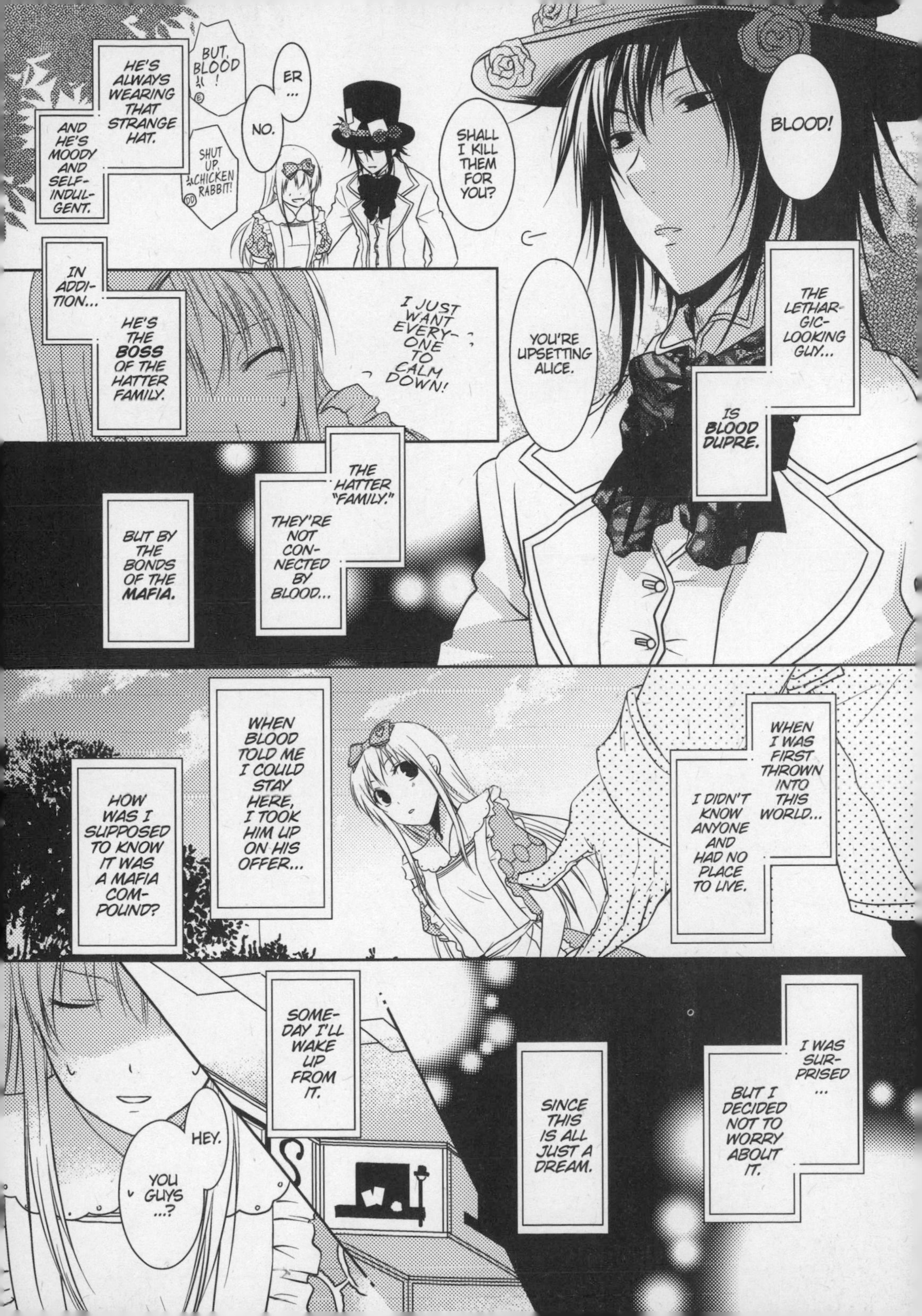
BLOOD!
THE LETHARGIC-LOOKING GUY...
YOU'RE UPSETTING ALICE.
IS BLOOD DUPRE.
SHALL I KILL THEM FOR YOU?
ER...
NO.
BUT, BLOOD!
SHUT UP, CHICKEN RABBIT!
HE'S ALWAYS WEARING THAT STRANGE HAT.
AND HE'S MOODY AND SELF-INDULGENT.
I JUST WANT EVERYONE TO CALM DOWN!
IN ADDITION...
HE'S THE BOSS OF THE HATTER FAMILY.
THE HATTER "FAMILY."
THEY'RE NOT CONNECTED BY BLOOD...
BUT BY THE BONDS OF THE MAFIA.
WHEN I WAS FIRST THROWN INTO THIS WORLD...
I DIDN'T KNOW ANYONE AND HAD NO PLACE TO LIVE.
WHEN BLOOD TOLD ME I COULD STAY HERE, I TOOK HIM UP ON HIS OFFER...
HOW WAS I SUPPOSED TO KNOW IT WAS A MAFIA COMPOUND?
I WAS SURPRISED...
BUT I DECIDED NOT TO WORRY ABOUT IT.
SINCE THIS IS ALL JUST A DREAM.
SOMEDAY I'LL WAKE UP FROM IT.
HEY.
YOU GUYS...?

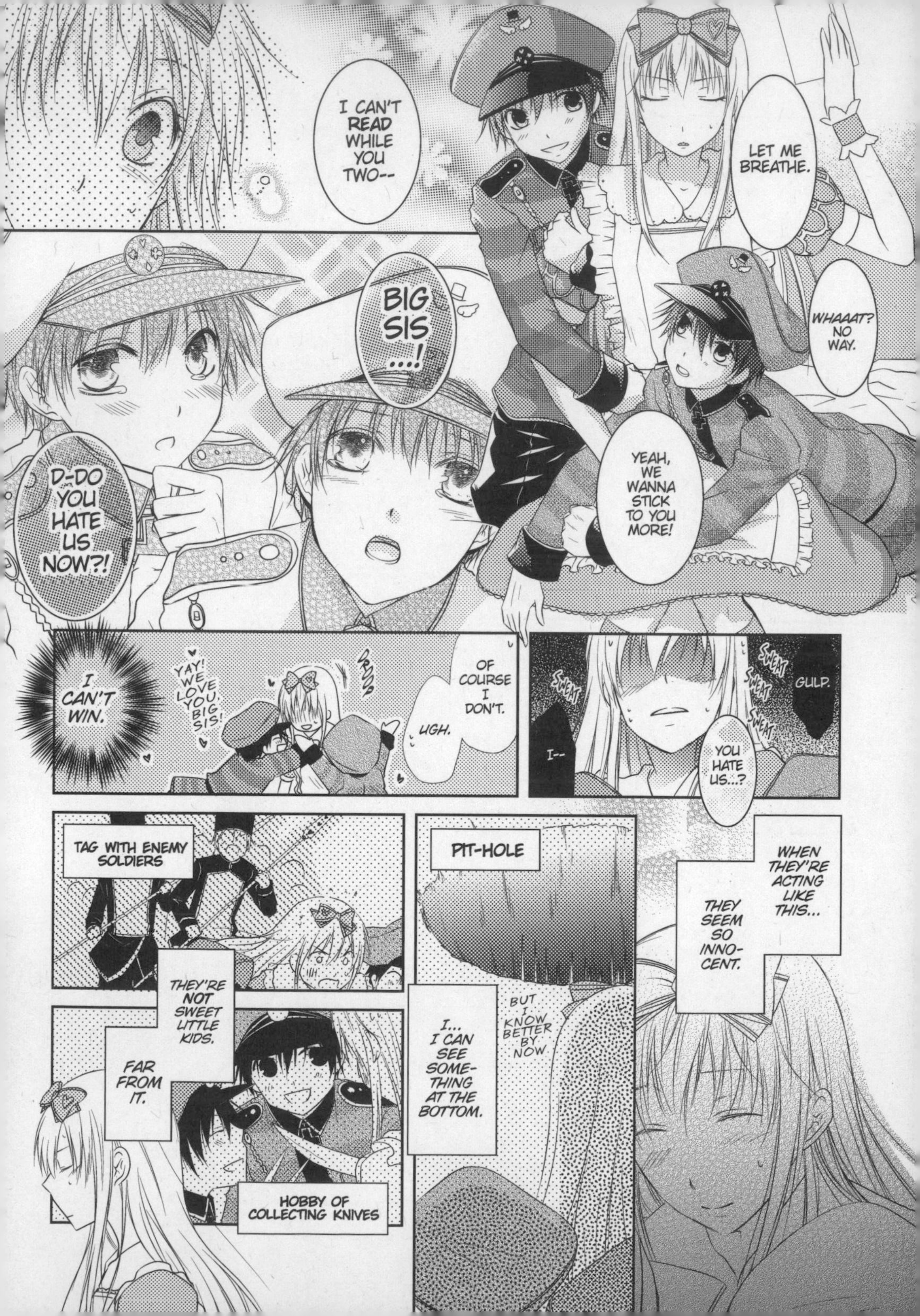

LET ME BREATHE.
I CAN'T READ WHILE YOU TWO--
WHAAAT? NO WAY.
YEAH, WE WANNA STICK TO YOU MORE!
BIG SIS...!
D-DO YOU HATE US NOW?!
GULP.
SWEAT SWEAT SWEAT SWEAT
YOU HATE US...?
I--
OF COURSE I DON'T.
UGH.
DROOP
YAY! WE LOVE YOU, BIG SIS!
I CAN'T WIN.
WHEN THEY'RE ACTING LIKE THIS...
THEY SEEM SO INNO-CENT.
BUT I KNOW BETTER BY NOW.
PIT-HOLE
I... I CAN SEE SOME-THING AT THE BOTTOM.
TAG WITH ENEMY SOLDIERS
THEY'RE NOT SWEET LITTLE KIDS.
FAR FROM IT.
HOBBY OF COLLECTING KNIVES

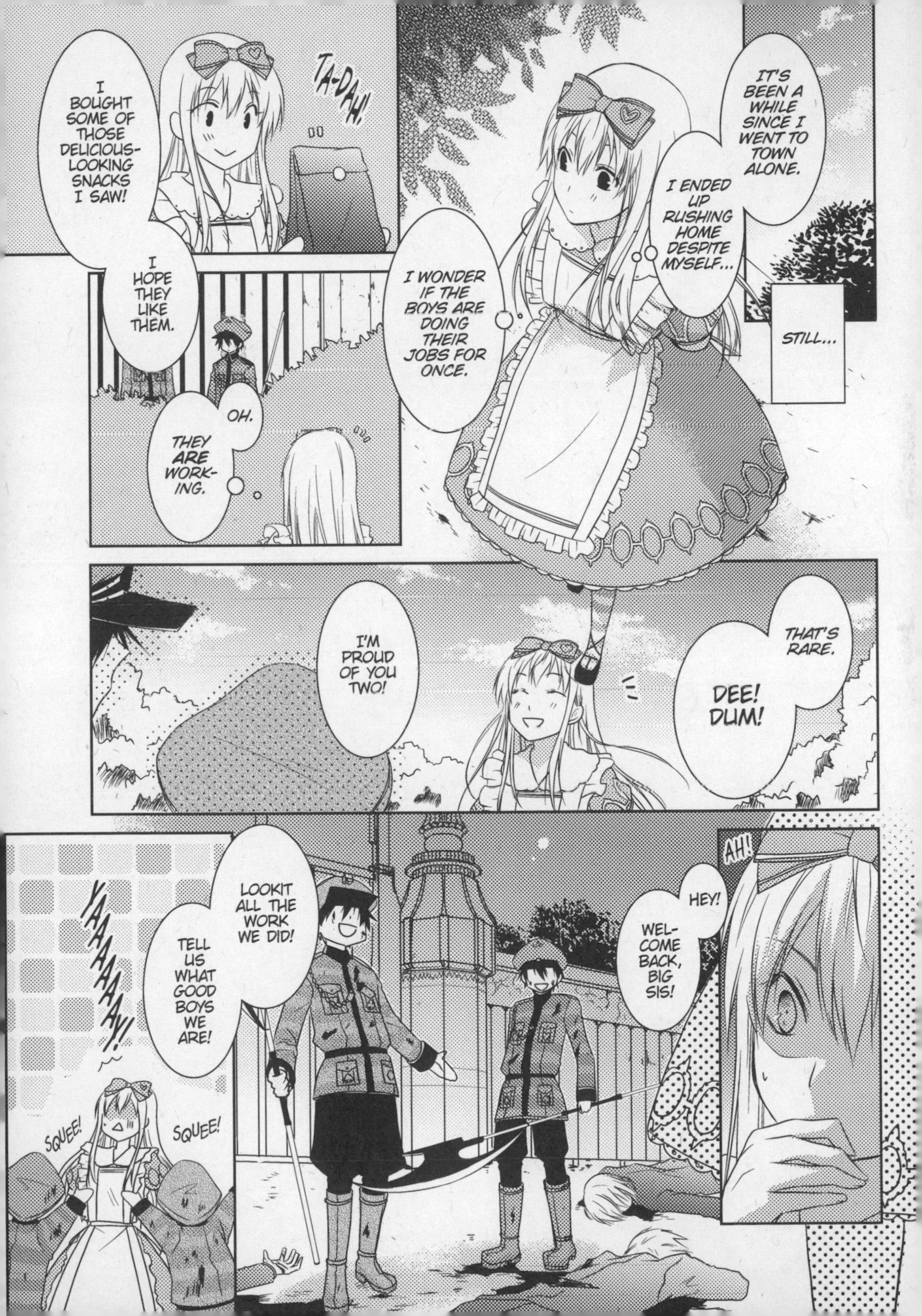
IT'S BEEN A WHILE SINCE I WENT TO TOWN ALONE.
I ENDED UP RUSHING HOME DESPITE MYSELF...
STILL...
I WONDER IF THE BOYS ARE DOING THEIR JOBS FOR ONCE.
TA-DAH!
I BOUGHT SOME OF THOSE DELICIOUS-LOOKING SNACKS I SAW!
I HOPE THEY LIKE THEM.
OH.
THEY ARE WORKING.
THAT'S RARE.
DEE! DUM!
I'M PROUD OF YOU TWO!
AH!
HEY!
WELCOME BACK, BIG SIS!
LOOKIT ALL THE WORK WE DID!
TELL US WHAT GOOD BOYS WE ARE!
YAAAAAAY!
SQUEE!
SQUEE!

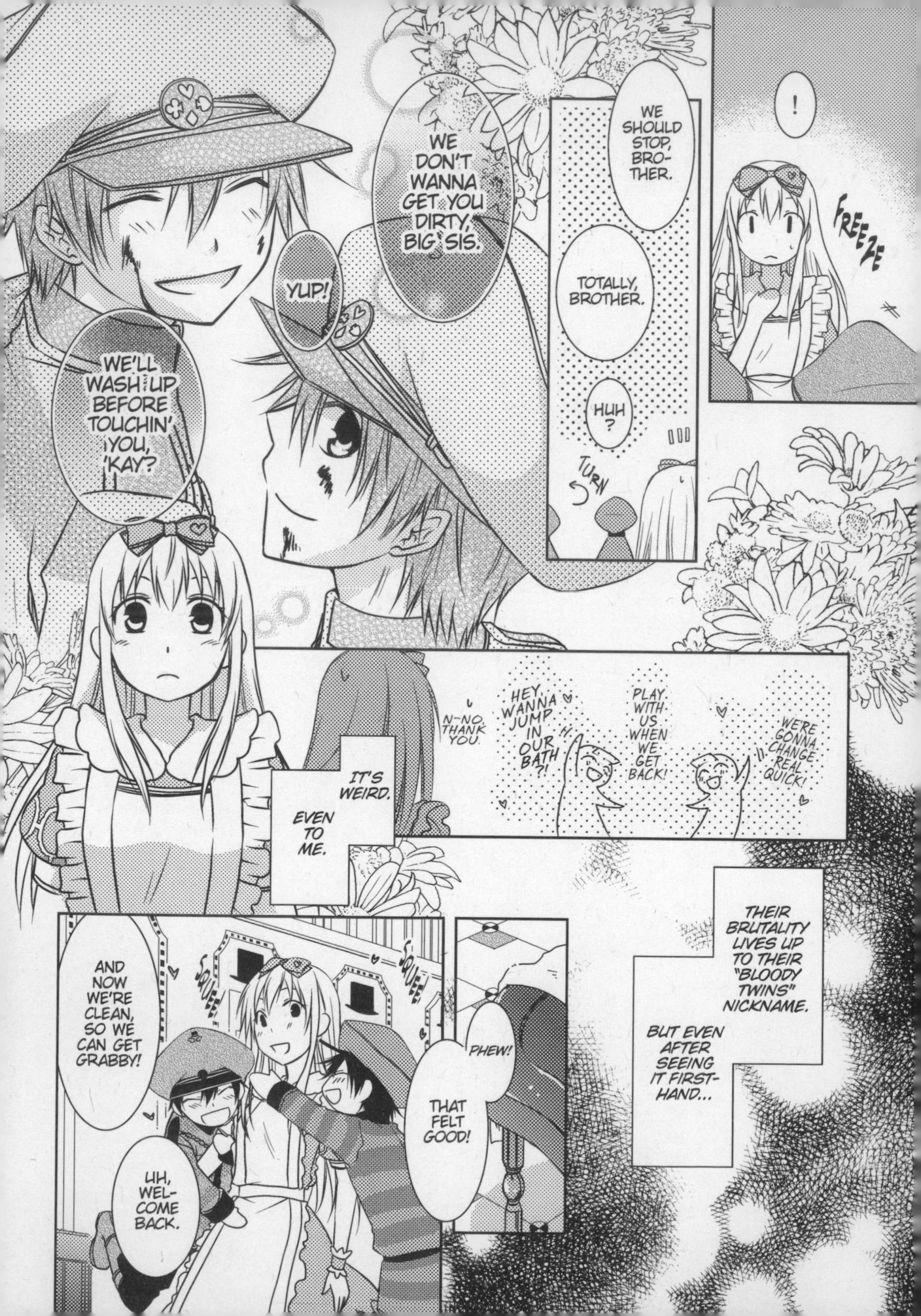
!
FREEZE
WE SHOULD STOP, BROTHER.
TOTALLY, BROTHER.
HUH?
TURN
WE DON'T WANNA GET YOU DIRTY, BIG SIS.
YUP!
WE'LL WASH UP BEFORE TOUCHIN' YOU, 'KAY?
WE'RE GONNA CHANGE REAL QUICK!
PLAY WITH US WHEN WE GET BACK!
HEY, WANNA JUMP IN OUR BATH?!
N-NO, THANK YOU.
IT'S WEIRD.
EVEN TO ME.
THEIR BRUTALITY LIVES UP TO THEIR "BLOODY TWINS" NICKNAME.
BUT EVEN AFTER SEEING IT FIRST-HAND...
PHEW!
THAT FELT GOOD!
SQUEE!
SQUEE!
AND NOW WE'RE CLEAN, SO WE CAN GET GRABBY!
UH, WELCOME BACK.

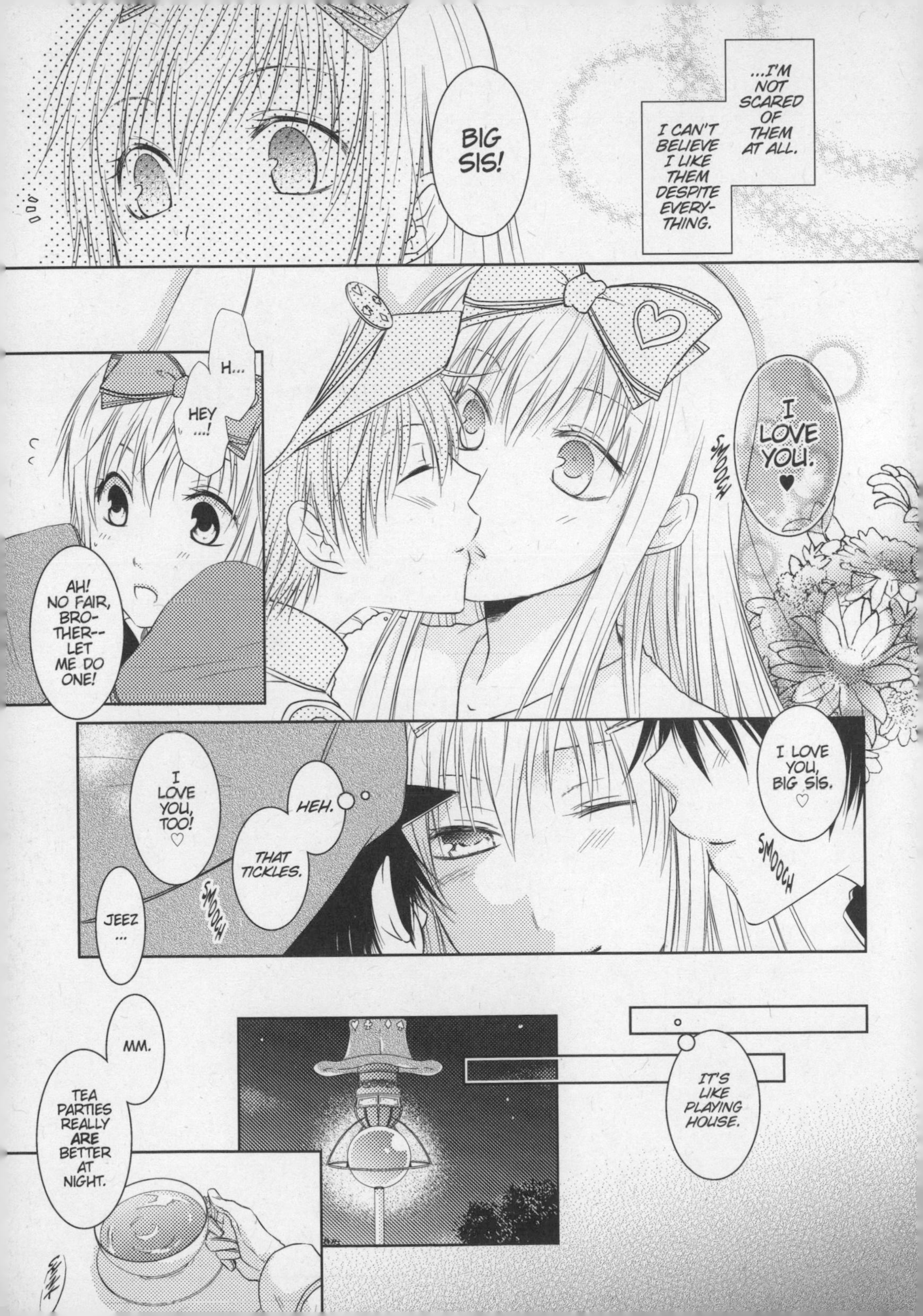
...I'M NOT SCARED OF THEM AT ALL.
I CAN'T BELIEVE I LIKE THEM DESPITE EVERY-THING.
BIG SIS!
I LOVE YOU. ♥
SMOOCH
H... HEY ...!
AH! NO FAIR, BROTHER--LET ME DO ONE!
I LOVE YOU, BIG SIS. ♡
SMOOCH
HEH. THAT TICKLES.
I LOVE YOU, TOO! ♡
SMOOCH
JEEZ ...
IT'S LIKE PLAYING HOUSE.
MM.
TEA PARTIES REALLY ARE BETTER AT NIGHT.

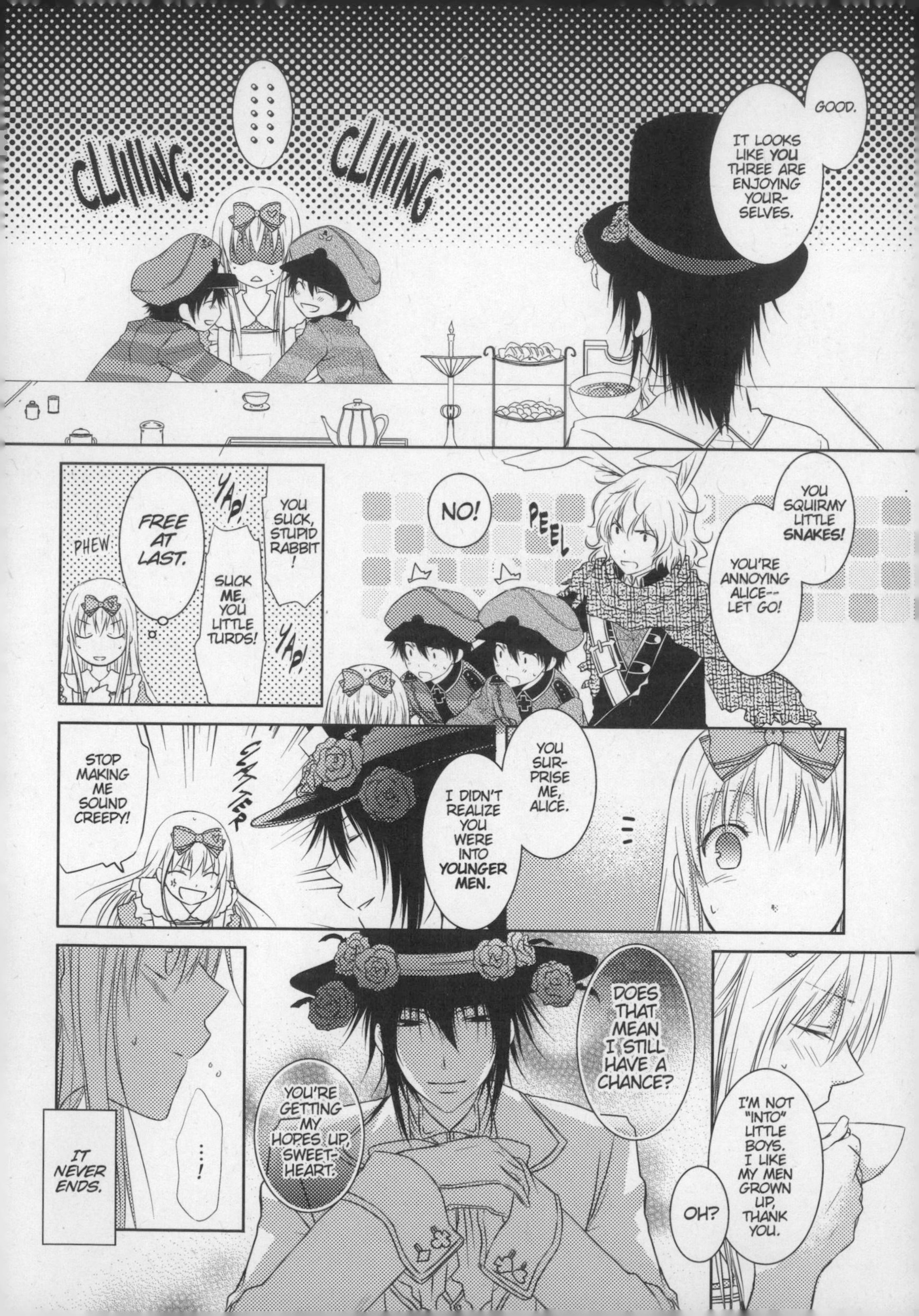
GOOD.
IT LOOKS LIKE YOU THREE ARE ENJOYING YOUR-SELVES.
CLIIING
......
CLIIING
YOU SQUIRMY LITTLE SNAKES!
YOU'RE ANNOYING ALICE-- LET GO!
PEEL
NO!
YOU SUCK, STUPID RABBIT!
YAP!
SUCK ME, YOU LITTLE TURDS!
YAP!
FREE AT LAST.
PHEW
...
YOU SUR-PRISE ME, ALICE.
I DIDN'T REALIZE YOU WERE INTO YOUNGER MEN.
CLATTER
STOP MAKING ME SOUND CREEPY!
I'M NOT "INTO" LITTLE BOYS. I LIKE MY MEN GROWN UP, THANK YOU.
OH?
DOES THAT MEAN I STILL HAVE A CHANCE?
YOU'RE GETTING MY HOPES UP, SWEET-HEART.
...!
IT NEVER ENDS.

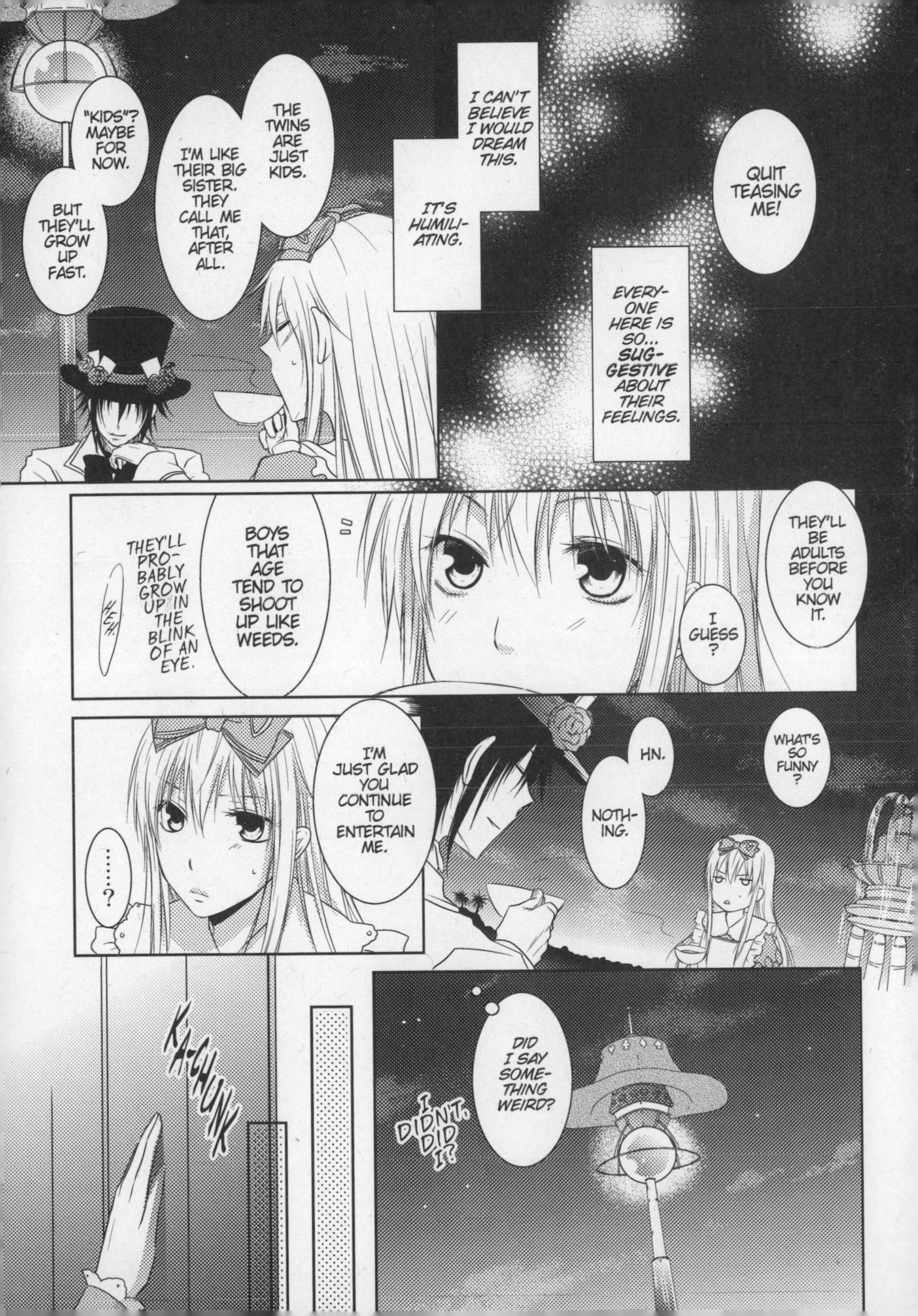
QUIT TEASING ME!
I CAN'T BELIEVE I WOULD DREAM THIS.
IT'S HUMILIATING.
EVERYONE HERE IS SO... **SUGGESTIVE** ABOUT THEIR FEELINGS.
THE TWINS ARE JUST KIDS.
I'M LIKE THEIR BIG SISTER. THEY CALL ME THAT, AFTER ALL.
"KIDS"? MAYBE FOR NOW.
BUT THEY'LL GROW UP FAST.
THEY'LL BE ADULTS BEFORE YOU KNOW IT.
I GUESS?
BOYS THAT AGE TEND TO SHOOT UP LIKE WEEDS.
HEH.
THEY'LL PROBABLY GROW UP IN THE BLINK OF AN EYE.
WHAT'S SO FUNNY?
HN.
NOTHING.
I'M JUST GLAD YOU CONTINUE TO ENTERTAIN ME.
......?
DID I SAY SOMETHING WEIRD?
I DIDN'T, DID I?
KA-CHUNK

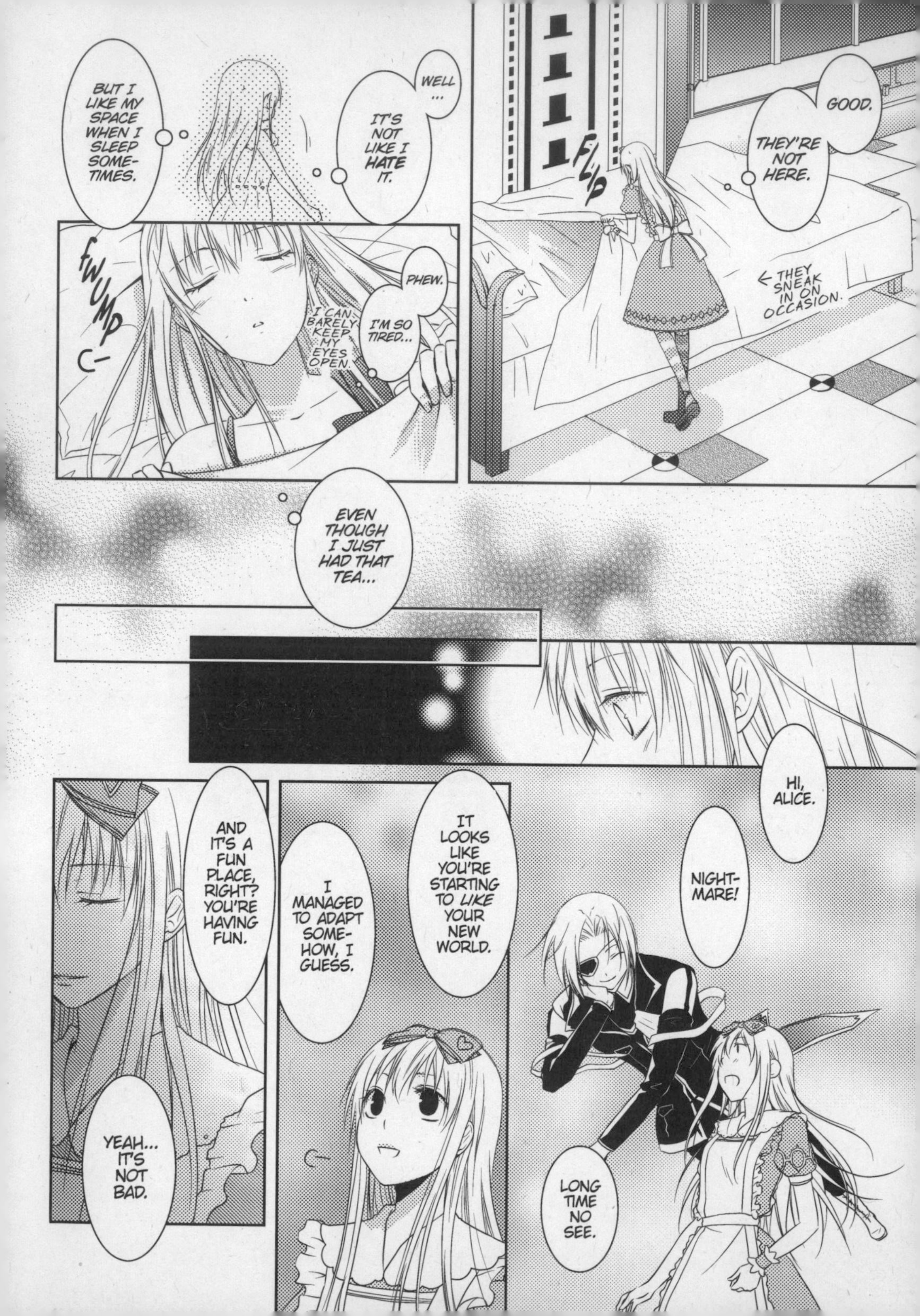
GOOD.
THEY'RE NOT HERE.
FLIP
← THEY SNEAK IN ON OCCASION.
WELL...
IT'S NOT LIKE I HATE IT.
BUT I LIKE MY SPACE WHEN I SLEEP SOMETIMES.
PHEW.
I'M SO TIRED...
I CAN BARELY KEEP MY EYES OPEN.
FWUMP
EVEN THOUGH I JUST HAD THAT TEA...
HI, ALICE.
NIGHTMARE!
LONG TIME NO SEE.
IT LOOKS LIKE YOU'RE STARTING TO LIKE YOUR NEW WORLD.
I MANAGED TO ADAPT SOMEHOW, I GUESS.
AND IT'S A FUN PLACE, RIGHT? YOU'RE HAVING FUN.
YEAH... IT'S NOT BAD.

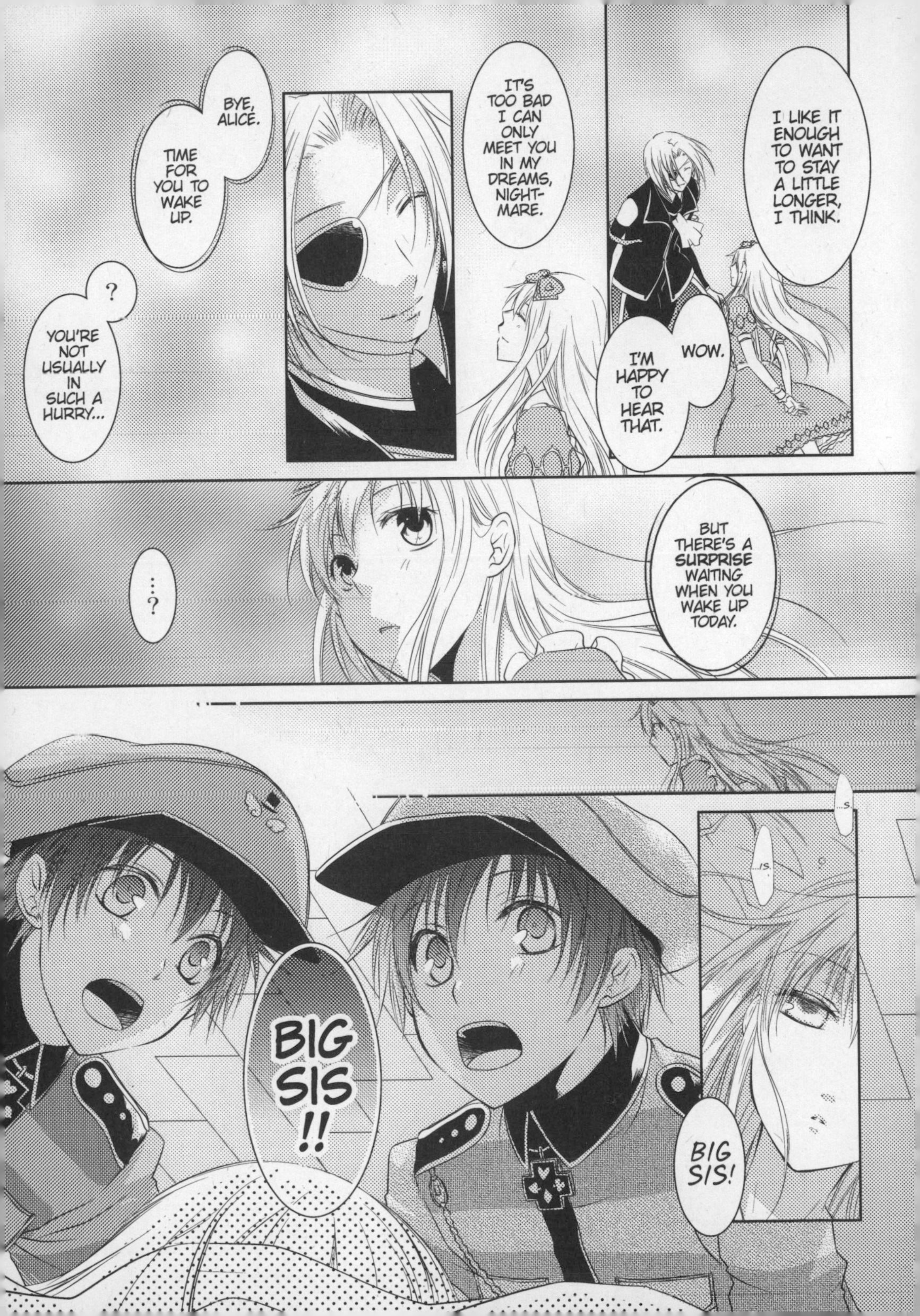
I LIKE IT ENOUGH TO WANT TO STAY A LITTLE LONGER, I THINK.
WOW.
I'M HAPPY TO HEAR THAT.
IT'S TOO BAD I CAN ONLY MEET YOU IN MY DREAMS, NIGHTMARE.
BYE, ALICE.
TIME FOR YOU TO WAKE UP.
?
YOU'RE NOT USUALLY IN SUCH A HURRY...
BUT THERE'S A **SURPRISE** WAITING WHEN YOU WAKE UP TODAY.
...?
...S.
...IS.
BIG SIS!
BIG SIS!!

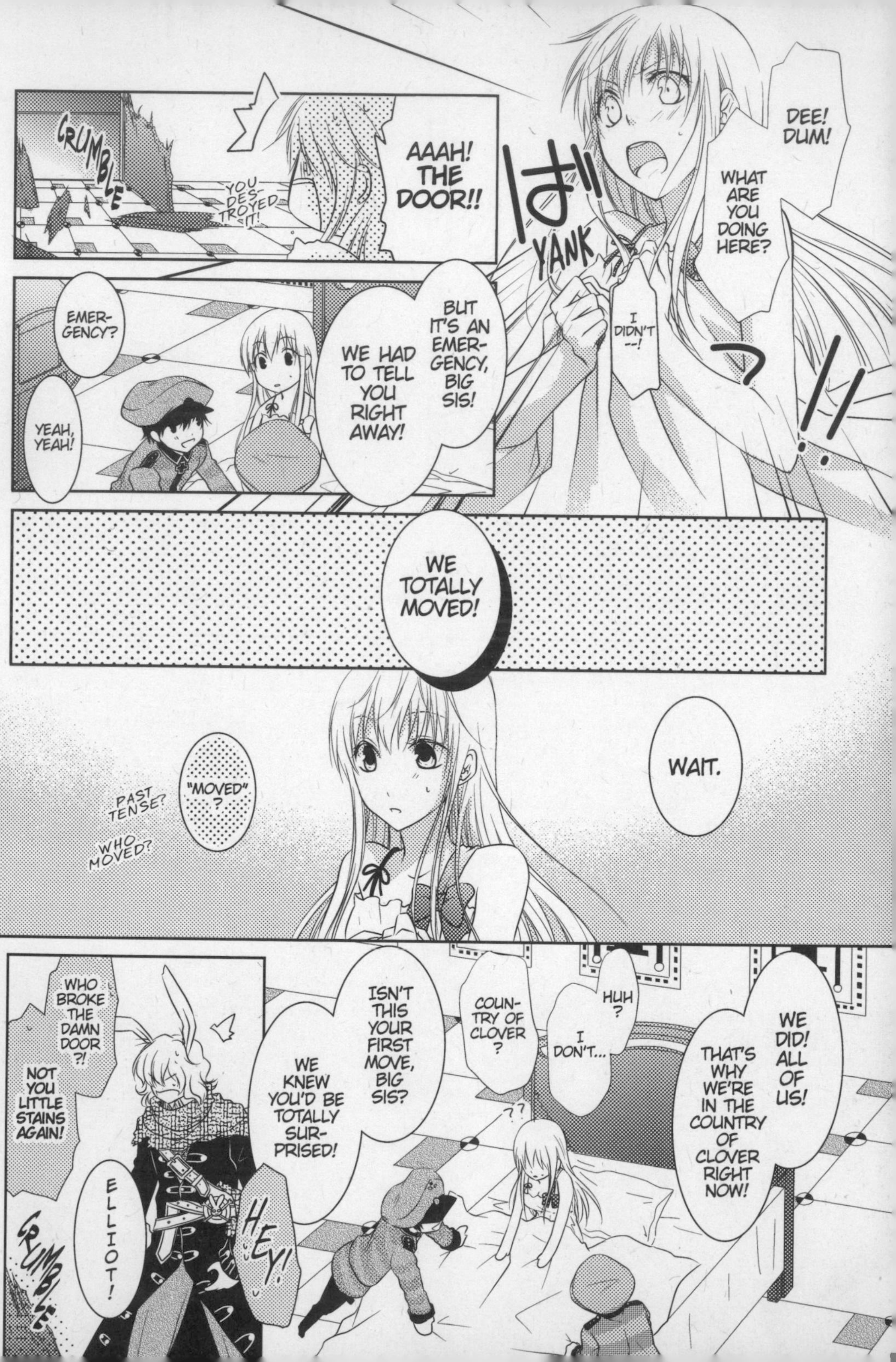
DEE! DUM!
WHAT ARE YOU DOING HERE?
ば
YANK
I DIDN'T--!
AAAH! THE DOOR!!
YOU DES-TROYED IT!
CRUMBLE
BUT IT'S AN EMER-GENCY, BIG SIS!
WE HAD TO TELL YOU RIGHT AWAY!
EMER-GENCY?
YEAH, YEAH!
WE TOTALLY MOVED!
WAIT.
"MOVED"?
PAST TENSE?
WHO MOVED?
WE DID! ALL OF US!
THAT'S WHY WE'RE IN THE COUNTRY OF CLOVER RIGHT NOW!
HUH?
I DON'T...
COUN-TRY OF CLOVER?
??
ISN'T THIS YOUR FIRST MOVE, BIG SIS?
WE KNEW YOU'D BE TOTALLY SUR-PRISED!
HEY!
ELLIOT!
WHO BROKE THE DAMN DOOR?!
NOT YOU LITTLE STAINS AGAIN!
CRUMBLE

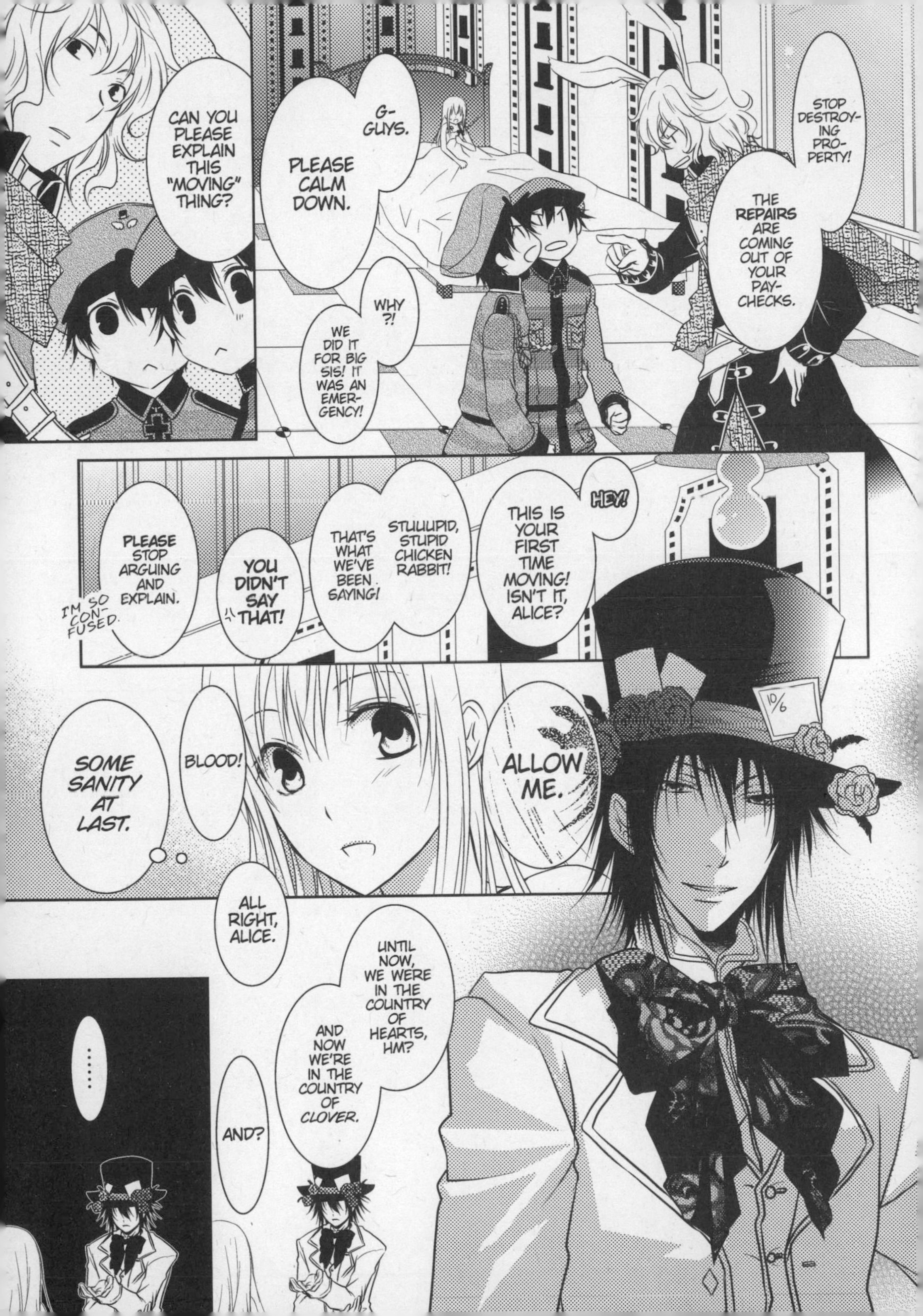
STOP DESTROYING PROPERTY!
THE REPAIRS ARE COMING OUT OF YOUR PAYCHECKS.
G-GUYS.
PLEASE CALM DOWN.
WHY?!
WE DID IT FOR BIG SIS! IT WAS AN EMERGENCY!
CAN YOU PLEASE EXPLAIN THIS "MOVING" THING?
HEY!
THIS IS YOUR FIRST TIME MOVING! ISN'T IT, ALICE?
STUUUPID, STUPID CHICKEN RABBIT!
THAT'S WHAT WE'VE BEEN SAYING!
YOU DIDN'T SAY THAT!
PLEASE STOP ARGUING AND EXPLAIN.
I'M SO CONFUSED.
ALLOW ME.
BLOOD!
SOME SANITY AT LAST.
ALL RIGHT, ALICE.
UNTIL NOW, WE WERE IN THE COUNTRY OF HEARTS, HM?
AND NOW WE'RE IN THE COUNTRY OF CLOVER.
AND?
......

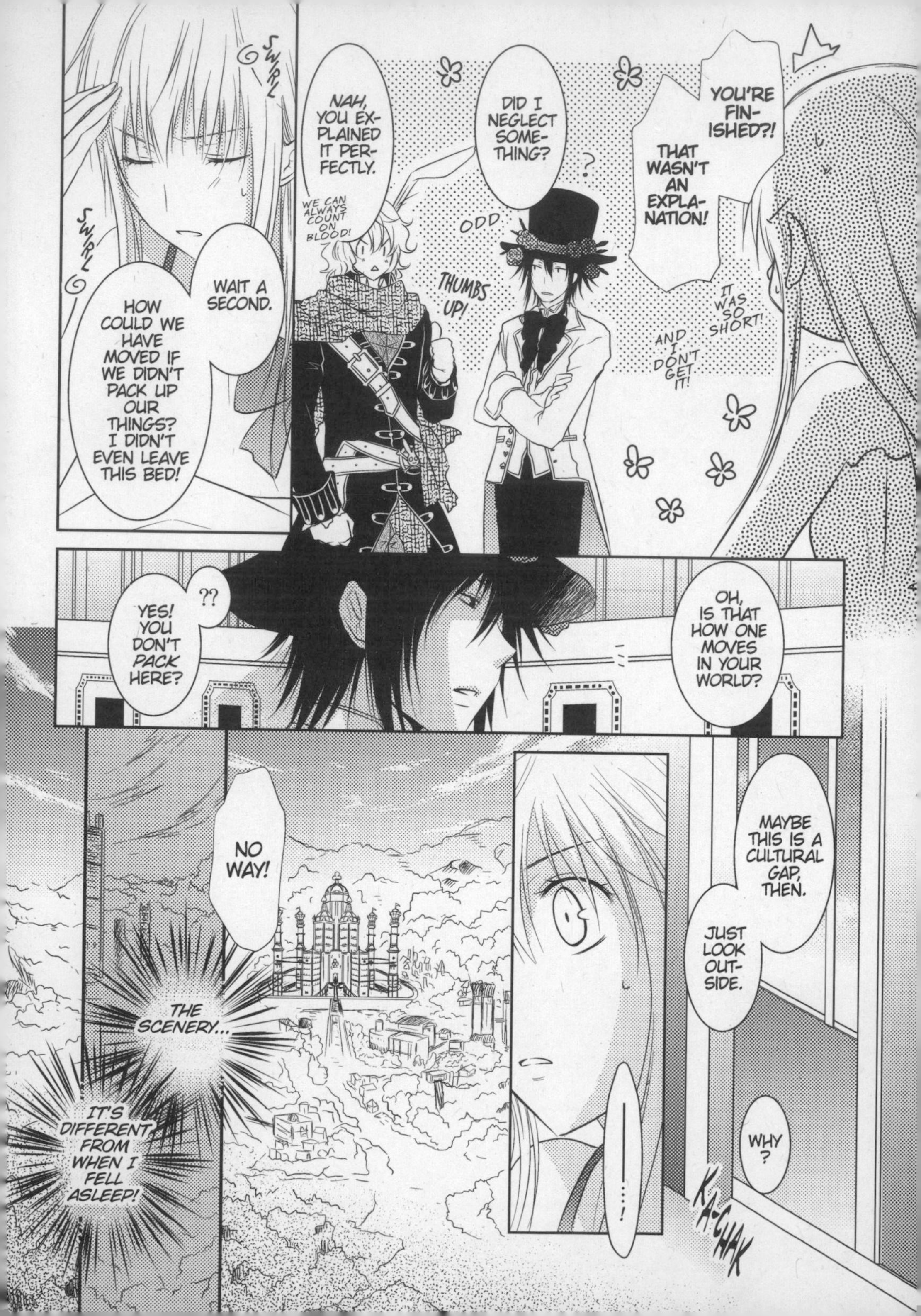
YOU'RE FINISHED?!
THAT WASN'T AN EXPLANATION!
IT WAS SO SHORT!
AND I DON'T GET IT!
DID I NEGLECT SOMETHING?
?
ODD
NAH, YOU EXPLAINED IT PERFECTLY.
WE CAN ALWAYS COUNT ON BLOOD!
THUMBS UP!
SWIRL
SWIRL
WAIT A SECOND.
HOW COULD WE HAVE MOVED IF WE DIDN'T PACK UP OUR THINGS? I DIDN'T EVEN LEAVE THIS BED!
OH, IS THAT HOW ONE MOVES IN YOUR WORLD?
YES! YOU DON'T PACK HERE?
??
MAYBE THIS IS A CULTURAL GAP, THEN.
JUST LOOK OUTSIDE.
WHY?
KA-CHAK
...!
NO WAY!
THE SCENERY...
IT'S DIFFERENT FROM WHEN I FELL ASLEEP!

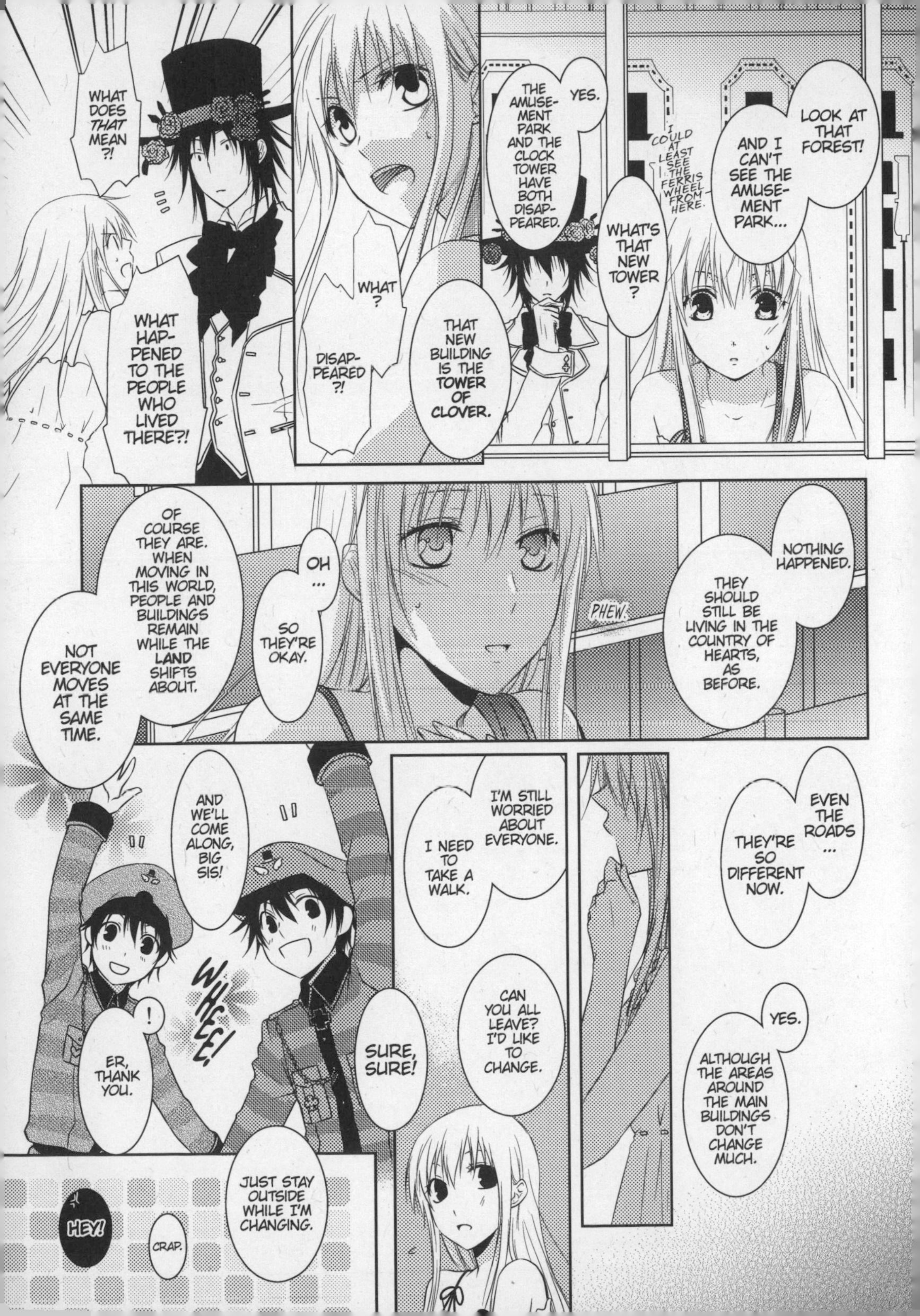
LOOK AT THAT FOREST!
AND I CAN'T SEE THE AMUSEMENT PARK...
I COULD AT LEAST SEE THE FERRIS WHEEL FROM HERE.
WHAT'S THAT NEW TOWER?
YES.
THE AMUSEMENT PARK AND THE CLOCK TOWER HAVE BOTH DISAPPEARED.
THAT NEW BUILDING IS THE TOWER OF CLOVER.
WHAT?
DISAPPEARED?!
WHAT DOES THAT MEAN?!
WHAT HAPPENED TO THE PEOPLE WHO LIVED THERE?!
NOTHING HAPPENED.
THEY SHOULD STILL BE LIVING IN THE COUNTRY OF HEARTS, AS BEFORE.
PHEW.
OH ...
SO THEY'RE OKAY.
OF COURSE THEY ARE. WHEN MOVING IN THIS WORLD, PEOPLE AND BUILDINGS REMAIN WHILE THE LAND SHIFTS ABOUT.
NOT EVERYONE MOVES AT THE SAME TIME.
EVEN THE ROADS ...
THEY'RE SO DIFFERENT NOW.
YES.
ALTHOUGH THE AREAS AROUND THE MAIN BUILDINGS DON'T CHANGE MUCH.
I'M STILL WORRIED ABOUT EVERYONE.
I NEED TO TAKE A WALK.
CAN YOU ALL LEAVE? I'D LIKE TO CHANGE.
SURE, SURE!
AND WE'LL COME ALONG, BIG SIS!
WHEE!
!
ER, THANK YOU.
JUST STAY OUTSIDE WHILE I'M CHANGING.
CRAP.
HEY!

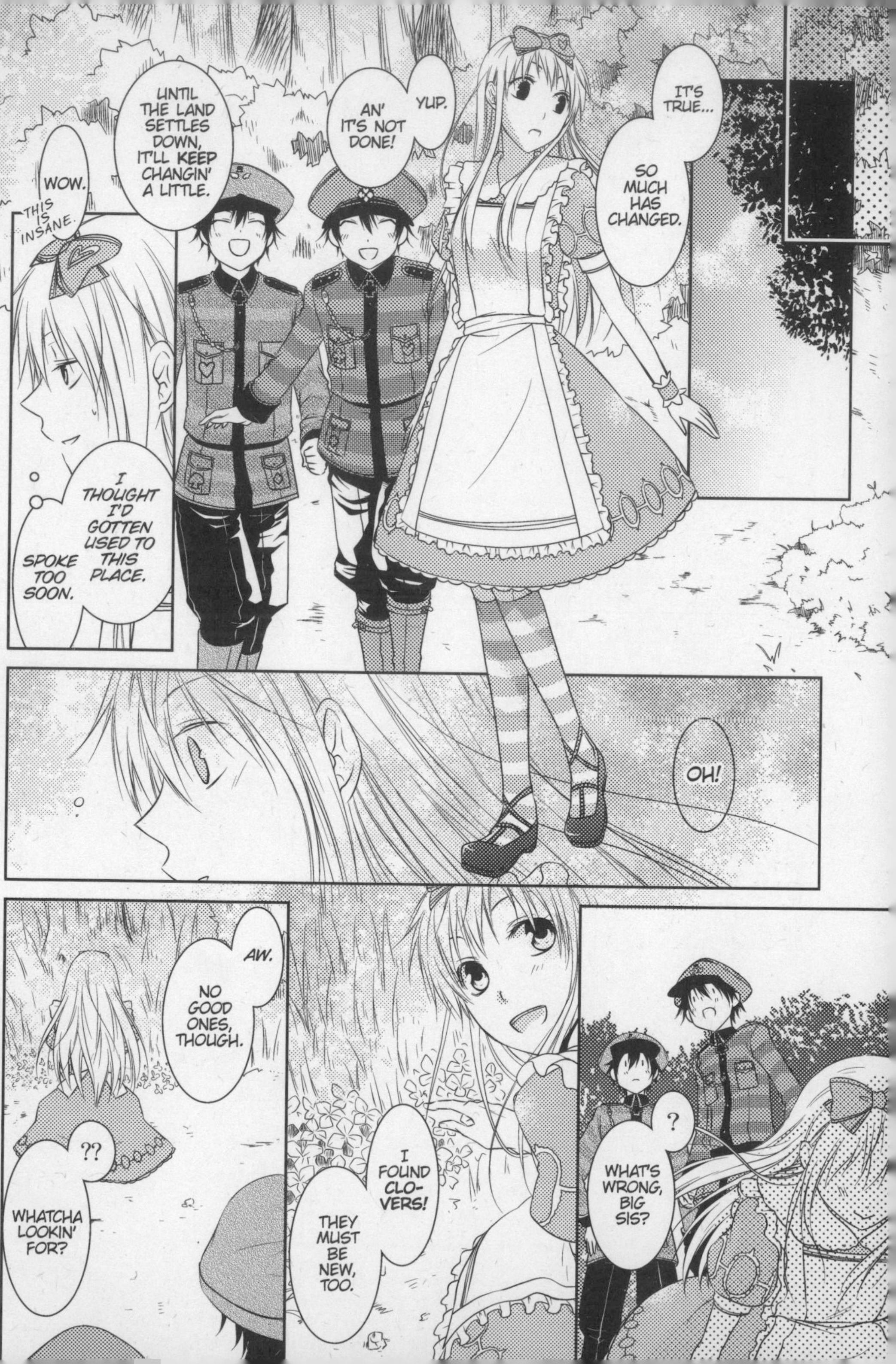
IT'S TRUE...
SO MUCH HAS CHANGED.
YUP.
AN' IT'S NOT DONE!
UNTIL THE LAND SETTLES DOWN, IT'LL KEEP CHANGIN' A LITTLE.
WOW.
THIS IS INSANE.
I THOUGHT I'D GOTTEN USED TO THIS PLACE.
SPOKE TOO SOON.
OH!
?
WHAT'S WRONG, BIG SIS?
I FOUND CLO-VERS!
THEY MUST BE NEW, TOO.
AW.
NO GOOD ONES, THOUGH.
??
WHATCHA LOOKIN' FOR?

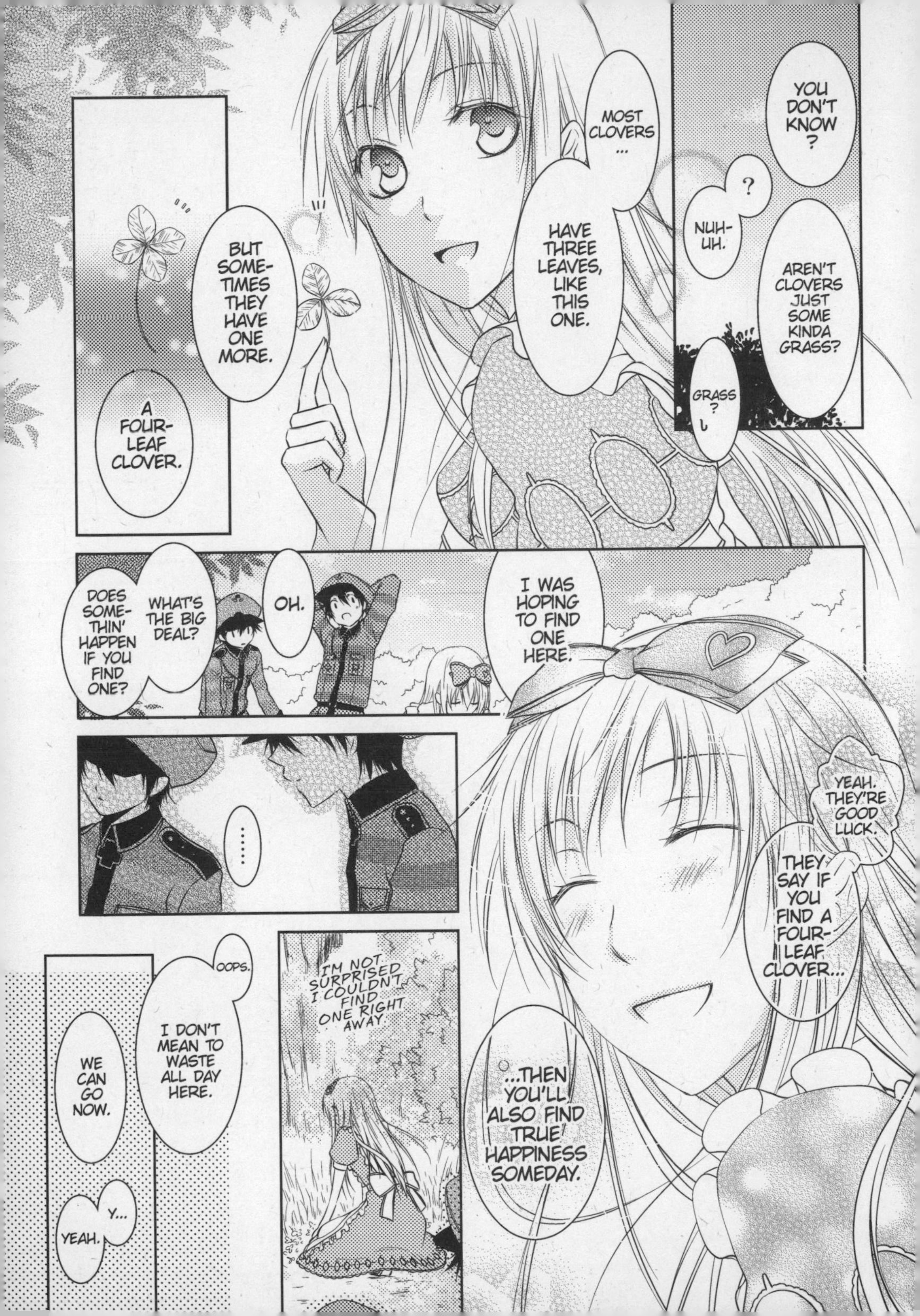
YOU DON'T KNOW?
?
NUH-UH.
AREN'T CLOVERS JUST SOME KINDA GRASS?
GRASS?
MOST CLOVERS...
HAVE THREE LEAVES, LIKE THIS ONE.
BUT SOME-TIMES THEY HAVE ONE MORE.
A FOUR-LEAF CLOVER.
I WAS HOPING TO FIND ONE HERE.
OH.
WHAT'S THE BIG DEAL?
DOES SOME-THIN' HAPPEN IF YOU FIND ONE?
YEAH. THEY'RE GOOD LUCK.
THEY SAY IF YOU FIND A FOUR-LEAF CLOVER...
...THEN YOU'LL ALSO FIND TRUE HAPPINESS SOMEDAY.
......
I'M NOT SURPRISED I COULDN'T FIND ONE RIGHT AWAY.
OOPS.
I DON'T MEAN TO WASTE ALL DAY HERE.
WE CAN GO NOW.
Y... YEAH.

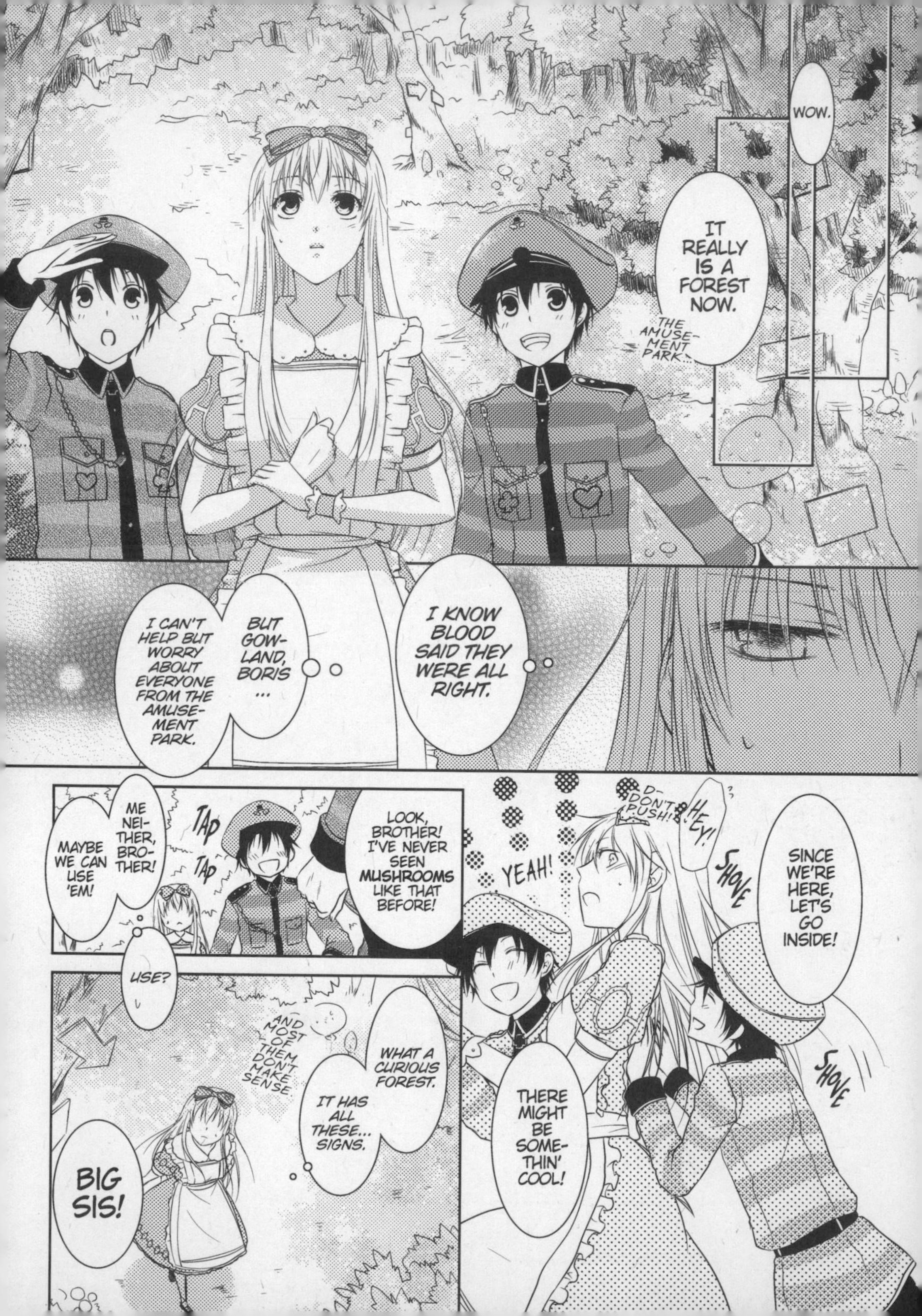
WOW.
IT REALLY IS A FOREST NOW.
THE AMUSEMENT PARK...
I KNOW BLOOD SAID THEY WERE ALL RIGHT.
BUT GOWLAND, BORIS...
I CAN'T HELP BUT WORRY ABOUT EVERYONE FROM THE AMUSEMENT PARK.
SINCE WE'RE HERE, LET'S GO INSIDE!
HEY!
D-DON'T PUSH!
SHOVE
YEAH!
SHOVE
THERE MIGHT BE SOMETHIN' COOL!
LOOK, BROTHER! I'VE NEVER SEEN MUSHROOMS LIKE THAT BEFORE!
TAP
TAP
ME NEITHER, BROTHER!
MAYBE WE CAN USE 'EM!
USE?
WHAT A CURIOUS FOREST.
IT HAS ALL THESE... SIGNS.
AND MOST OF THEM DON'T MAKE SENSE.
BIG SIS!

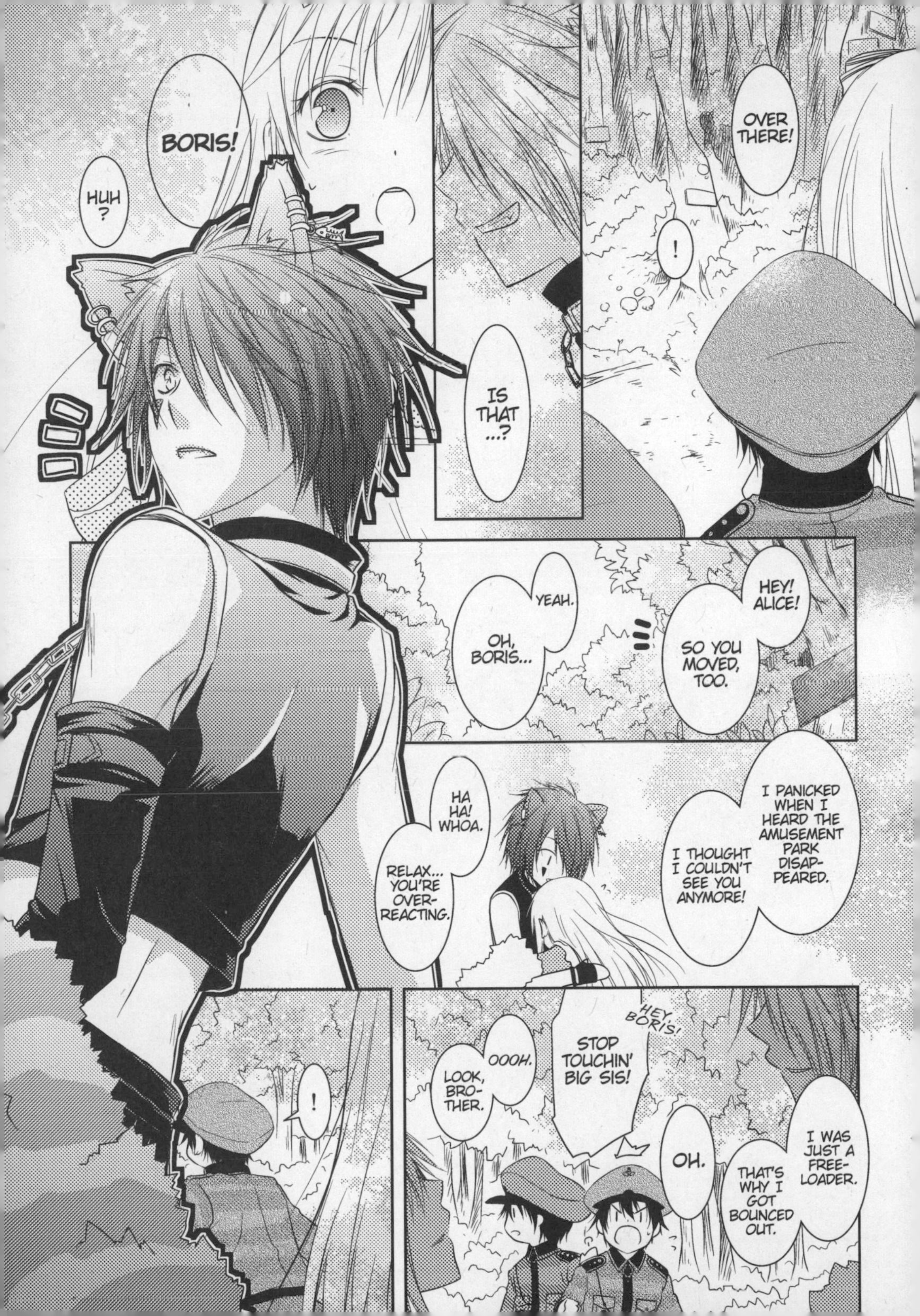

OVER THERE!
!
IS THAT ...?
BORIS!
HUH ?
HEY! ALICE!
SO YOU MOVED, TOO.
OH, BORIS...
YEAH.
I PANICKED WHEN I HEARD THE AMUSEMENT PARK DISAPPEARED.
I THOUGHT I COULDN'T SEE YOU ANYMORE!
HA HA! WHOA.
RELAX... YOU'RE OVER-REACTING.
HEY, BORIS!
STOP TOUCHIN' BIG SIS!
OOOH.
LOOK, BROTHER.
I WAS JUST A FREE-LOADER.
THAT'S WHY I GOT BOUNCED OUT.
OH.
!

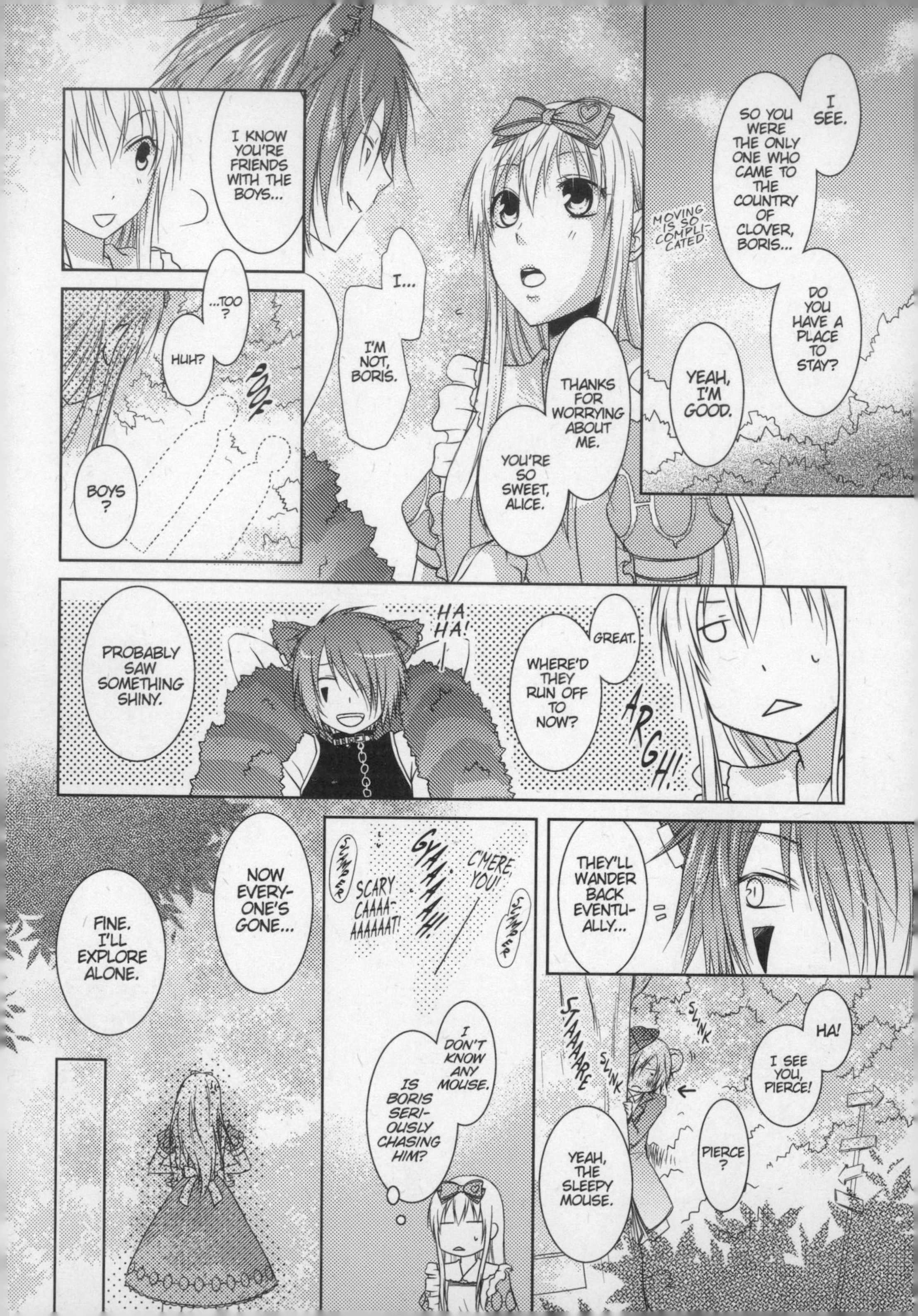

I SEE.
SO YOU WERE THE ONLY ONE WHO CAME TO THE COUNTRY OF CLOVER, BORIS...
MOVING IS SO COMPLICATED.
DO YOU HAVE A PLACE TO STAY?
YEAH, I'M GOOD.
THANKS FOR WORRYING ABOUT ME.
YOU'RE SO SWEET, ALICE.
I...
I'M NOT, BORIS.
I KNOW YOU'RE FRIENDS WITH THE BOYS...
...TOO?
HUH?
POOF
BOYS?
GREAT.
WHERE'D THEY RUN OFF TO NOW?
ARGH!
HA HA!
PROBABLY SAW SOMETHING SHINY.
THEY'LL WANDER BACK EVENTUALLY...
C'MERE, YOU!
GYAAAAAAH!!
SCARY CAAAA-AAAAAAT!
SIMPER
SIMPER
NOW EVERYONE'S GONE...
FINE. I'LL EXPLORE ALONE.
HA!
I SEE YOU, PIERCE!
SLINK
SLINK
STAAAARE
PIERCE?
YEAH, THE SLEEPY MOUSE.
I DON'T KNOW ANY MOUSE.
IS BORIS SERIOUSLY CHASING HIM?

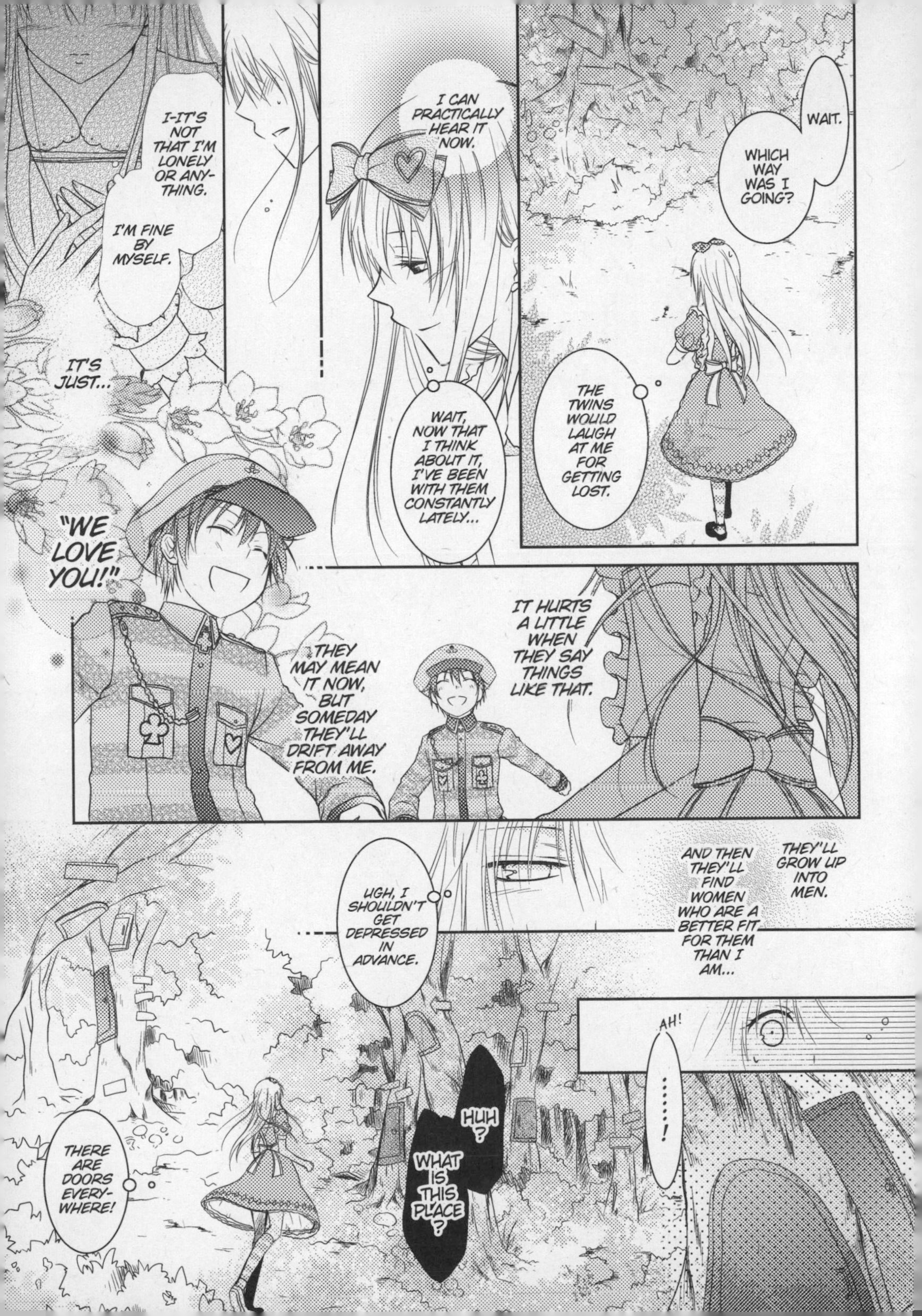
WAIT.
WHICH WAY WAS I GOING?
THE TWINS WOULD LAUGH AT ME FOR GETTING LOST.
I CAN PRACTICALLY HEAR IT NOW.
WAIT, NOW THAT I THINK ABOUT IT, I'VE BEEN WITH THEM CONSTANTLY LATELY...
I-IT'S NOT THAT I'M LONELY OR ANY-THING.
I'M FINE BY MYSELF.
IT'S JUST...
"WE LOVE YOU!"
IT HURTS A LITTLE WHEN THEY SAY THINGS LIKE THAT.
THEY MAY MEAN IT NOW, BUT SOMEDAY THEY'LL DRIFT AWAY FROM ME.
THEY'LL GROW UP INTO MEN.
AND THEN THEY'LL FIND WOMEN WHO ARE A BETTER FIT FOR THEM THAN I AM...
UGH, I SHOULDN'T GET DEPRESSED IN ADVANCE.
AH!
......!
HUH?
WHAT IS THIS PLACE?
THERE ARE DOORS EVERY-WHERE!

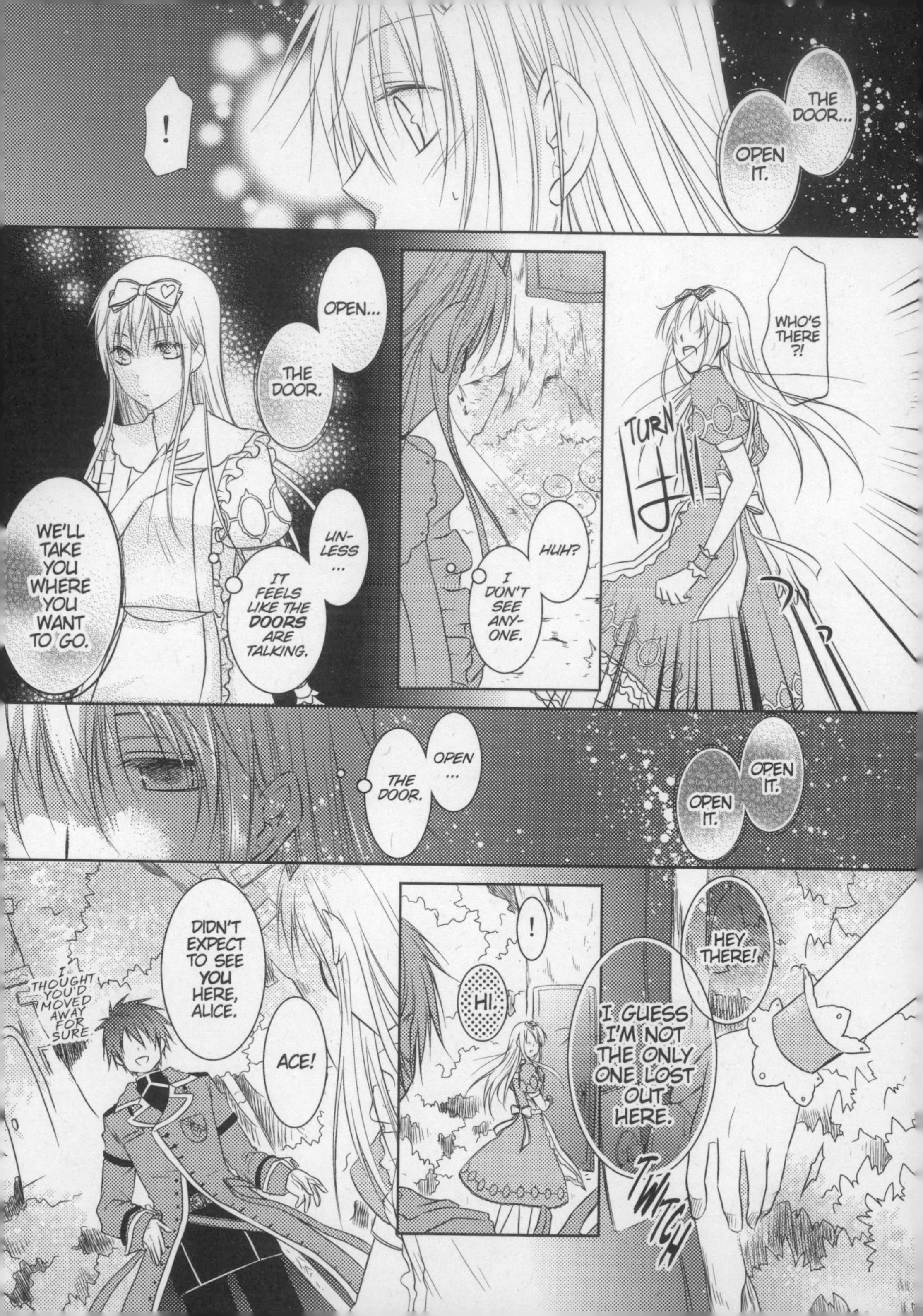
THE DOOR...
OPEN IT.
!
WHO'S THERE ?!
TURN
HUH?
I DON'T SEE ANY-ONE.
OPEN...
THE DOOR.
UN-LESS ...
IT FEELS LIKE THE DOORS ARE TALKING.
WE'LL TAKE YOU WHERE YOU WANT TO GO.
OPEN IT.
OPEN IT.
OPEN ...
THE DOOR.
HEY THERE!
I GUESS I'M NOT THE ONLY ONE LOST OUT HERE.
TWITCH
!
HI.
DIDN'T EXPECT TO SEE YOU HERE, ALICE.
ACE!
I THOUGHT YOU'D MOVED AWAY FOR SURE.

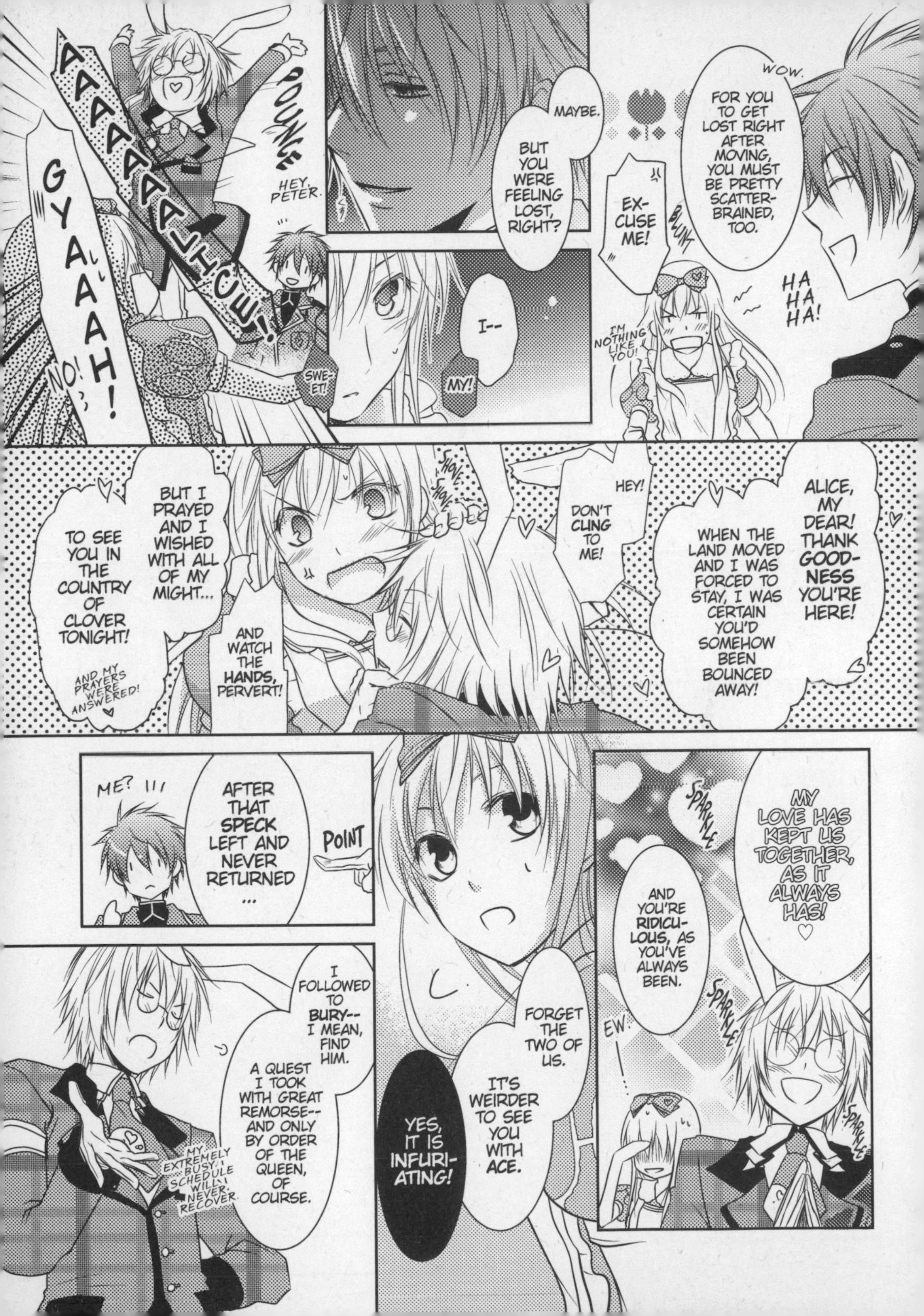
WOW.
FOR YOU TO GET LOST RIGHT AFTER MOVING, YOU MUST BE PRETTY SCATTER-BRAINED, TOO.
HA HA HA!
BLINK
EX-CUSE ME!
I'M NOTHING LIKE YOU!
MAYBE.
BUT YOU WERE FEELING LOST, RIGHT?
I--
MY!
SWE-ET!
POUNCE
HEY, PETER.
AAAAAAAALICE!
GYAAAAH!
NO!
ALICE, MY DEAR! THANK GOODNESS YOU'RE HERE!
WHEN THE LAND MOVED AND I WAS FORCED TO STAY, I WAS CERTAIN YOU'D SOMEHOW BEEN BOUNCED AWAY!
HEY!
DON'T CLING TO ME!
SHOVE SHOVE
AND WATCH THE HANDS, PERVERT!
BUT I PRAYED AND I WISHED WITH ALL OF MY MIGHT...
TO SEE YOU IN THE COUNTRY OF CLOVER TONIGHT!
AND MY PRAYERS WERE ANSWERED!
SPARKLE
MY LOVE HAS KEPT US TOGETHER, AS IT ALWAYS HAS!
AND YOU'RE RIDICULOUS, AS YOU'VE ALWAYS BEEN.
SPARKLE
EW.
SPARKLE
FORGET THE TWO OF US.
IT'S WEIRDER TO SEE YOU WITH ACE.
AFTER THAT SPECK LEFT AND NEVER RETURNED...
POINT
ME?
I FOLLOWED TO BURY-- I MEAN, FIND HIM.
A QUEST I TOOK WITH GREAT REMORSE-- AND ONLY BY ORDER OF THE QUEEN, OF COURSE.
MY EXTREMELY BUSY SCHEDULE WILL NEVER RECOVER.
YES, IT IS INFURIATING!

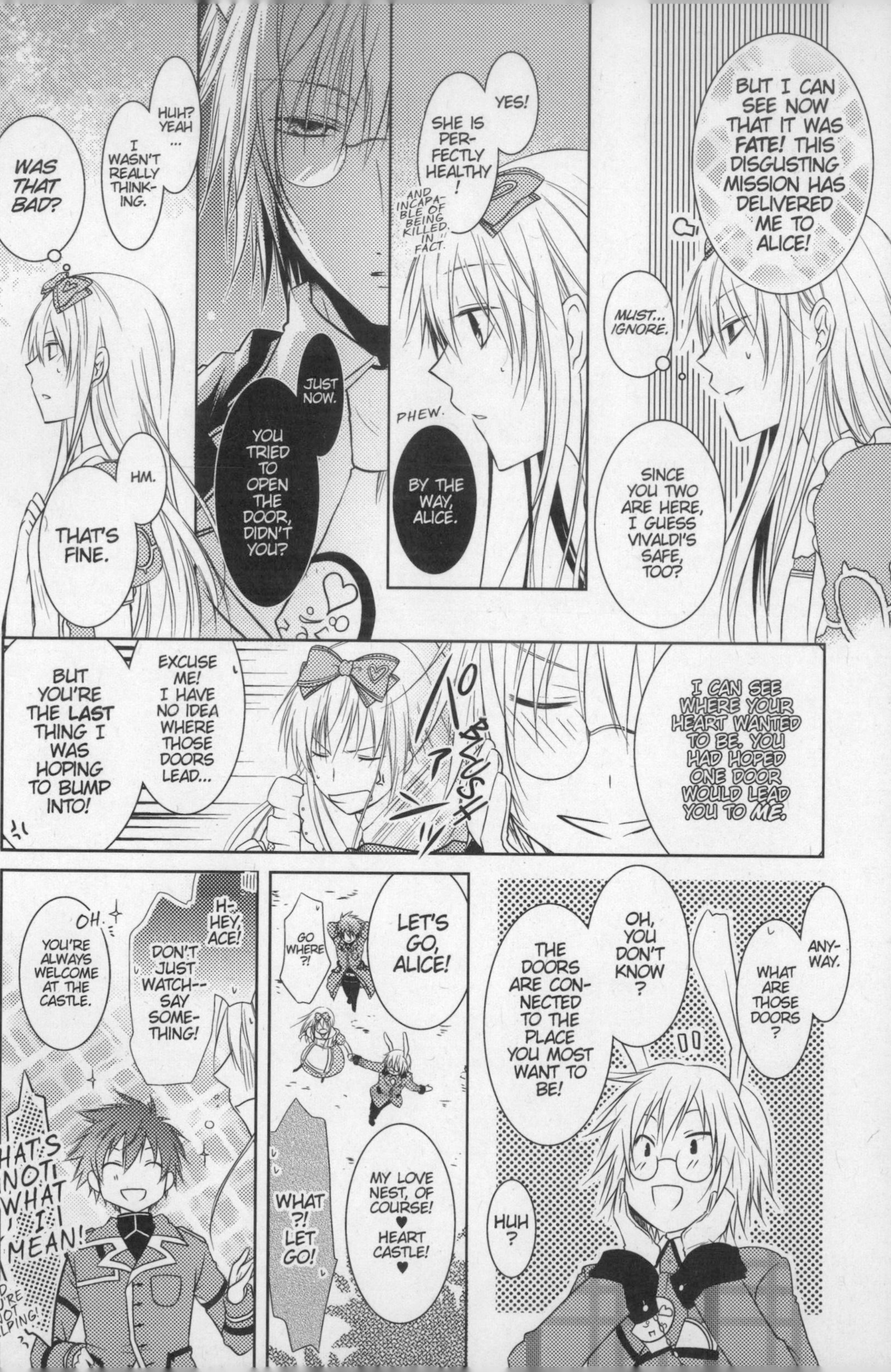
BUT I CAN SEE NOW THAT IT WAS FATE! THIS DISGUSTING MISSION HAS DELIVERED ME TO ALICE!
MUST... IGNORE.
SINCE YOU TWO ARE HERE, I GUESS VIVALDI'S SAFE, TOO?
YES!
SHE IS PERFECTLY HEALTHY!
AND INCAPABLE OF BEING KILLED, IN FACT.
PHEW.
BY THE WAY, ALICE.
JUST NOW.
YOU TRIED TO OPEN THE DOOR, DIDN'T YOU?
HUH? YEAH...
I WASN'T REALLY THINKING.
WAS THAT BAD?
HM.
THAT'S FINE.
I CAN SEE WHERE YOUR HEART WANTED TO BE. YOU HAD HOPED ONE DOOR WOULD LEAD YOU TO ME.
BLUSH
EXCUSE ME! I HAVE NO IDEA WHERE THOSE DOORS LEAD...
BUT YOU'RE THE LAST THING I WAS HOPING TO BUMP INTO!
ANYWAY.
WHAT ARE THOSE DOORS?
OH, YOU DON'T KNOW?
THE DOORS ARE CONNECTED TO THE PLACE YOU MOST WANT TO BE!
HUH?
LET'S GO, ALICE!
GO WHERE?!
MY LOVE NEST, OF COURSE! ♥ HEART CASTLE! ♥
WHAT?! LET GO!
H-HEY, ACE!
DON'T JUST WATCH--SAY SOMETHING!
OH.
YOU'RE ALWAYS WELCOME AT THE CASTLE.
THAT'S NOT WHAT I MEAN!
AND YOU'RE NOT HELPING!

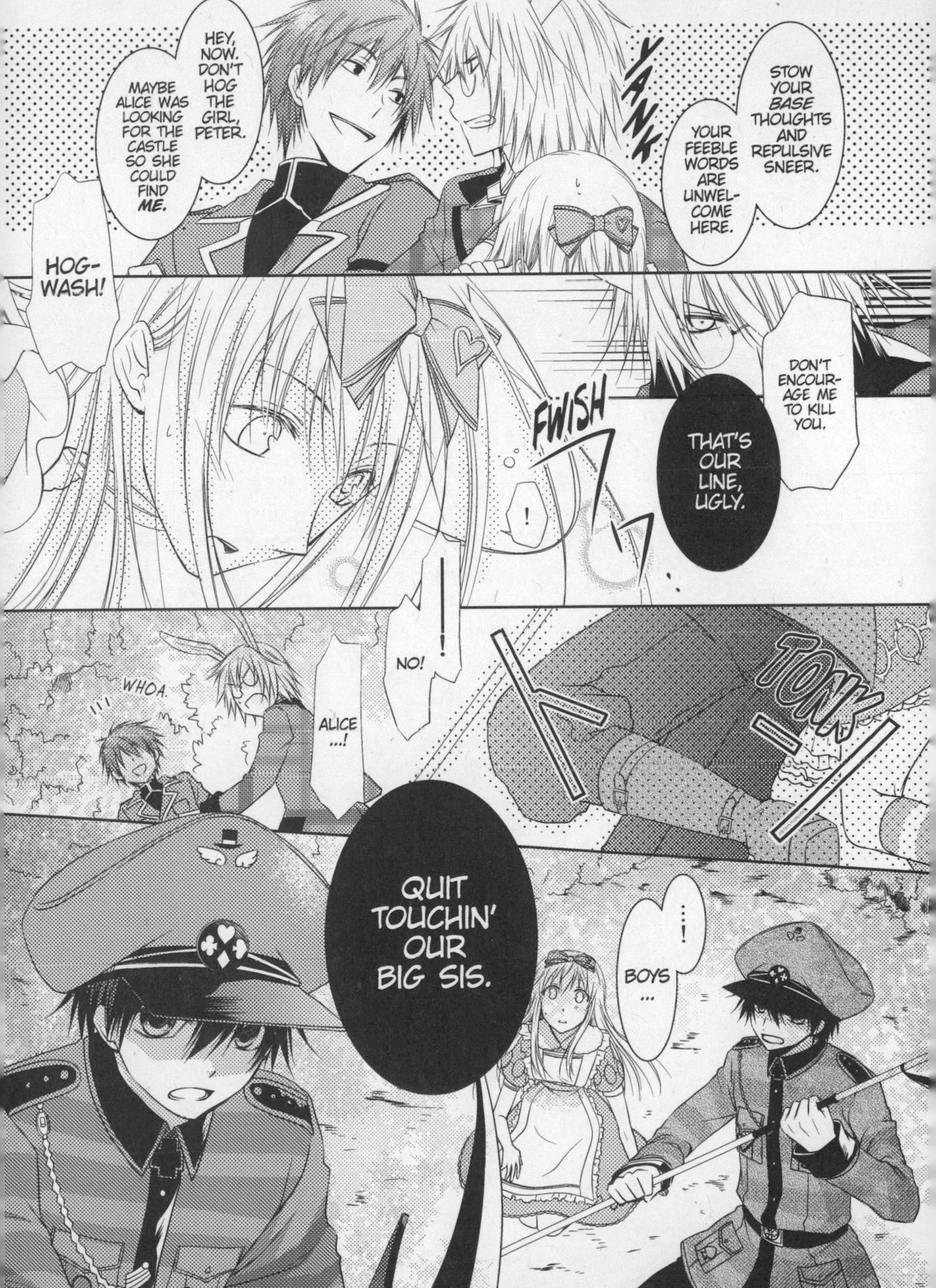
STOW YOUR BASE THOUGHTS AND REPULSIVE SNEER.
YOUR FEEBLE WORDS ARE UNWELCOME HERE.
YANK
HEY, NOW. DON'T HOG THE GIRL, PETER.
MAYBE ALICE WAS LOOKING FOR THE CASTLE SO SHE COULD FIND ME.
HOG-WASH!
DON'T ENCOURAGE ME TO KILL YOU.
THAT'S OUR LINE, UGLY.
FWISH
!
TONK
!
NO!
ALICE ...!
WHOA.
...!
BOYS ...
QUIT TOUCHIN' OUR BIG SIS.

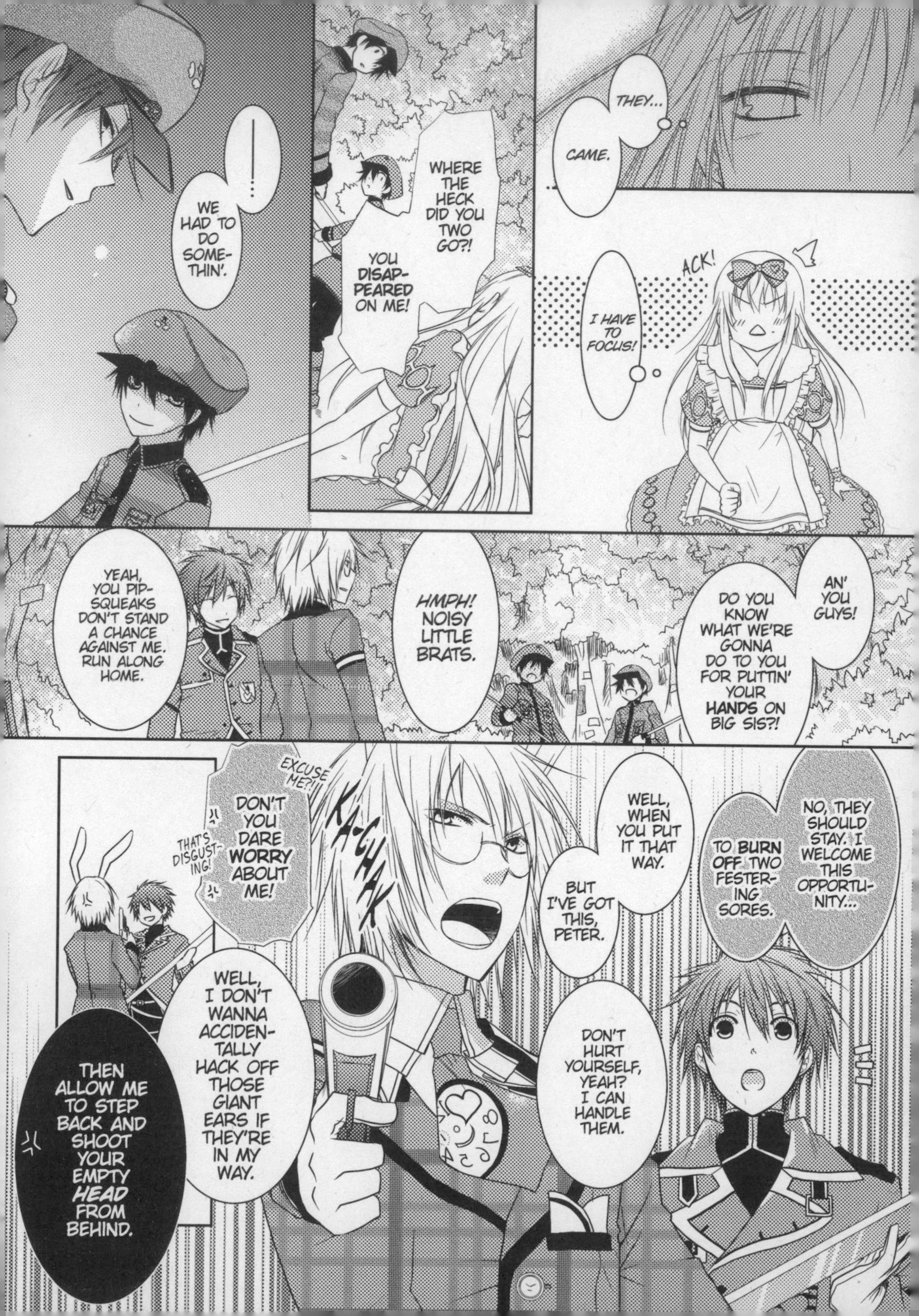
THEY... CAME.
ACK!
I HAVE TO FOCUS!
WHERE THE HECK DID YOU TWO GO?!
YOU DISAPPEARED ON ME!
...!
WE HAD TO DO SOMETHIN'.
AN' YOU GUYS!
DO YOU KNOW WHAT WE'RE GONNA DO TO YOU FOR PUTTIN' YOUR HANDS ON BIG SIS?!
HMPH! NOISY LITTLE BRATS.
YEAH, YOU PIPSQUEAKS DON'T STAND A CHANCE AGAINST ME. RUN ALONG HOME.
NO, THEY SHOULD STAY. I WELCOME THIS OPPORTUNITY...
TO BURN OFF TWO FESTERING SORES.
WELL, WHEN YOU PUT IT THAT WAY.
BUT I'VE GOT THIS, PETER.
DON'T HURT YOURSELF, YEAH? I CAN HANDLE THEM.
KA-CHAK
WELL, I DON'T WANNA ACCIDENTALLY HACK OFF THOSE GIANT EARS IF THEY'RE IN MY WAY.
EXCUSE ME?!
DON'T YOU DARE WORRY ABOUT ME!
THAT'S DISGUSTING!
THEN ALLOW ME TO STEP BACK AND SHOOT YOUR EMPTY HEAD FROM BEHIND.

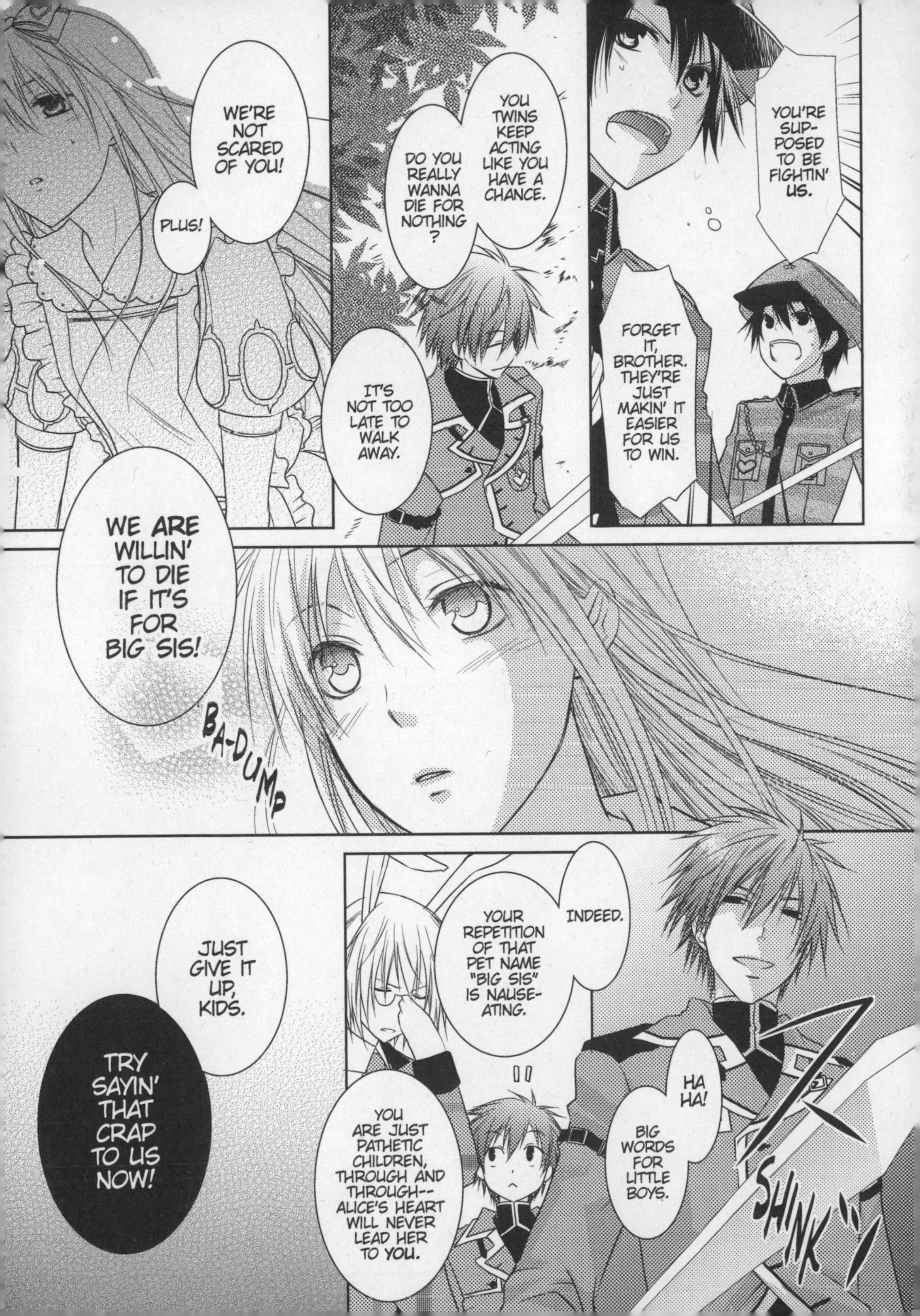
YOU'RE SUP-POSED TO BE FIGHTIN' US.
FORGET IT, BROTHER. THEY'RE JUST MAKIN' IT EASIER FOR US TO WIN.
YOU TWINS KEEP ACTING LIKE YOU HAVE A CHANCE.
DO YOU REALLY WANNA DIE FOR NOTHING?
IT'S NOT TOO LATE TO WALK AWAY.
WE'RE NOT SCARED OF YOU!
PLUS!
WE ARE WILLIN' TO DIE IF IT'S FOR BIG SIS!
BA-DUMP
INDEED.
YOUR REPETITION OF THAT PET NAME "BIG SIS" IS NAUSE-ATING.
HA HA!
BIG WORDS FOR LITTLE BOYS.
YOU ARE JUST PATHETIC CHILDREN, THROUGH AND THROUGH-- ALICE'S HEART WILL NEVER LEAD HER TO YOU.
SHINK
JUST GIVE IT UP, KIDS.
TRY SAYIN' THAT CRAP TO US NOW!

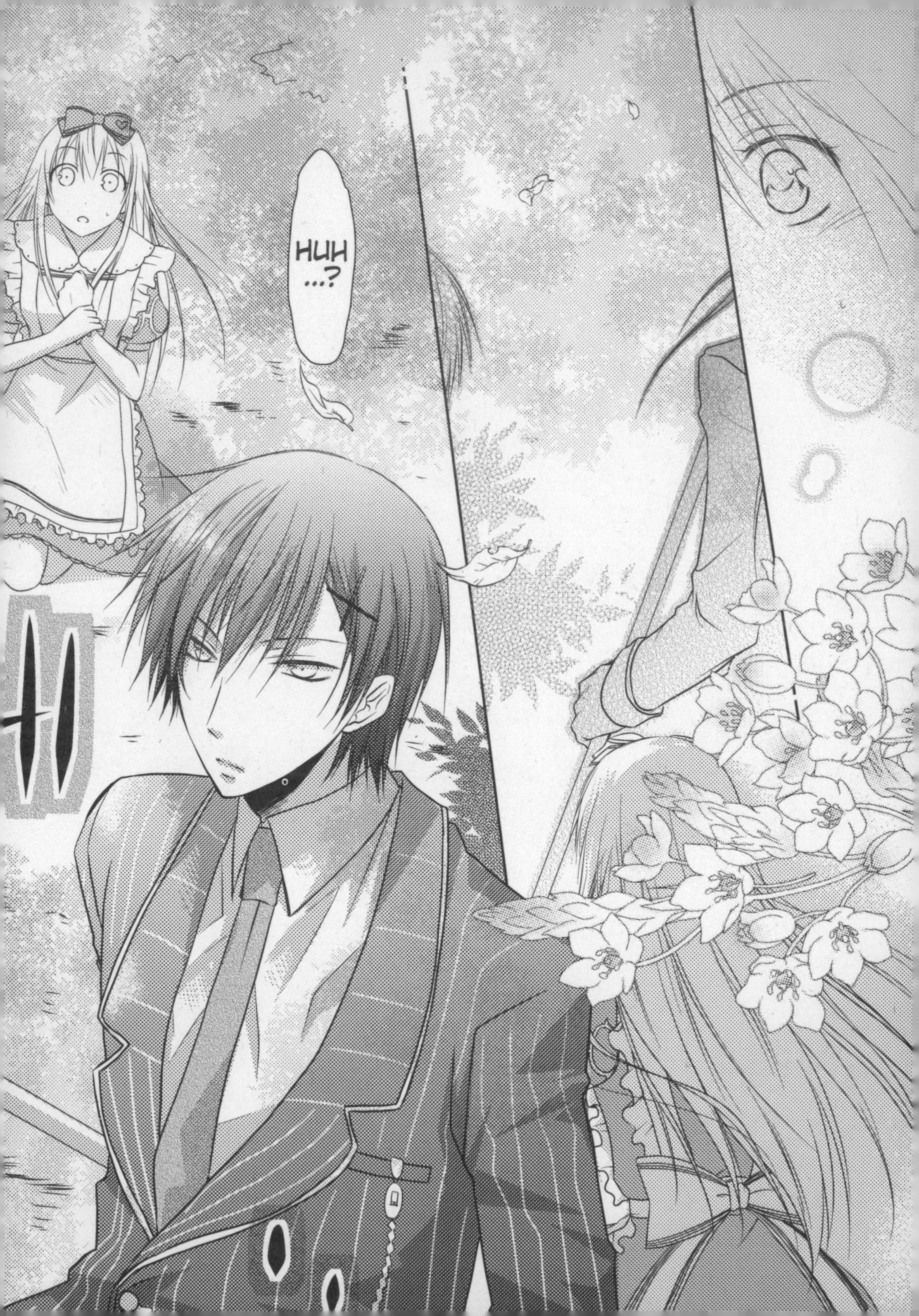
HUH ...?

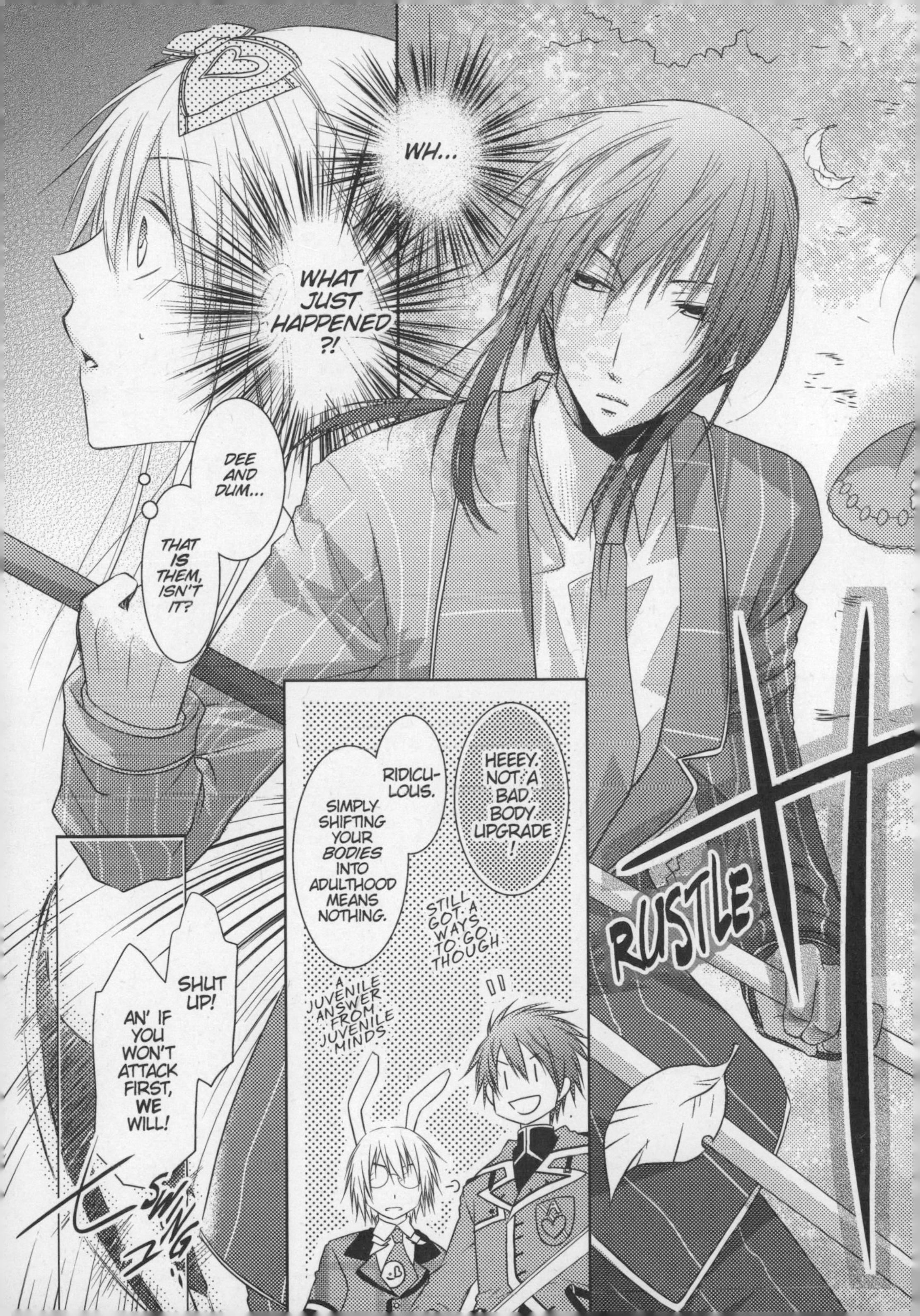
WH...
RUSTLE
WHAT JUST HAPPENED ?!
DEE AND DUM...
THAT IS THEM, ISN'T IT?
HEEEY. NOT A BAD BODY UPGRADE!
RIDICULOUS.
SIMPLY SHIFTING YOUR BODIES INTO ADULTHOOD MEANS NOTHING.
STILL GOT A WAYS TO GO THOUGH
A JUVENILE ANSWER FROM JUVENILE MINDS.
SHUT UP!
AN' IF YOU WON'T ATTACK FIRST, WE WILL!
SWING

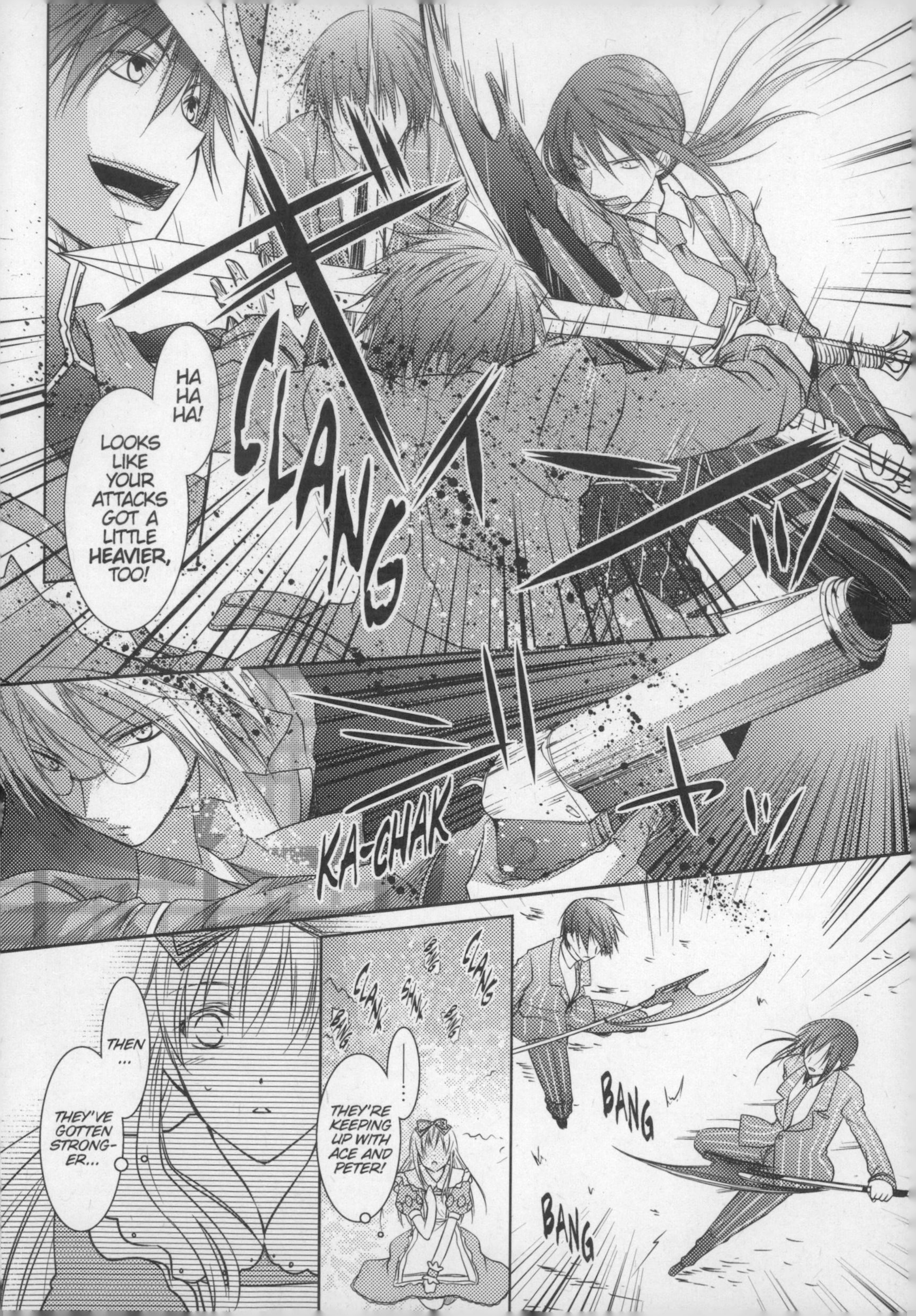
CLANG
HA HA HA! LOOKS LIKE YOUR ATTACKS GOT A LITTLE HEAVIER, TOO!
KA-CHAK
BANG
BANG
CLANG
BANG
SHINK
BANG
CLANK
BANG
...!
THEY'RE KEEPING UP WITH ACE AND PETER!
THEN ...
THEY'VE GOTTEN STRONGER...

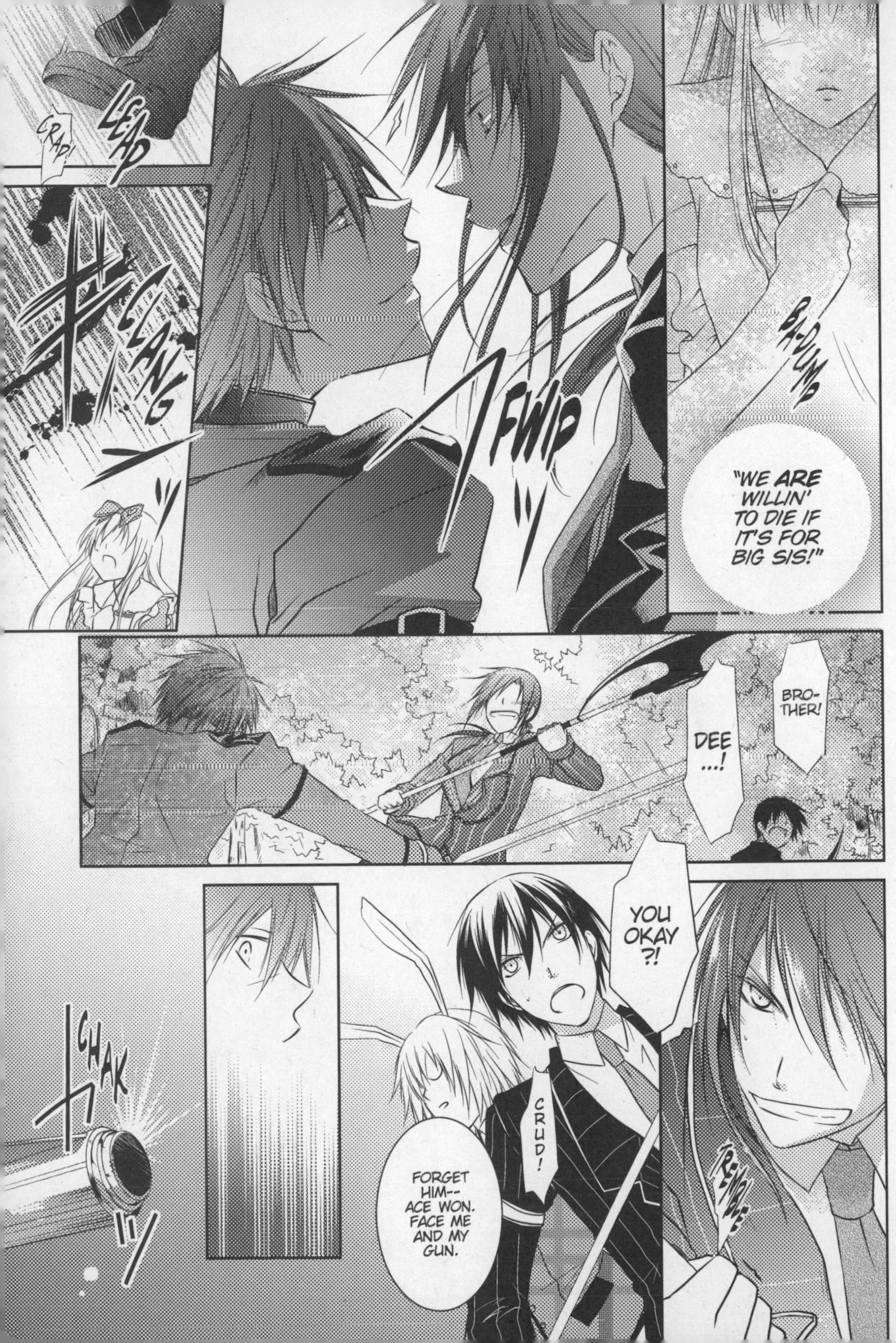
BA-DUMP
"WE ARE WILLIN' TO DIE IF IT'S FOR BIG SIS!"
FWIP
LEAP
CRAP!
CLANG
BRO-THER!
DEE ...!
YOU OKAY ?!
TREMBLE
CRUD!
FORGET HIM-- ACE WON. FACE ME AND MY GUN.
CHAK

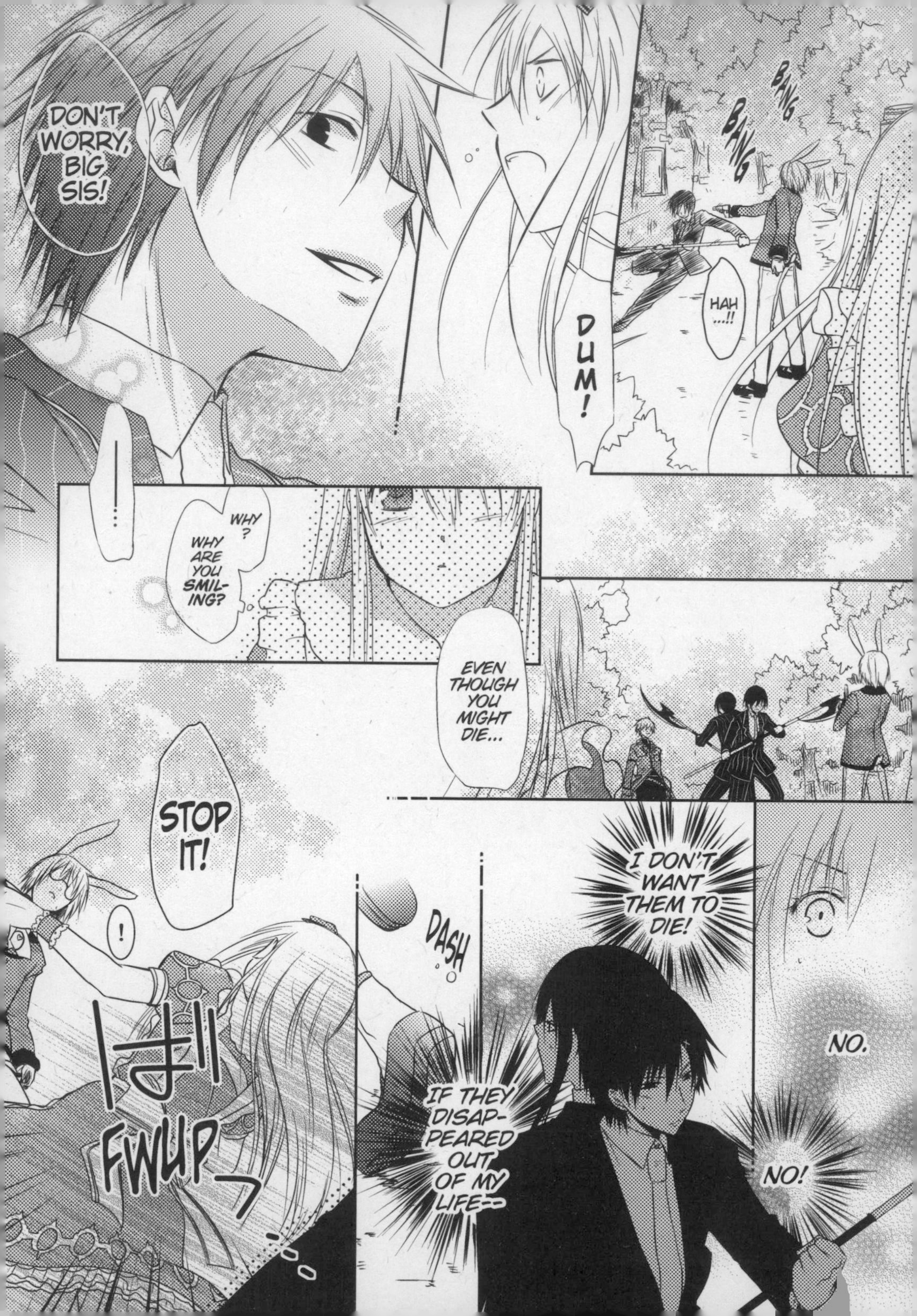
BANG
BANG
HAH ...!!
DUM!
DON'T WORRY, BIG SIS!
......
WHY? WHY ARE YOU SMILING?
EVEN THOUGH YOU MIGHT DIE...
NO.
NO!
I DON'T WANT THEM TO DIE!
IF THEY DISAP-PEARED OUT OF MY LIFE--
DASH
STOP IT!
!
ばっ
FWUP

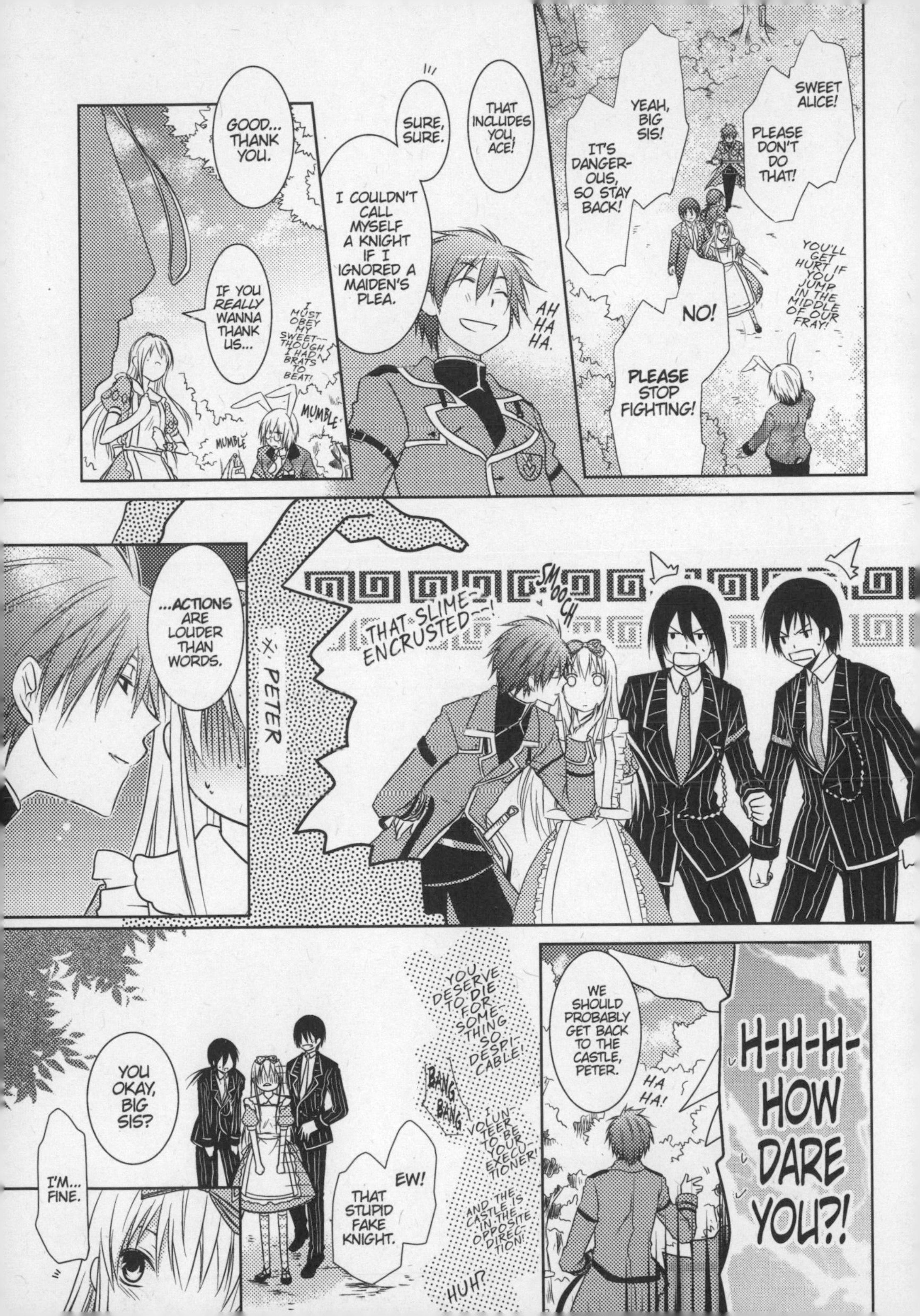
SWEET ALICE!
PLEASE DON'T DO THAT!
YEAH, BIG SIS!
IT'S DANGER-OUS, SO STAY BACK!
YOU'LL GET HURT IF YOU JUMP IN THE MIDDLE OF OUR FRAY!
NO!
PLEASE STOP FIGHTING!
THAT INCLUDES YOU, ACE!
SURE, SURE.
I COULDN'T CALL MYSELF A KNIGHT IF I IGNORED A MAIDEN'S PLEA.
AH HA HA.
GOOD... THANK YOU.
IF YOU REALLY WANNA THANK US...
I MUST OBEY MY SWEET--THOUGH I HAD BRATS TO BEAT!
MUMBLE
MUMBLE
SMOOCH
THAT SLIME-ENCRUSTED--!
※ PETER
...ACTIONS ARE LOUDER THAN WORDS.
H-H-H-HOW DARE YOU?!
WE SHOULD PROBABLY GET BACK TO THE CASTLE, PETER.
HA HA!
YOU DESERVE TO DIE FOR SOMETHING SO DESPICABLE!
BANG BANG
I VOLUNTEER TO BE YOUR EXECUTIONER!
AND THE CASTLE IS IN THE OPPOSITE DIRECTION!
HUH?
EW!
THAT STUPID FAKE KNIGHT.
YOU OKAY, BIG SIS?
I'M... FINE.

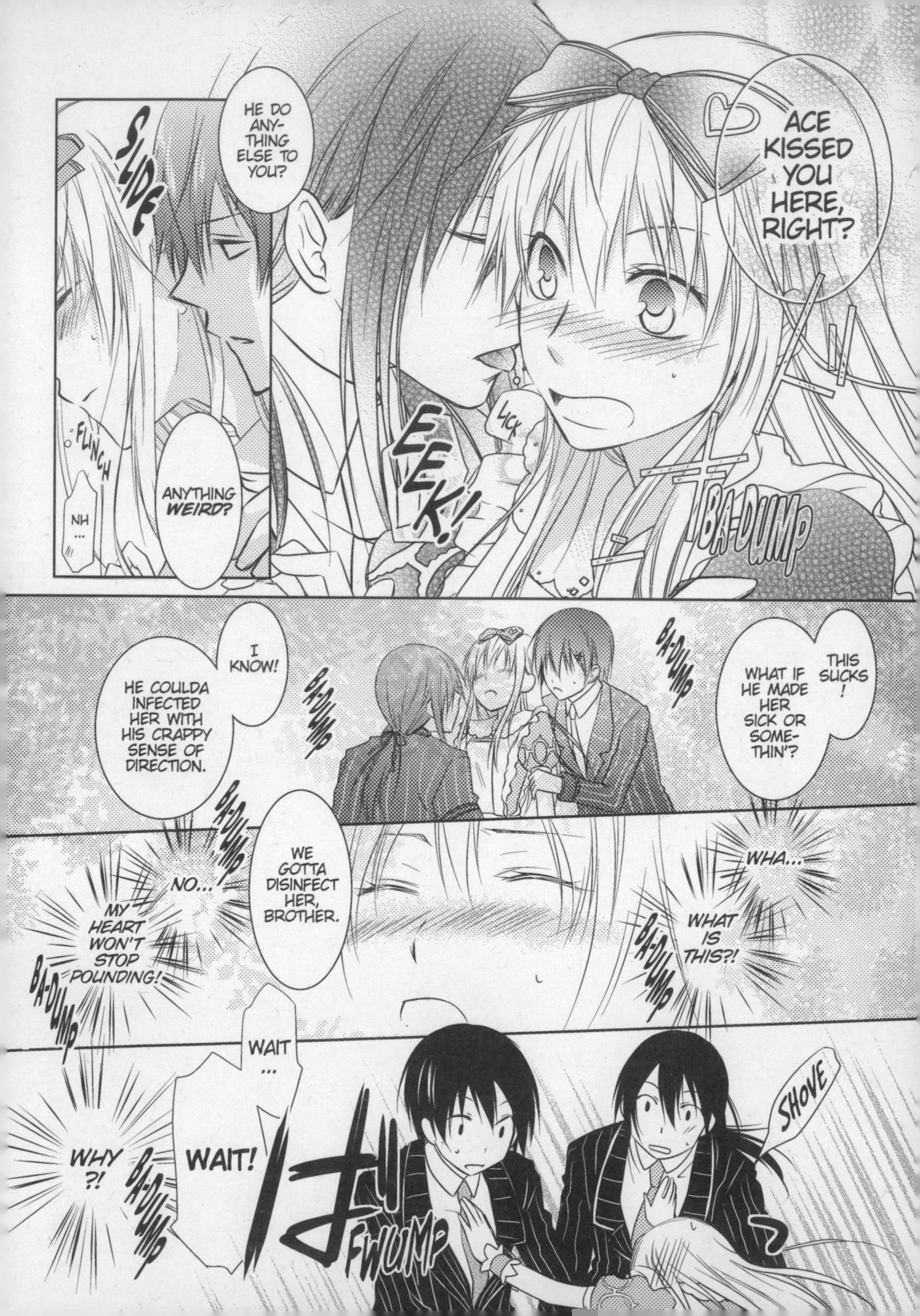
ACE KISSED YOU HERE, RIGHT?
BA-DUMP
LICK
EEK!
HE DO ANYTHING ELSE TO YOU?
SLIDE
ANYTHING WEIRD?
FLINCH
NH...
THIS SUCKS!
WHAT IF HE MADE HER SICK OR SOMETHIN'?
BA-DUMP
I KNOW!
HE COULDA INFECTED HER WITH HIS CRAPPY SENSE OF DIRECTION.
BA-DUMP
WHA...
WHAT IS THIS?!
BA-DUMP
WE GOTTA DISINFECT HER, BROTHER.
BA-DUMP
NO...
MY HEART WON'T STOP POUNDING!
BA-DUMP
SHOVE
FWUMP
WAIT...
WAIT!
WHY?!
BA-DUMP

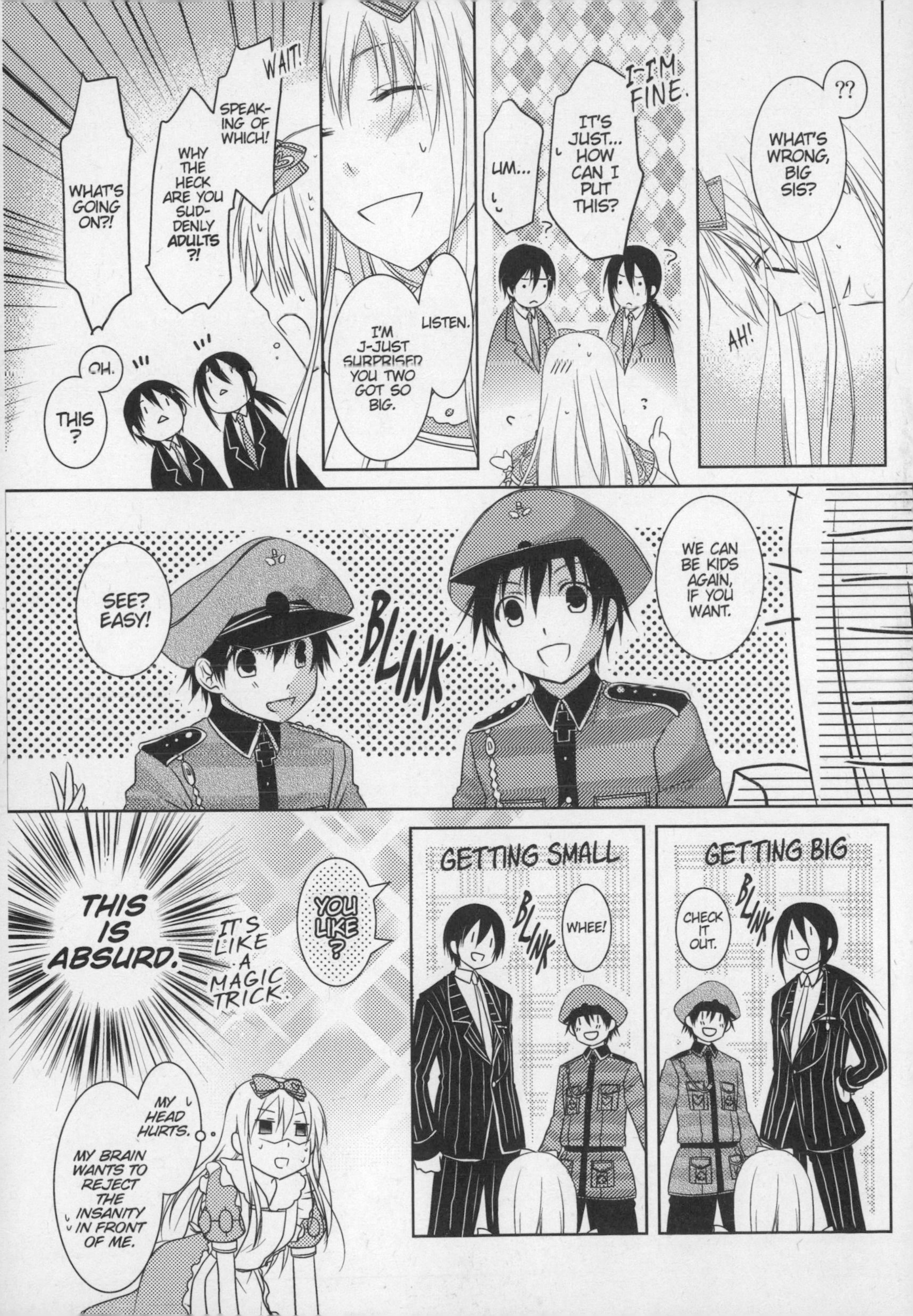
??
WHAT'S WRONG, BIG SIS?
AH!
I-I'M FINE.
IT'S JUST... HOW CAN I PUT THIS?
UM...
LISTEN.
I'M J-JUST SURPRISED YOU TWO GOT SO BIG.
WAIT!
SPEAKING OF WHICH!
WHY THE HECK ARE YOU SUDDENLY ADULTS?!
WHAT'S GOING ON?!
OH.
THIS?
WE CAN BE KIDS AGAIN, IF YOU WANT.
BLINK
SEE? EASY!
GETTING BIG
BLINK
CHECK IT OUT.
GETTING SMALL
WHEE!
BLINK
YOU LIKE?
IT'S LIKE A MAGIC TRICK.
THIS IS ABSURD.
MY HEAD HURTS.
MY BRAIN WANTS TO REJECT THE INSANITY IN FRONT OF ME.

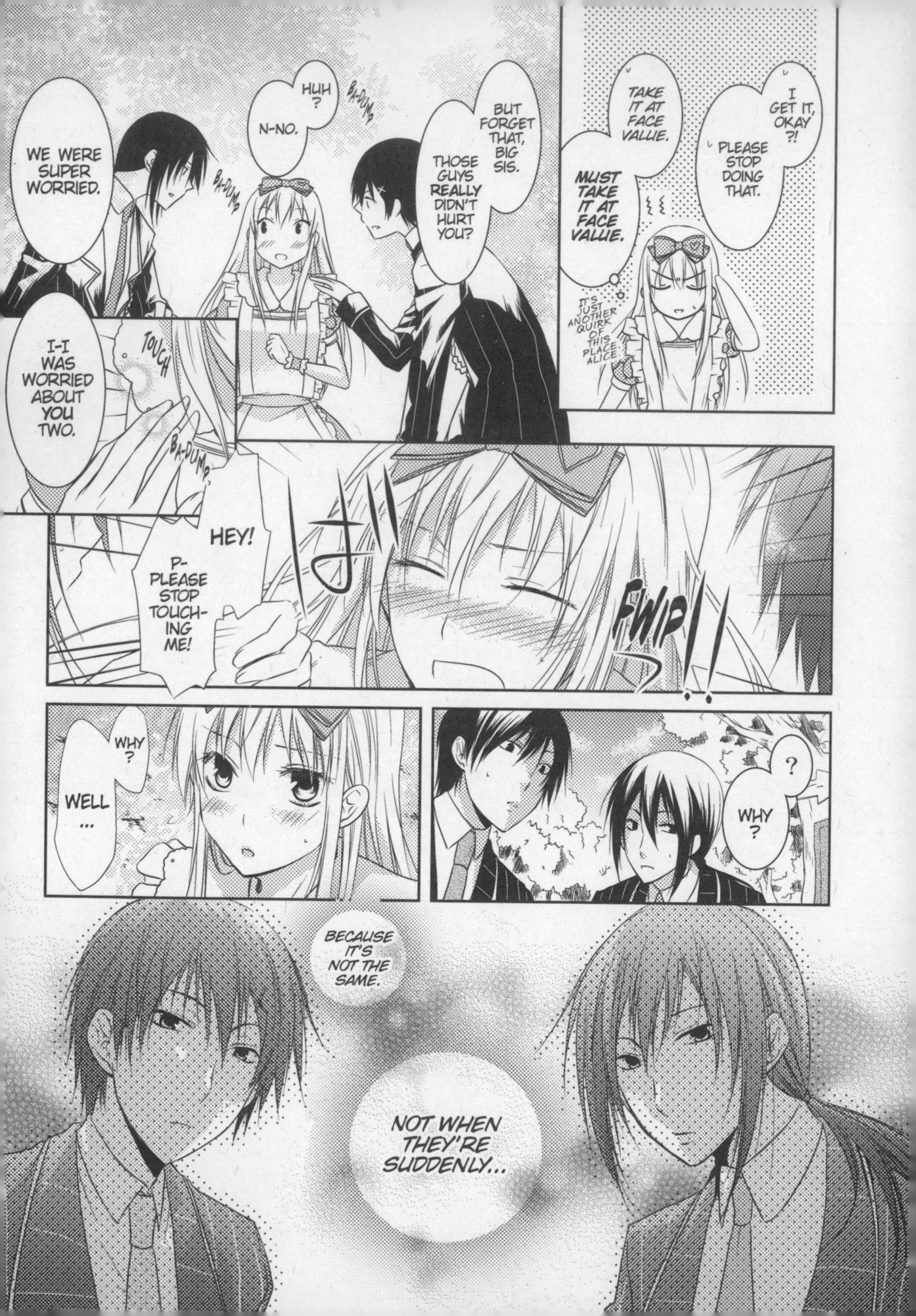
I GET IT, OKAY ?!
PLEASE STOP DOING THAT.
TAKE IT AT FACE VALUE.
MUST TAKE IT AT FACE VALUE.
IT'S JUST ANOTHER QUIRK OF THIS PLACE, ALICE.
BUT FORGET THAT, BIG SIS.
THOSE GUYS REALLY DIDN'T HURT YOU?
BA-DUMP
HUH ?
N-NO.
BA-DUMP
WE WERE SUPER WORRIED.
BA-DUMP
TOUCH
I-I WAS WORRIED ABOUT YOU TWO.
BA-DUMP
FWIP!!
HEY!
P-PLEASE STOP TOUCHING ME!
?
WHY ?
WHY ?
WELL ...
BECAUSE IT'S NOT THE SAME.
NOT WHEN THEY'RE SUDDENLY...

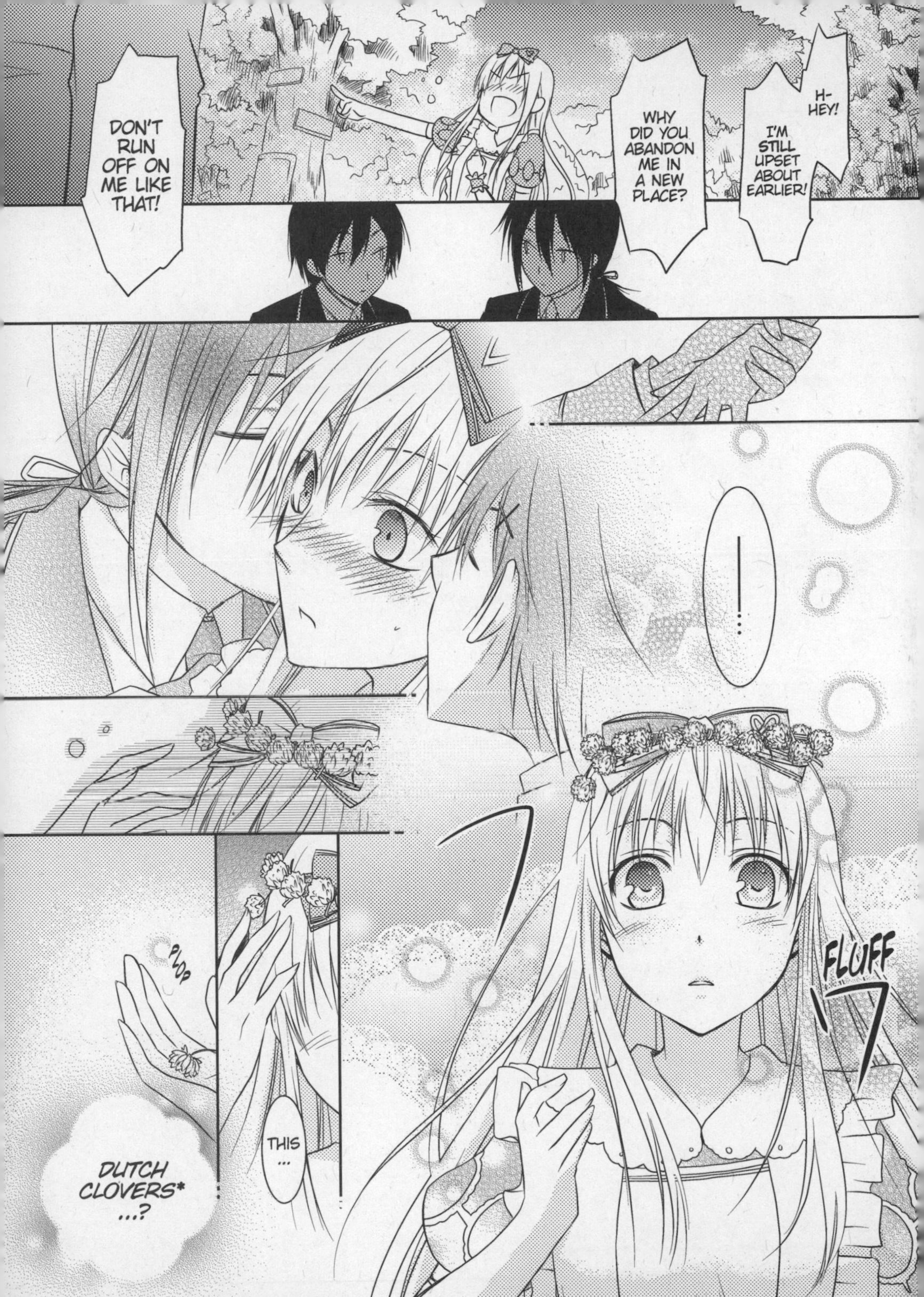
H-HEY!
I'M STILL UPSET ABOUT EARLIER!
WHY DID YOU ABANDON ME IN A NEW PLACE?
DON'T RUN OFF ON ME LIKE THAT!
!
FLUFF
PLOP
THIS ...
DUTCH CLOVERS* ...?

*Dutch clovers are a type of clover that produce little white flowers.

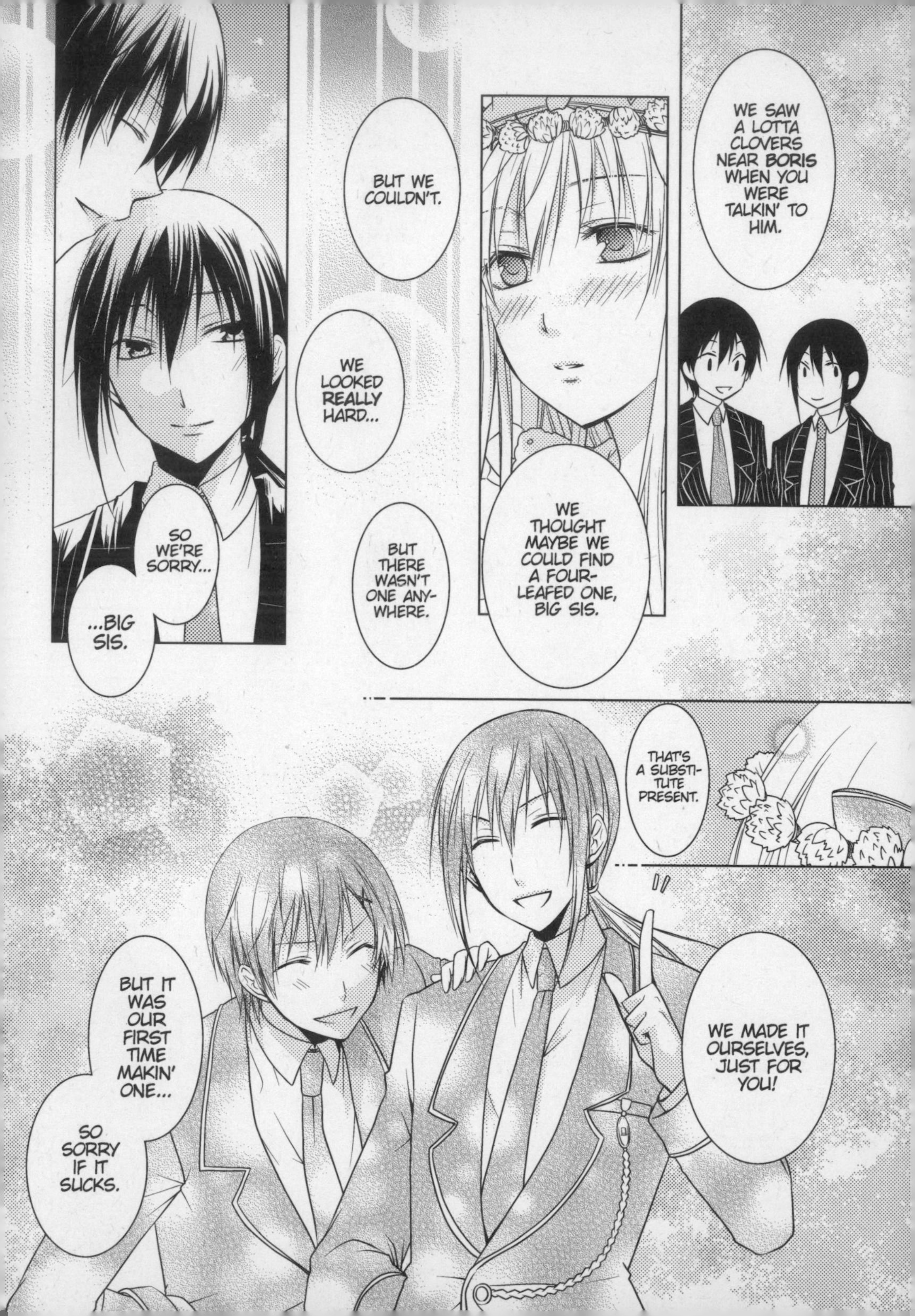
WE SAW A LOTTA CLOVERS NEAR BORIS WHEN YOU WERE TALKIN' TO HIM.
WE THOUGHT MAYBE WE COULD FIND A FOUR-LEAFED ONE, BIG SIS.
BUT THERE WASN'T ONE ANYWHERE.
WE LOOKED REALLY HARD...
BUT WE COULDN'T.
SO WE'RE SORRY...
...BIG SIS.
THAT'S A SUBSTITUTE PRESENT.
WE MADE IT OURSELVES, JUST FOR YOU!
BUT IT WAS OUR FIRST TIME MAKIN' ONE...
SO SORRY IF IT SUCKS.

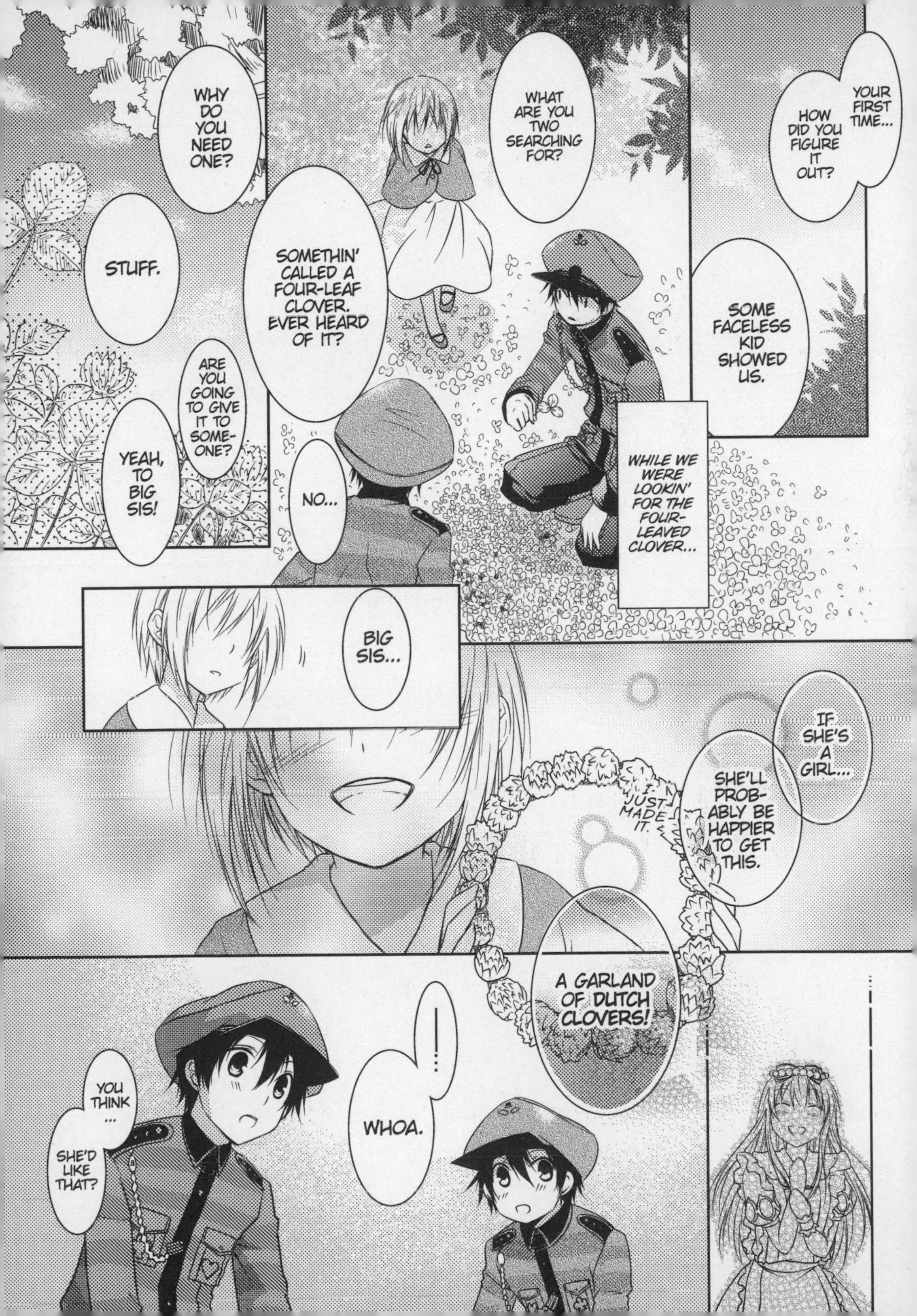
YOUR FIRST TIME...
HOW DID YOU FIGURE IT OUT?
SOME FACELESS KID SHOWED US.
WHAT ARE YOU TWO SEARCHING FOR?
SOMETHIN' CALLED A FOUR-LEAF CLOVER. EVER HEARD OF IT?
WHILE WE WERE LOOKIN' FOR THE FOUR-LEAVED CLOVER...
WHY DO YOU NEED ONE?
STUFF.
ARE YOU GOING TO GIVE IT TO SOME-ONE?
YEAH, TO BIG SIS!
NO...
BIG SIS...
IF SHE'S A GIRL...
SHE'LL PROBABLY BE HAPPIER TO GET THIS.
I-JUST MADE IT.
A GARLAND OF DUTCH CLOVERS!
...!
WHOA.
YOU THINK ...
SHE'D LIKE THAT?

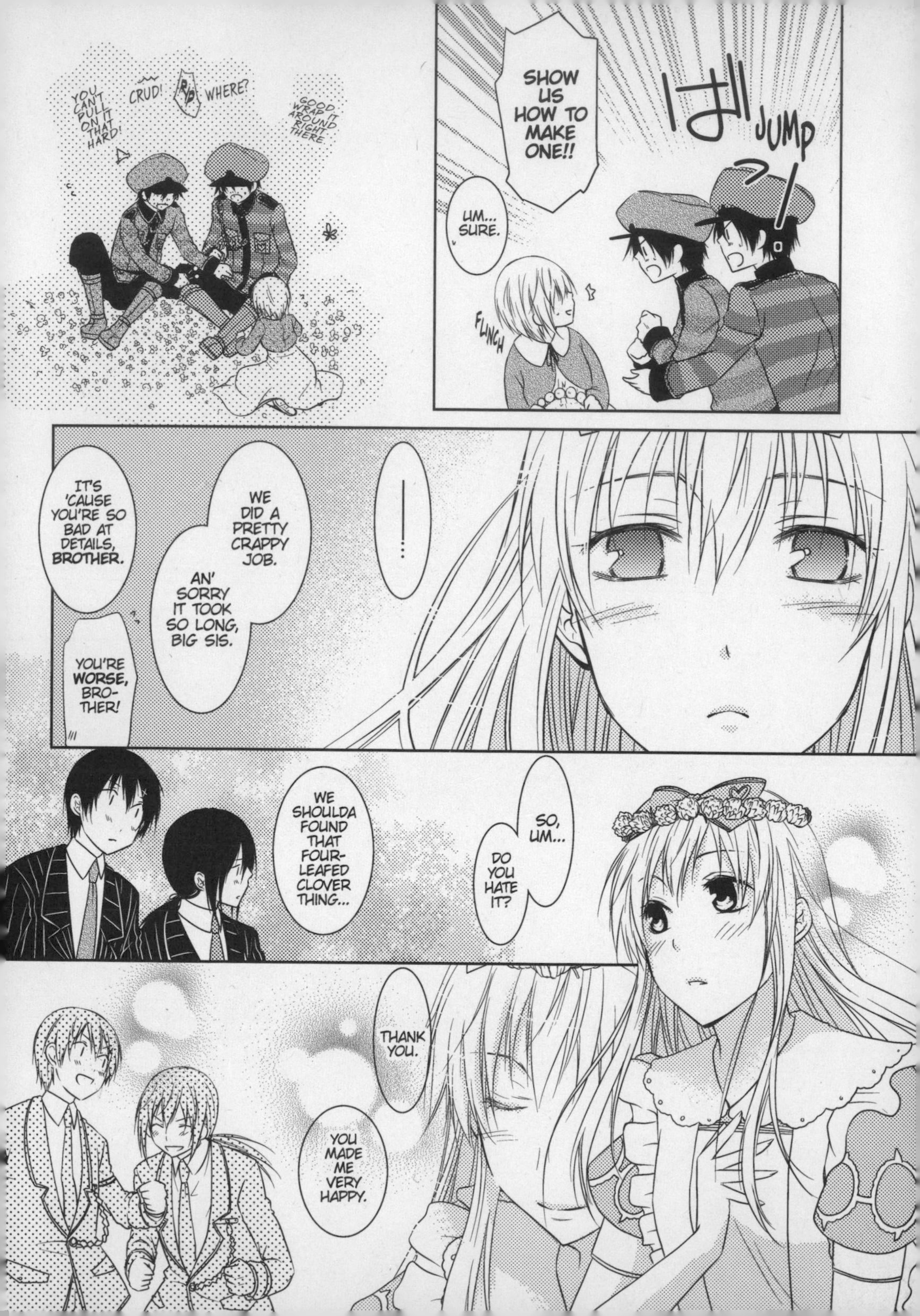
SHOW US HOW TO MAKE ONE!!
はッ JUMP
UM... SURE.
FLINCH
GOOD, WRAP IT AROUND RIGHT THERE
WHERE?
CRUD!
YOU CAN'T PULL ON IT THAT HARD!
—!...
WE DID A PRETTY CRAPPY JOB.
IT'S 'CAUSE YOU'RE SO BAD AT DETAILS, BROTHER.
AN' SORRY IT TOOK SO LONG, BIG SIS.
YOU'RE WORSE, BROTHER!
SO, UM...
DO YOU HATE IT?
WE SHOULDA FOUND THAT FOUR-LEAFED CLOVER THING...
THANK YOU.
YOU MADE ME VERY HAPPY.

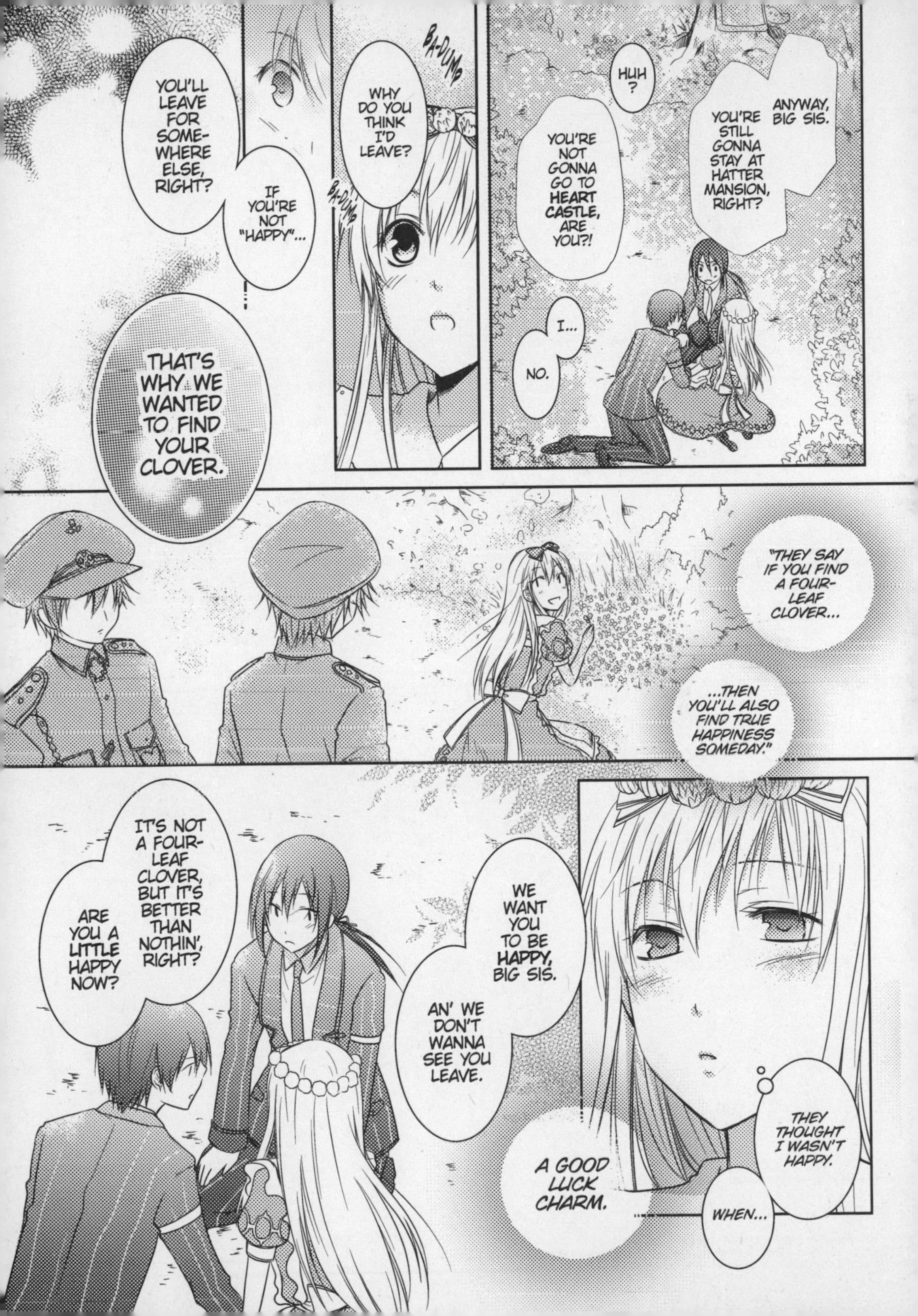
ANYWAY, BIG SIS.
YOU'RE STILL GONNA STAY AT HATTER MANSION, RIGHT?
HUH?
YOU'RE NOT GONNA GO TO HEART CASTLE, ARE YOU?!
I...
NO.
BA-DUMP
WHY DO YOU THINK I'D LEAVE?
BA-DUMP
YOU'LL LEAVE FOR SOME-WHERE ELSE, RIGHT?
IF YOU'RE NOT "HAPPY"...
THAT'S WHY WE WANTED TO FIND YOUR CLOVER.
"THEY SAY IF YOU FIND A FOUR-LEAF CLOVER...
...THEN YOU'LL ALSO FIND TRUE HAPPINESS SOMEDAY."
THEY THOUGHT I WASN'T HAPPY.
WHEN...
A GOOD LUCK CHARM.
WE WANT YOU TO BE HAPPY, BIG SIS.
AN' WE DON'T WANNA SEE YOU LEAVE.
IT'S NOT A FOUR-LEAF CLOVER, BUT IT'S BETTER THAN NOTHIN', RIGHT?
ARE YOU A LITTLE HAPPY NOW?

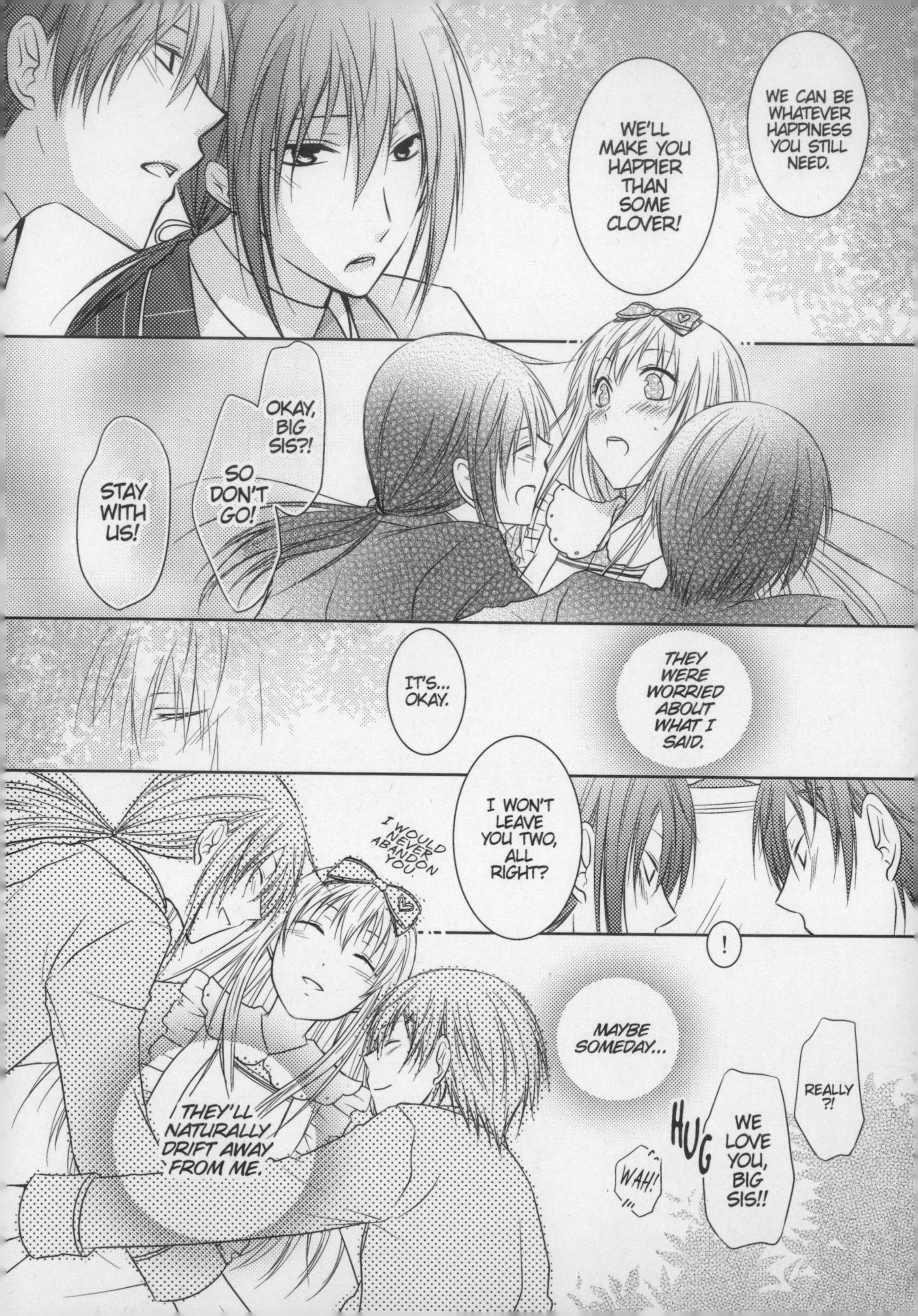
WE CAN BE WHATEVER HAPPINESS YOU STILL NEED.
WE'LL MAKE YOU HAPPIER THAN SOME CLOVER!
OKAY, BIG SIS?!
SO DON'T GO!
STAY WITH US!
THEY WERE WORRIED ABOUT WHAT I SAID.
IT'S... OKAY.
I WON'T LEAVE YOU TWO, ALL RIGHT?
I WOULD NEVER ABANDON YOU.
!
MAYBE SOMEDAY...
REALLY ?!
WE LOVE YOU, BIG SIS!!
HUG
WAH!
THEY'LL NATURALLY DRIFT AWAY FROM ME.

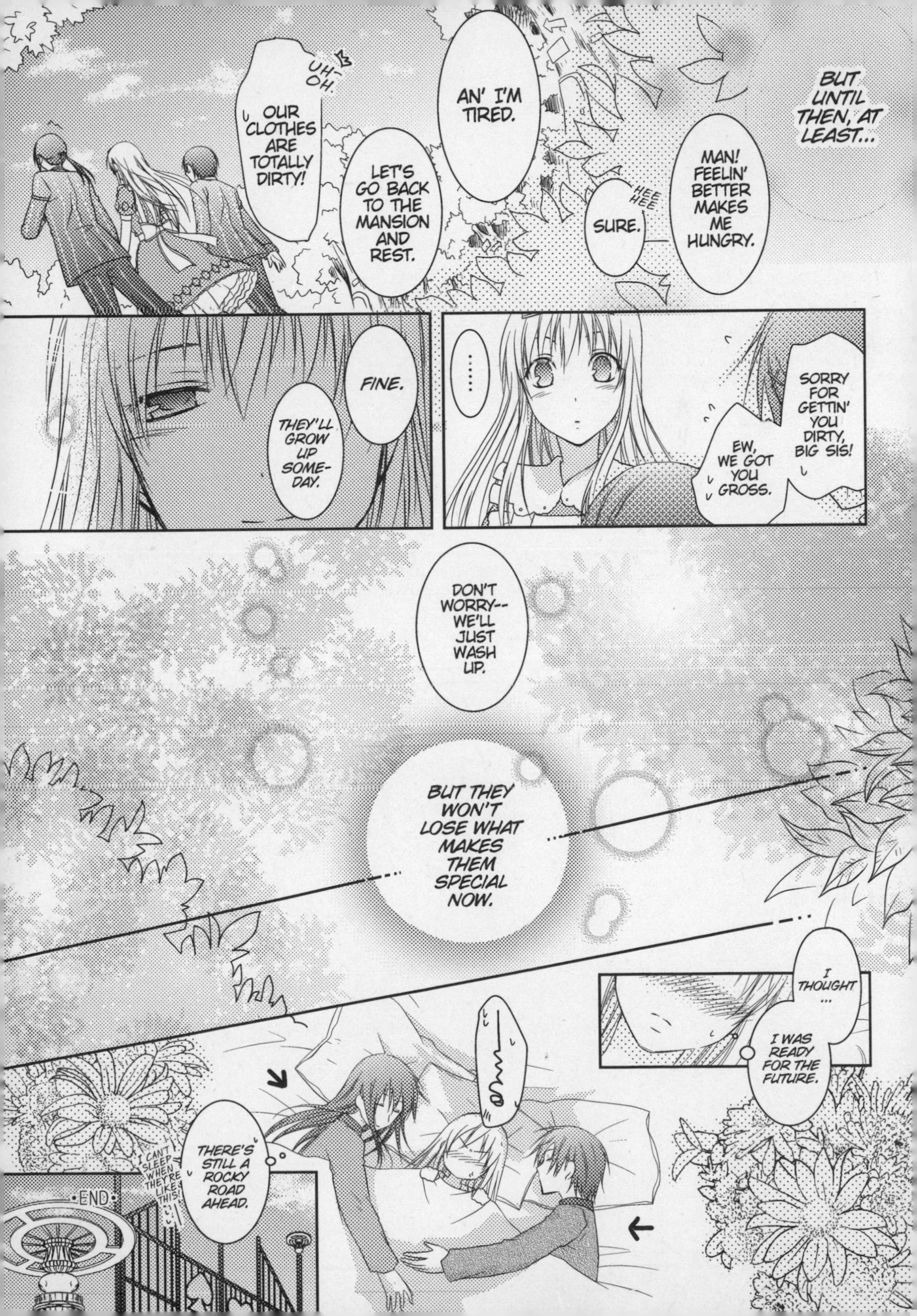
BUT UNTIL THEN, AT LEAST...
MAN! FEELIN' BETTER MAKES ME HUNGRY.
HEE HEE
SURE.
AN' I'M TIRED.
LET'S GO BACK TO THE MANSION AND REST.
UH-OH.
OUR CLOTHES ARE TOTALLY DIRTY!
SORRY FOR GETTIN' YOU DIRTY, BIG SIS!
EW, WE GOT YOU GROSS.
......
FINE.
THEY'LL GROW UP SOME-DAY.
DON'T WORRY-- WE'LL JUST WASH UP.
BUT THEY WON'T LOSE WHAT MAKES THEM SPECIAL NOW.
I THOUGHT ...
I WAS READY FOR THE FUTURE.
THERE'S STILL A ROCKY ROAD AHEAD.
I CAN'T SLEEP WHEN THEY'RE LIKE THIS!
•END•

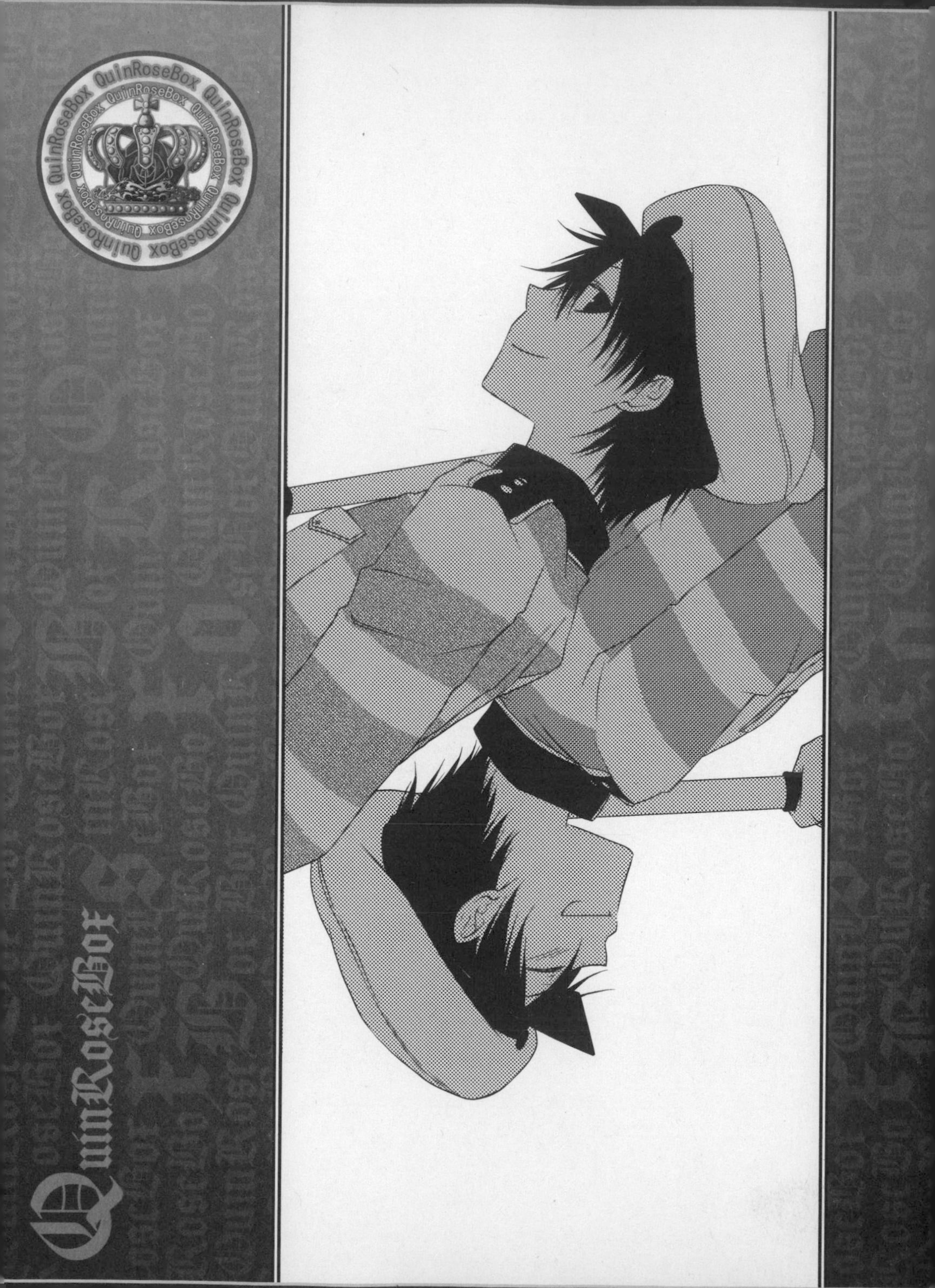
QuinRoseBox

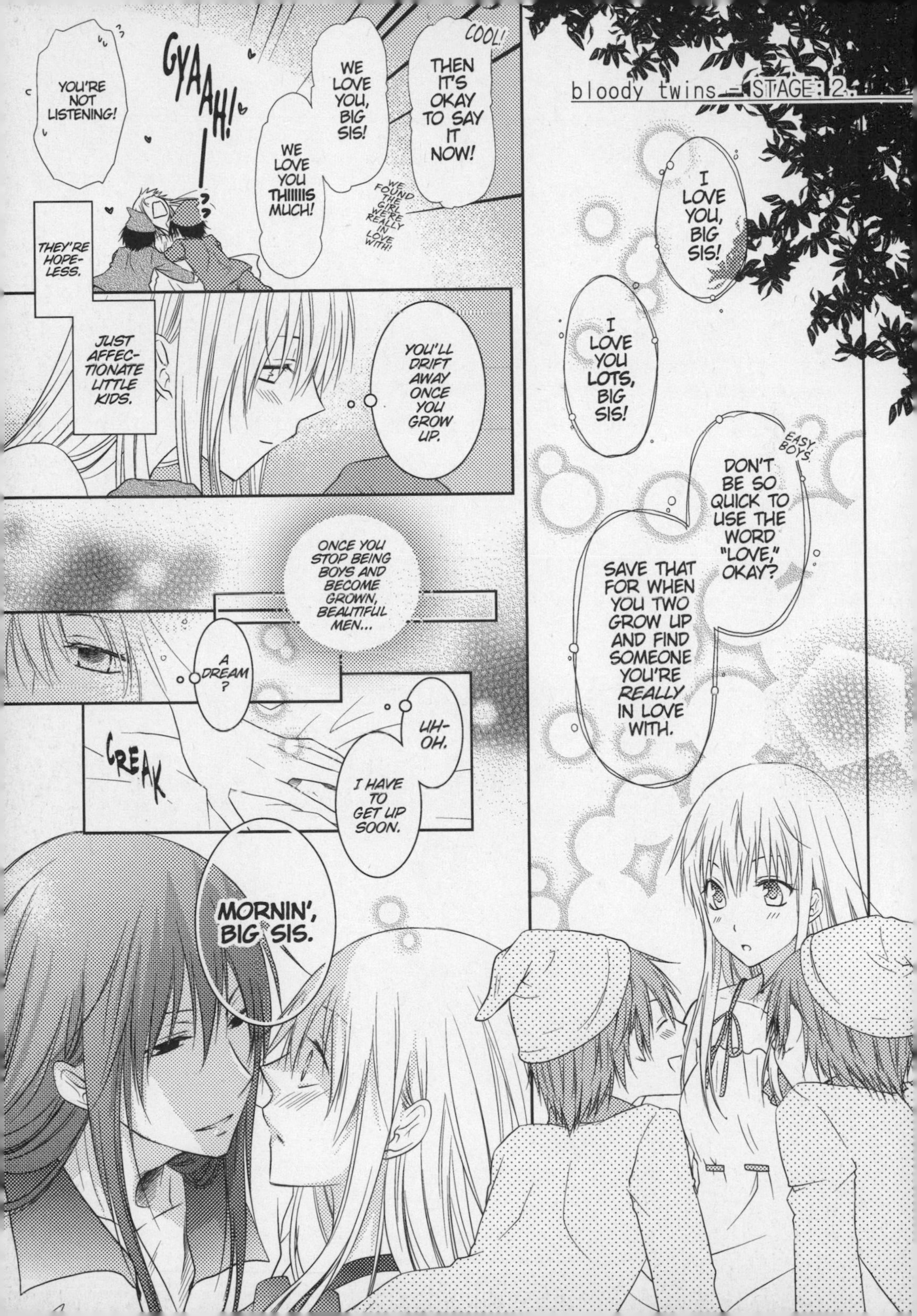
bloody twins - STAGE: 2.
I LOVE YOU, BIG SIS!
I LOVE YOU LOTS, BIG SIS!
EASY, BOYS.
DON'T BE SO QUICK TO USE THE WORD "LOVE," OKAY?
SAVE THAT FOR WHEN YOU TWO GROW UP AND FIND SOMEONE YOU'RE *REALLY* IN LOVE WITH.
COOL!
THEN IT'S OKAY TO SAY IT NOW!
WE LOVE YOU, BIG SIS!
WE FOUND THE GIRL WE'RE REALLY IN LOVE WITH!
WE LOVE YOU THIIIIIS MUCH!
GYAAAH!
YOU'RE NOT LISTENING!
THEY'RE HOPELESS.
JUST AFFECTIONATE LITTLE KIDS.
YOU'LL DRIFT AWAY ONCE YOU GROW UP.
ONCE YOU STOP BEING BOYS AND BECOME GROWN, BEAUTIFUL MEN...
A DREAM?
UH-OH.
I HAVE TO GET UP SOON.
CREAK
MORNIN', BIG SIS.

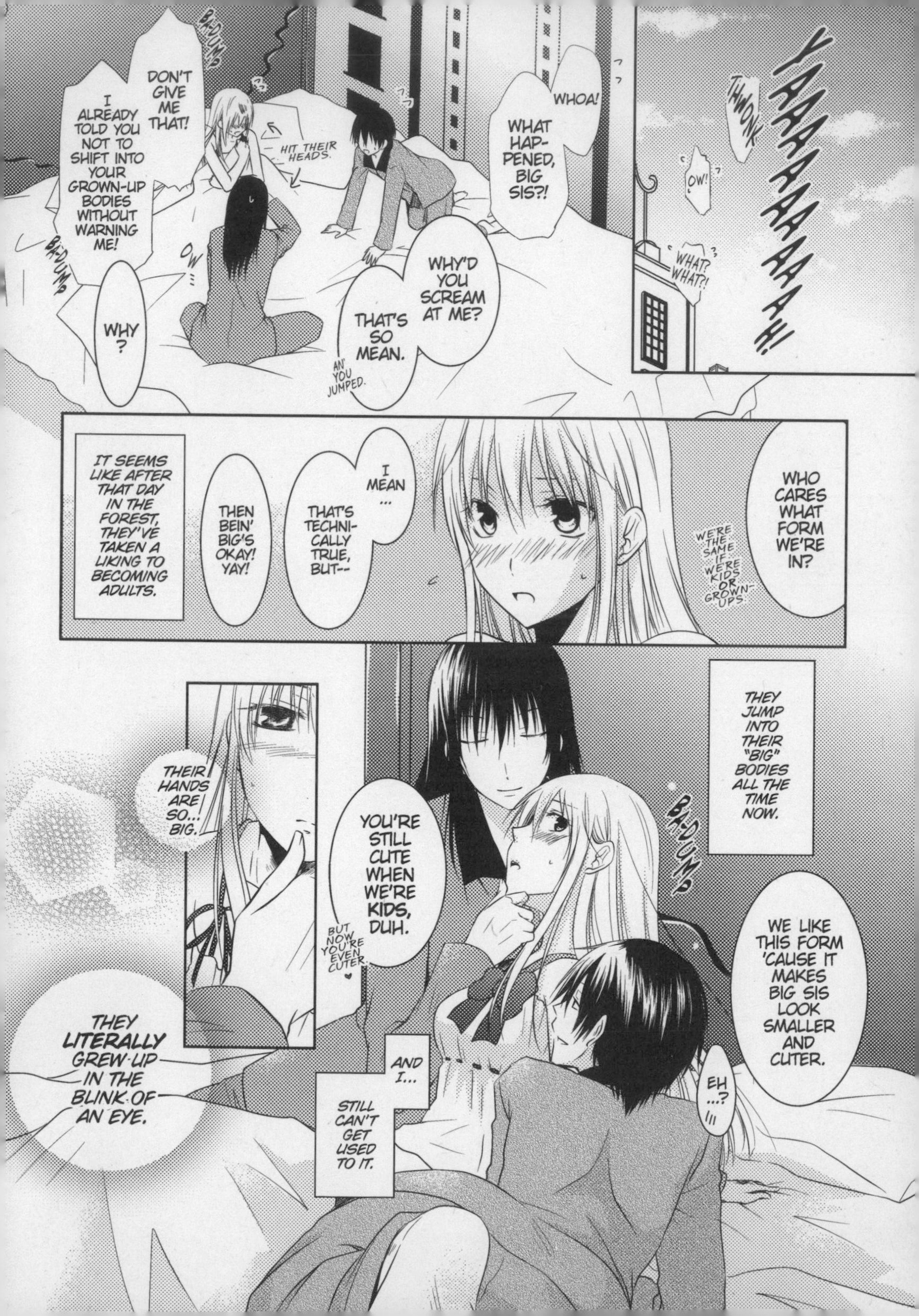
YAAAAAAAAAAAH!!
THWONK
OW!
WHAT? WHAT?!
WHOA!
WHAT HAPPENED, BIG SIS?!
BADUMP
DON'T GIVE ME THAT!
I ALREADY TOLD YOU NOT TO SHIFT INTO YOUR GROWN-UP BODIES WITHOUT WARNING ME!
HIT THEIR HEADS.
WHY'D YOU SCREAM AT ME?
THAT'S SO MEAN.
AN' YOU JUMPED.
OW
WHY?
BADUMP
WHO CARES WHAT FORM WE'RE IN?
WE'RE THE SAME IF WE'RE KIDS OR GROWN-UPS.
I MEAN...
THAT'S TECHNICALLY TRUE, BUT--
THEN BEIN' BIG'S OKAY! YAY!
IT SEEMS LIKE AFTER THAT DAY IN THE FOREST, THEY'VE TAKEN A LIKING TO BECOMING ADULTS.
THEY JUMP INTO THEIR "BIG" BODIES ALL THE TIME NOW.
BADUMP
WE LIKE THIS FORM 'CAUSE IT MAKES BIG SIS LOOK SMALLER AND CUTER.
YOU'RE STILL CUTE WHEN WE'RE KIDS, DUH.
BUT NOW YOU'RE EVEN CUTER.
EH...?
AND I...
STILL CAN'T GET USED TO IT.
THEIR HANDS ARE SO... BIG.
THEY LITERALLY GREW-UP IN THE BLINK OF AN EYE.

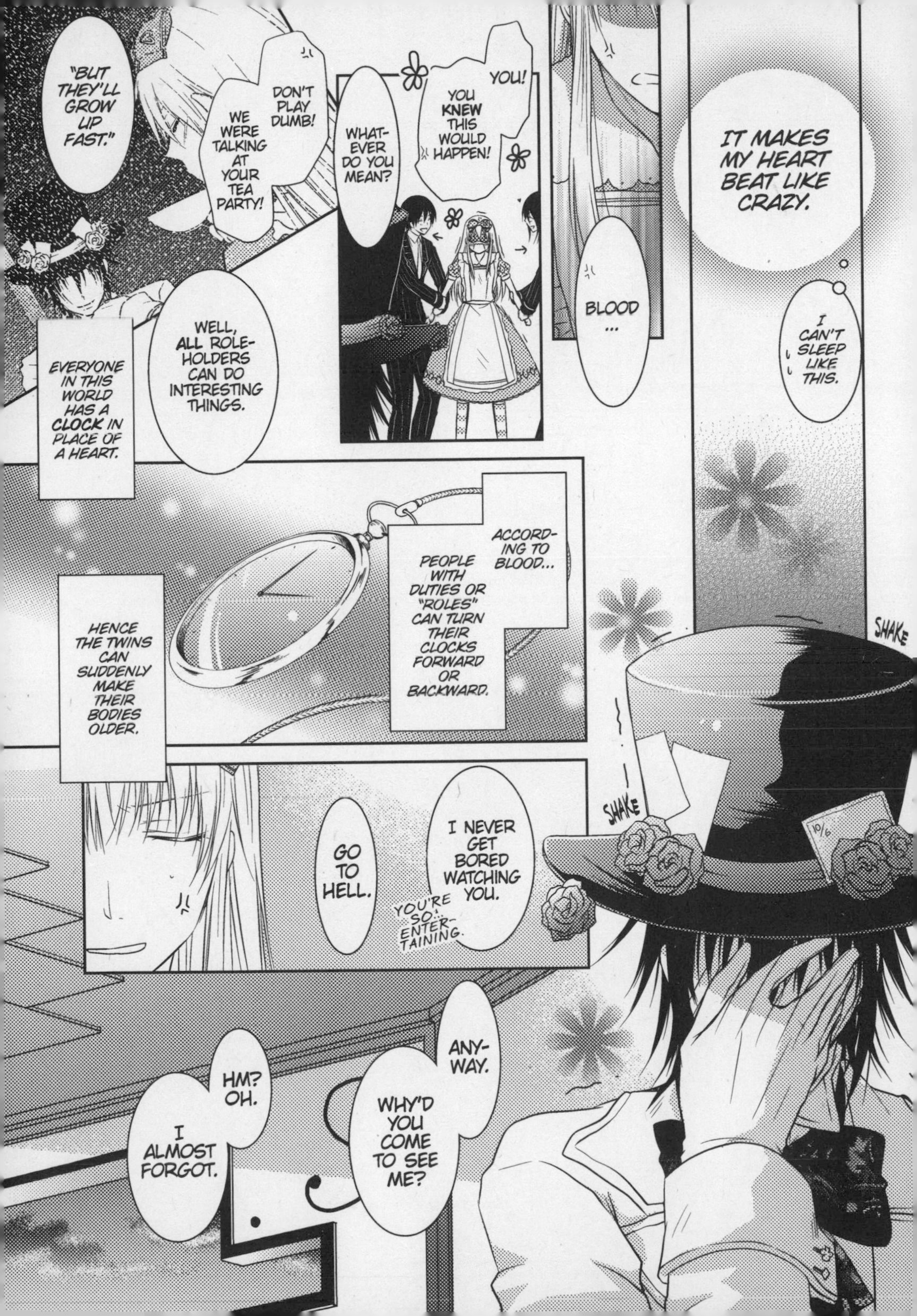
IT MAKES MY HEART BEAT LIKE CRAZY.
I CAN'T SLEEP LIKE THIS.
BLOOD...
YOU! YOU KNEW THIS WOULD HAPPEN!
WHATEVER DO YOU MEAN?
DON'T PLAY DUMB! WE WERE TALKING AT YOUR TEA PARTY!
"BUT THEY'LL GROW UP FAST."
WELL, ALL ROLE-HOLDERS CAN DO INTERESTING THINGS.
EVERYONE IN THIS WORLD HAS A CLOCK IN PLACE OF A HEART.
ACCORDING TO BLOOD...
PEOPLE WITH DUTIES OR "ROLES" CAN TURN THEIR CLOCKS FORWARD OR BACKWARD.
HENCE THE TWINS CAN SUDDENLY MAKE THEIR BODIES OLDER.
SHAKE
SHAKE
I NEVER GET BORED WATCHING YOU.
YOU'RE SO... ENTERTAINING.
GO TO HELL.
ANYWAY.
WHY'D YOU COME TO SEE ME?
HM? OH.
I ALMOST FORGOT.

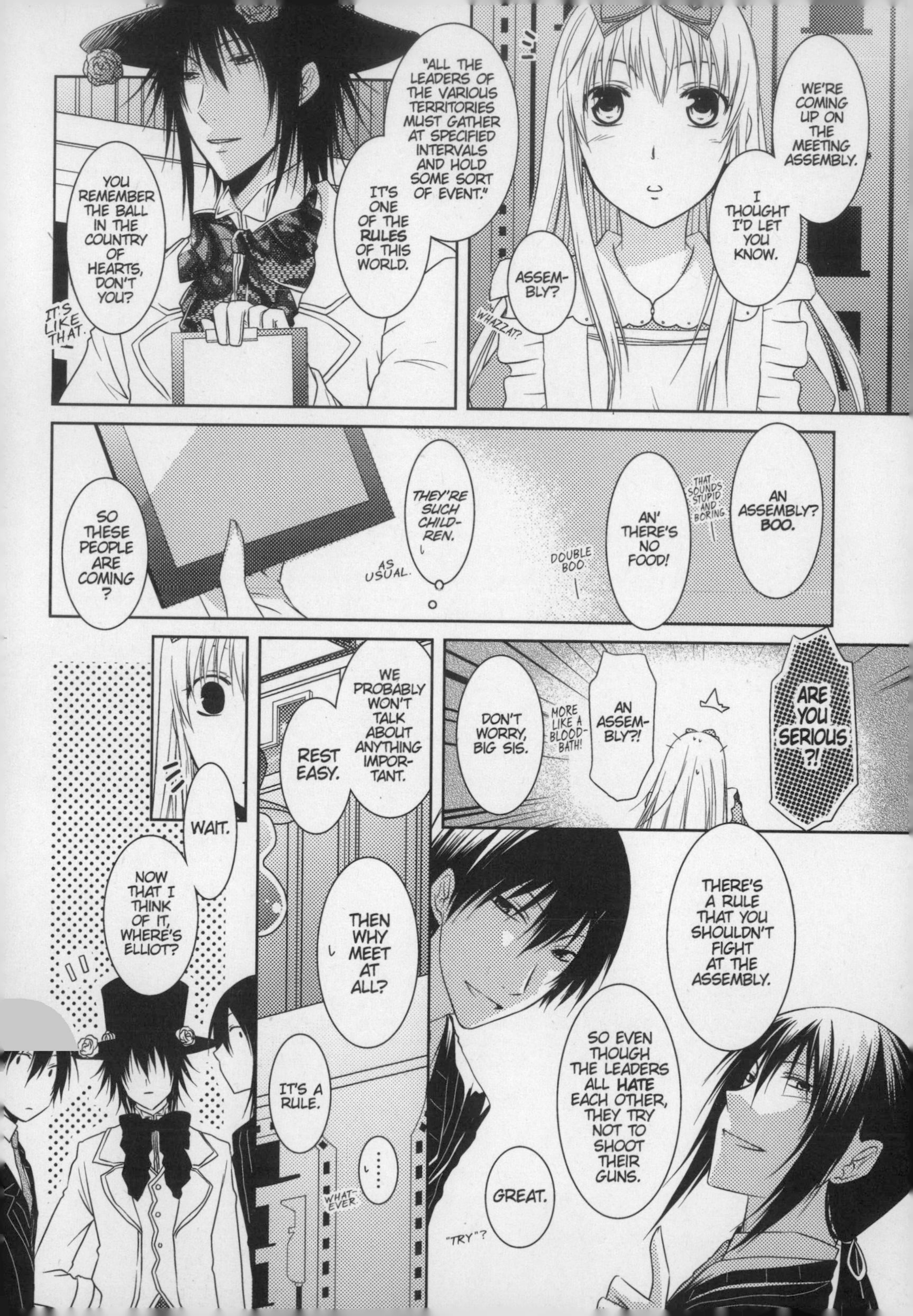
WE'RE COMING UP ON THE MEETING ASSEMBLY.
I THOUGHT I'D LET YOU KNOW.
ASSEM-BLY?
WHAZZAT?
"ALL THE LEADERS OF THE VARIOUS TERRITORIES MUST GATHER AT SPECIFIED INTERVALS AND HOLD SOME SORT OF EVENT."
IT'S ONE OF THE RULES OF THIS WORLD.
YOU REMEMBER THE BALL IN THE COUNTRY OF HEARTS, DON'T YOU?
IT'S LIKE THAT.
AN ASSEMBLY? BOO.
THAT SOUNDS STUPID AND BORING
AN' THERE'S NO FOOD!
DOUBLE BOO.
THEY'RE SUCH CHILD-REN.
AS USUAL.
SO THESE PEOPLE ARE COMING?
ARE YOU SERIOUS?!
AN ASSEM-BLY?!
MORE LIKE A BLOOD-BATH!
DON'T WORRY, BIG SIS.
THERE'S A RULE THAT YOU SHOULDN'T FIGHT AT THE ASSEMBLY.
SO EVEN THOUGH THE LEADERS ALL HATE EACH OTHER, THEY TRY NOT TO SHOOT THEIR GUNS.
GREAT.
"TRY"?
WE PROBABLY WON'T TALK ABOUT ANYTHING IMPOR-TANT.
REST EASY.
THEN WHY MEET AT ALL?
IT'S A RULE.
......
WHAT-EVER
WAIT.
NOW THAT I THINK OF IT, WHERE'S ELLIOT?

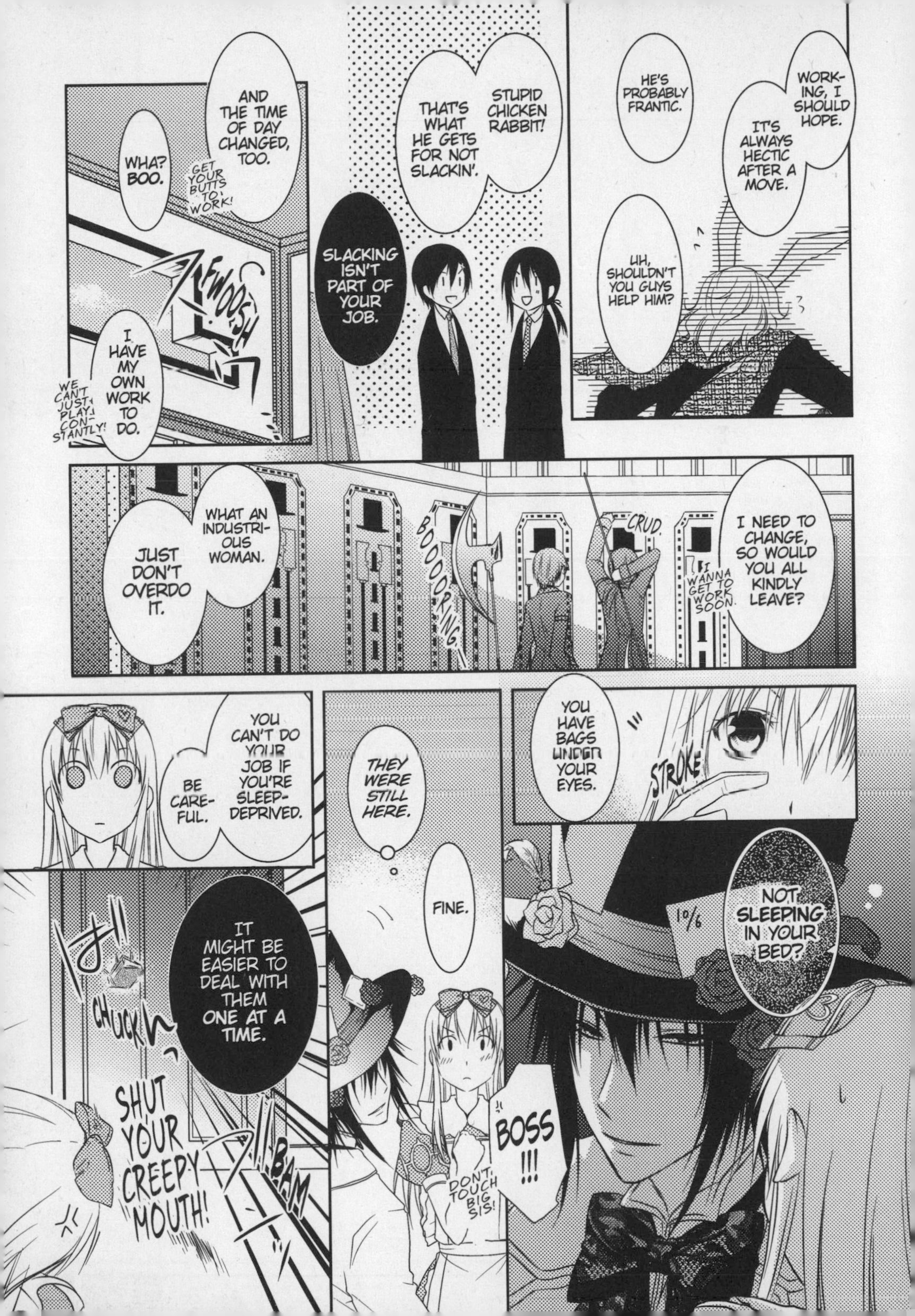

WORKING, I SHOULD HOPE.
HE'S PROBABLY FRANTIC.
IT'S ALWAYS HECTIC AFTER A MOVE.
UH, SHOULDN'T YOU GUYS HELP HIM?
STUPID CHICKEN RABBIT!
THAT'S WHAT HE GETS FOR NOT SLACKIN'.
SLACKING ISN'T PART OF YOUR JOB.
AND THE TIME OF DAY CHANGED, TOO.
WHA? BOO.
GET YOUR BUTTS TO WORK!
FWOOSH
I HAVE MY OWN WORK TO DO.
WE CAN'T JUST PLAY CONSTANTLY!
I NEED TO CHANGE, SO WOULD YOU ALL KINDLY LEAVE?
CRUD.
I WANNA GET TO WORK SOON.
BOOOORING
WHAT AN INDUSTRIOUS WOMAN.
JUST DON'T OVERDO IT.
YOU HAVE BAGS UNDER YOUR EYES.
STROKE
NOT SLEEPING IN YOUR BED?
THEY WERE STILL HERE.
FINE.
BOSS!!!
DON'T TOUCH BIG SIS!
YOU CAN'T DO YOUR JOB IF YOU'RE SLEEP-DEPRIVED.
BE CAREFUL.
IT MIGHT BE EASIER TO DEAL WITH THEM ONE AT A TIME.
CHUCK
SHUT YOUR CREEPY MOUTH!
BAM

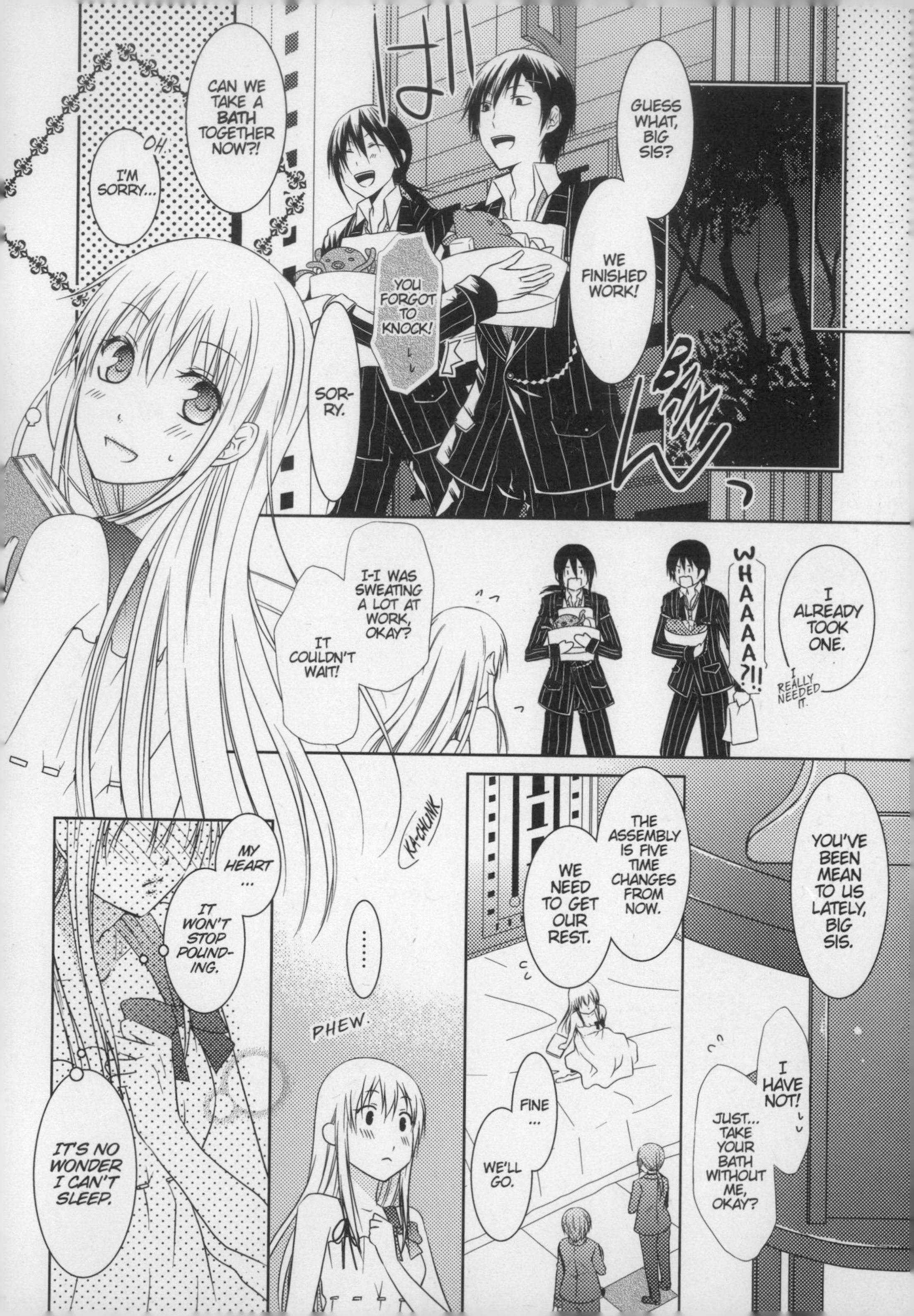
GUESS WHAT, BIG SIS?
WE FINISHED WORK!
BAM
CAN WE TAKE A BATH TOGETHER NOW?!
YOU FORGOT TO KNOCK!
SORRY.
OH... I'M SORRY...
I ALREADY TOOK ONE.
I REALLY NEEDED IT.
WHAAAAA?!!
I-I WAS SWEATING A LOT AT WORK, OKAY?
IT COULDN'T WAIT!
YOU'VE BEEN MEAN TO US LATELY, BIG SIS.
I HAVE NOT!
JUST... TAKE YOUR BATH WITHOUT ME, OKAY?
THE ASSEMBLY IS FIVE TIME CHANGES FROM NOW.
WE NEED TO GET OUR REST.
FINE...
WE'LL GO.
KA-CHUNK
......
PHEW.
MY HEART...
IT WON'T STOP POUNDING.
IT'S NO WONDER I CAN'T SLEEP.

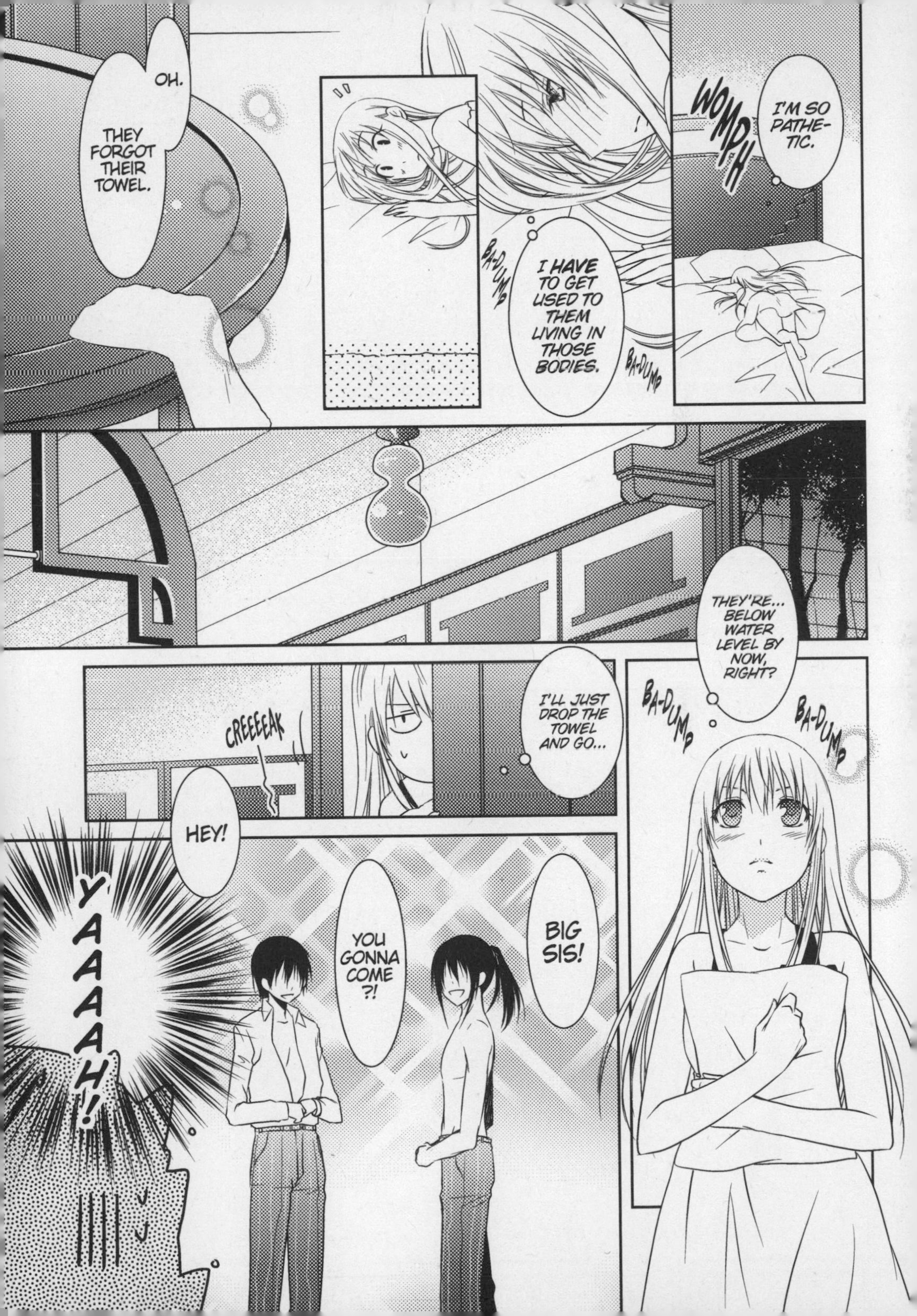
WOMPH
I'M SO PATHETIC.
I HAVE TO GET USED TO THEM LIVING IN THOSE BODIES.
BA-DUMP
BA-DUMP
OH.
THEY FORGOT THEIR TOWEL.
THEY'RE... BELOW WATER LEVEL BY NOW, RIGHT?
BA-DUMP
BA-DUMP
I'LL JUST DROP THE TOWEL AND GO...
CREEEEAK
HEY!
BIG SIS!
YOU GONNA COME?!
YAAAAAH!!

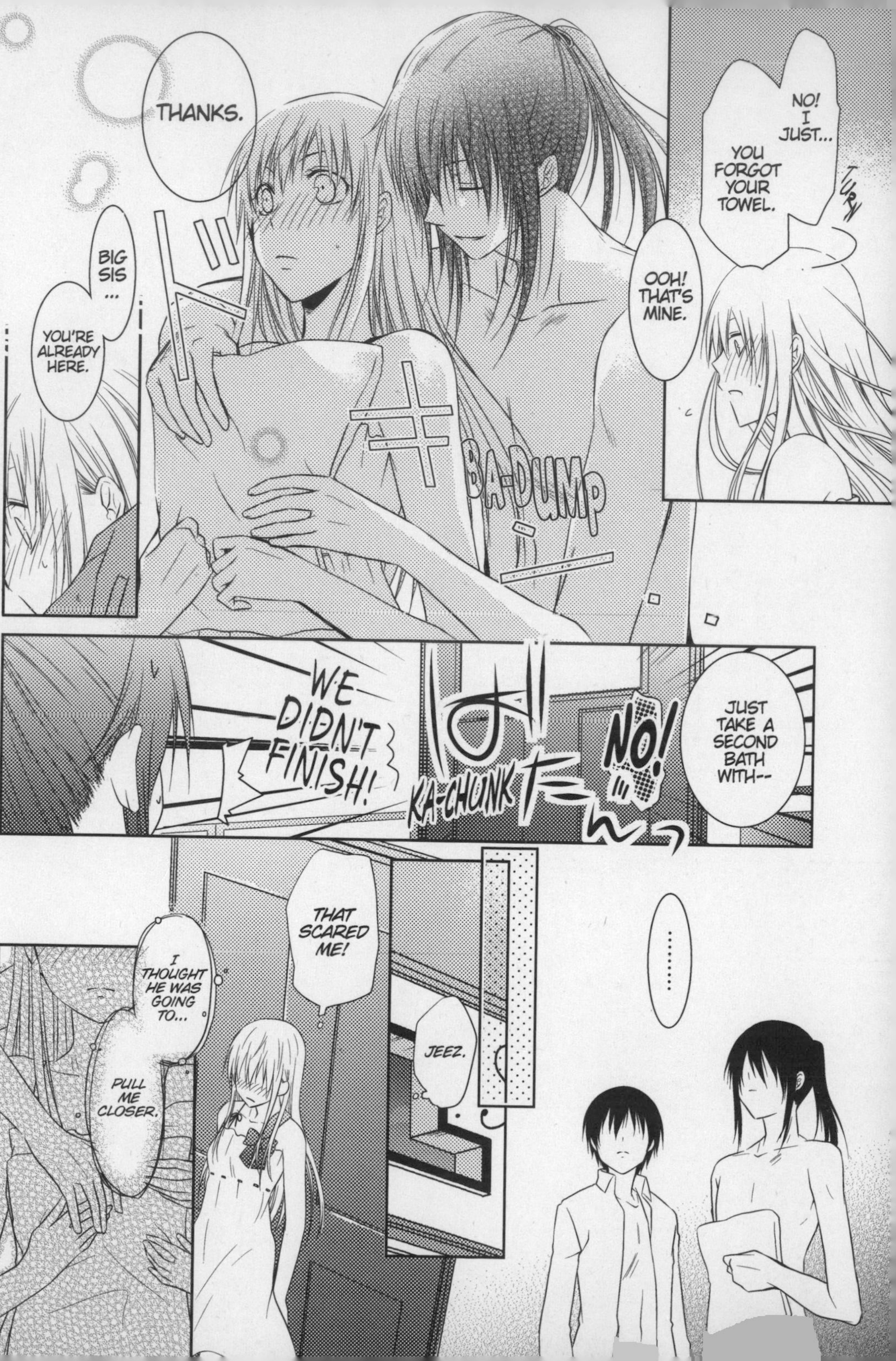
NO! I JUST... YOU FORGOT YOUR TOWEL.
TURN
OOH! THAT'S MINE.
THANKS.
BA-DUMP
BIG SIS...
YOU'RE ALREADY HERE.
JUST TAKE A SECOND BATH WITH--
NO!
KA-CHUNK
WE DIDN'T FINISH!
......
JEEZ.
THAT SCARED ME!
I THOUGHT HE WAS GOING TO...
PULL ME CLOSER.

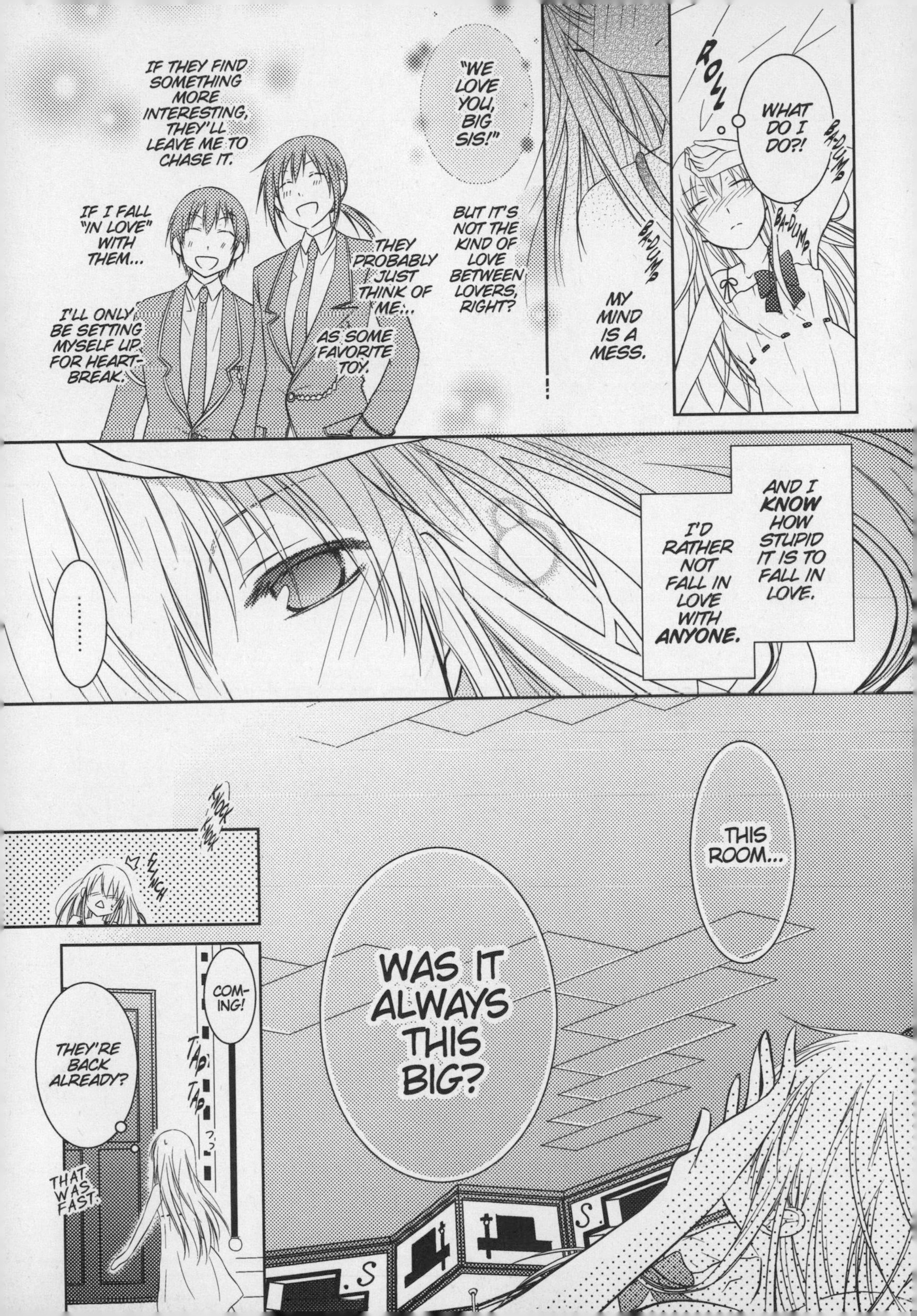
ROLL
WHAT DO I DO?!
BA-DUMP
BA-DUMP
BA-DUMP
MY MIND IS A MESS.
"WE LOVE YOU, BIG SIS!"
BUT IT'S NOT THE KIND OF LOVE BETWEEN LOVERS, RIGHT?
THEY PROBABLY JUST THINK OF ME...
AS SOME FAVORITE TOY.
IF THEY FIND SOMETHING MORE INTERESTING, THEY'LL LEAVE ME TO CHASE IT.
IF I FALL "IN LOVE" WITH THEM...
I'LL ONLY BE SETTING MYSELF UP FOR HEART-BREAK.
AND I KNOW HOW STUPID IT IS TO FALL IN LOVE.
I'D RATHER NOT FALL IN LOVE WITH ANYONE.
......
THIS ROOM...
WAS IT ALWAYS THIS BIG?
KNOCK KNOCK
FLINCH
COMING!
TAP TAP
THEY'RE BACK ALREADY?
THAT WAS FAST.

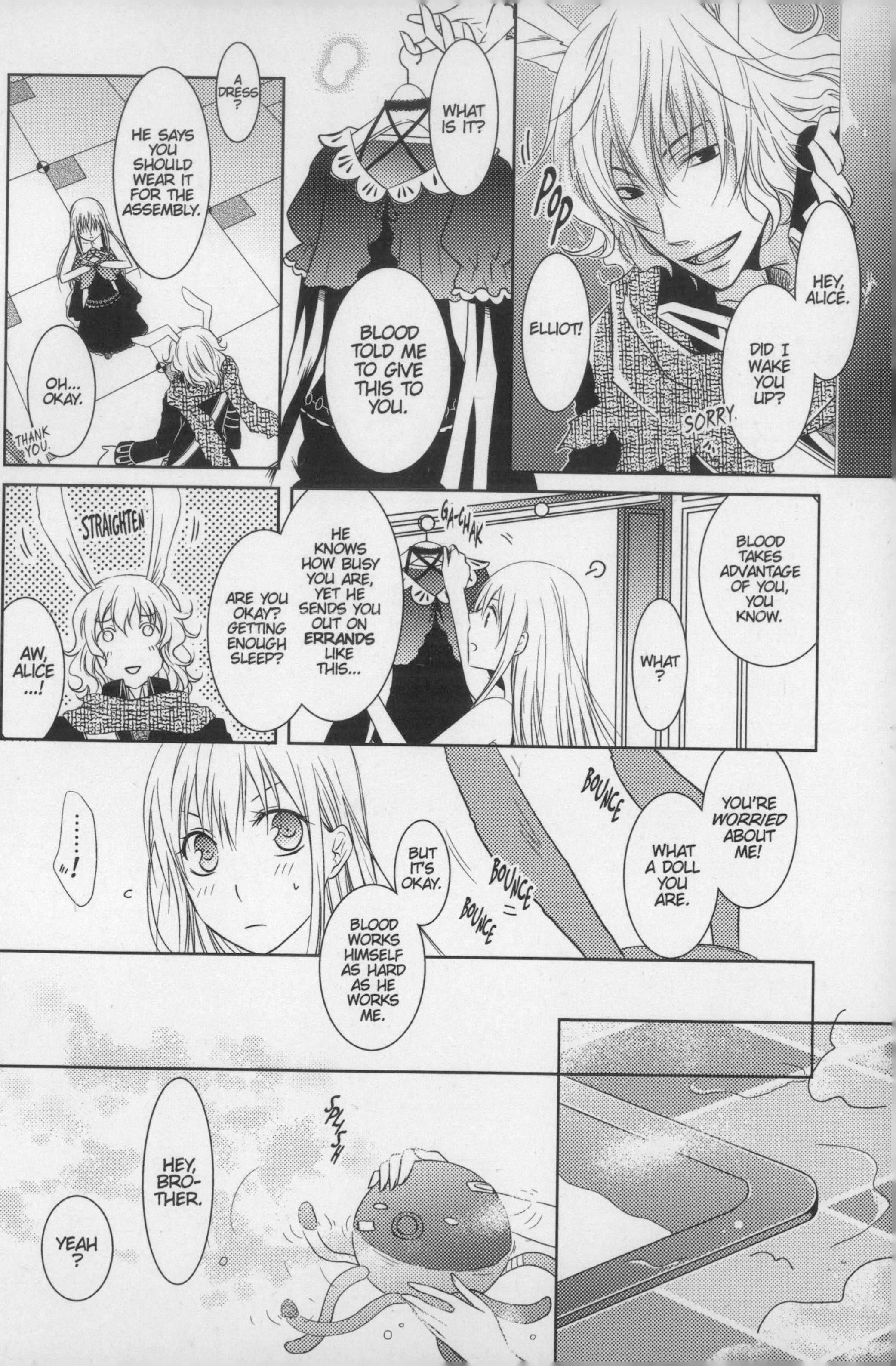

HEY, ALICE.
DID I WAKE YOU UP?
SORRY.
POP
ELLIOT!
WHAT IS IT?
A DRESS?
BLOOD TOLD ME TO GIVE THIS TO YOU.
HE SAYS YOU SHOULD WEAR IT FOR THE ASSEMBLY.
OH... OKAY.
THANK YOU.
BLOOD TAKES ADVANTAGE OF YOU, YOU KNOW.
WHAT?
GA-CHAK
HE KNOWS HOW BUSY YOU ARE, YET HE SENDS YOU OUT ON ERRANDS LIKE THIS...
ARE YOU OKAY? GETTING ENOUGH SLEEP?
STRAIGHTEN
AW, ALICE ...!
YOU'RE WORRIED ABOUT ME!
WHAT A DOLL YOU ARE.
BOUNCE
BOUNCE
BOUNCE
BUT IT'S OKAY.
BLOOD WORKS HIMSELF AS HARD AS HE WORKS ME.
......!
SPLISH
HEY, BROTHER.
YEAH?

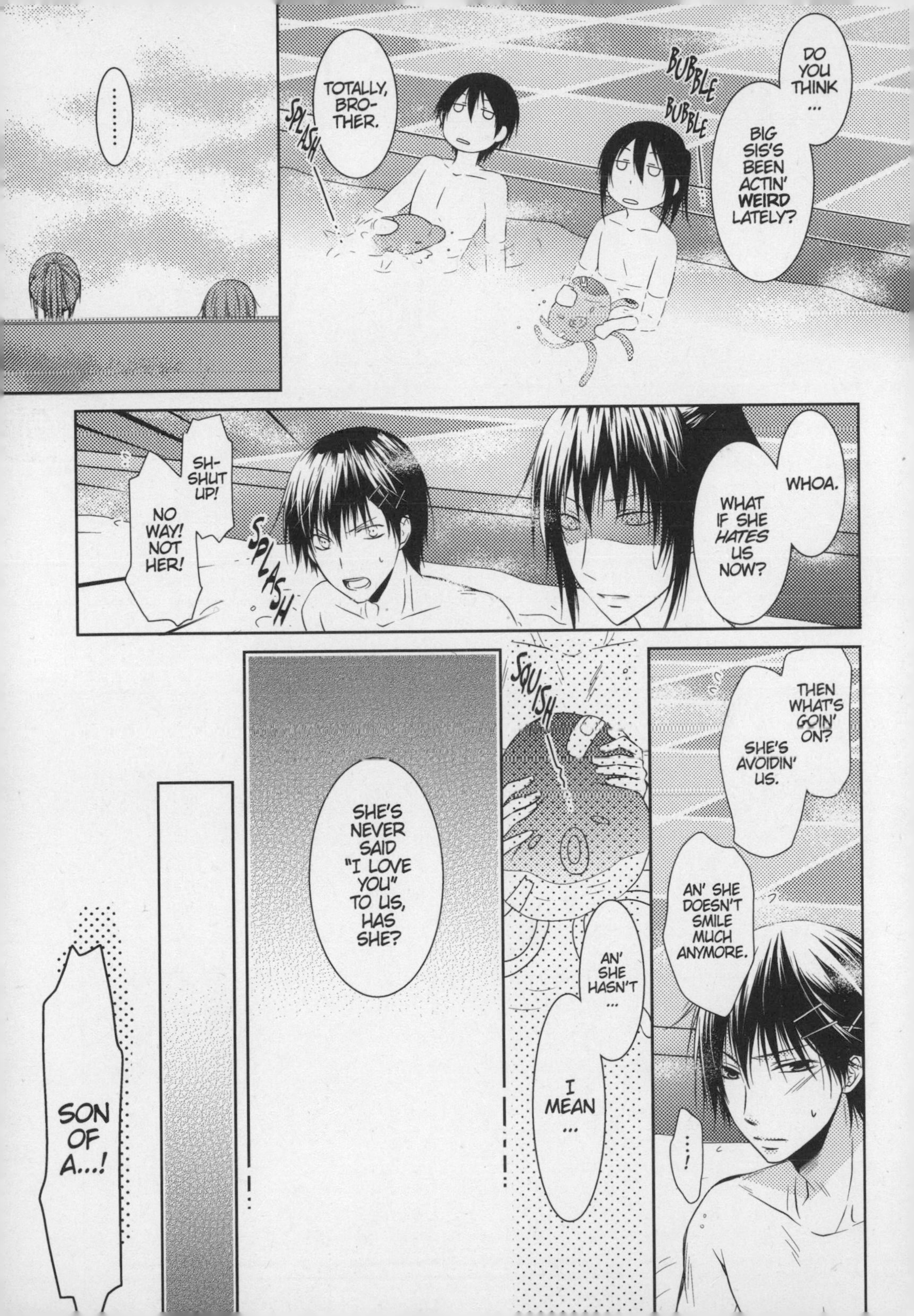
DO YOU THINK ... BIG SIS'S BEEN ACTIN' WEIRD LATELY?
BUBBLE BUBBLE
TOTALLY, BROTHER.
SPLASH
......
WHOA.
WHAT IF SHE HATES US NOW?
SH-SHUT UP!
NO WAY! NOT HER!
SPLASH
THEN WHAT'S GOIN' ON?
SHE'S AVOIDIN' US.
AN' SHE DOESN'T SMILE MUCH ANYMORE.
...!
SQUISH
AN' SHE HASN'T ...
I MEAN ...
SHE'S NEVER SAID "I LOVE YOU" TO US, HAS SHE?
SON OF A...!

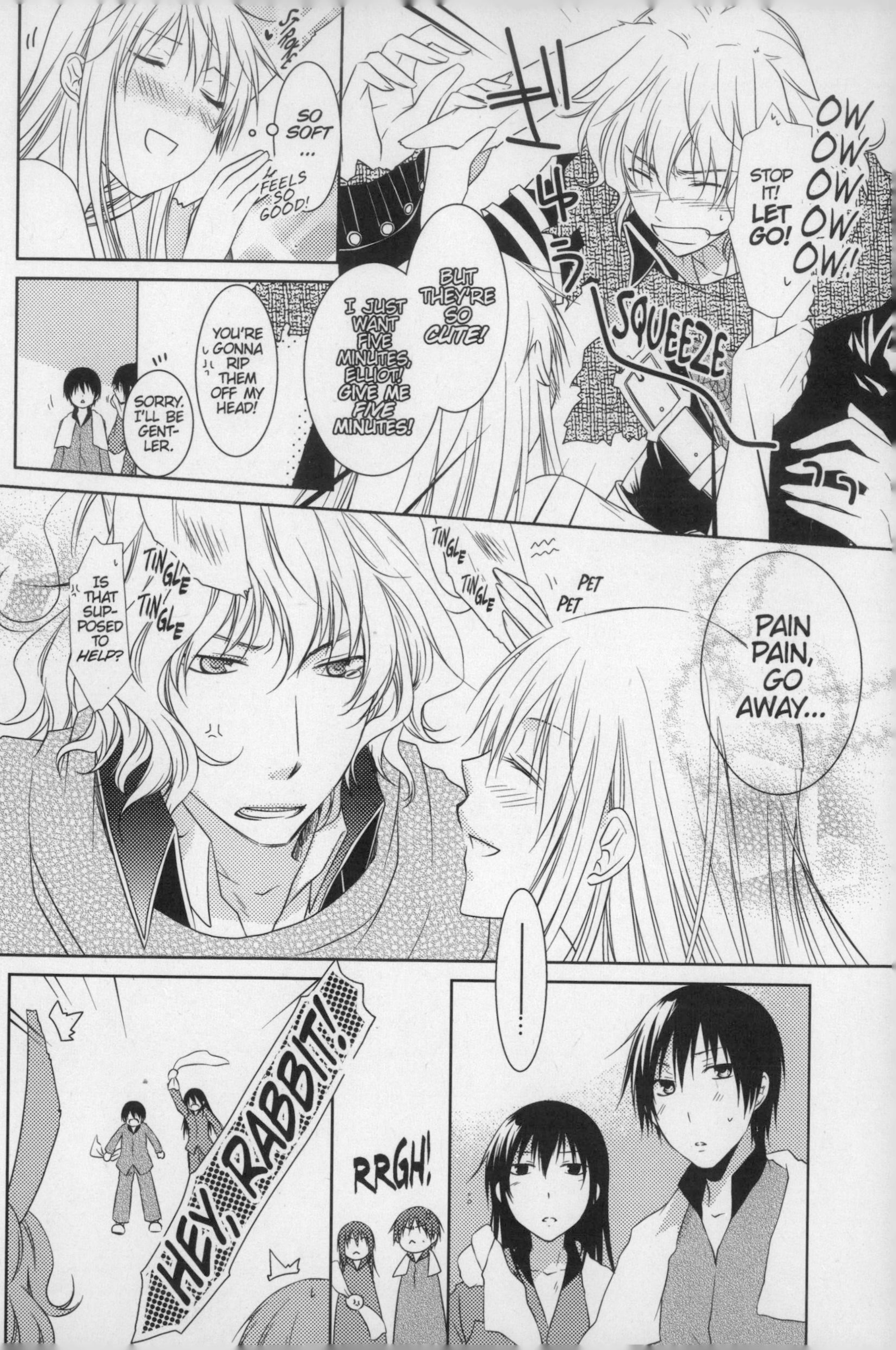
OW OW OW OW OW!
STOP IT! LET GO!
SQUEEZE
BUT THEY'RE SO CUTE!
I JUST WANT FIVE MINUTES, ELLIOT! GIVE ME FIVE MINUTES!
STROKE
SO SOFT ... FEELS SO GOOD!
YOU'RE GONNA RIP THEM OFF MY HEAD!
SORRY. I'LL BE GENT-LER.
PET PET
PAIN PAIN, GO AWAY...
TINGLE TINGLE
TINGLE TINGLE
IS THAT SUP-POSED TO HELP?
......
RRGH!
HEY, RABBIT!

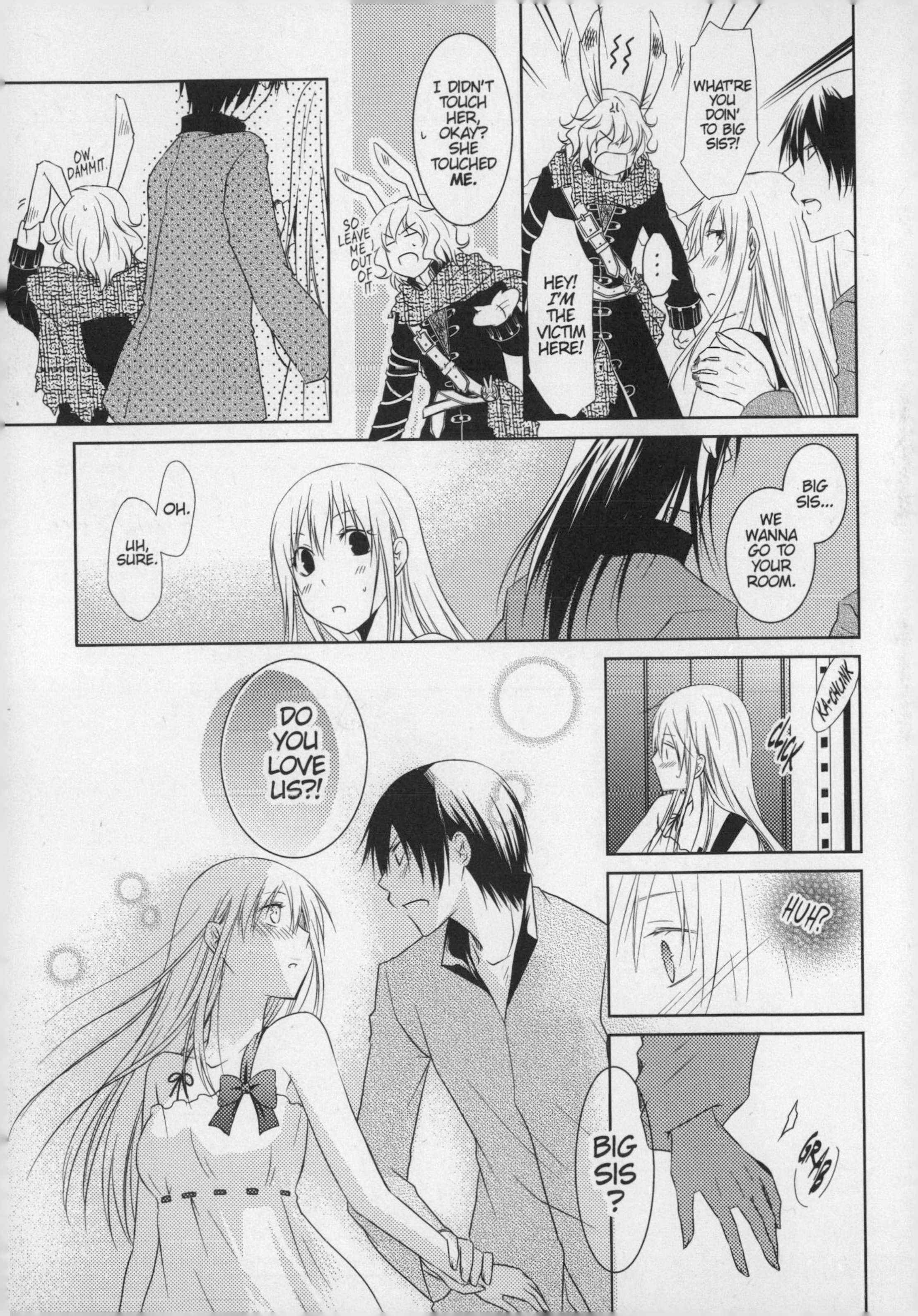
WHAT'RE YOU DOIN' TO BIG SIS?!
...
HEY! I'M THE VICTIM HERE!
I DIDN'T TOUCH HER, OKAY? SHE TOUCHED ME.
SO LEAVE ME OUT OF IT.
OW. DAMMIT.
BIG SIS... WE WANNA GO TO YOUR ROOM.
OH.
UH, SURE.
KA-CHUNK
CLICK
HUH?
GRAB
BIG SIS?
DO YOU LOVE US?!

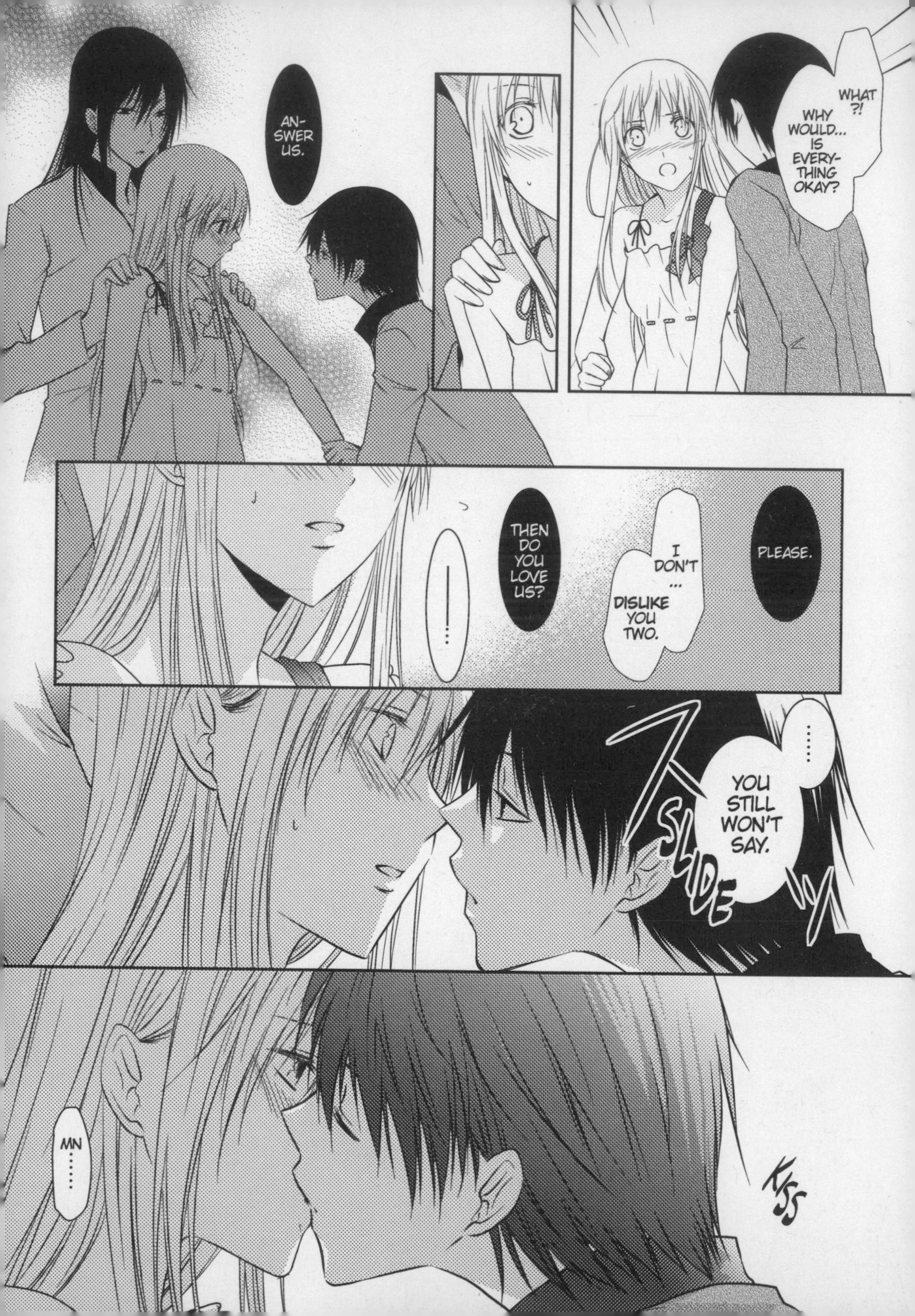
WHAT?! WHY WOULD... IS EVERYTHING OKAY?
ANSWER US.
PLEASE.
I DON'T ... DISLIKE YOU TWO.
THEN DO YOU LOVE US?
......
......
YOU STILL WON'T SAY.
SLIDE
KISS
MN......

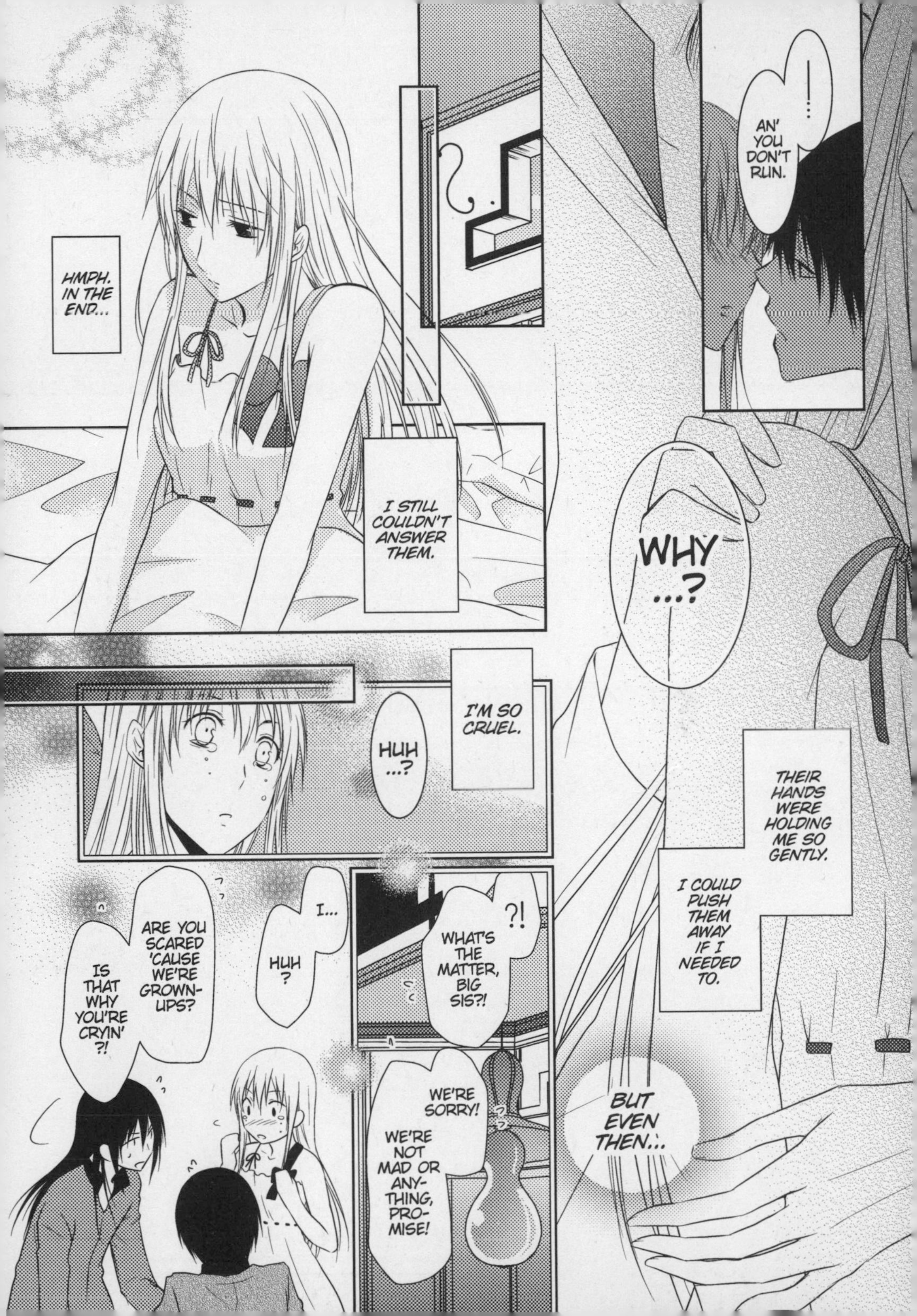
!...
AN' YOU DON'T RUN.
WHY ...?
THEIR HANDS WERE HOLDING ME SO GENTLY.
I COULD PUSH THEM AWAY IF I NEEDED TO.
BUT EVEN THEN...
HMPH. IN THE END...
I STILL COULDN'T ANSWER THEM.
I'M SO CRUEL.
HUH ...?
?!
WHAT'S THE MATTER, BIG SIS?!
WE'RE SORRY!
WE'RE NOT MAD OR ANY-THING, PRO-MISE!
I...
HUH ?
ARE YOU SCARED 'CAUSE WE'RE GROWN-UPS?
IS THAT WHY YOU'RE CRYIN' ?!

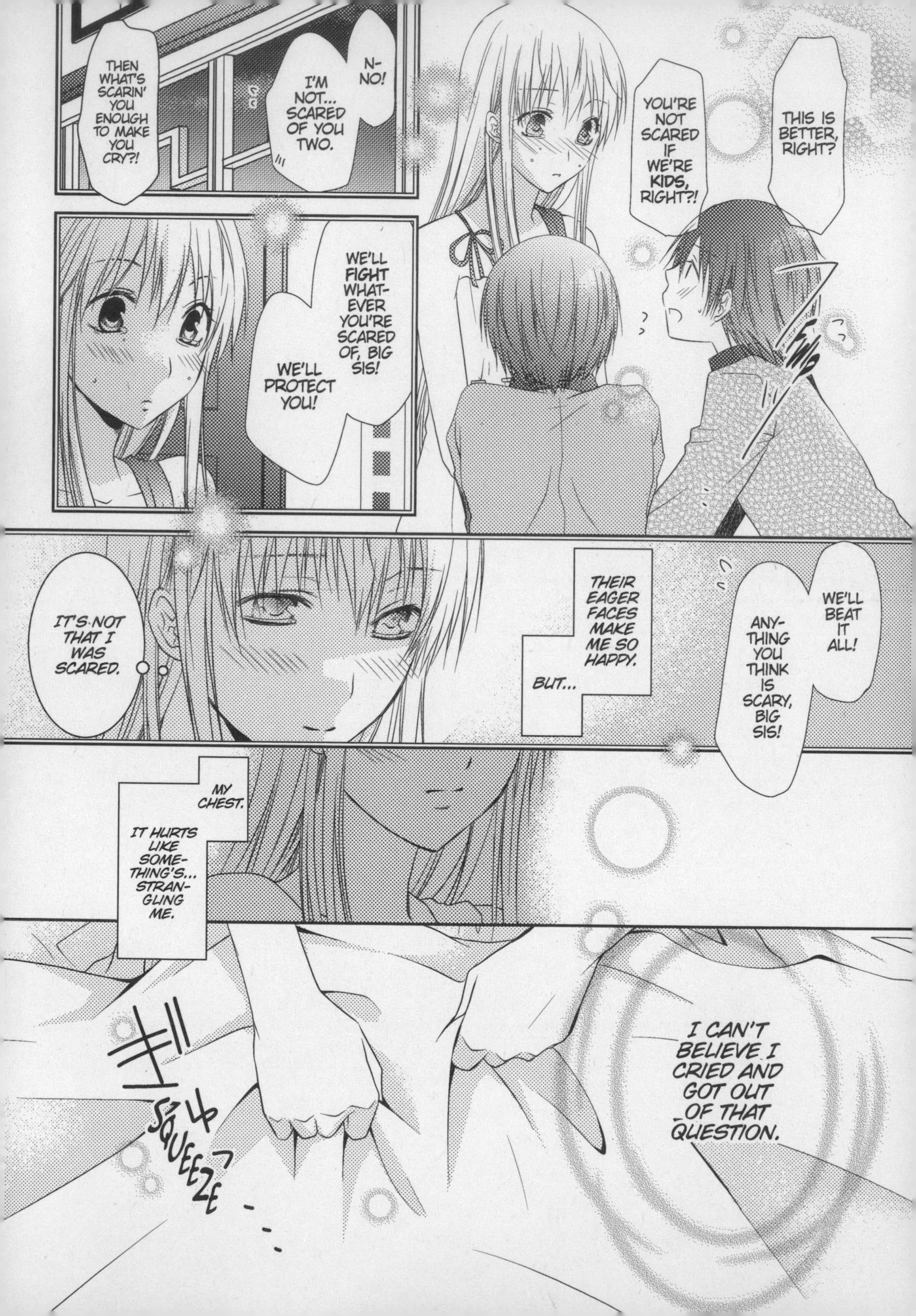
THIS IS BETTER, RIGHT?
YOU'RE NOT SCARED IF WE'RE **KIDS**, RIGHT?!
FWIP
N-NO!
I'M NOT... SCARED OF YOU TWO.
THEN WHAT'S SCARIN' YOU ENOUGH TO MAKE YOU CRY?!
WE'LL **FIGHT** WHATEVER YOU'RE SCARED OF, BIG SIS!
WE'LL PROTECT YOU!
WE'LL BEAT IT ALL!
ANYTHING YOU THINK IS SCARY, BIG SIS!
THEIR EAGER FACES MAKE ME SO HAPPY.
BUT...
IT'S NOT THAT I WAS SCARED.
MY CHEST.
IT HURTS LIKE SOMETHING'S... STRANGLING ME.
I CAN'T BELIEVE I CRIED AND GOT OUT OF THAT QUESTION.
SQUEEZE

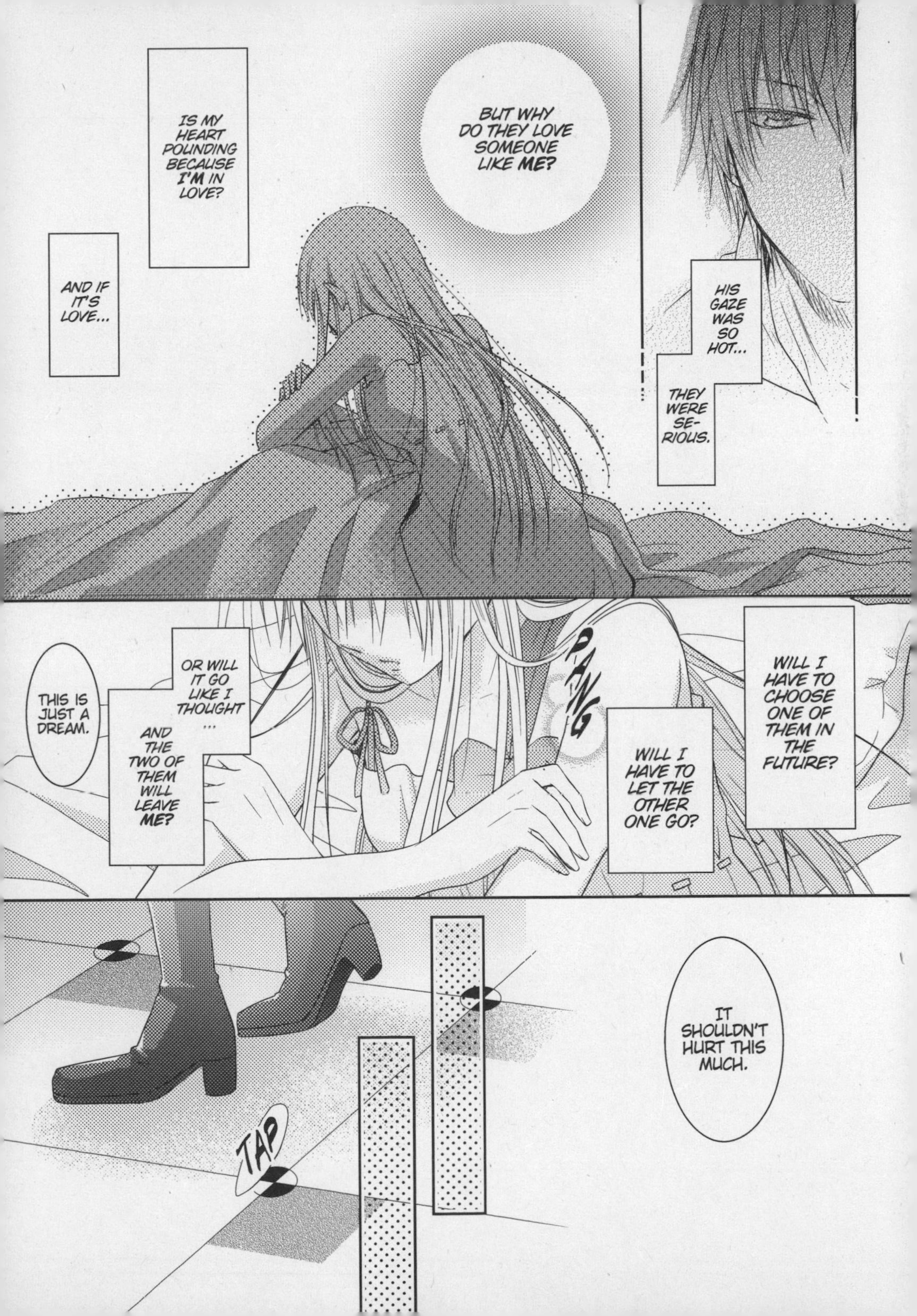
HIS GAZE WAS SO HOT...
THEY WERE SE-RIOUS.
BUT WHY DO THEY LOVE SOMEONE LIKE **ME**?
IS MY HEART POUNDING BECAUSE **I'M** IN LOVE?
AND IF IT'S LOVE...
WILL I HAVE TO CHOOSE ONE OF THEM IN THE FUTURE?
PANG
WILL I HAVE TO LET THE OTHER ONE GO?
OR WILL IT GO LIKE I THOUGHT...
AND THE TWO OF THEM WILL LEAVE **ME**?
THIS IS JUST A DREAM.
IT SHOULDN'T HURT THIS MUCH.
TAP

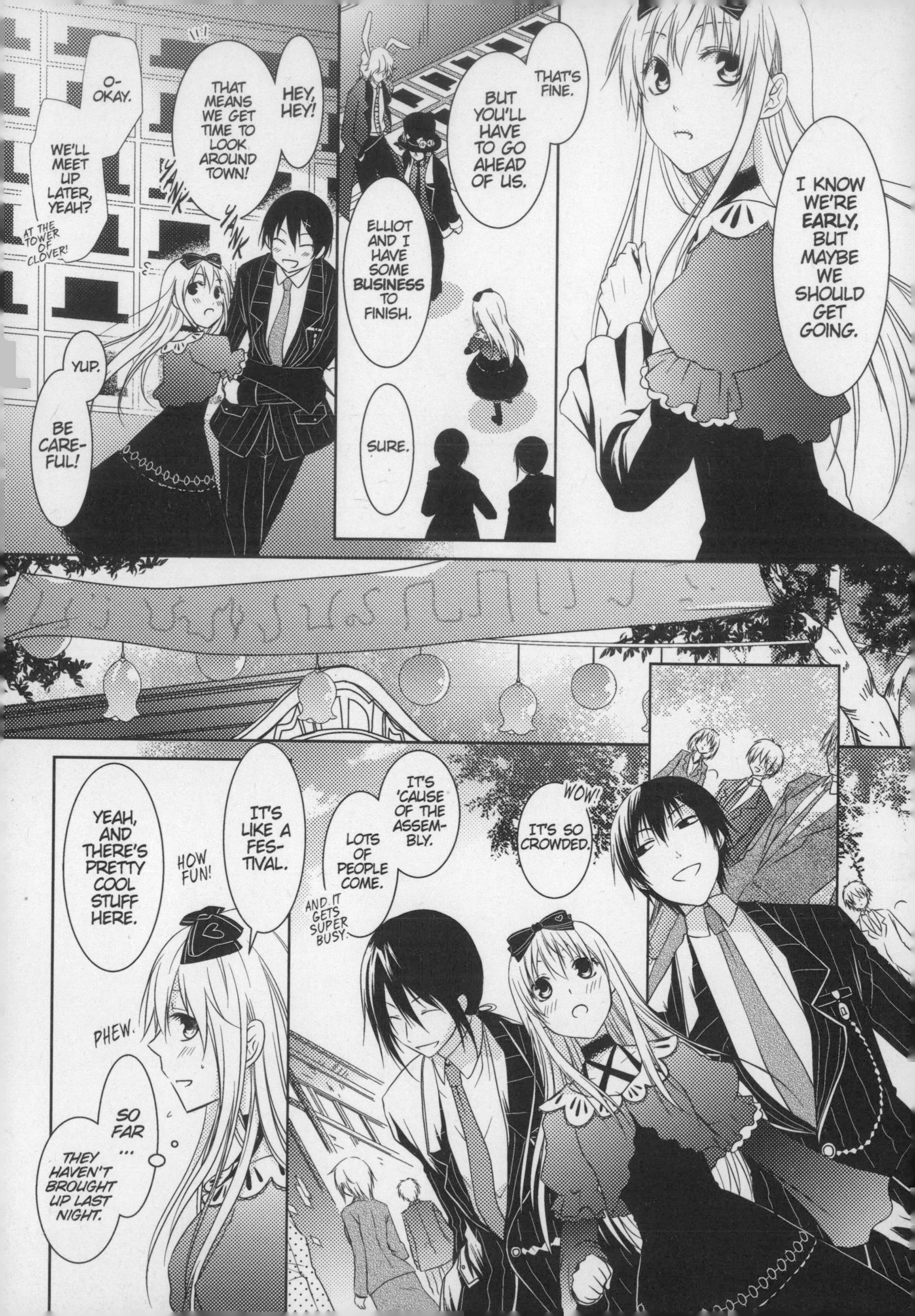
I KNOW WE'RE EARLY, BUT MAYBE WE SHOULD GET GOING.
THAT'S FINE.
BUT YOU'LL HAVE TO GO AHEAD OF US.
ELLIOT AND I HAVE SOME BUSINESS TO FINISH.
SURE.
HEY, HEY!
THAT MEANS WE GET TIME TO LOOK AROUND TOWN!
YANK
YANK
O-OKAY.
WE'LL MEET UP LATER, YEAH?
AT THE TOWER OF CLOVER!
YUP.
BE CAREFUL!
WOW!
IT'S SO CROWDED.
IT'S 'CAUSE OF THE ASSEMBLY.
LOTS OF PEOPLE COME.
AND IT GETS SUPER BUSY.
IT'S LIKE A FESTIVAL.
HOW FUN!
YEAH, AND THERE'S PRETTY COOL STUFF HERE.
PHEW.
SO FAR...
THEY HAVEN'T BROUGHT UP LAST NIGHT.

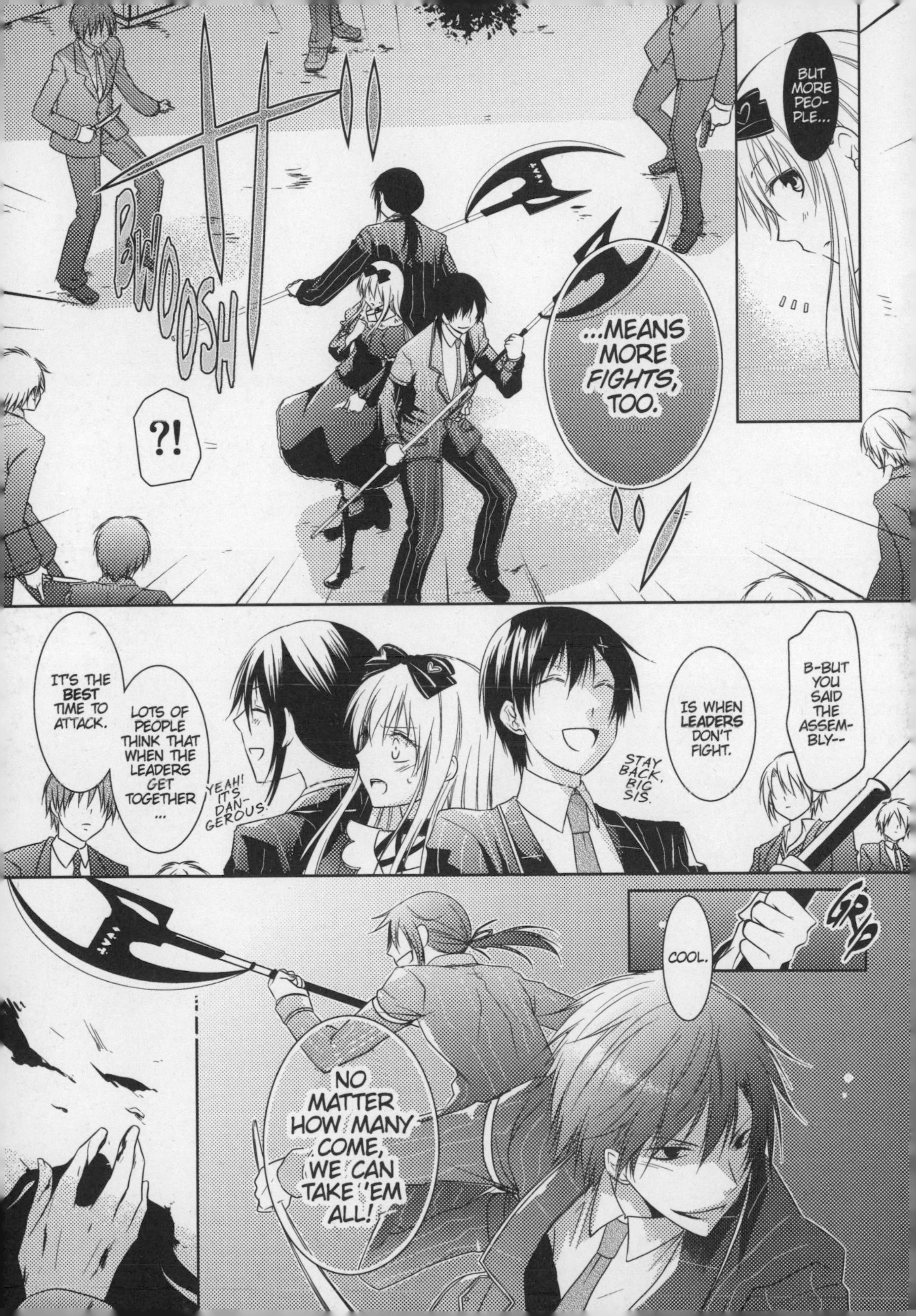
BUT MORE PEO-PLE...
...MEANS MORE FIGHTS, TOO.
BWOOSH
?!
B-BUT YOU SAID THE ASSEM-BLY--
IS WHEN LEADERS DON'T FIGHT.
STAY BACK, BIG SIS.
YEAH! IT'S DAN-GEROUS.
LOTS OF PEOPLE THINK THAT WHEN THE LEADERS GET TOGETHER ...
IT'S THE BEST TIME TO ATTACK.
GRIP
COOL.
NO MATTER HOW MANY COME, WE CAN TAKE 'EM ALL!

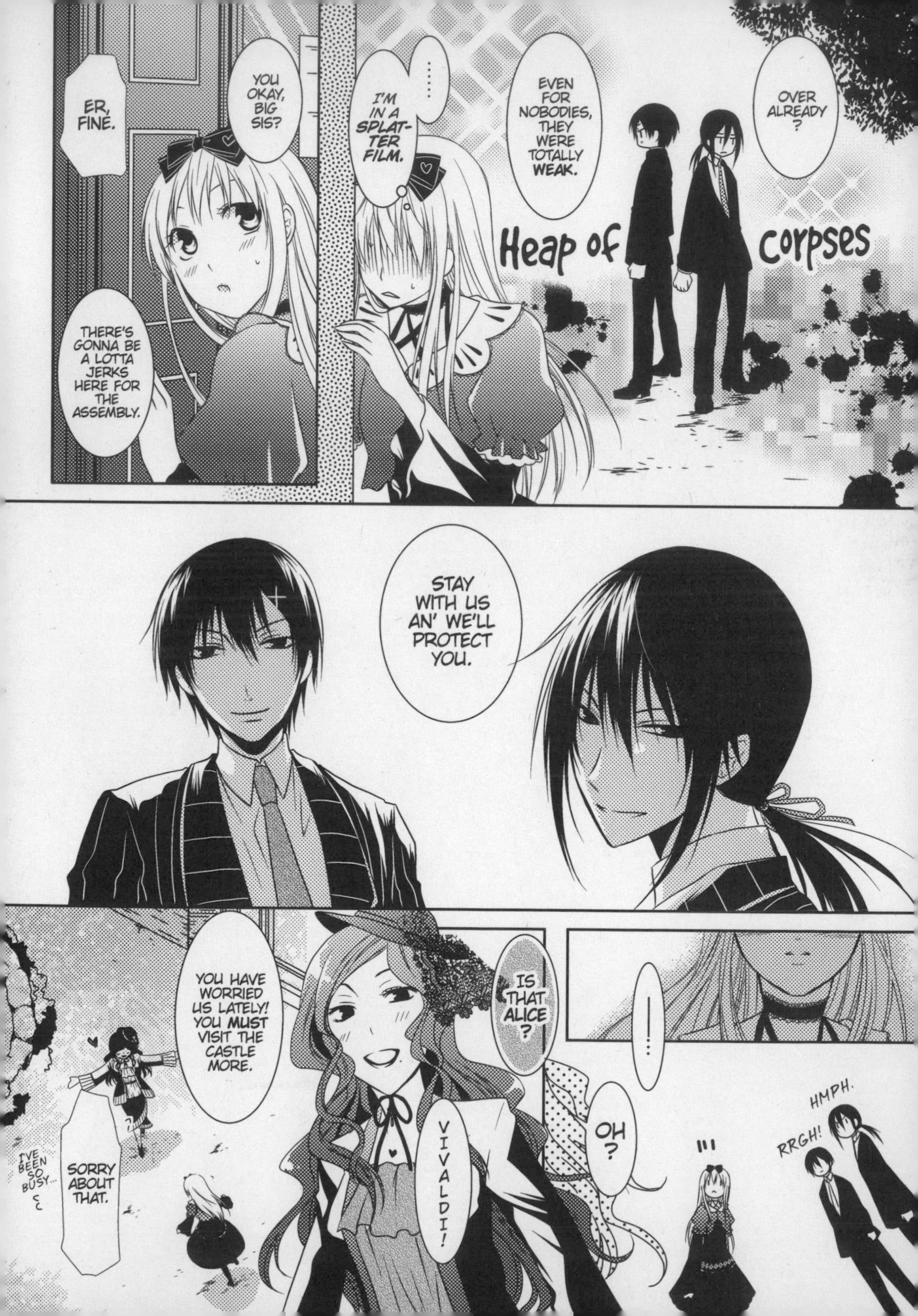
OVER ALREADY?
EVEN FOR NOBODIES, THEY WERE TOTALLY WEAK.
Heap of corpses
......
I'M IN A SPLATTER FILM.
YOU OKAY, BIG SIS?
ER, FINE.
THERE'S GONNA BE A LOTTA JERKS HERE FOR THE ASSEMBLY.
STAY WITH US AN' WE'LL PROTECT YOU.
!...
IS THAT ALICE?
OH?
HMPH.
RRGH!
VIVALDI!
YOU HAVE WORRIED US LATELY! YOU MUST VISIT THE CASTLE MORE.
SORRY ABOUT THAT.
I'VE BEEN SO BUSY...

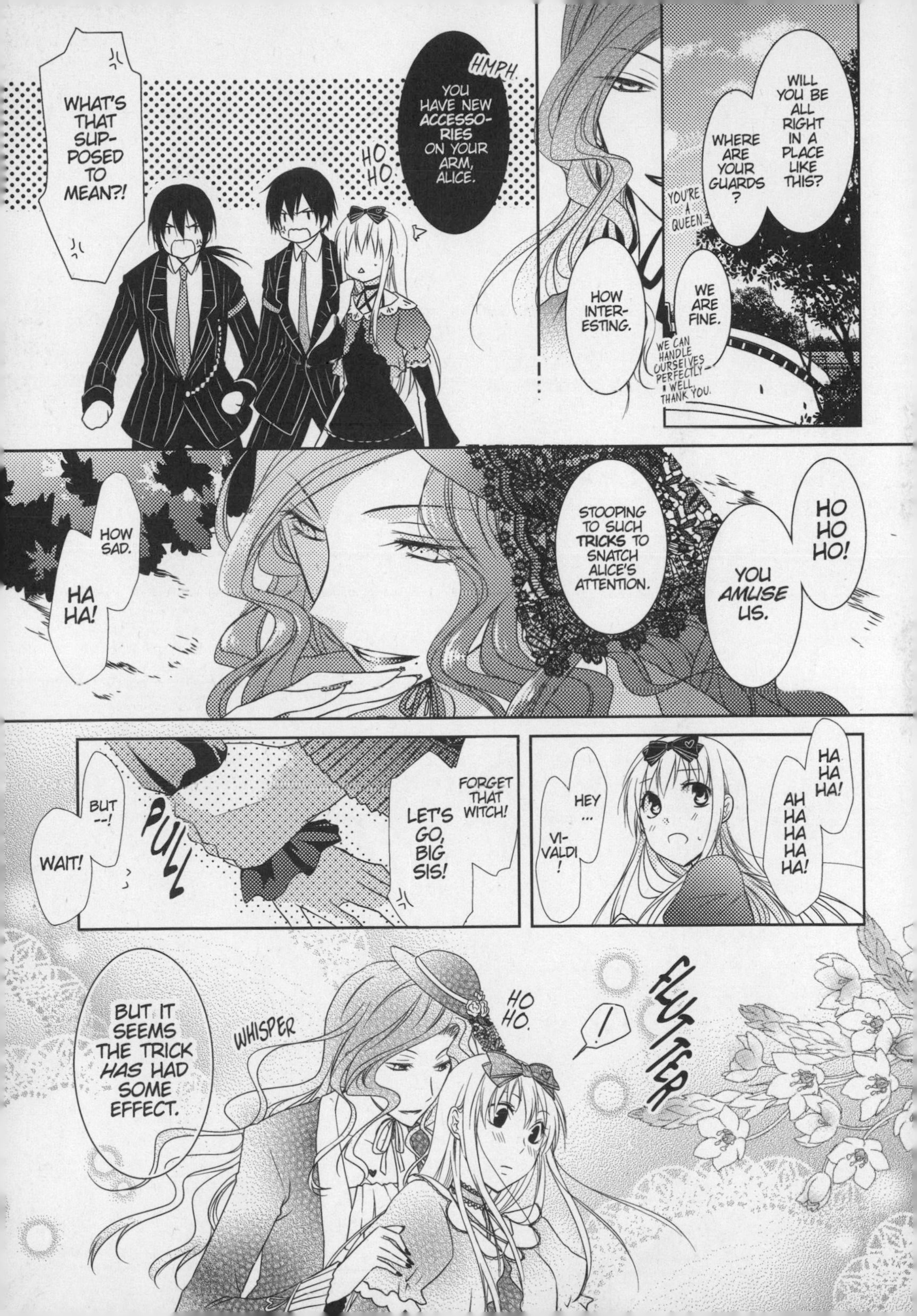
WILL YOU BE ALL RIGHT IN A PLACE LIKE THIS?
WHERE ARE YOUR GUARDS?
YOU'RE A QUEEN...
WE ARE FINE.
WE CAN HANDLE OURSELVES PERFECTLY WELL, THANK YOU.
HOW INTER-ESTING.
HMPH.
YOU HAVE NEW ACCESSO-RIES ON YOUR ARM, ALICE.
HO HO.
WHAT'S THAT SUP-POSED TO MEAN?!
HO HO HO!
YOU AMUSE US.
STOOPING TO SUCH TRICKS TO SNATCH ALICE'S ATTENTION.
HOW SAD.
HA HA!
HA HA HA!
AH HA HA HA HA HA!
HEY... VI-VALDI!
FORGET THAT WITCH!
LET'S GO, BIG SIS!
PULL
BUT --!
WAIT!
FLUTTER
!
HO HO.
WHISPER
BUT IT SEEMS THE TRICK HAS HAD SOME EFFECT.

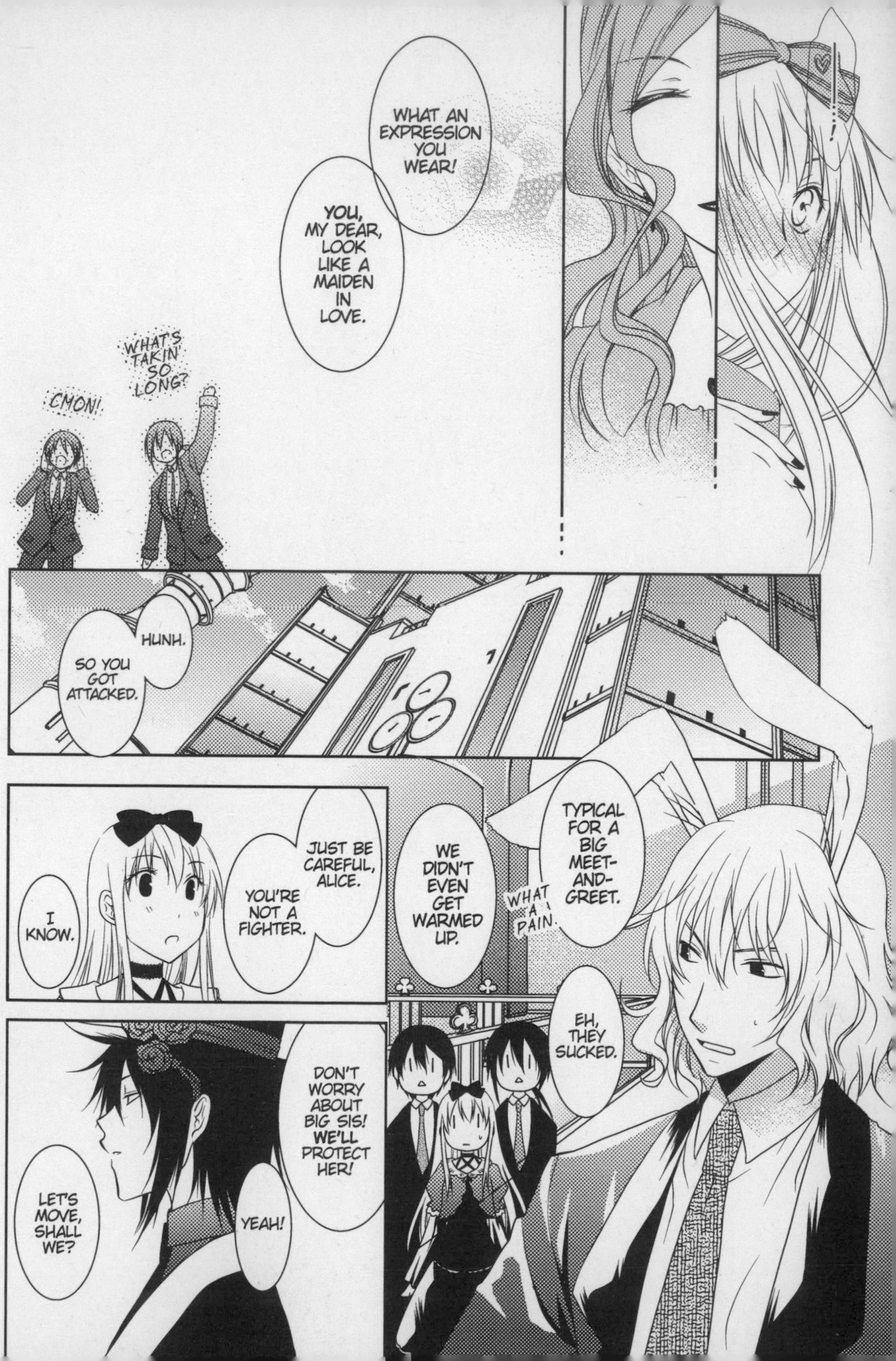
WHAT AN EXPRESSION YOU WEAR!
YOU, MY DEAR, LOOK LIKE A MAIDEN IN LOVE.
WHAT'S TAKIN' SO LONG?
C'MON!
HUNH.
SO YOU GOT ATTACKED.
TYPICAL FOR A BIG MEET-AND-GREET.
WHAT A PAIN.
WE DIDN'T EVEN GET WARMED UP.
JUST BE CAREFUL, ALICE.
YOU'RE NOT A FIGHTER.
I KNOW.
EH, THEY SUCKED.
DON'T WORRY ABOUT BIG SIS! WE'LL PROTECT HER!
YEAH!
LET'S MOVE, SHALL WE?

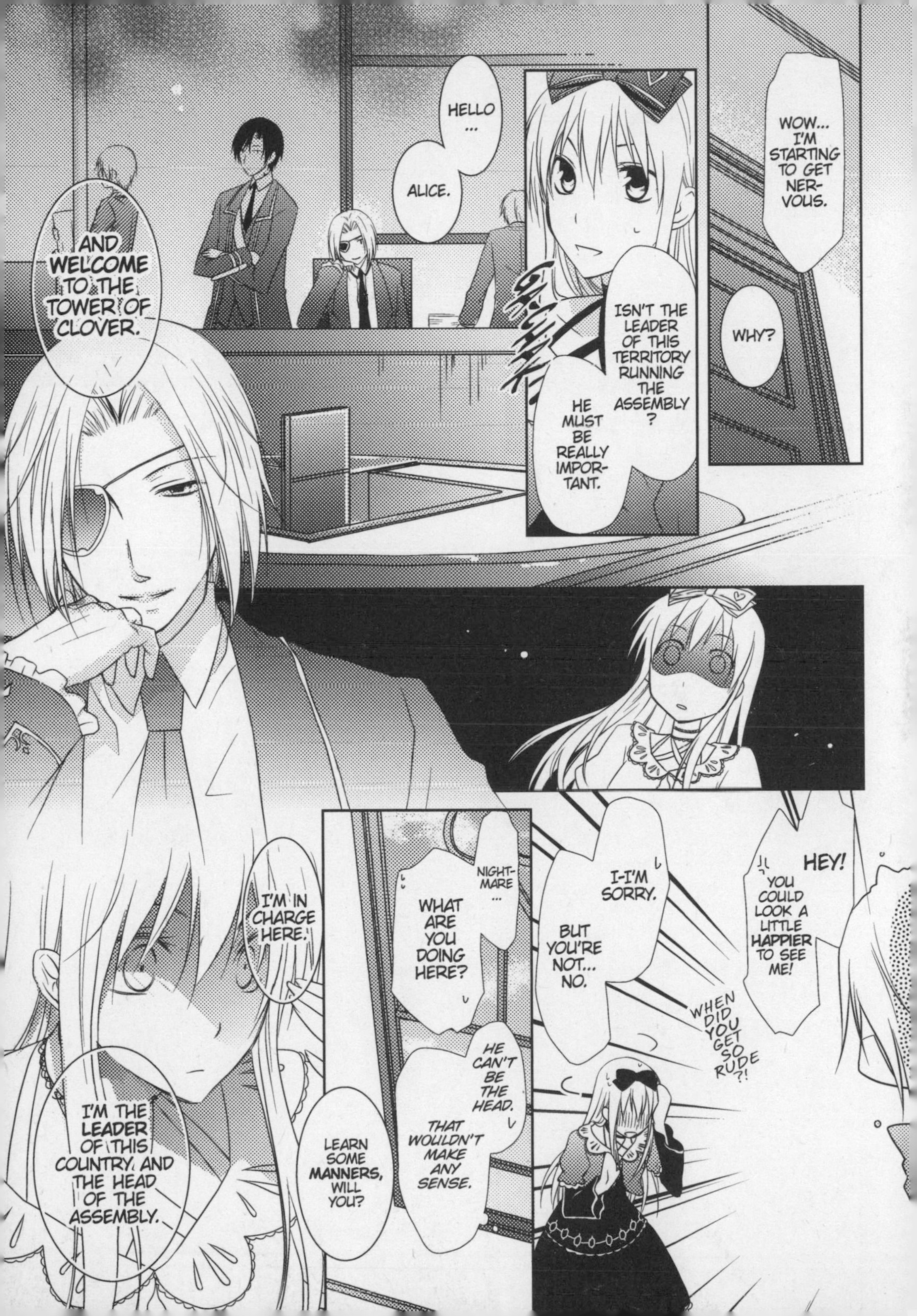
WOW... I'M STARTING TO GET NERVOUS.
WHY?
ISN'T THE LEADER OF THIS TERRITORY RUNNING THE ASSEMBLY?
HE MUST BE REALLY IMPORTANT.
GACHAK
HELLO...
ALICE.
AND WELCOME TO THE TOWER OF CLOVER.
HEY!
YOU COULD LOOK A LITTLE HAPPIER TO SEE ME!
WHEN DID YOU GET SO RUDE?!
I-I'M SORRY.
BUT YOU'RE NOT... NO.
NIGHTMARE...
WHAT ARE YOU DOING HERE?
HE CAN'T BE THE HEAD.
THAT WOULDN'T MAKE ANY SENSE.
LEARN SOME MANNERS, WILL YOU?
I'M IN CHARGE HERE.
I'M THE LEADER OF THIS COUNTRY AND THE HEAD OF THE ASSEMBLY.

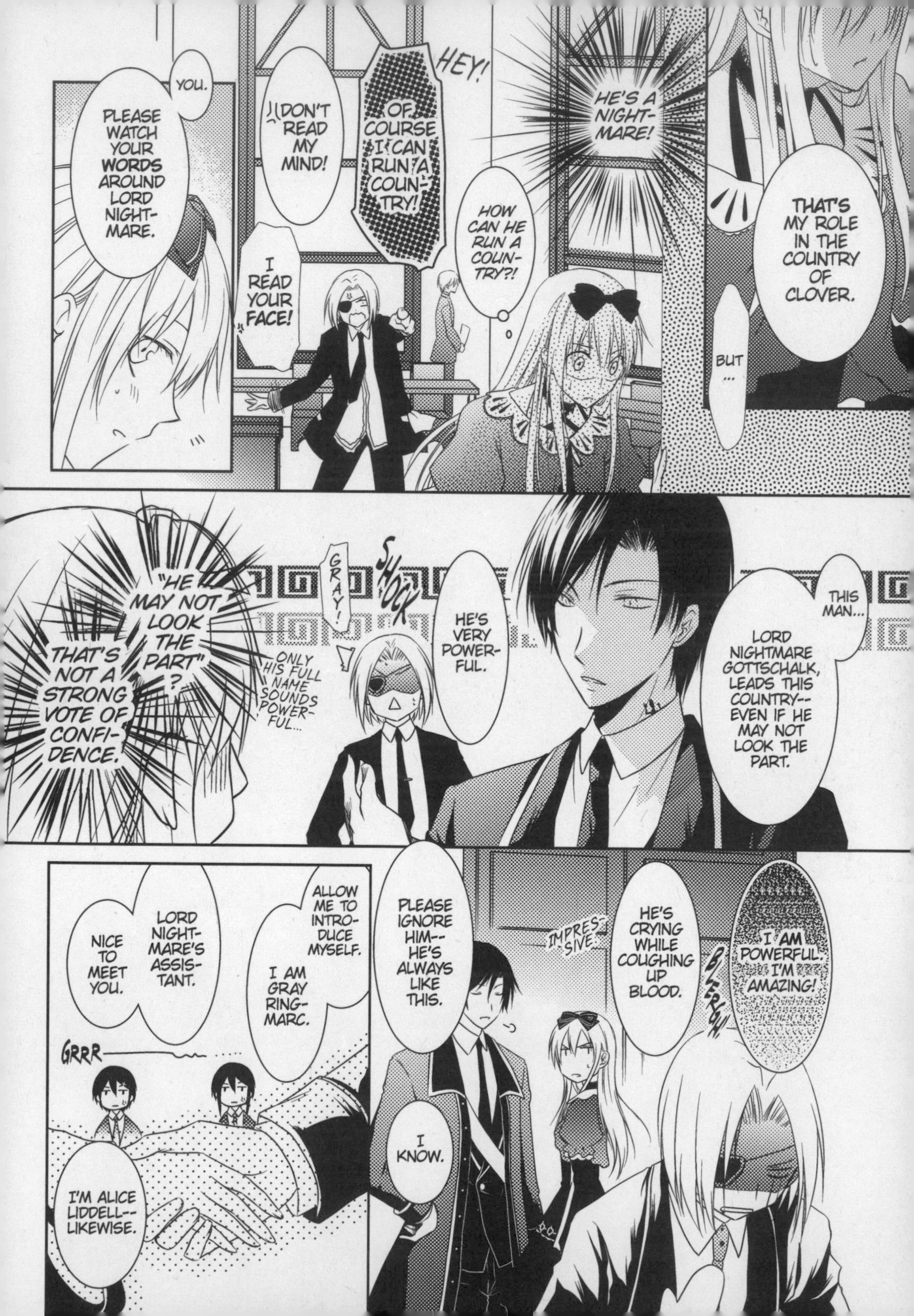
THAT'S MY ROLE IN THE COUNTRY OF CLOVER.
BUT...
HE'S A NIGHTMARE!
HOW CAN HE RUN A COUNTRY?!
HEY!
OF COURSE I CAN RUN A COUNTRY!
DON'T READ MY MIND!
I READ YOUR FACE!
YOU.
PLEASE WATCH YOUR WORDS AROUND LORD NIGHTMARE.
THIS MAN...
LORD NIGHTMARE GOTTSCHALK, LEADS THIS COUNTRY--EVEN IF HE MAY NOT LOOK THE PART.
HE'S VERY POWERFUL.
SHOCK
GRAY!
ONLY HIS FULL NAME SOUNDS POWERFUL...
"HE MAY NOT LOOK THE PART"?
THAT'S NOT A STRONG VOTE OF CONFIDENCE.
I AM POWERFUL. I'M AMAZING!
HE'S CRYING WHILE COUGHING UP BLOOD.
IMPRESSIVE.
PLEASE IGNORE HIM--HE'S ALWAYS LIKE THIS.
I KNOW.
ALLOW ME TO INTRODUCE MYSELF.
I AM GRAY RINGMARC.
LORD NIGHTMARE'S ASSISTANT.
NICE TO MEET YOU.
GRRR
I'M ALICE LIDDELL--LIKEWISE.

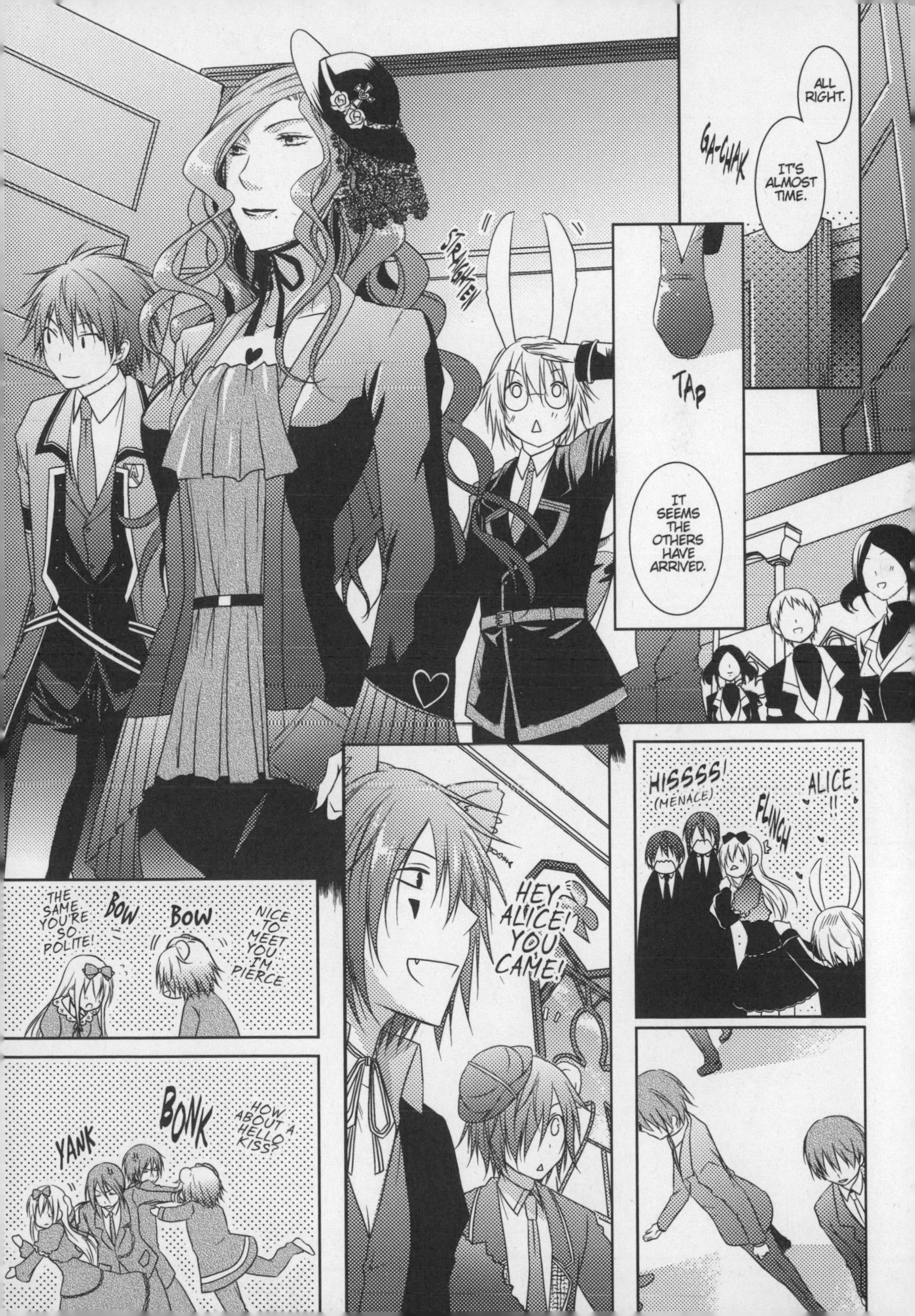
ALL RIGHT.
IT'S ALMOST TIME.
GA-CHAK
TAP
IT SEEMS THE OTHERS HAVE ARRIVED.
STRAIGHTEN
ALICE!!
FLINCH
HISSSS! (MENACE)
HEY, ALICE! YOU CAME!
NICE TO MEET YOU I'M PIERCE
BOW
BOW
THE SAME YOU'RE SO POLITE!
HOW ABOUT A HELLO KISS?
BONK
YANK

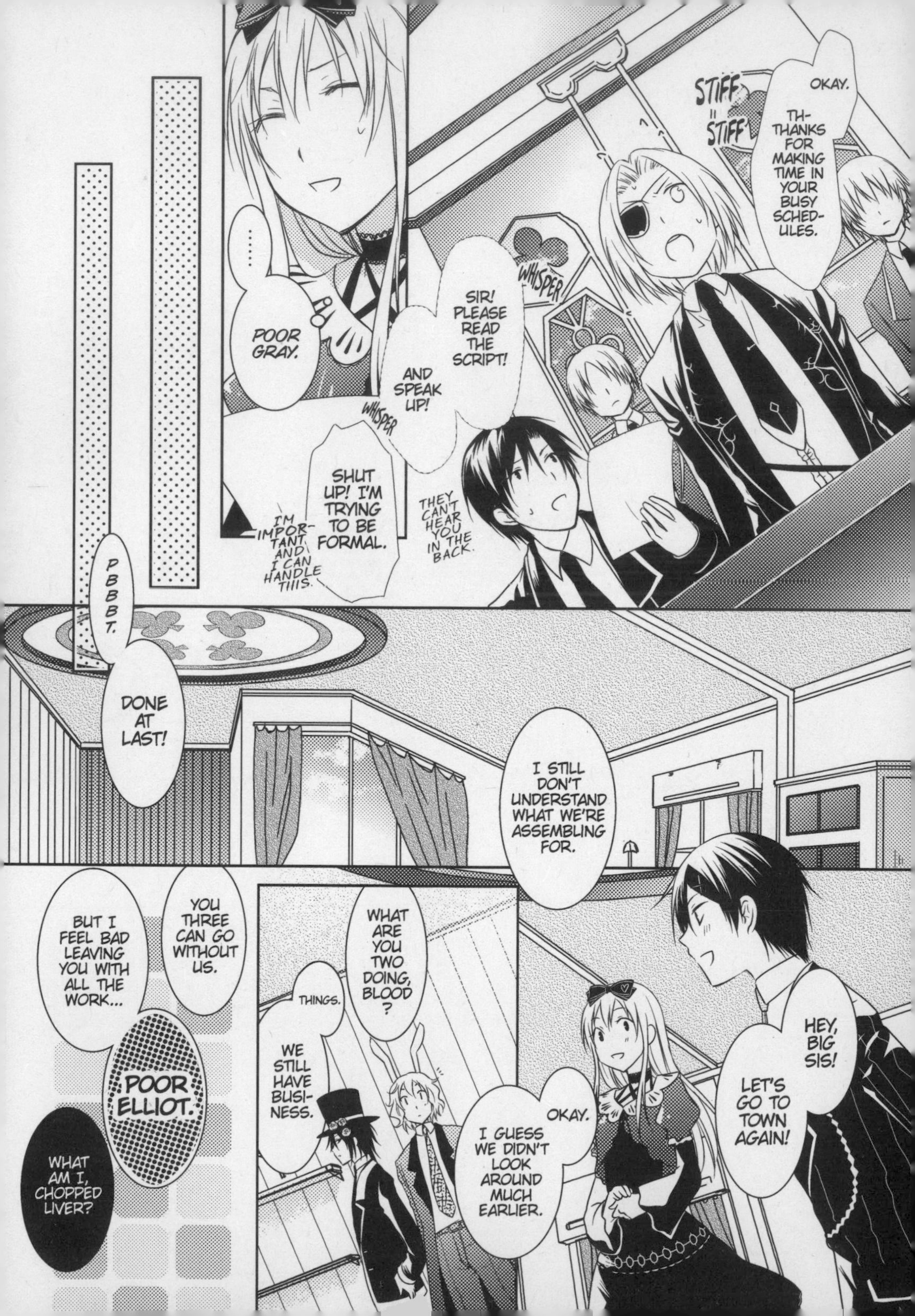
STIFF STIFF
OKAY.
TH-THANKS FOR MAKING TIME IN YOUR BUSY SCHED-ULES.
WHISPER
SIR! PLEASE READ THE SCRIPT!
AND SPEAK UP!
WHISPER
THEY CAN'T HEAR YOU IN THE BACK.
SHUT UP! I'M TRYING TO BE FORMAL.
I'M IMPOR-TANT AND I CAN HANDLE THIIS.
......
POOR GRAY.
PBBBT.
I STILL DON'T UNDERSTAND WHAT WE'RE ASSEMBLING FOR.
DONE AT LAST!
HEY, BIG SIS!
LET'S GO TO TOWN AGAIN!
OKAY.
I GUESS WE DIDN'T LOOK AROUND MUCH EARLIER.
WHAT ARE YOU TWO DOING, BLOOD?
THINGS.
WE STILL HAVE BUSI-NESS.
YOU THREE CAN GO WITHOUT US.
BUT I FEEL BAD LEAVING YOU WITH ALL THE WORK...
POOR ELLIOT.
WHAT AM I, CHOPPED LIVER?

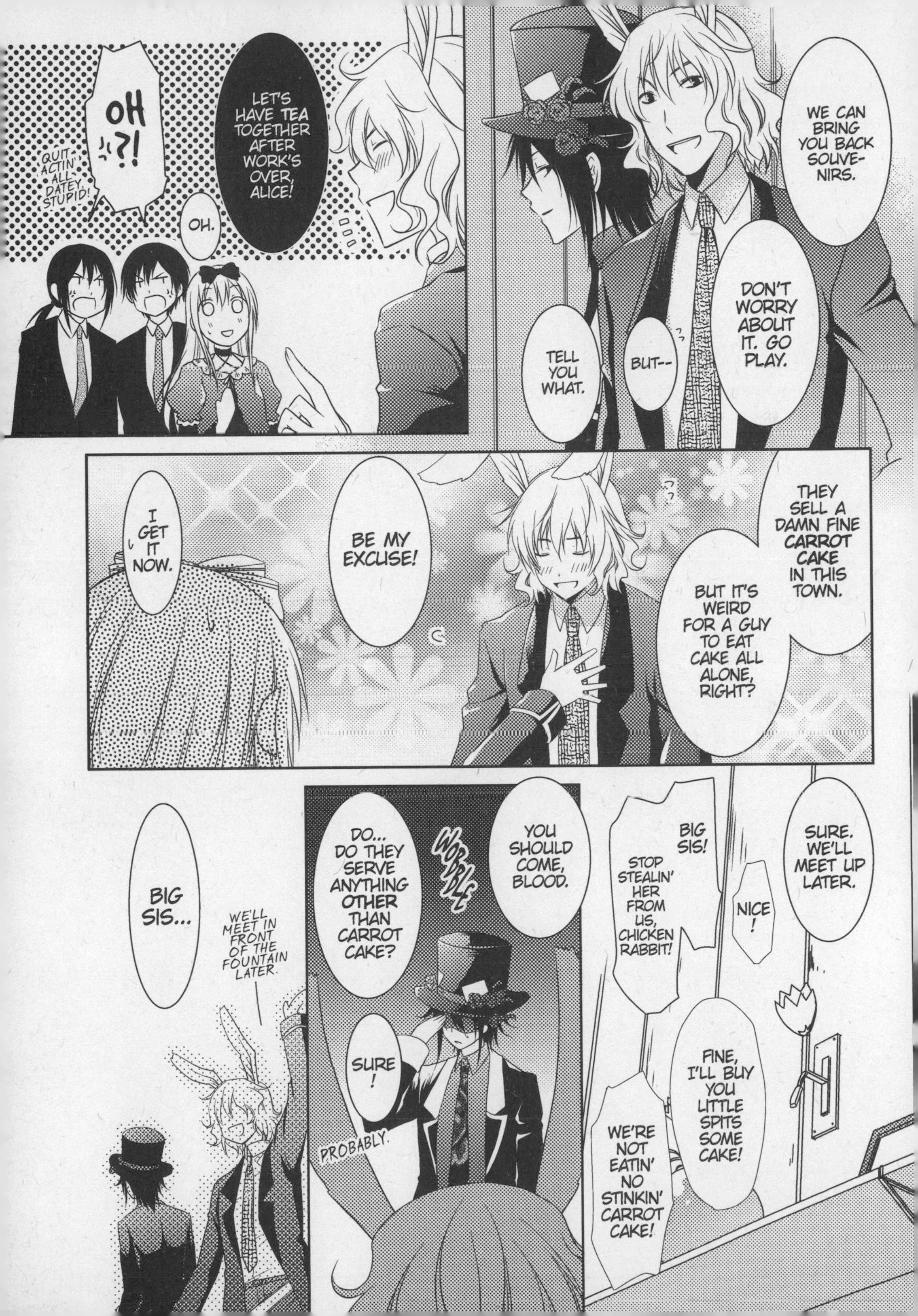
WE CAN BRING YOU BACK SOUVENIRS.
DON'T WORRY ABOUT IT. GO PLAY.
BUT--
TELL YOU WHAT.
LET'S HAVE TEA TOGETHER AFTER WORK'S OVER, ALICE!
OH ?!
QUIT ACTIN' ALL DATEY, STUPID!
OH.
THEY SELL A DAMN FINE CARROT CAKE IN THIS TOWN.
BUT IT'S WEIRD FOR A GUY TO EAT CAKE ALL ALONE, RIGHT?
BE MY EXCUSE!
I GET IT NOW.
SURE. WE'LL MEET UP LATER.
NICE!
BIG SIS!
STOP STEALIN' HER FROM US, CHICKEN RABBIT!
FINE, I'LL BUY YOU LITTLE SPITS SOME CAKE!
WE'RE NOT EATIN' NO STINKIN' CARROT CAKE!
YOU SHOULD COME, BLOOD.
WOBBLE
DO... DO THEY SERVE ANYTHING OTHER THAN CARROT CAKE?
SURE!
PROBABLY.
BIG SIS...
WE'LL MEET IN FRONT OF THE FOUNTAIN LATER.

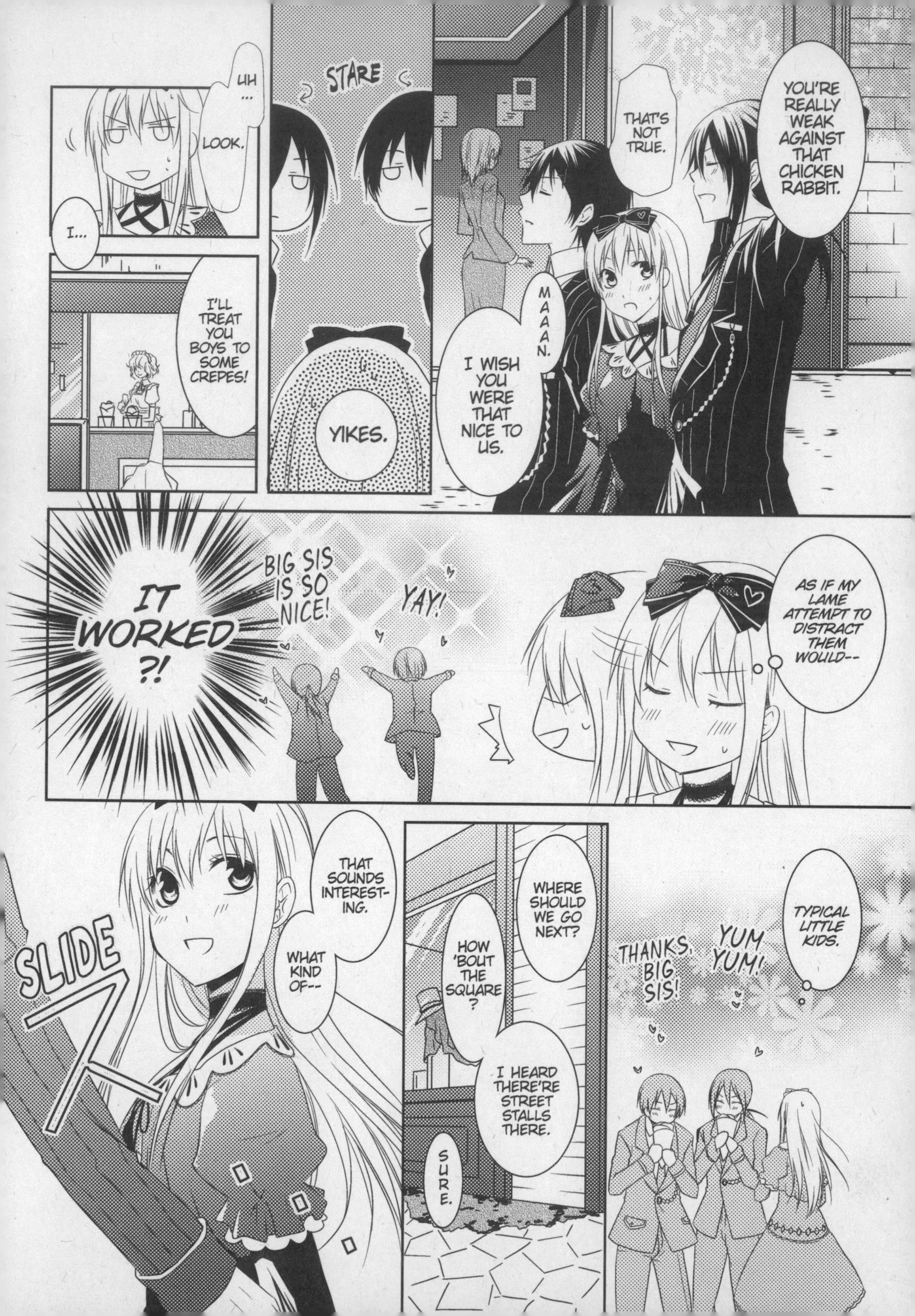
YOU'RE REALLY WEAK AGAINST THAT CHICKEN RABBIT.
THAT'S NOT TRUE.
MAAAN.
I WISH YOU WERE THAT NICE TO US.
STARE
YIKES.
UH ...
LOOK.
I...
I'LL TREAT YOU BOYS TO SOME CREPES!
AS IF MY LAME ATTEMPT TO DISTRACT THEM WOULD--
YAY!
BIG SIS IS SO NICE!
IT WORKED ?!
TYPICAL LITTLE KIDS.
YUM YUM!
THANKS, BIG SIS!
WHERE SHOULD WE GO NEXT?
HOW 'BOUT THE SQUARE ?
I HEARD THERE'RE STREET STALLS THERE.
SURE.
THAT SOUNDS INTERESTING.
WHAT KIND OF--
SLIDE

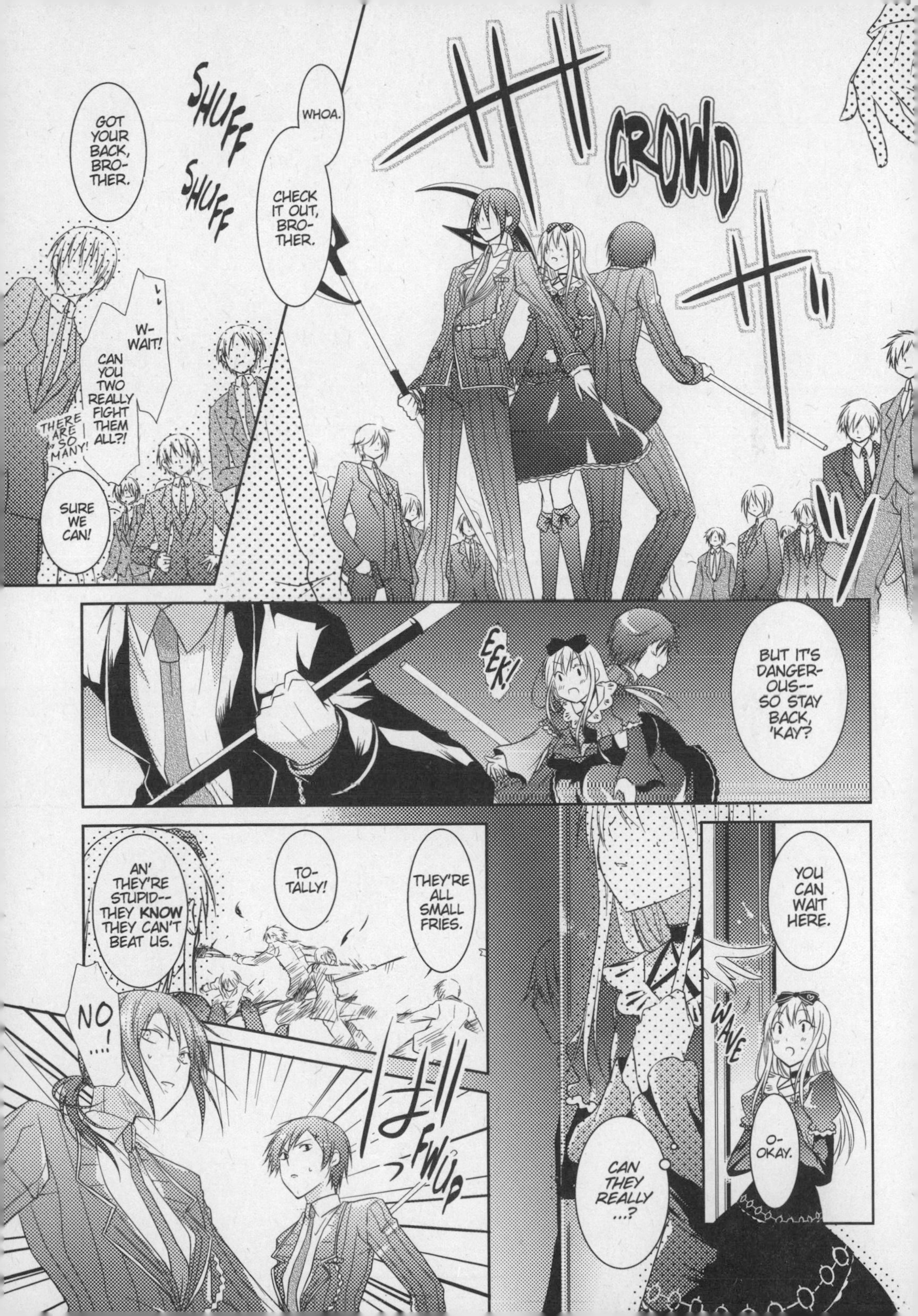
CROWD
WHOA.
CHECK IT OUT, BROTHER.
SHUFF SHUFF
GOT YOUR BACK, BROTHER.
W-WAIT! CAN YOU TWO REALLY FIGHT THEM ALL?!
THERE ARE SO MANY!
SURE WE CAN!
BUT IT'S DANGEROUS-- SO STAY BACK, 'KAY?
EEK!
YOU CAN WAIT HERE.
WAVE
O-OKAY.
CAN THEY REALLY ...?
THEY'RE ALL SMALL FRIES.
TO-TALLY!
AN' THEY'RE STUPID-- THEY KNOW THEY CAN'T BEAT US.
FWUP
NO...!

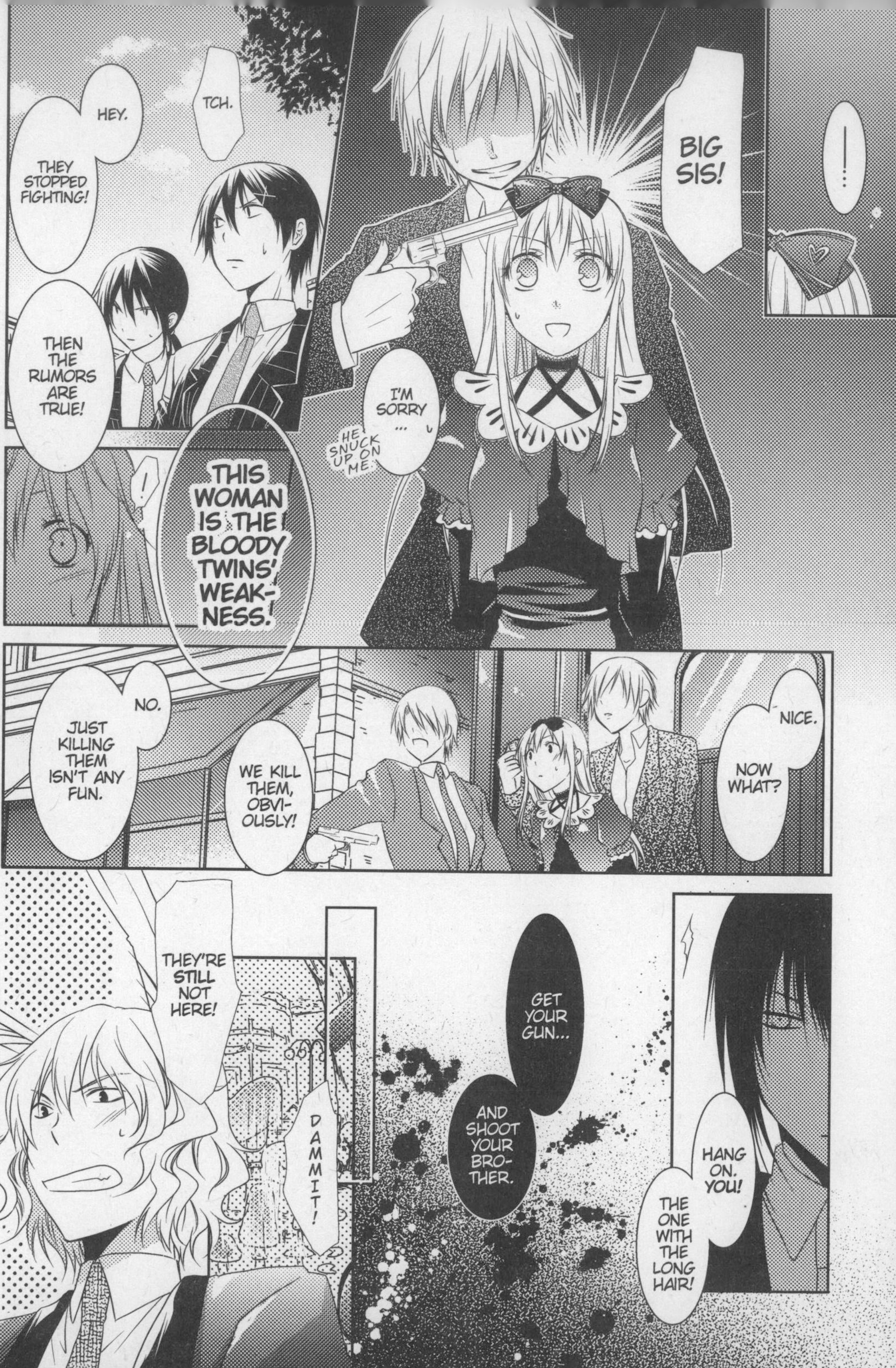
!...
BIG SIS!
I'M SORRY...
HE SNUCK UP ON ME.
HEY.
TCH.
THEY STOPPED FIGHTING!
THEN THE RUMORS ARE TRUE!
!
THIS WOMAN IS THE BLOODY TWINS' WEAKNESS!
NICE.
NOW WHAT?
WE KILL THEM, OBVIOUSLY!
NO.
JUST KILLING THEM ISN'T ANY FUN.
HANG ON. YOU!
THE ONE WITH THE LONG HAIR!
GET YOUR GUN...
AND SHOOT YOUR BROTHER.
THEY'RE STILL NOT HERE!
DAMMIT!

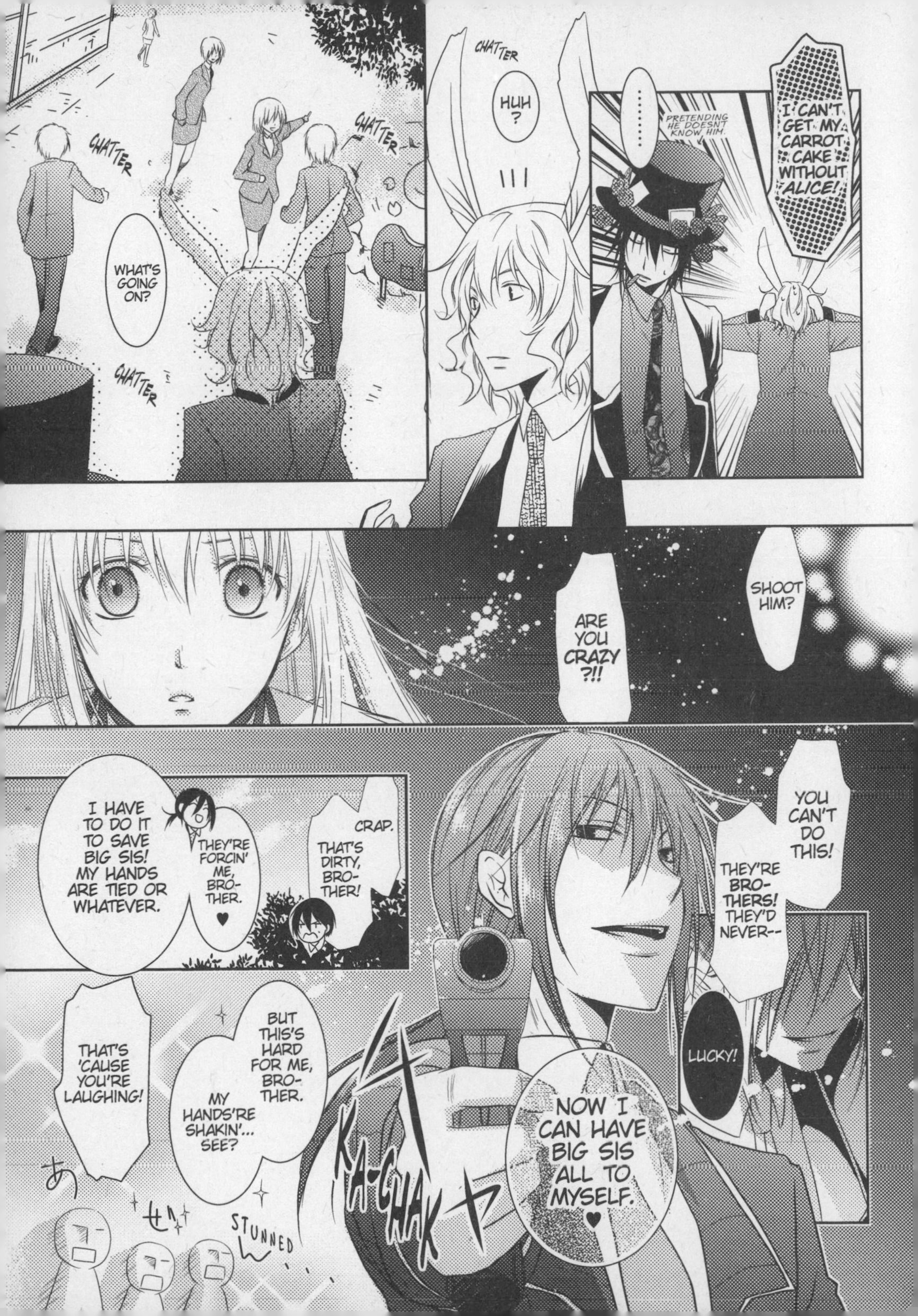
I CAN'T GET MY CARROT CAKE WITHOUT ALICE!
...
PRETENDING HE DOESN'T KNOW HIM.
CHATTER
HUH?
CHATTER
WHAT'S GOING ON?
CHATTER
CHATTER
SHOOT HIM?
ARE YOU CRAZY?!!
YOU CAN'T DO THIS!
THEY'RE BROTHERS! THEY'D NEVER--
LUCKY!
NOW I CAN HAVE BIG SIS ALL TO MYSELF. ♥
KA-CHAK
CRAP. THAT'S DIRTY, BROTHER!
THEY'RE FORCIN' ME, BROTHER. ♥
I HAVE TO DO IT TO SAVE BIG SIS! MY HANDS ARE TIED OR WHATEVER.
BUT THIS'S HARD FOR ME, BROTHER.
MY HANDS'RE SHAKIN'... SEE?
THAT'S 'CAUSE YOU'RE LAUGHING!
STUNNED

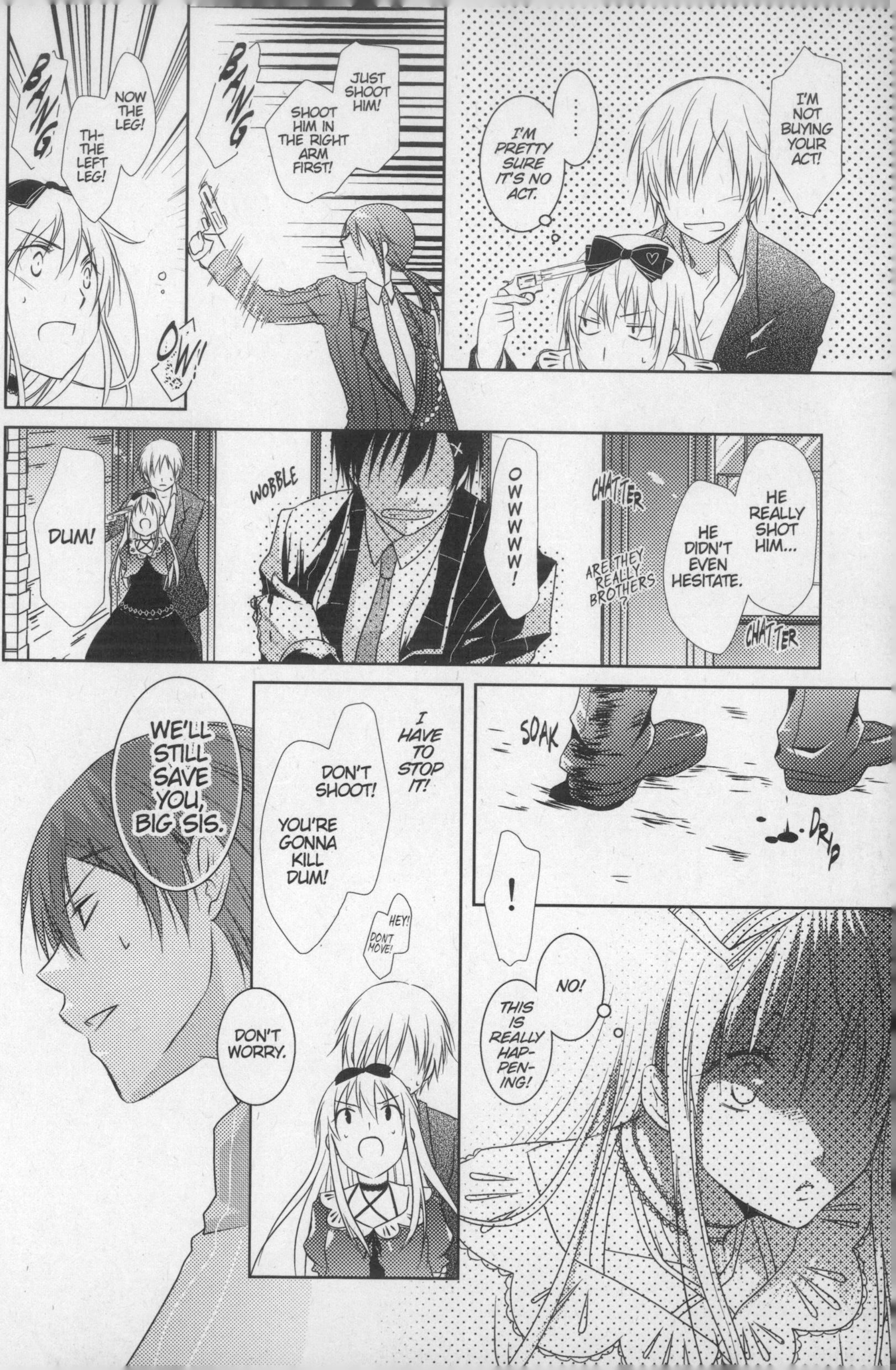
I'M NOT BUYING YOUR ACT!
...
I'M PRETTY SURE IT'S NO ACT.
JUST SHOOT HIM!
SHOOT HIM IN THE RIGHT ARM FIRST!
BANG
BANG
NOW THE LEG!
TH-THE LEFT LEG!
OW!
HE REALLY SHOT HIM...
HE DIDN'T EVEN HESITATE.
CHATTER
ARE THEY REALLY BROTHERS?
CHATTER
OWWWWWW!
WOBBLE
DUM!
SOAK
DRIP
!
NO!
THIS IS REALLY HAP-PEN-ING!
I HAVE TO STOP IT!
DON'T SHOOT!
YOU'RE GONNA KILL DUM!
HEY!
DON'T MOVE!
DON'T WORRY.
WE'LL STILL SAVE YOU, BIG SIS.

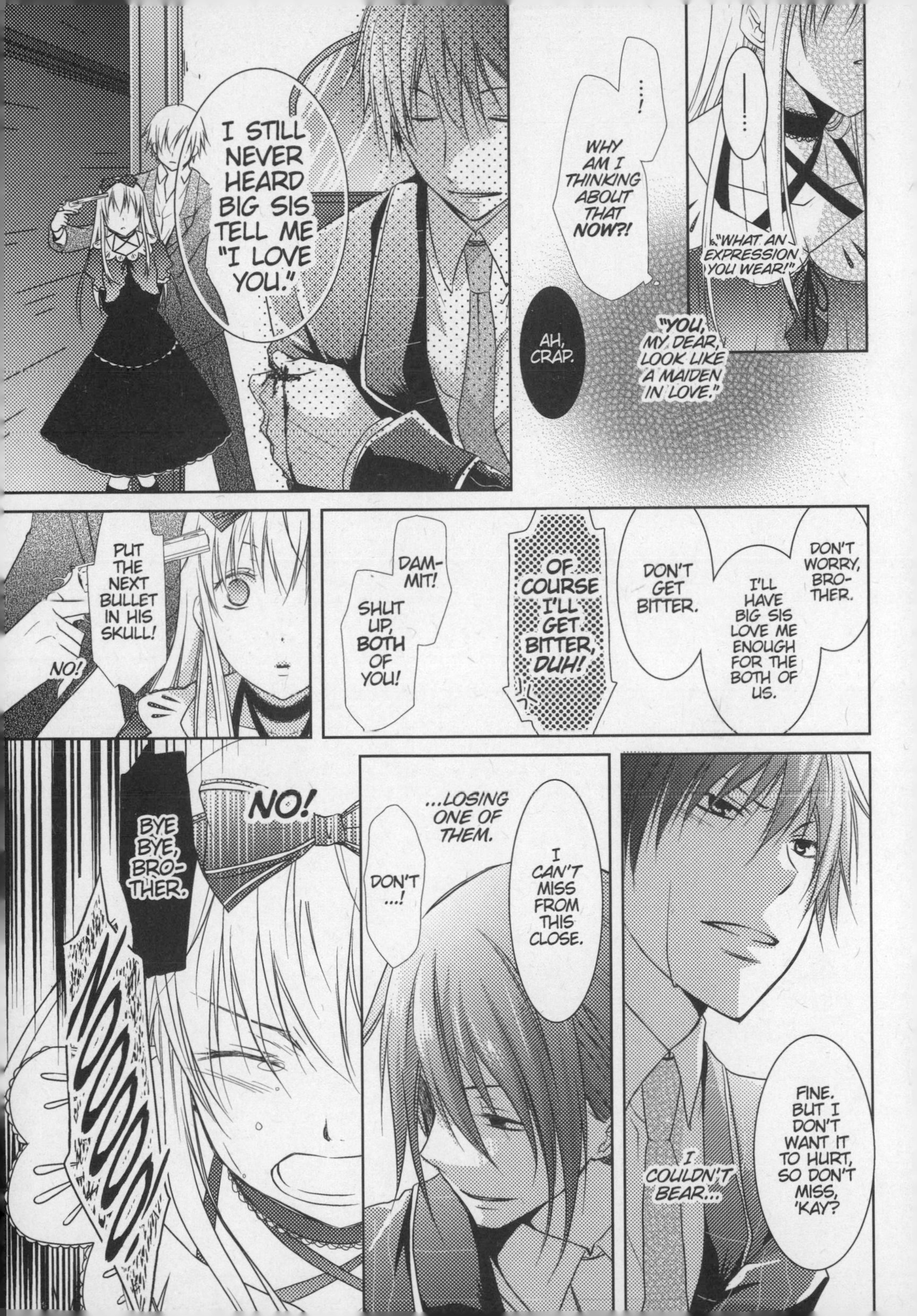
…!
"WHAT AN EXPRESSION YOU WEAR!"
"YOU, MY DEAR, LOOK LIKE A MAIDEN IN LOVE."
…!
WHY AM I THINKING ABOUT THAT NOW?!
AH, CRAP.
I STILL NEVER HEARD BIG SIS TELL ME "I LOVE YOU."
DON'T WORRY, BROTHER.
I'LL HAVE BIG SIS LOVE ME ENOUGH FOR THE BOTH OF US.
DON'T GET BITTER.
OF COURSE I'LL GET BITTER, DUH!
DAMMIT!
SHUT UP, BOTH OF YOU!
PUT THE NEXT BULLET IN HIS SKULL!
NO!
FINE. BUT I DON'T WANT IT TO HURT, SO DON'T MISS, 'KAY?
I COULDN'T BEAR...
I CAN'T MISS FROM THIS CLOSE.
...LOSING ONE OF THEM.
DON'T ...!
NO!
BYE BYE, BROTHER.

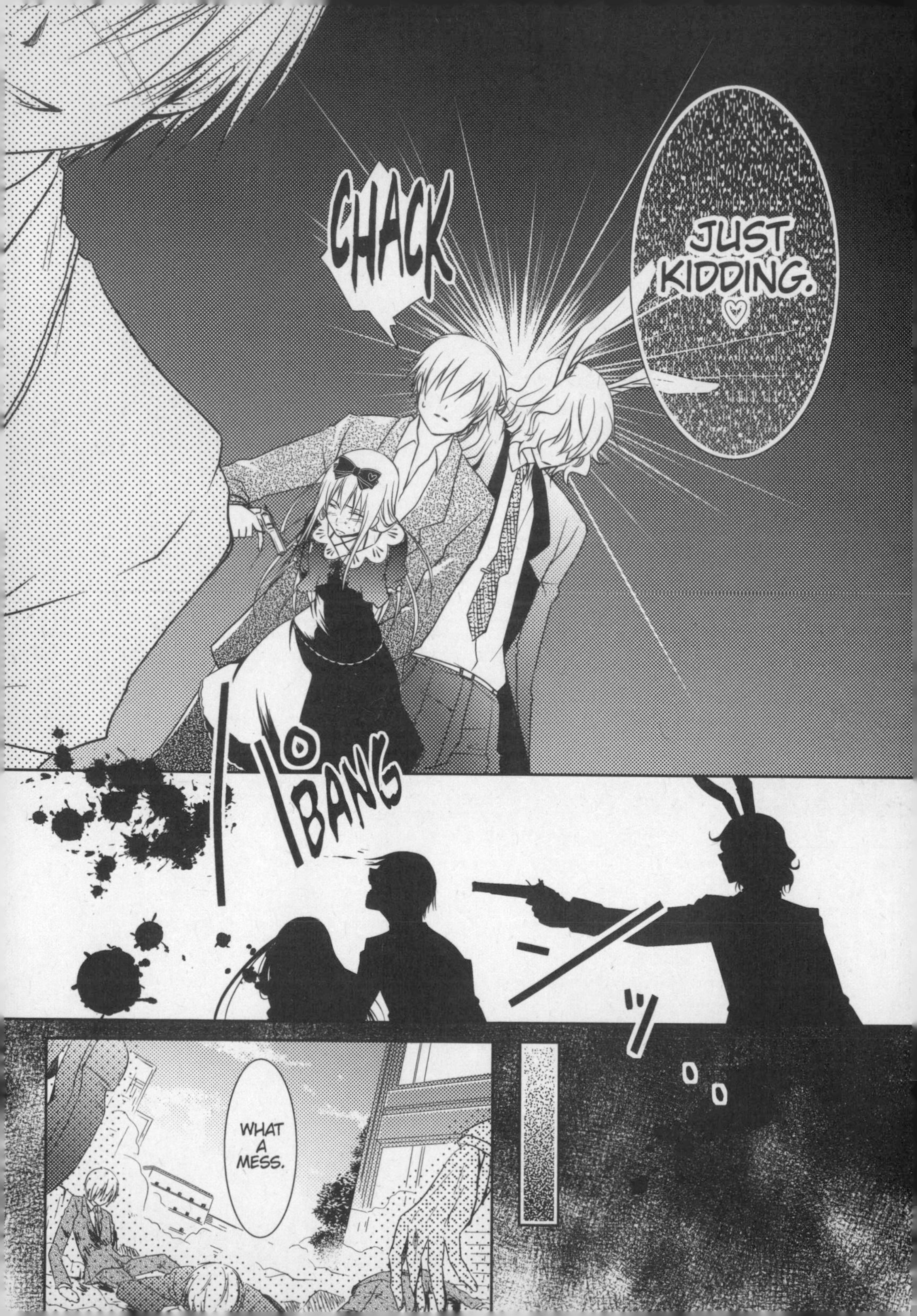
JUST KIDDING. ♡
CHACK
BANG
WHAT A MESS.

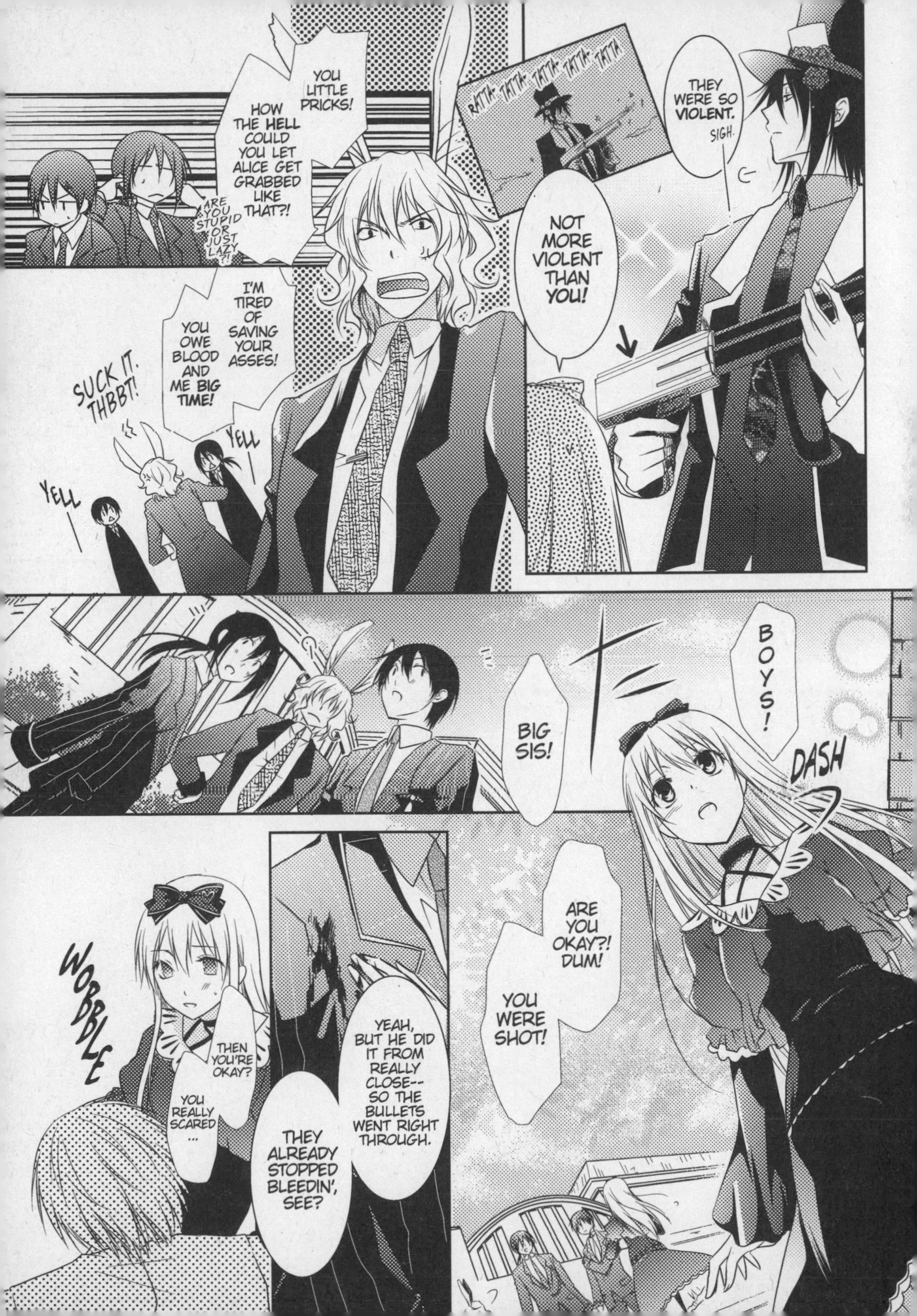
THEY WERE SO VIOLENT.
SIGH.
RATTA- TATTA- TATTA- TATTA- TATTA
NOT MORE VIOLENT THAN YOU!
YOU LITTLE PRICKS!
HOW THE HELL COULD YOU LET ALICE GET GRABBED LIKE THAT?!
ARE YOU STUPID OR JUST LAZY?!
I'M TIRED OF SAVING YOUR ASSES!
YOU OWE BLOOD AND ME BIG TIME!
SUCK IT. THBBT!
YELL
YELL
BOYS!
DASH
BIG SIS!
ARE YOU OKAY?! DUM!
YOU WERE SHOT!
YEAH, BUT HE DID IT FROM REALLY CLOSE-- SO THE BULLETS WENT RIGHT THROUGH.
THEY ALREADY STOPPED BLEEDIN', SEE?
THEN YOU'RE OKAY?
YOU REALLY SCARED ...
WOBBLE

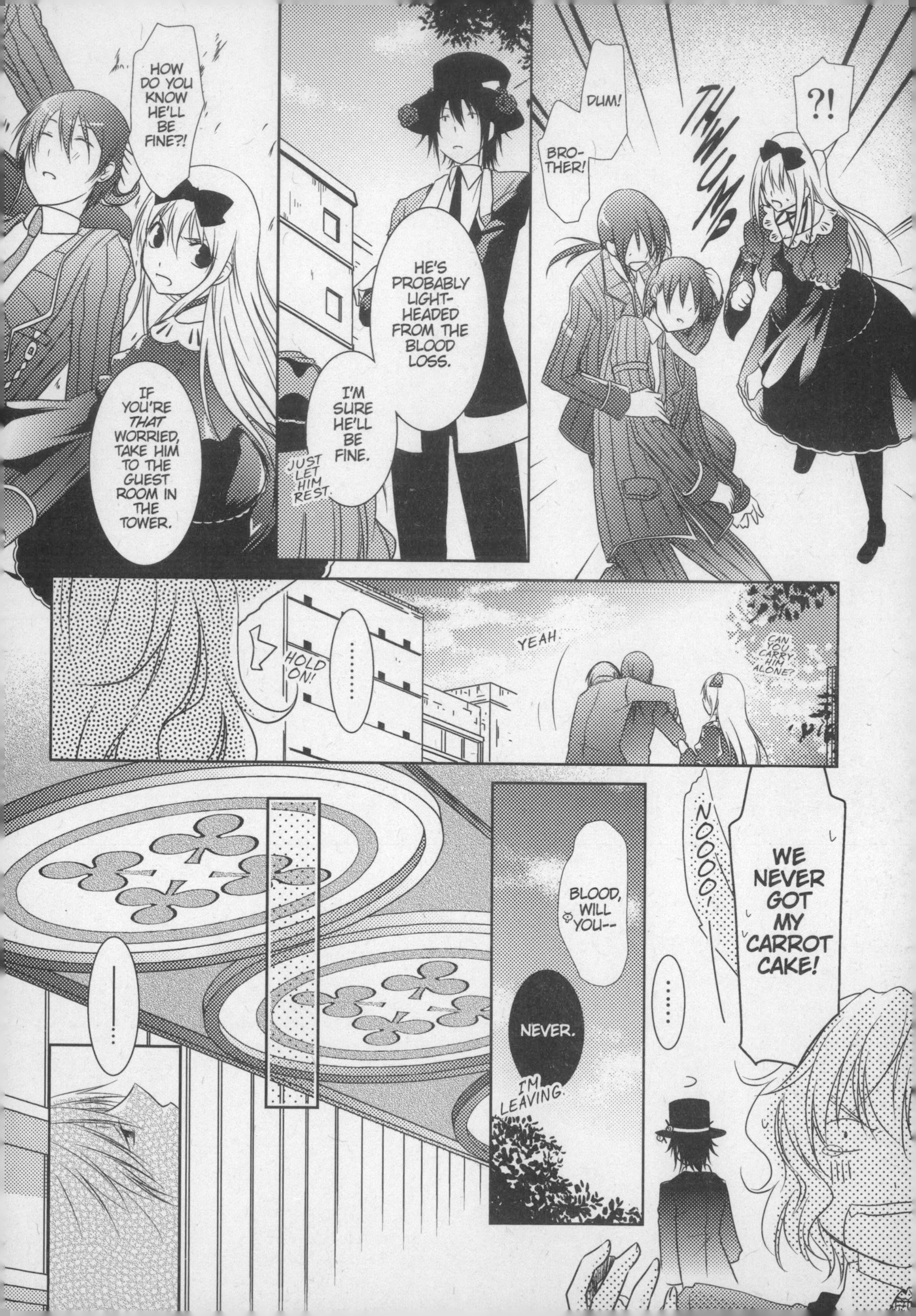
?!
DUM!
BRO-THER!
THWUMP
HE'S PROBABLY LIGHT-HEADED FROM THE BLOOD LOSS.
I'M SURE HE'LL BE FINE.
JUST LET HIM REST.
HOW DO YOU KNOW HE'LL BE FINE?!
IF YOU'RE *THAT* WORRIED, TAKE HIM TO THE GUEST ROOM IN THE TOWER.
CAN YOU CARRY HIM ALONE?
YEAH.
......
HOLD ON!
NOOOO!
WE NEVER GOT MY CARROT CAKE!
BLOOD, WILL YOU--
......
NEVER.
I'M LEAVING.
...!

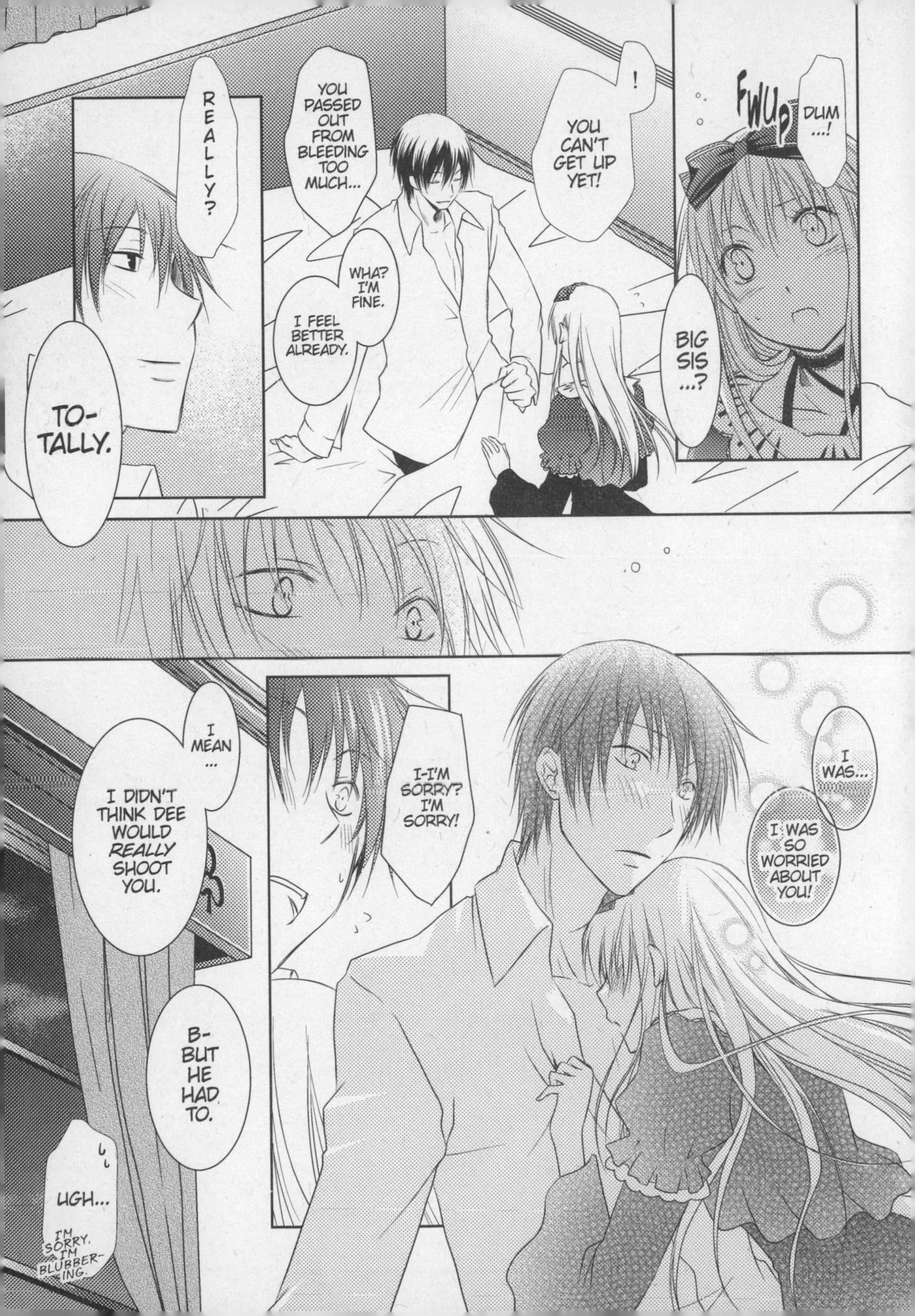
FWUP
DUM ...!
BIG SIS ...?
!
YOU CAN'T GET UP YET!
YOU PASSED OUT FROM BLEEDING TOO MUCH...
WHA? I'M FINE.
I FEEL BETTER ALREADY.
REALLY?
TO-TALLY.
I WAS...!
I WAS SO WORRIED ABOUT YOU!
I-I'M SORRY? I'M SORRY!
WHA?
I MEAN ...
I DIDN'T THINK DEE WOULD *REALLY* SHOOT YOU.
B-BUT HE HAD TO.
UGH...
I'M SORRY. I'M BLUBBER-ING.

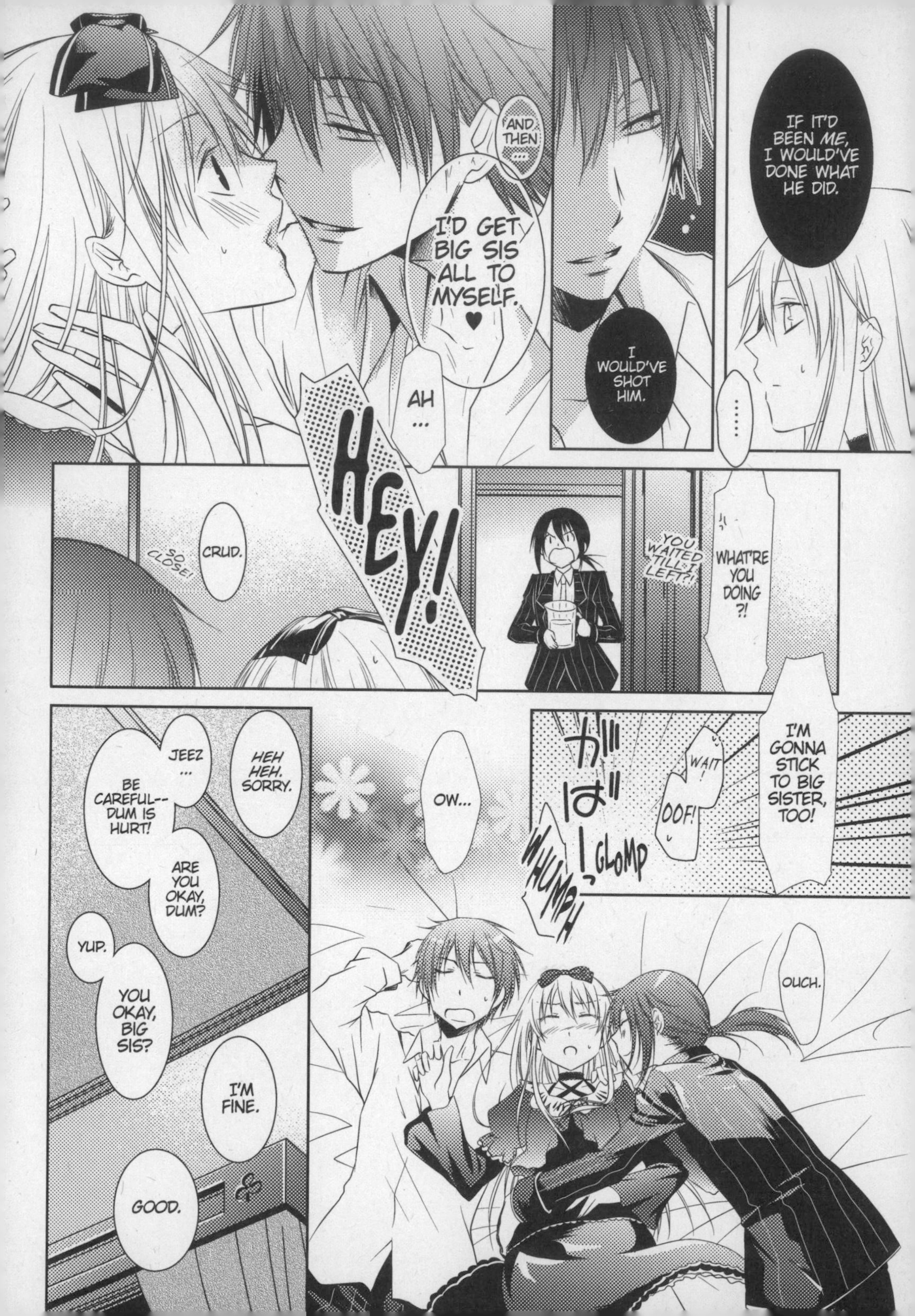

IF IT'D BEEN ME, I WOULD'VE DONE WHAT HE DID.
.....
I WOULD'VE SHOT HIM.
AND THEN ...
I'D GET BIG SIS ALL TO MYSELF. ♥
AH ...
WHAT'RE YOU DOING ?!
YOU WAITED TILL I LEFT?!
HEY!
CRUD.
SO CLOSE!
I'M GONNA STICK TO BIG SISTER, TOO!
WAIT!
OOF!
がば!
GLOMP
WHUMPH
OUCH.
OW...
HEH HEH. SORRY.
JEEZ ...
BE CAREFUL-- DUM IS HURT!
ARE YOU OKAY, DUM?
YUP.
YOU OKAY, BIG SIS?
I'M FINE.
GOOD.

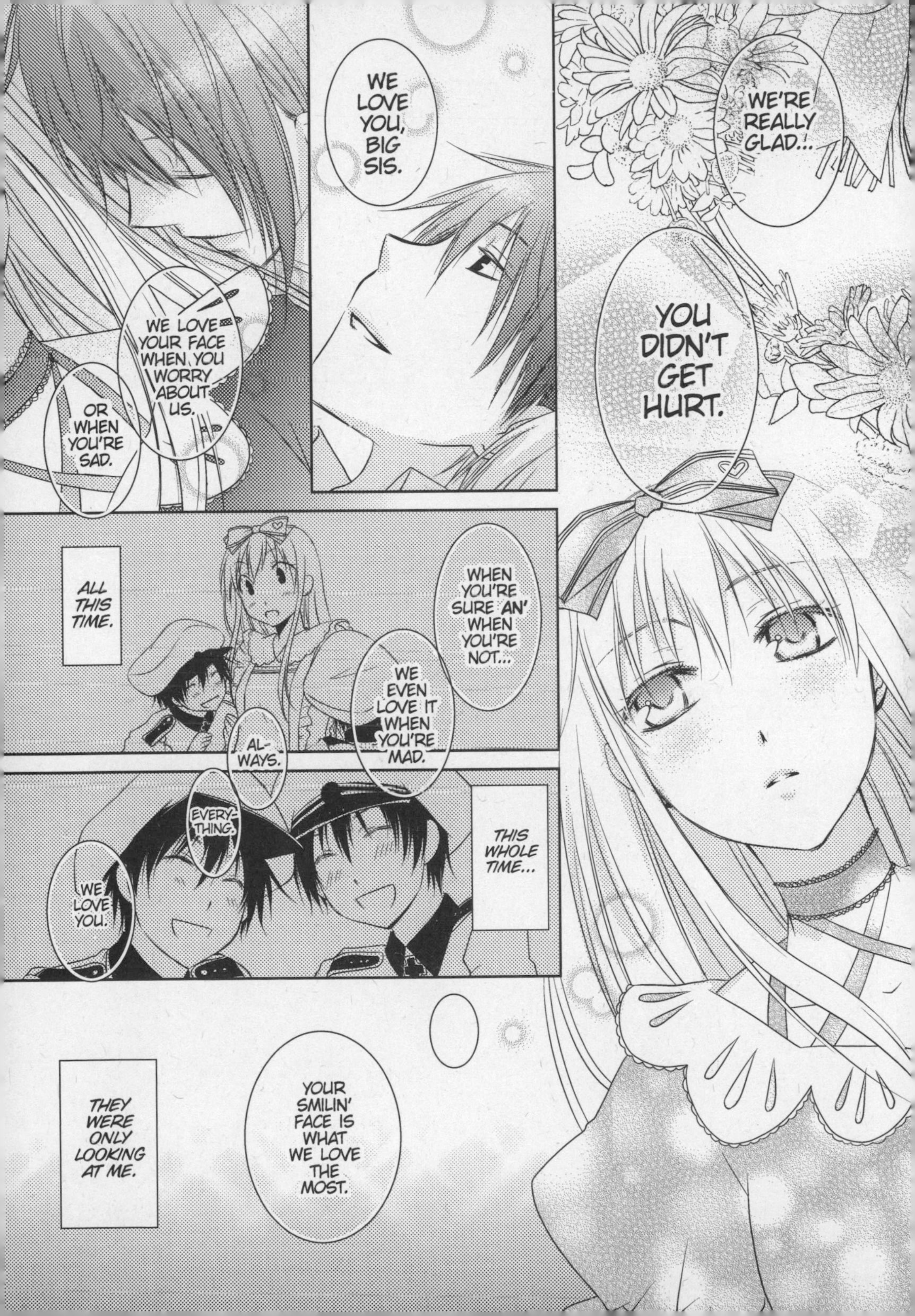
WE'RE REALLY GLAD...
YOU DIDN'T GET HURT.
WE LOVE YOU, BIG SIS.
WE LOVE YOUR FACE WHEN YOU WORRY ABOUT US.
OR WHEN YOU'RE SAD.
WHEN YOU'RE SURE AN' WHEN YOU'RE NOT...
WE EVEN LOVE IT WHEN YOU'RE MAD.
ALL THIS TIME.
AL-WAYS.
THIS WHOLE TIME...
EVERY-THING.
WE LOVE YOU.
YOUR SMILIN' FACE IS WHAT WE LOVE THE MOST.
THEY WERE ONLY LOOKING AT ME.

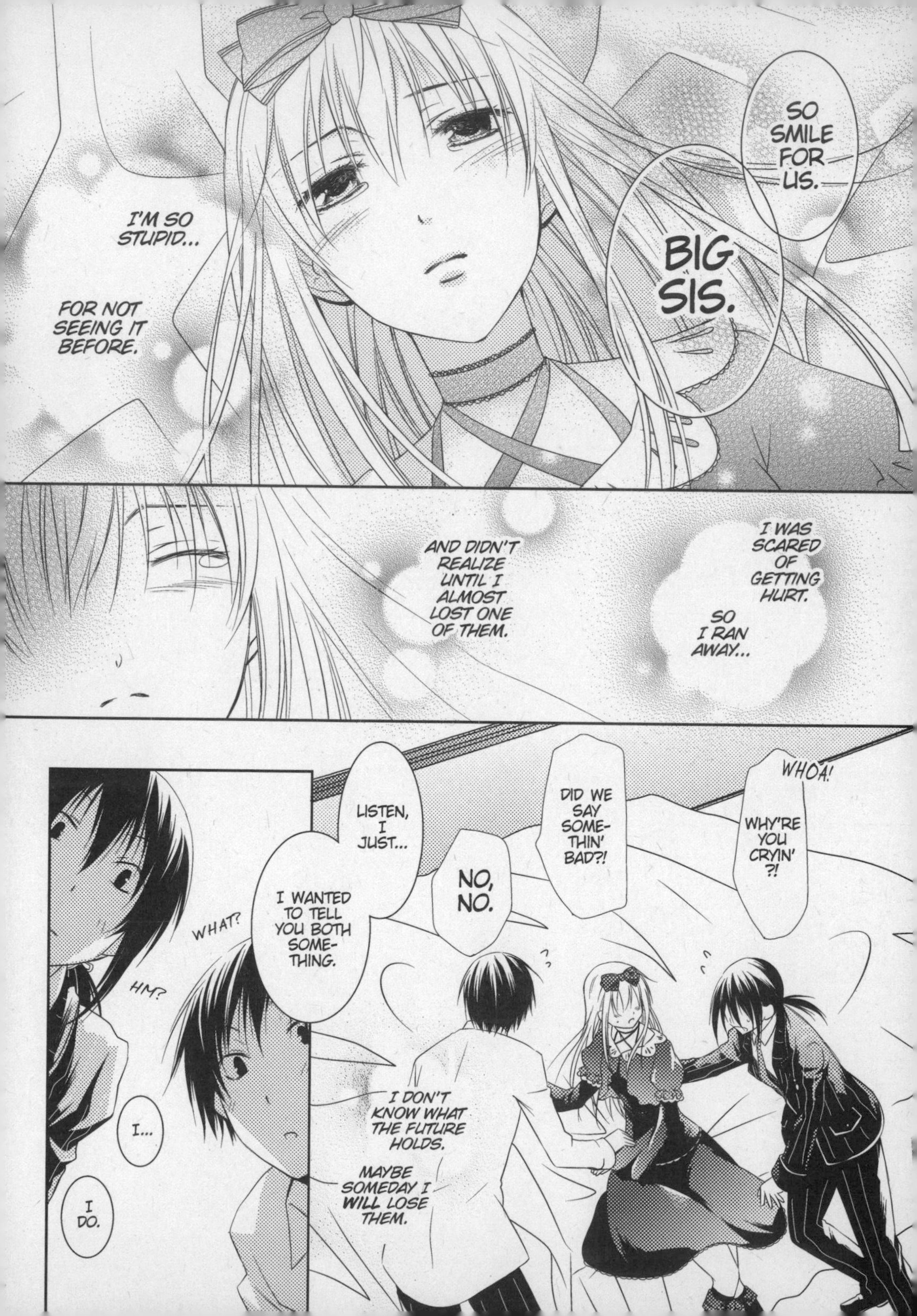
SO SMILE FOR US.
BIG SIS.
I'M SO STUPID...
FOR NOT SEEING IT BEFORE.
I WAS SCARED OF GETTING HURT.
SO I RAN AWAY...
AND DIDN'T REALIZE UNTIL I ALMOST LOST ONE OF THEM.
WHOA!
WHY'RE YOU CRYIN'?!
DID WE SAY SOME-THIN' BAD?!
NO, NO.
LISTEN, I JUST...
I WANTED TO TELL YOU BOTH SOME-THING.
WHAT?
HM?
I DON'T KNOW WHAT THE FUTURE HOLDS.
MAYBE SOMEDAY I WILL LOSE THEM.
I...
I DO.

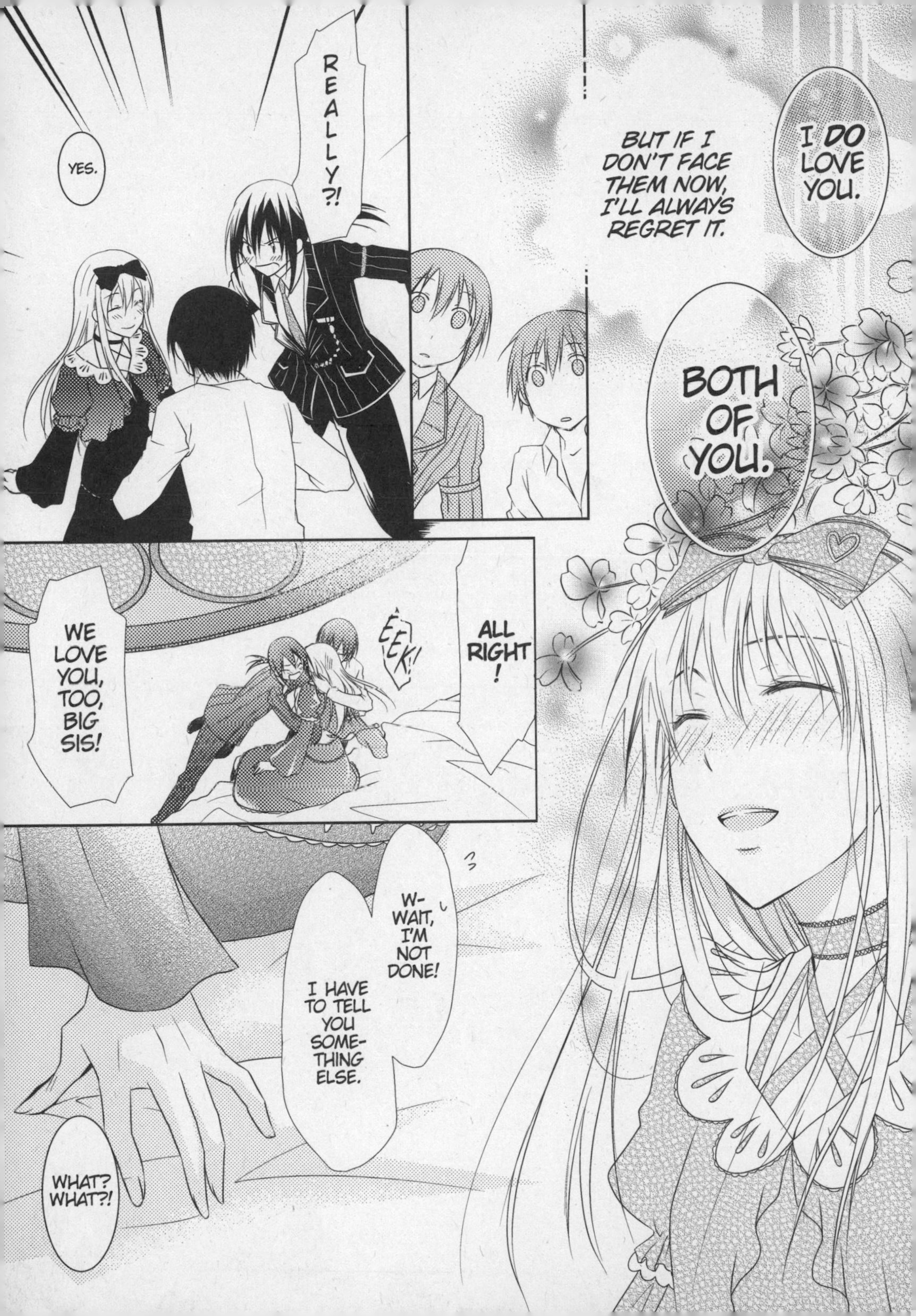
I DO LOVE YOU.
BUT IF I DON'T FACE THEM NOW, I'LL ALWAYS REGRET IT.
BOTH OF YOU.
REALLY?!
YES.
ALL RIGHT!
EEK!
WE LOVE YOU, TOO, BIG SIS!
W-WAIT, I'M NOT DONE!
I HAVE TO TELL YOU SOMETHING ELSE.
WHAT? WHAT?!

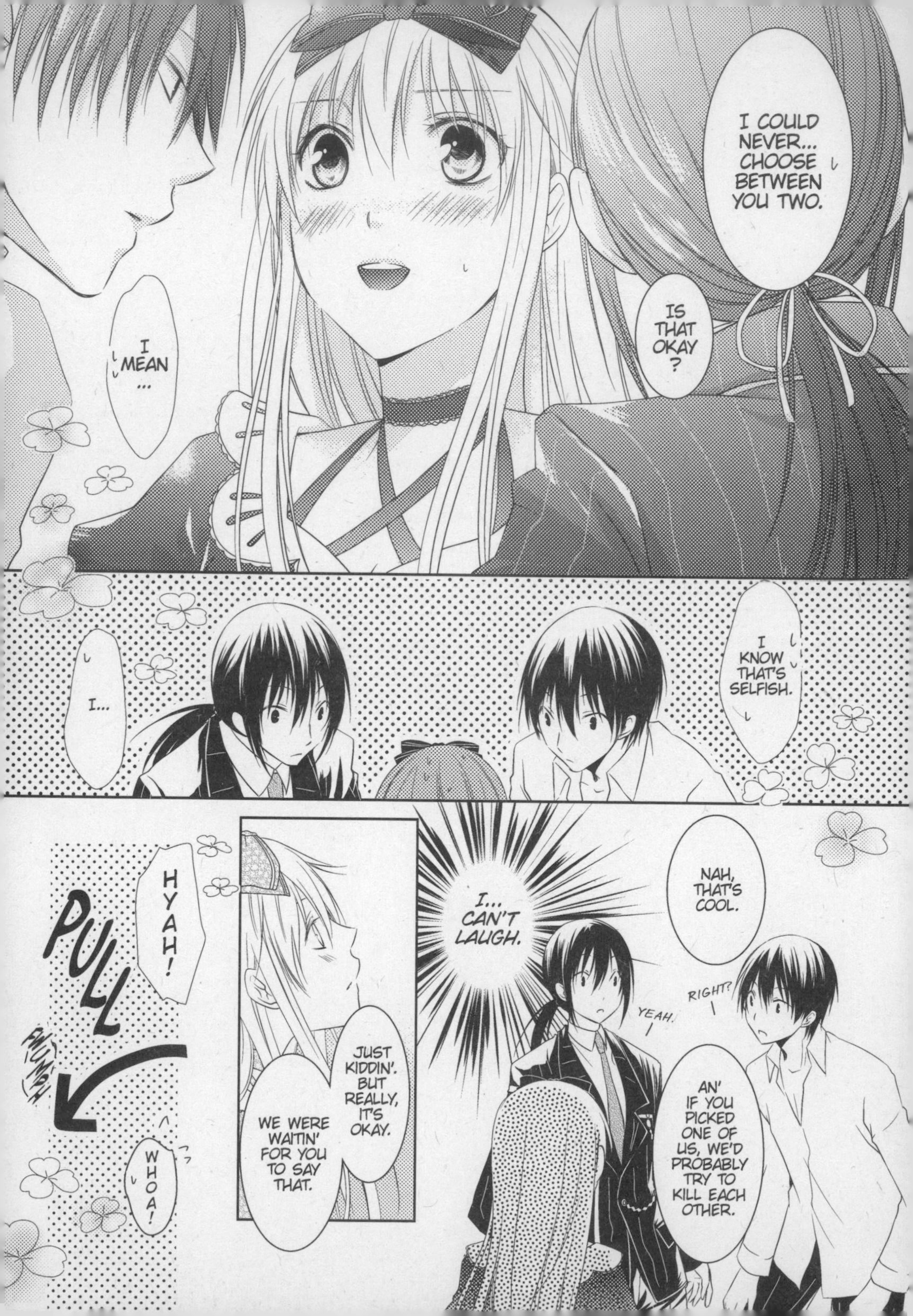
I COULD NEVER... CHOOSE BETWEEN YOU TWO.
IS THAT OKAY?
I MEAN...
I KNOW THAT'S SELFISH.
I...
NAH, THAT'S COOL.
I... CAN'T LAUGH.
RIGHT?
YEAH.
AN' IF YOU PICKED ONE OF US, WE'D PROBABLY TRY TO KILL EACH OTHER.
JUST KIDDIN'. BUT REALLY, IT'S OKAY.
WE WERE WAITIN' FOR YOU TO SAY THAT.
HYAH!
PULL
WHOA!

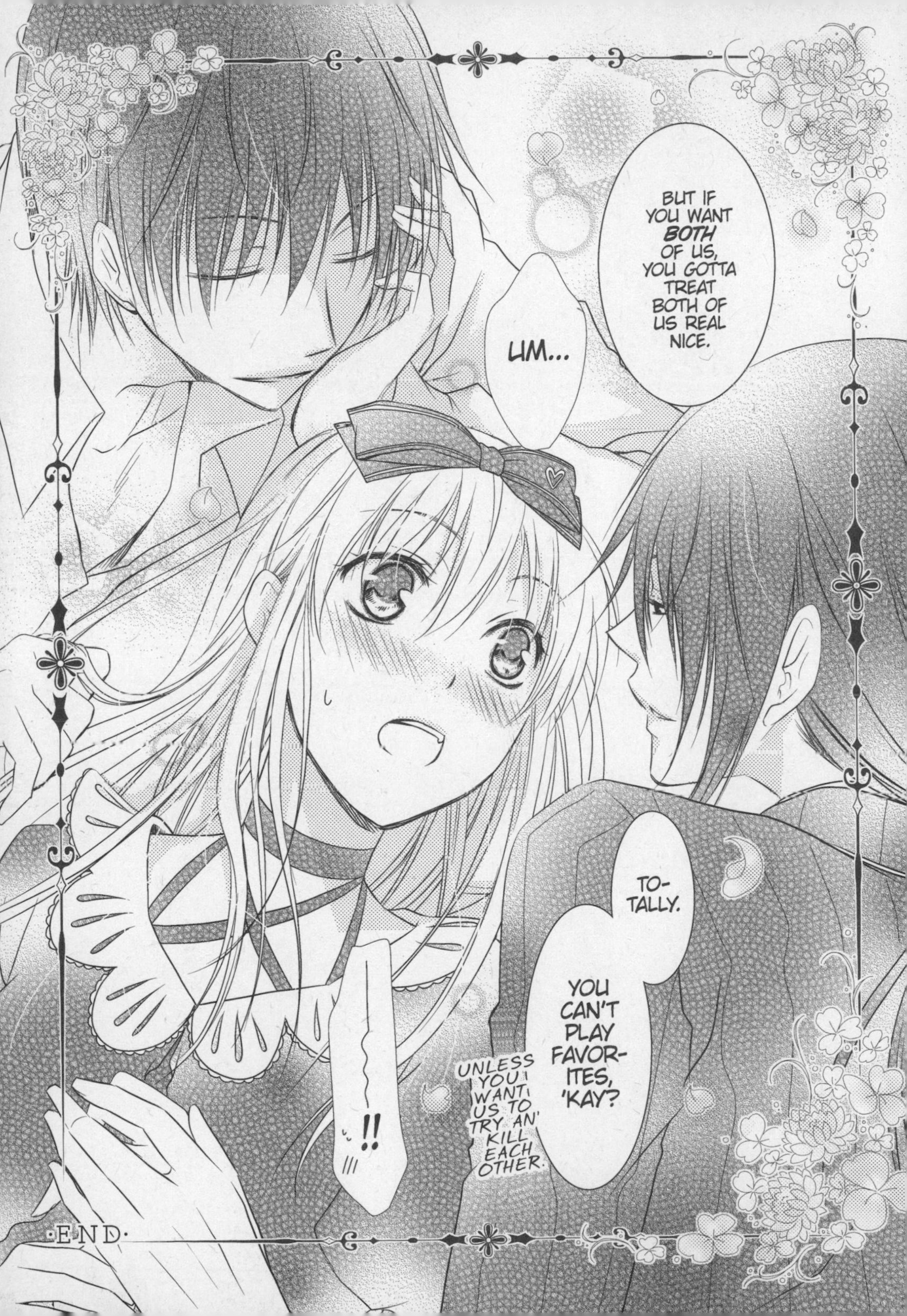
BUT IF YOU WANT ***BOTH*** OF US, YOU GOTTA TREAT BOTH OF US REAL NICE.
UM...
TO-TALLY.
YOU CAN'T PLAY FAVOR-ITES, 'KAY?
UNLESS YOU WANT US TO TRY AN' KILL EACH OTHER.
!!
·END·

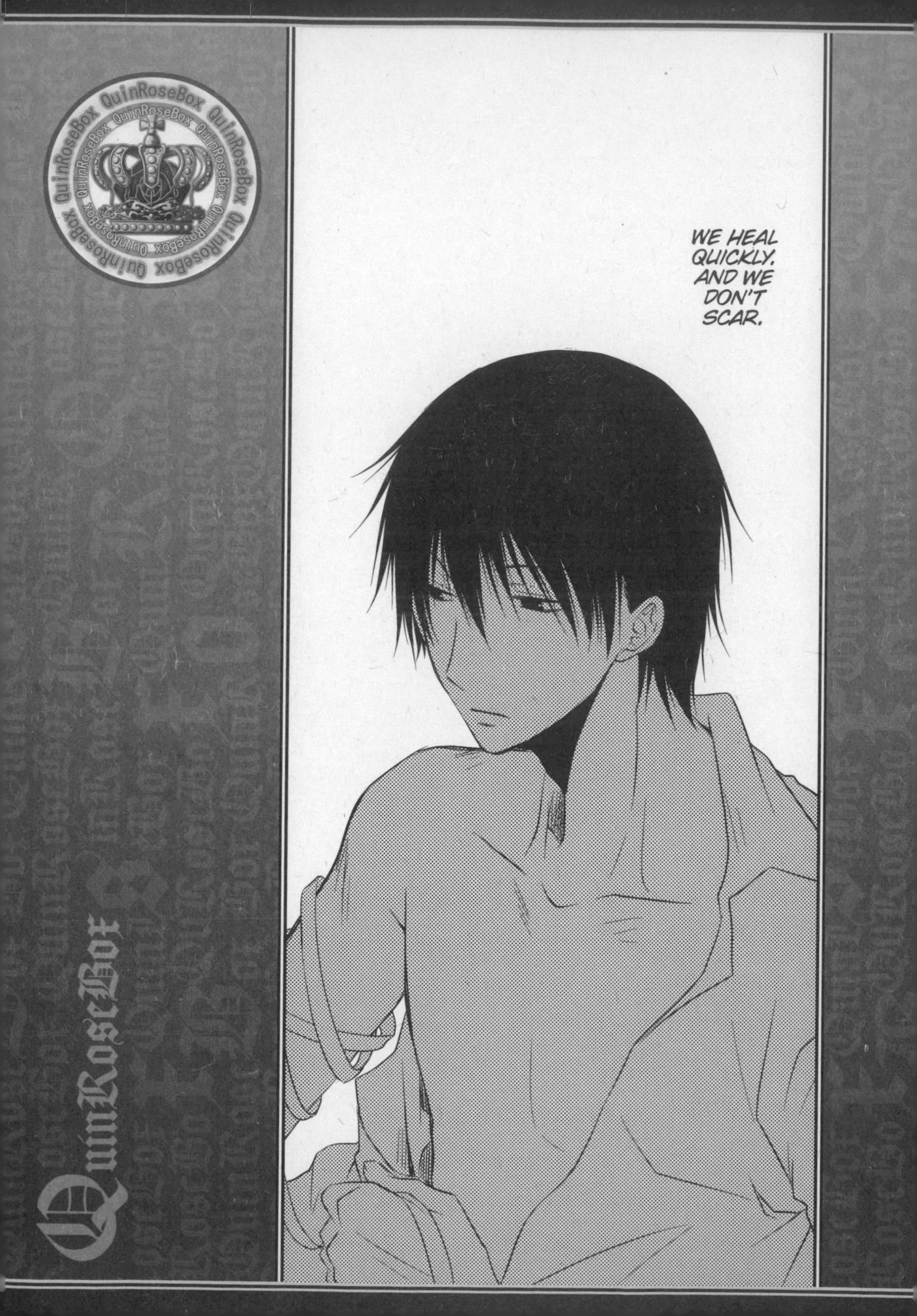
WE HEAL QUICKLY. AND WE DON'T SCAR.

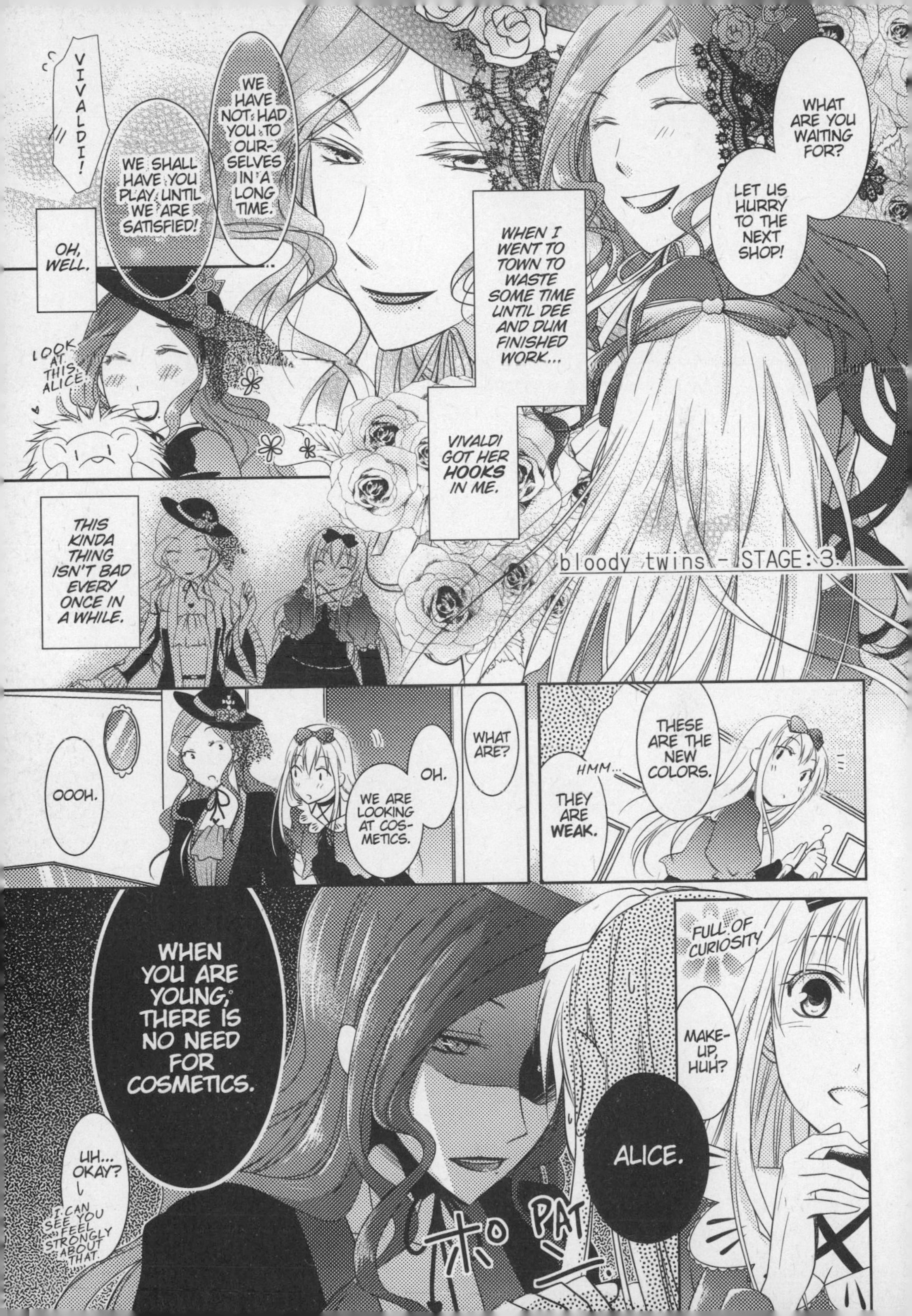
WHAT ARE YOU WAITING FOR?
LET US HURRY TO THE NEXT SHOP!
WE HAVE NOT HAD YOU TO OURSELVES IN A LONG TIME.
WE SHALL HAVE YOU PLAY UNTIL WE ARE SATISFIED!
VIVALDI!
OH, WELL.
WHEN I WENT TO TOWN TO WASTE SOME TIME UNTIL DEE AND DUM FINISHED WORK...
VIVALDI GOT HER HOOKS IN ME.
LOOK AT THIS ALICE.
THIS KINDA THING ISN'T BAD EVERY ONCE IN A WHILE.
bloody twins - STAGE: 3
THESE ARE THE NEW COLORS.
HMM...
THEY ARE WEAK.
WHAT ARE?
OH.
WE ARE LOOKING AT COSMETICS.
OOOH.
FULL OF CURIOSITY
MAKE-UP, HUH?
ALICE.
WHEN YOU ARE YOUNG, THERE IS NO NEED FOR COSMETICS.
UH... OKAY?
I CAN SEE YOU FEEL STRONGLY ABOUT THAT.
PAT

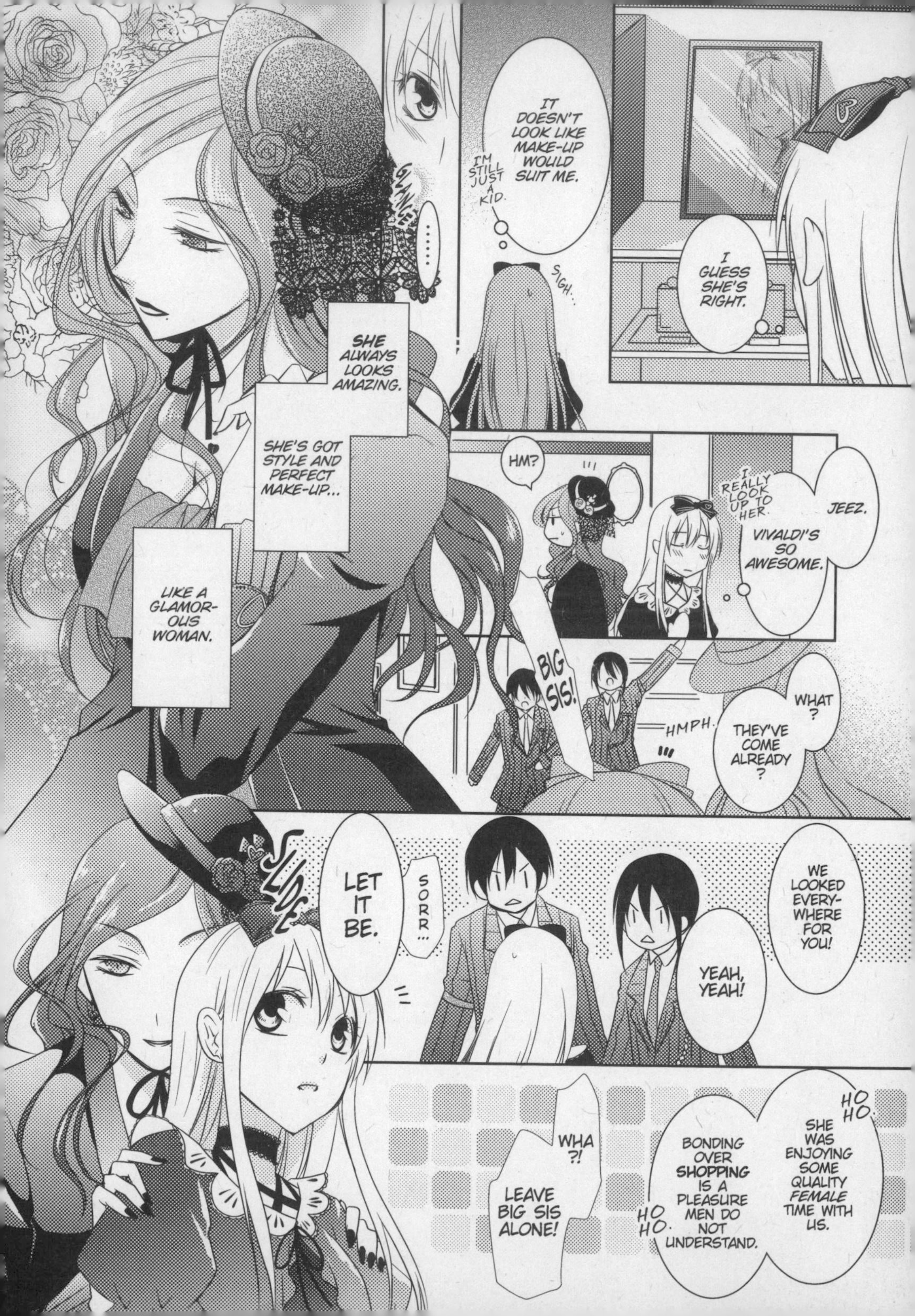
I GUESS SHE'S RIGHT.
IT DOESN'T LOOK LIKE MAKE-UP WOULD SUIT ME.
I'M STILL JUST A KID.
SIGH...
GLANCE
......
SHE ALWAYS LOOKS AMAZING.
SHE'S GOT STYLE AND PERFECT MAKE-UP...
LIKE A GLAMOROUS WOMAN.
I REALLY LOOK UP TO HER.
JEEZ. VIVALDI'S SO AWESOME.
HM?
WHAT? THEY'VE COME ALREADY?
HMPH.
BIG SIS!
WE LOOKED EVERYWHERE FOR YOU!
YEAH, YEAH!
SORR...
LET IT BE.
SLIDE
HO HO.
SHE WAS ENJOYING SOME QUALITY FEMALE TIME WITH US.
BONDING OVER SHOPPING IS A PLEASURE MEN DO NOT UNDERSTAND.
HO HO.
WHA?!
LEAVE BIG SIS ALONE!

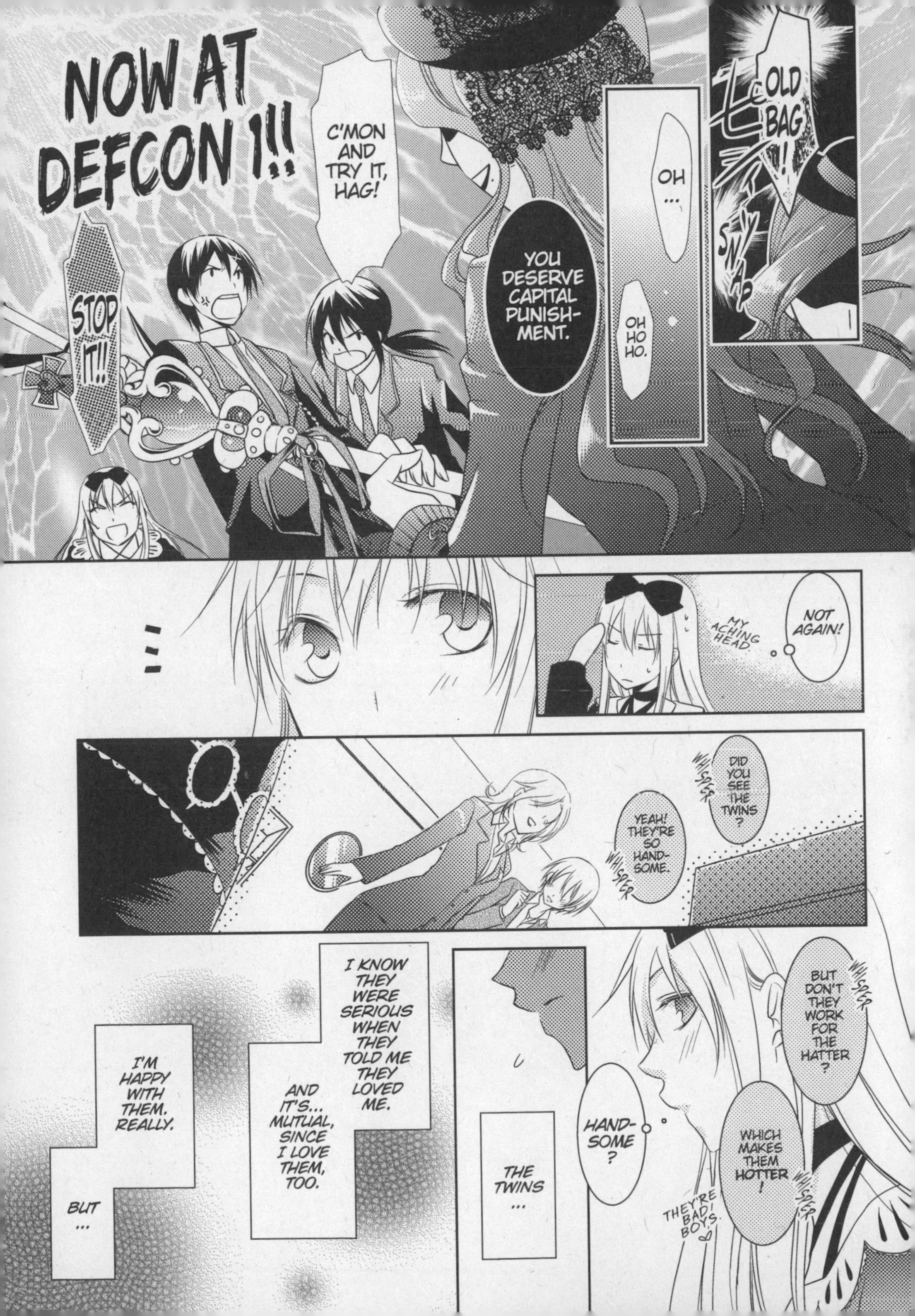
OLD BAG!
SNAP
OH... OH HO HO.
YOU DESERVE CAPITAL PUNISH-MENT.
C'MON AND TRY IT, HAG!
NOW AT DEFCON 1!!
STOP IT!!
NOT AGAIN!
MY ACHING HEAD
...
WHISPER
DID YOU SEE THE TWINS?
YEAH! THEY'RE SO HAND-SOME.
WHISPER
WHISPER
BUT DON'T THEY WORK FOR THE HATTER?
WHICH MAKES THEM HOTTER!
WHISPER
THEY'RE BAD BOYS.
HAND-SOME?
THE TWINS...
I KNOW THEY WERE SERIOUS WHEN THEY TOLD ME THEY LOVED ME.
AND IT'S... MUTUAL, SINCE I LOVE THEM, TOO.
I'M HAPPY WITH THEM. REALLY.
BUT...

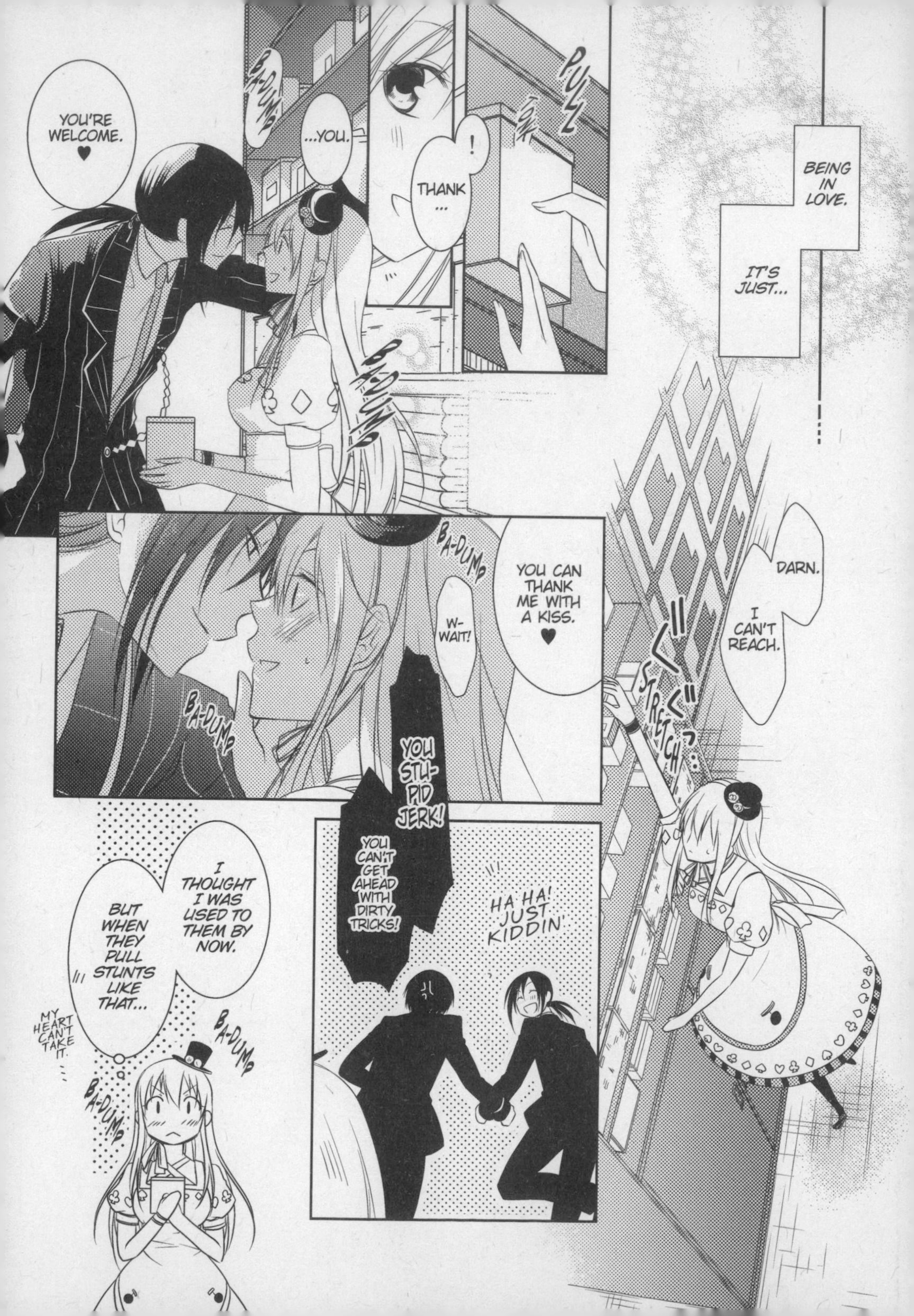
BEING IN LOVE.
IT'S JUST...
DARN.
I CAN'T REACH.
STRETCH
PULL
!
THANK...
...YOU.
BA-DUMP
YOU'RE WELCOME. ♥
BA-DUMP
YOU CAN THANK ME WITH A KISS. ♥
BA-DUMP
W-WAIT!
BA-DUMP
YOU STUPID JERK!
YOU CAN'T GET AHEAD WITH DIRTY TRICKS!
HA HA! JUST KIDDIN'
I THOUGHT I WAS USED TO THEM BY NOW.
BUT WHEN THEY PULL STUNTS LIKE THAT...
MY HEART CAN'T TAKE IT.
BA-DUMP
BA-DUMP

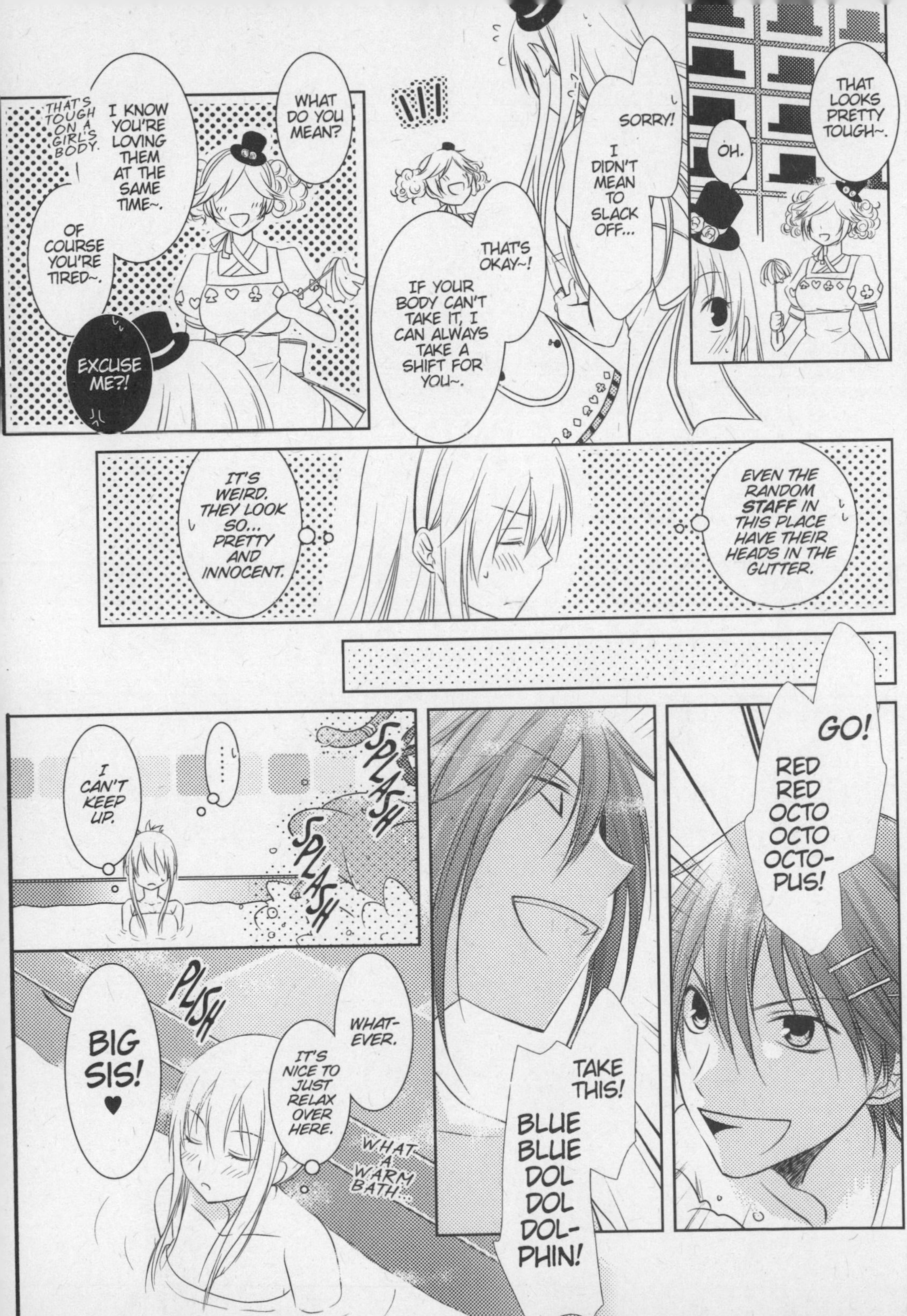
THAT LOOKS PRETTY TOUGH~.
OH.
SORRY!
I DIDN'T MEAN TO SLACK OFF...
THAT'S OKAY~!
IF YOUR BODY CAN'T TAKE IT, I CAN ALWAYS TAKE A SHIFT FOR YOU~.
WHAT DO YOU MEAN?
I KNOW YOU'RE LOVING THEM AT THE SAME TIME~.
THAT'S TOUGH ON A GIRL'S BODY.
OF COURSE YOU'RE TIRED~.
EXCUSE ME?!
EVEN THE RANDOM STAFF IN THIS PLACE HAVE THEIR HEADS IN THE GUTTER.
IT'S WEIRD. THEY LOOK SO... PRETTY AND INNOCENT.
GO!
RED RED OCTO OCTO OCTO-PUS!
TAKE THIS!
BLUE BLUE DOL DOL DOL-PHIN!
SPLASH
SPLASH
SPLASH
......
I CAN'T KEEP UP.
PLISH
BIG SIS! ♥
WHAT-EVER.
IT'S NICE TO JUST RELAX OVER HERE.
WHAT A WARM BATH...

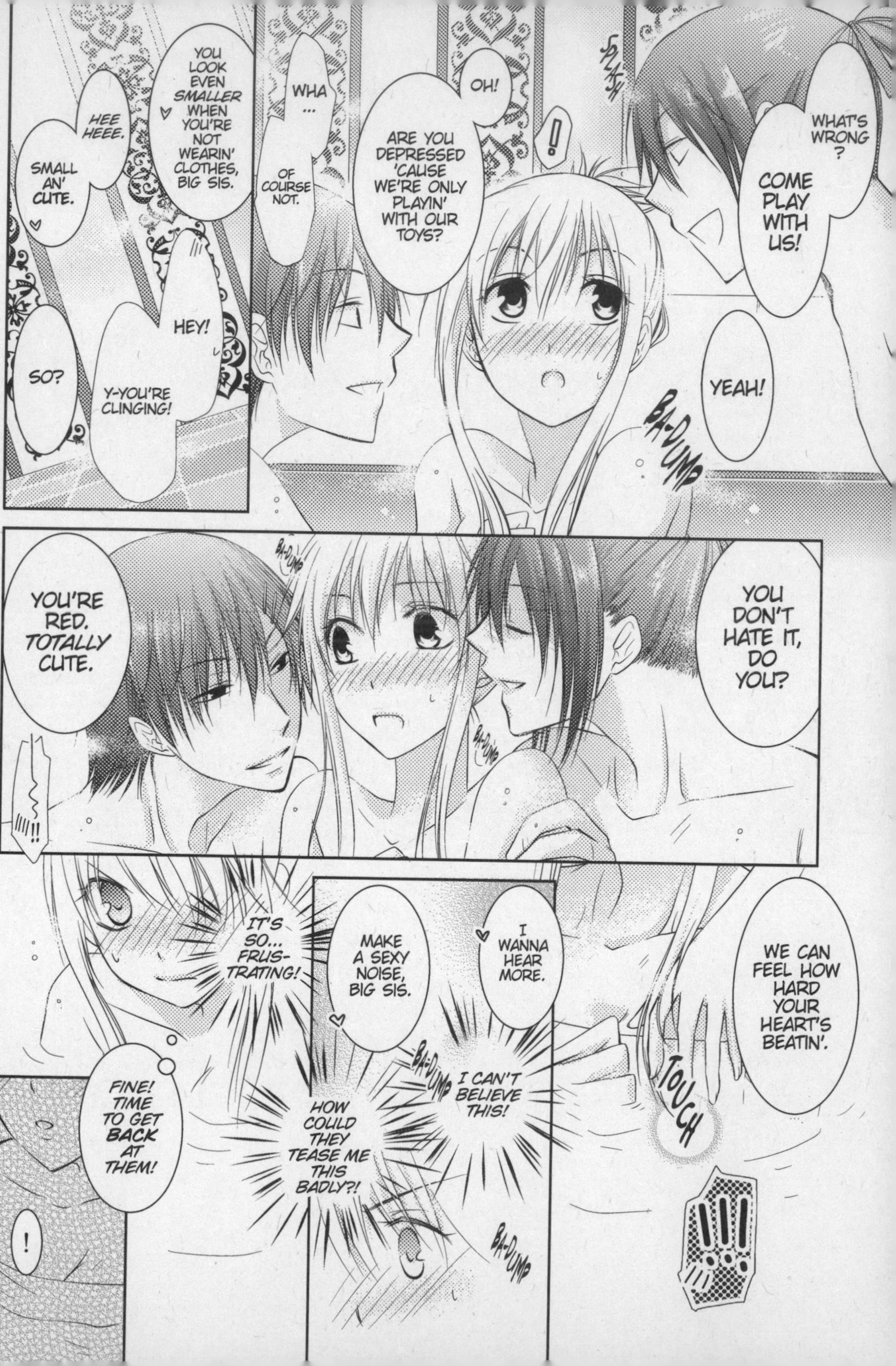
SPLKSH
WHAT'S WRONG?
COME PLAY WITH US!
OH!
ARE YOU DEPRESSED 'CAUSE WE'RE ONLY PLAYIN' WITH OUR TOYS?
!
WHA...
OF COURSE NOT.
YEAH!
BA-DUMP
YOU LOOK EVEN SMALLER WHEN YOU'RE NOT WEARIN' CLOTHES, BIG SIS.
HEE HEEE.
SMALL AN' CUTE.
HEY!
Y-YOU'RE CLINGING!
SO?
YOU DON'T HATE IT, DO YOU?
BA-DUMP
YOU'RE RED. TOTALLY CUTE.
BA-DUMP
WE CAN FEEL HOW HARD YOUR HEART'S BEATIN'.
TOUCH
I WANNA HEAR MORE.
MAKE A SEXY NOISE, BIG SIS.
BA-DUMP
I CAN'T BELIEVE THIS!
HOW COULD THEY TEASE ME THIS BADLY?!
BA-DUMP
IT'S SO... FRUS-TRATING!
FINE! TIME TO GET BACK AT THEM!
!

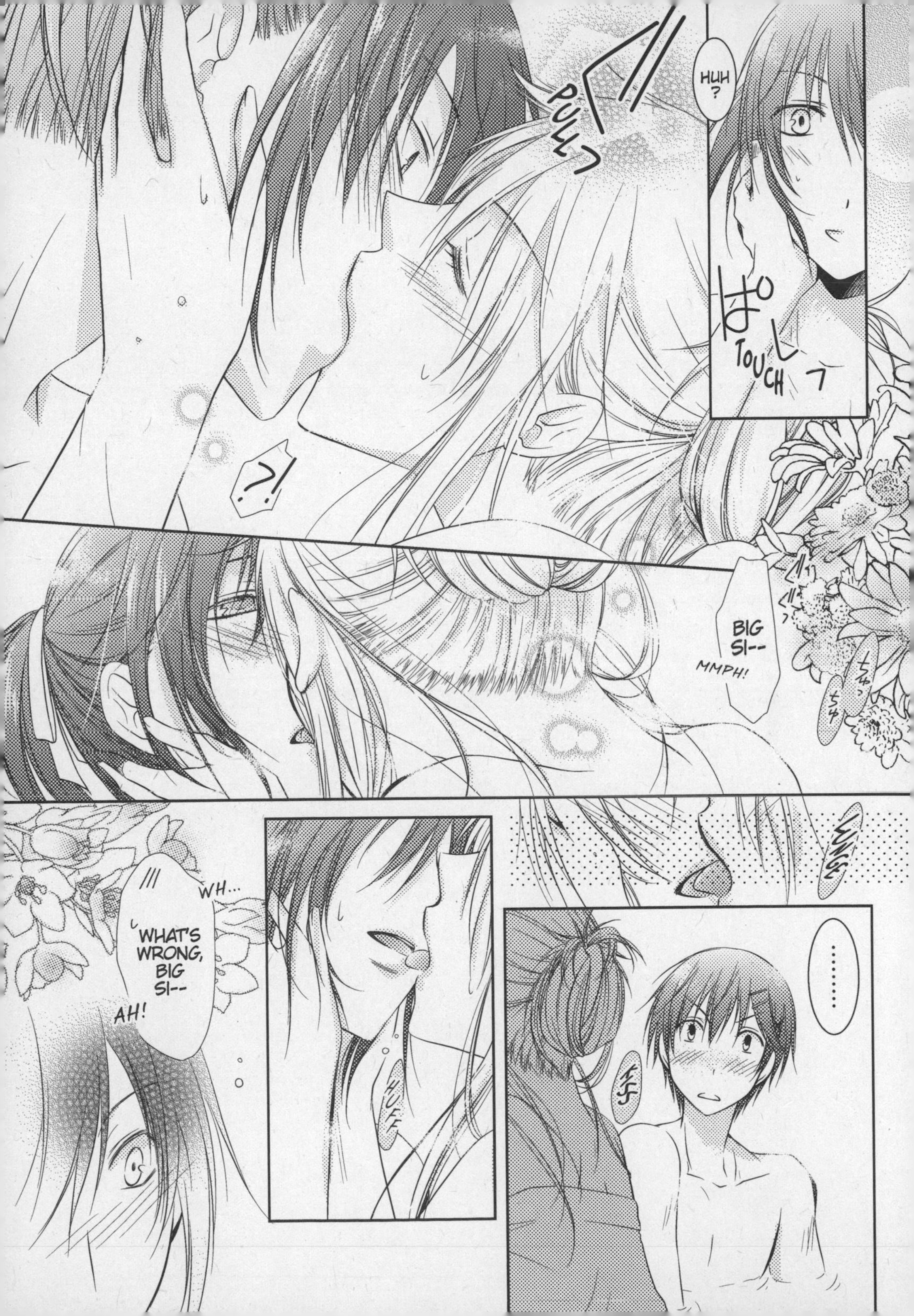
HUH?
ぱし
TOUCH
PULL
?!
BIG SI--
MMPH!
ちゅっ
ちゅ
LUNGE
......
KISS
HUFF
WH...
WHAT'S WRONG, BIG SI--
AH!

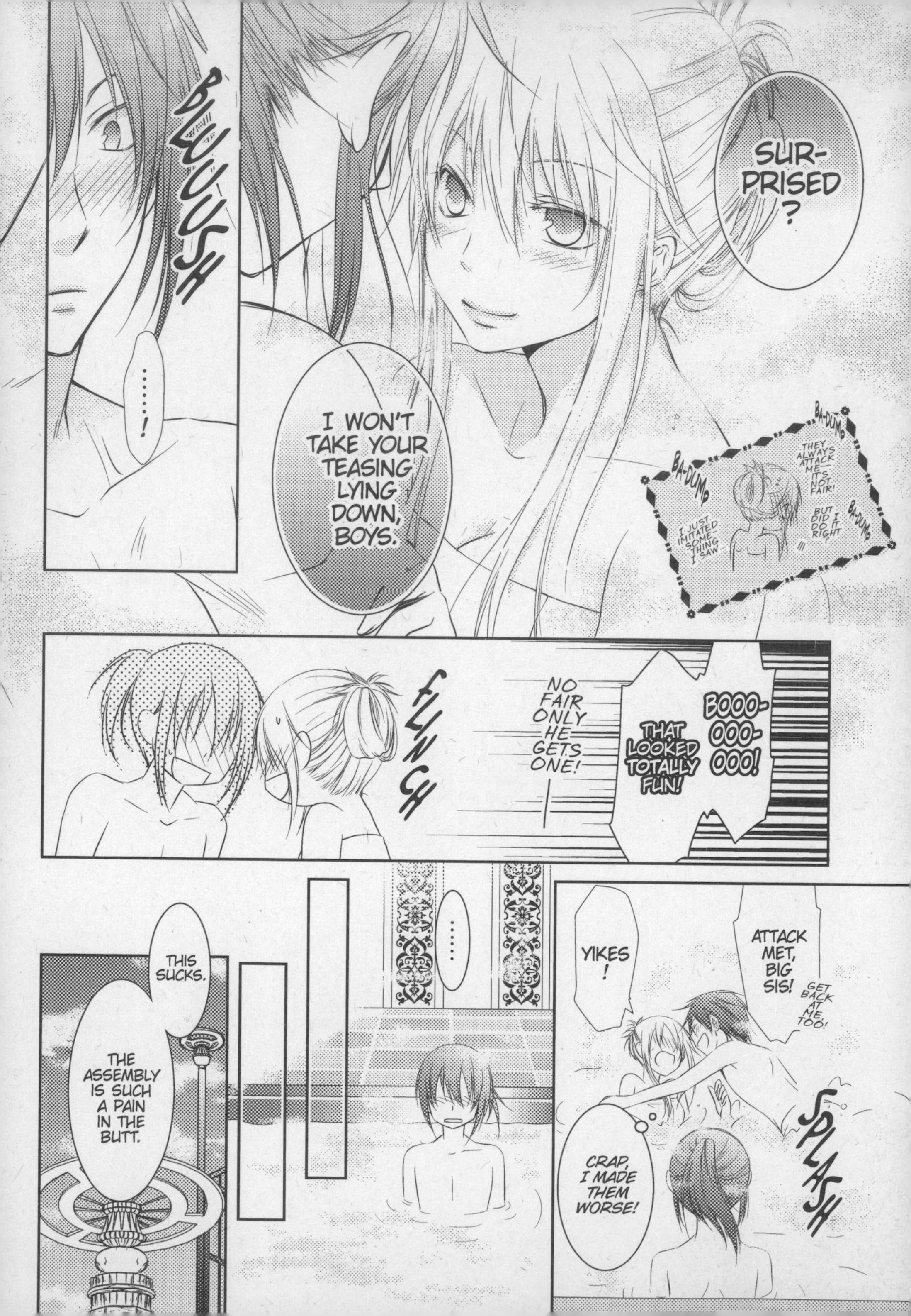
SUR-PRISED?
I WON'T TAKE YOUR TEASING LYING DOWN, BOYS.
BA-DUMP
BA-DUMP
BA-DUMP
THEY ALWAYS ATTACK ME—IT'S NOT FAIR!
BUT DID I DO IT RIGHT?
I JUST IMITATED SOMETHING I SAW
BLUUUSH
......!
BOOO-OOO-OOO!
THAT LOOKED TOTALLY FUN!
NO FAIR ONLY HE GETS ONE!
FLINCH
YIKES!
ATTACK MET, BIG SIS!
GET BACK AT ME, TOO!
SPLASH
CRAP, I MADE THEM WORSE!
......
THIS SUCKS.
THE ASSEMBLY IS SUCH A PAIN IN THE BUTT.

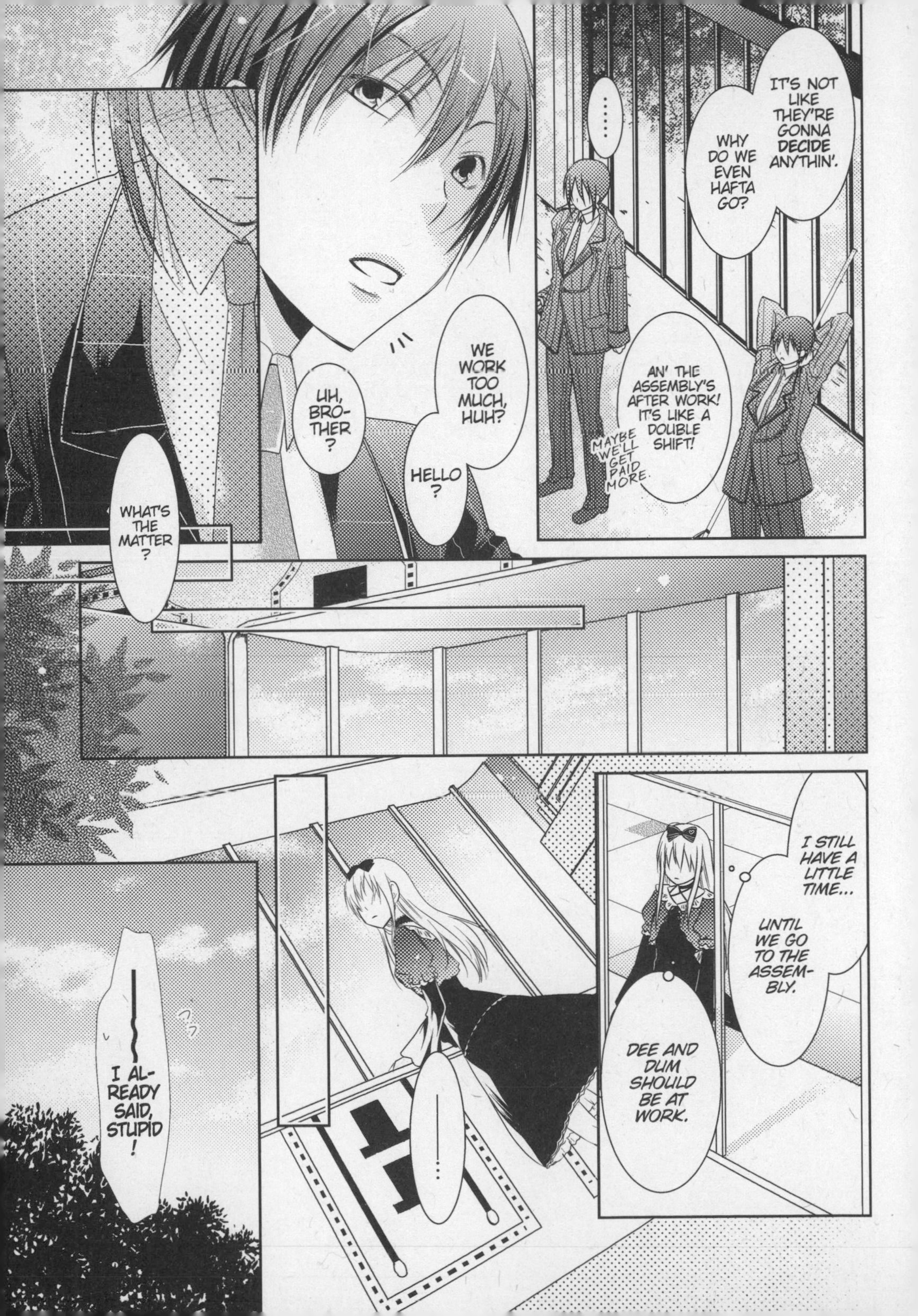
IT'S NOT LIKE THEY'RE GONNA DECIDE ANYTHIN'.
WHY DO WE EVEN HAFTA GO?
......
AN' THE ASSEMBLY'S AFTER WORK! IT'S LIKE A DOUBLE SHIFT!
MAYBE WE'LL GET PAID MORE.
WE WORK TOO MUCH, HUH?
UH, BROTHER?
HELLO?
WHAT'S THE MATTER?
I STILL HAVE A LITTLE TIME...
UNTIL WE GO TO THE ASSEMBLY.
DEE AND DUM SHOULD BE AT WORK.
......
I AL-READY SAID, STUPID!

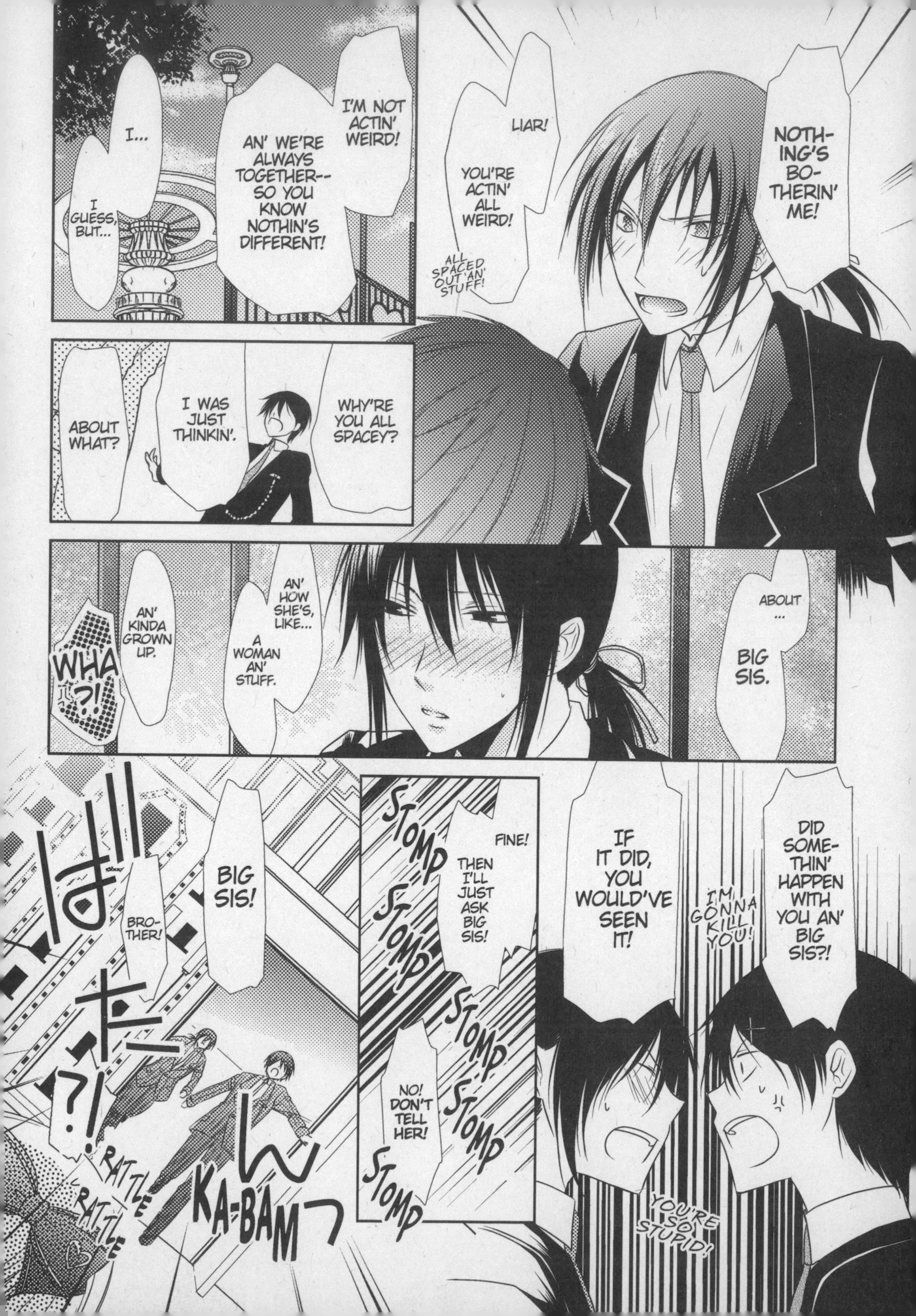
NOTH-ING'S BO-THERIN' ME!
LIAR!
YOU'RE ACTIN' ALL WEIRD!
ALL SPACED OUT AN' STUFF!
I'M NOT ACTIN' WEIRD!
AN' WE'RE ALWAYS TOGETHER-- SO YOU KNOW NOTHIN'S DIFFERENT!
I...
I GUESS, BUT...
WHY'RE YOU ALL SPACEY?
I WAS JUST THINKIN'.
ABOUT WHAT?
ABOUT ...
BIG SIS.
AN' HOW SHE'S, LIKE...
A WOMAN AN' STUFF.
AN' KINDA GROWN UP.
WHA?!
DID SOME-THIN' HAPPEN WITH YOU AN' BIG SIS?!
I'M GONNA KILL YOU!
IF IT DID, YOU WOULD'VE SEEN IT!
YOU'RE SO STUPID!
FINE!
THEN I'LL JUST ASK BIG SIS!
STOMP STOMP STOMP STOMP STOMP STOMP
NO! DON'T TELL HER!
BIG SIS!
BRO-THER!
RATTLE RATTLE
KA-BAM

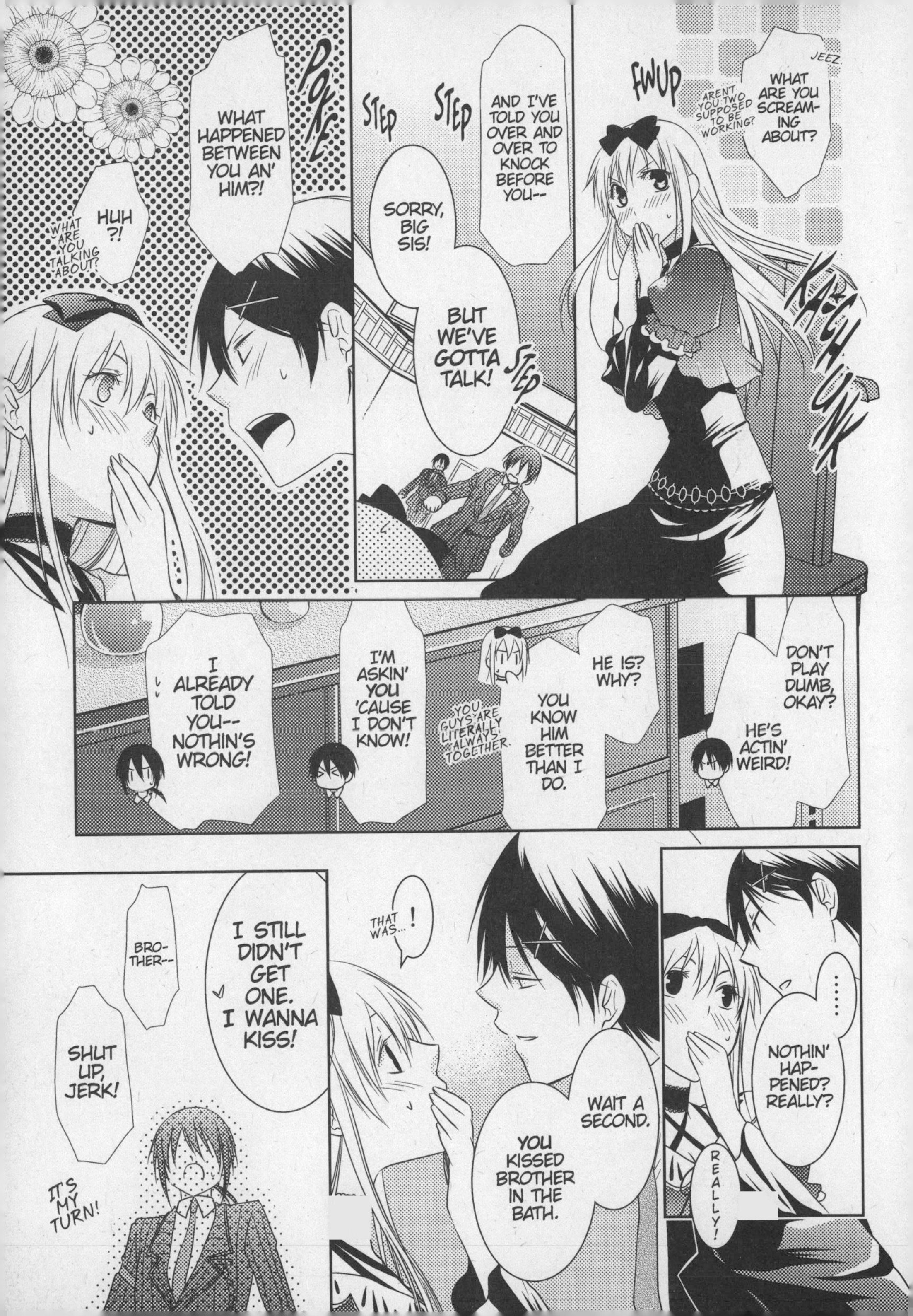
JEEZ.
WHAT ARE YOU SCREAM-ING ABOUT?
AREN'T YOU TWO SUPPOSED TO BE WORKING?
FWUP
KA-CHUNK
AND I'VE TOLD YOU OVER AND OVER TO KNOCK BEFORE YOU--
STEP
STEP
SORRY, BIG SIS!
BUT WE'VE GOTTA TALK!
STEP
POKE
WHAT HAPPENED BETWEEN YOU AN' HIM?!
HUH ?!
WHAT ARE YOU TALKING ABOUT?
DON'T PLAY DUMB, OKAY?
HE'S ACTIN' WEIRD!
HE IS? WHY?
YOU KNOW HIM BETTER THAN I DO.
YOU GUYS ARE LITERALLY ALWAYS TOGETHER.
I'M ASKIN' YOU 'CAUSE I DON'T KNOW!
I ALREADY TOLD YOU-- NOTHIN'S WRONG!
......
NOTHIN' HAP-PENED? REALLY?
REALLY!
WAIT A SECOND.
YOU KISSED BROTHER IN THE BATH.
THAT WAS...!
I STILL DIDN'T GET ONE. I WANNA KISS!
BRO-THER--
SHUT UP, JERK!
IT'S MY TURN!

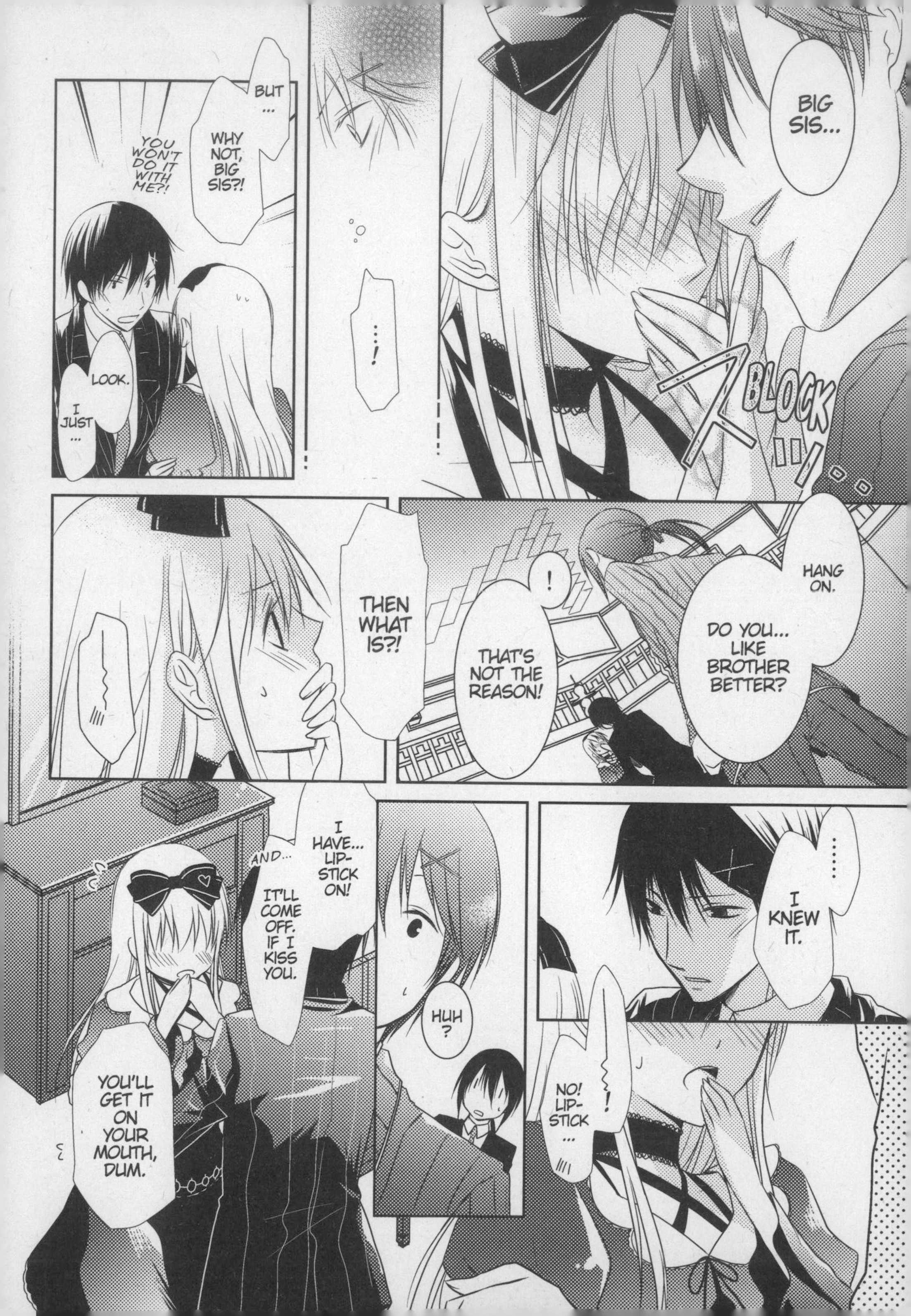
BIG SIS...
BLOCK
...!
BUT ... WHY NOT, BIG SIS?!
YOU WON'T DO IT WITH ME?!
LOOK. I JUST ...
HANG ON.
DO YOU... LIKE BROTHER BETTER?
!
THAT'S NOT THE REASON!
THEN WHAT IS?!
......
I KNEW IT.
NO! LIP-STICK ...
HUH?
I HAVE... LIP-STICK ON!
AND... IT'LL COME OFF. IF I KISS YOU.
YOU'LL GET IT ON YOUR MOUTH, DUM.

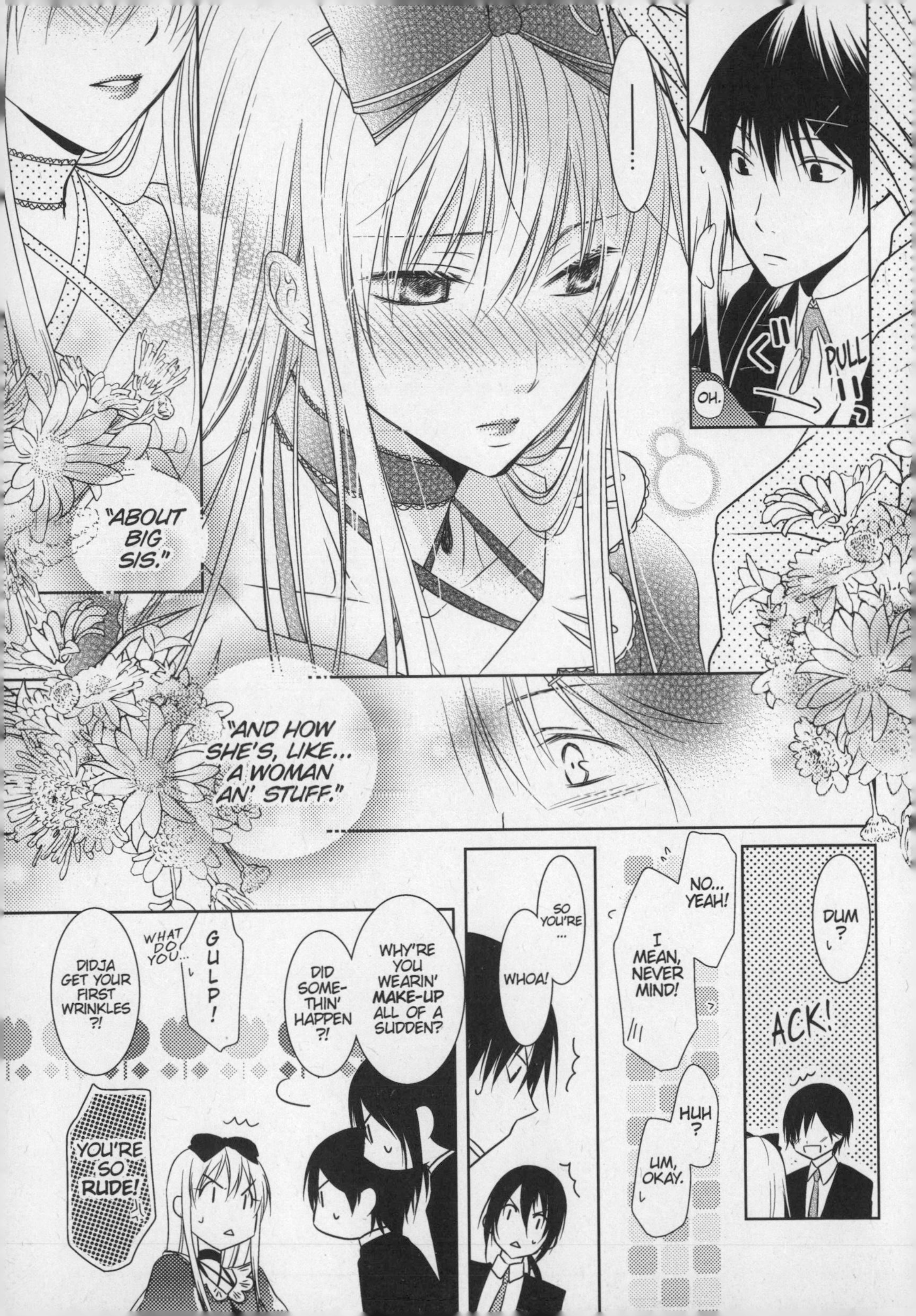
PULL
OH.
!...
"ABOUT BIG SIS."
"AND HOW SHE'S, LIKE... A WOMAN AN' STUFF."
DUM?
ACK!
NO... YEAH!
I MEAN, NEVER MIND!
HUH?
UM, OKAY.
SO YOU'RE...
WHOA!
WHY'RE YOU WEARIN' MAKE-UP ALL OF A SUDDEN?
DID SOME-THIN' HAPPEN?!
WHAT DO YOU...
GULP!
DIDJA GET YOUR FIRST WRINKLES?!
YOU'RE SO RUDE!

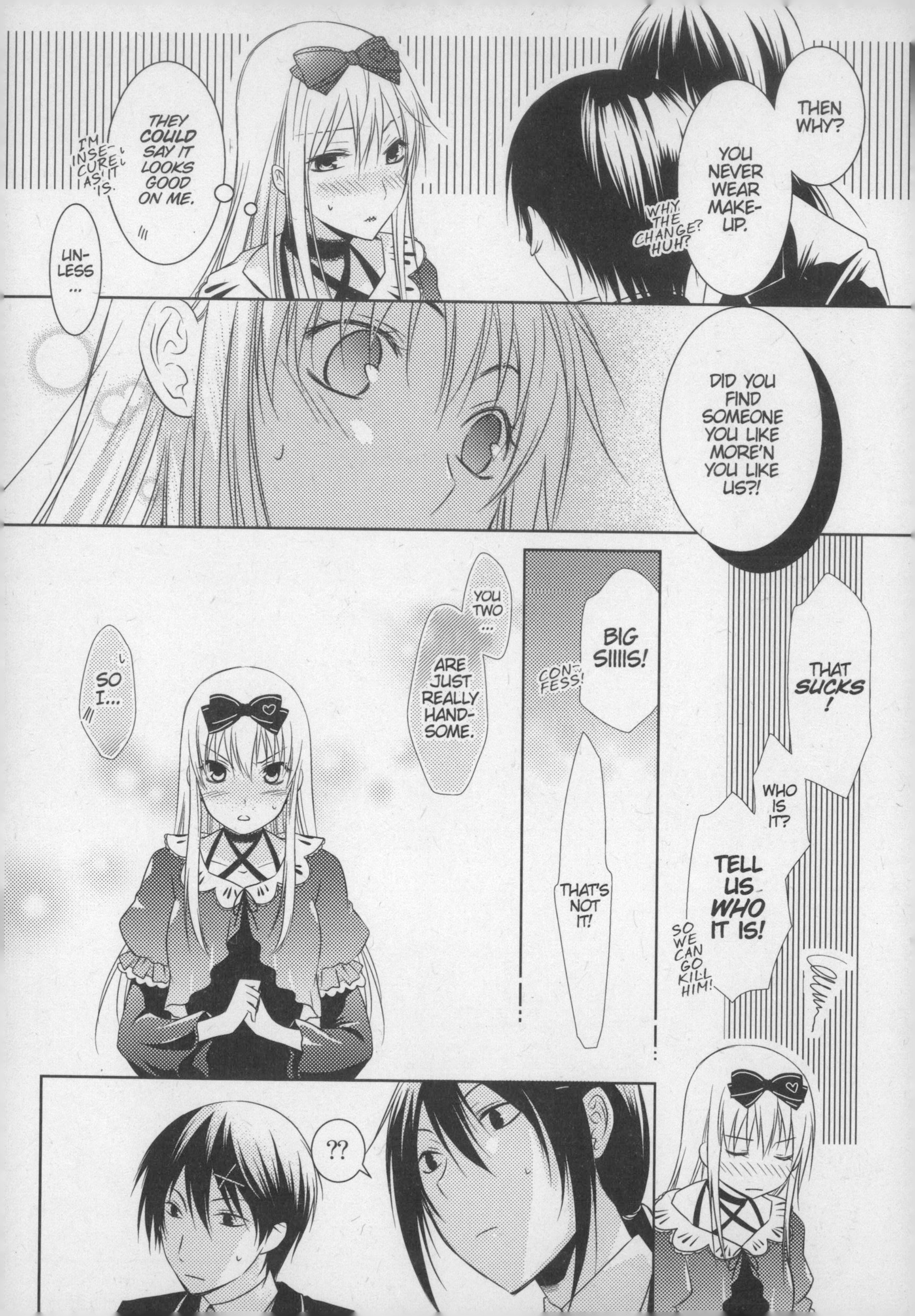
THEN WHY?
YOU NEVER WEAR MAKE-UP.
WHY THE CHANGE? HUH?
THEY COULD SAY IT LOOKS GOOD ON ME.
I'M INSE-CURE AS IT IS.
UN-LESS ...
DID YOU FIND SOMEONE YOU LIKE MORE'N YOU LIKE US?!
THAT SUCKS!
WHO IS IT?
TELL US WHO IT IS!
SO WE CAN GO KILL HIM!
BIG SIIIIS!
CON-FESS!
THAT'S NOT IT!
YOU TWO ...
ARE JUST REALLY HAND-SOME.
SO I...
??

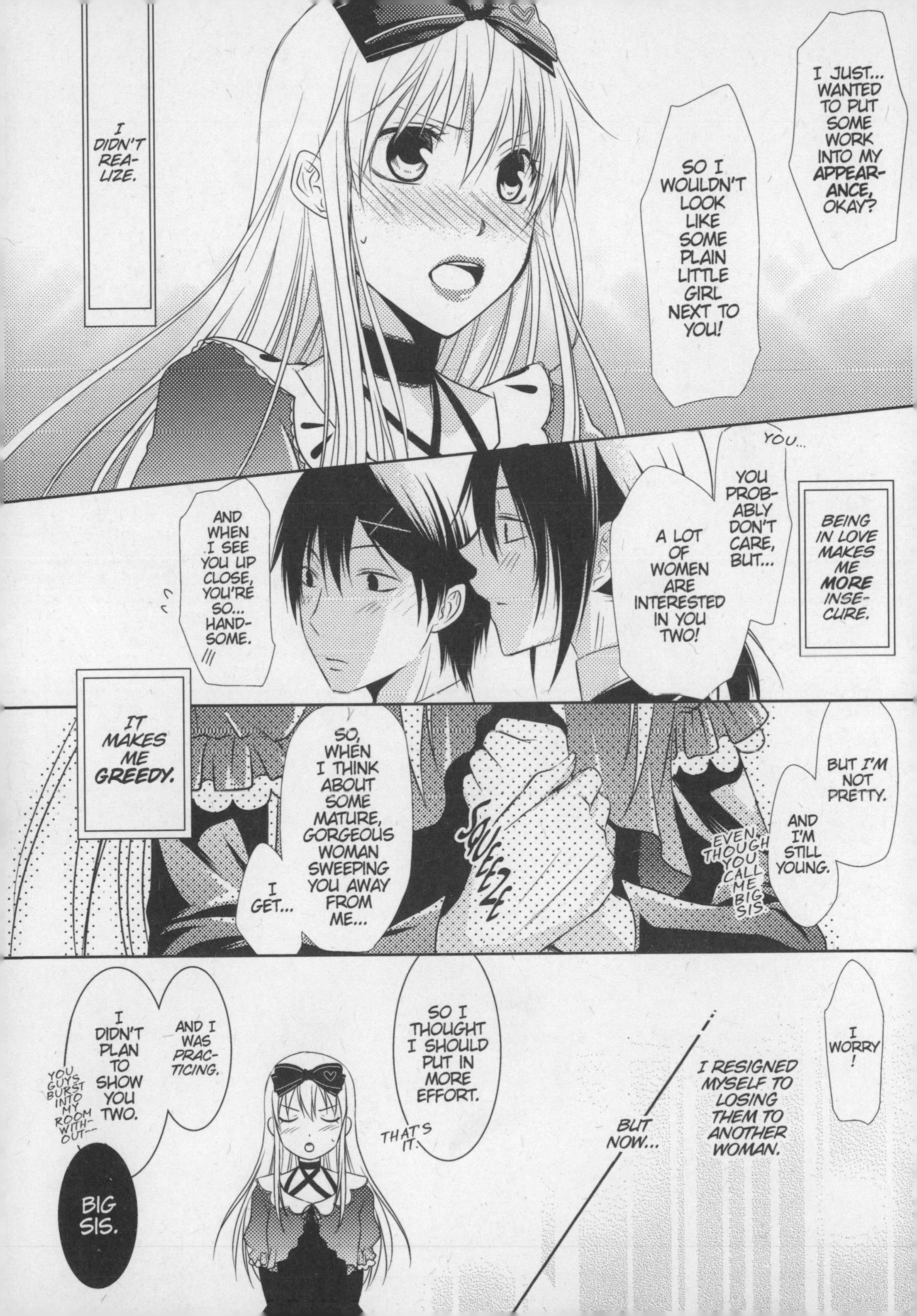
I JUST... WANTED TO PUT SOME WORK INTO MY APPEARANCE, OKAY?
SO I WOULDN'T LOOK LIKE SOME PLAIN LITTLE GIRL NEXT TO YOU!
I DIDN'T REALIZE.
BEING IN LOVE MAKES ME MORE INSECURE.
YOU...
YOU PROBABLY DON'T CARE, BUT...
A LOT OF WOMEN ARE INTERESTED IN YOU TWO!
AND WHEN I SEE YOU UP CLOSE, YOU'RE SO... HANDSOME.
BUT I'M NOT PRETTY.
AND I'M STILL YOUNG.
EVEN THOUGH YOU CALL ME BIG SIS.
SQUEEZE
SO, WHEN I THINK ABOUT SOME MATURE, GORGEOUS WOMAN SWEEPING YOU AWAY FROM ME...
I GET...
IT MAKES ME GREEDY.
I WORRY!
I RESIGNED MYSELF TO LOSING THEM TO ANOTHER WOMAN.
BUT NOW...
SO I THOUGHT I SHOULD PUT IN MORE EFFORT.
THAT'S IT.
AND I WAS PRACTICING.
I DIDN'T PLAN TO SHOW YOU TWO.
YOU GUYS BURST INTO MY ROOM WITHOUT--
BIG SIS.

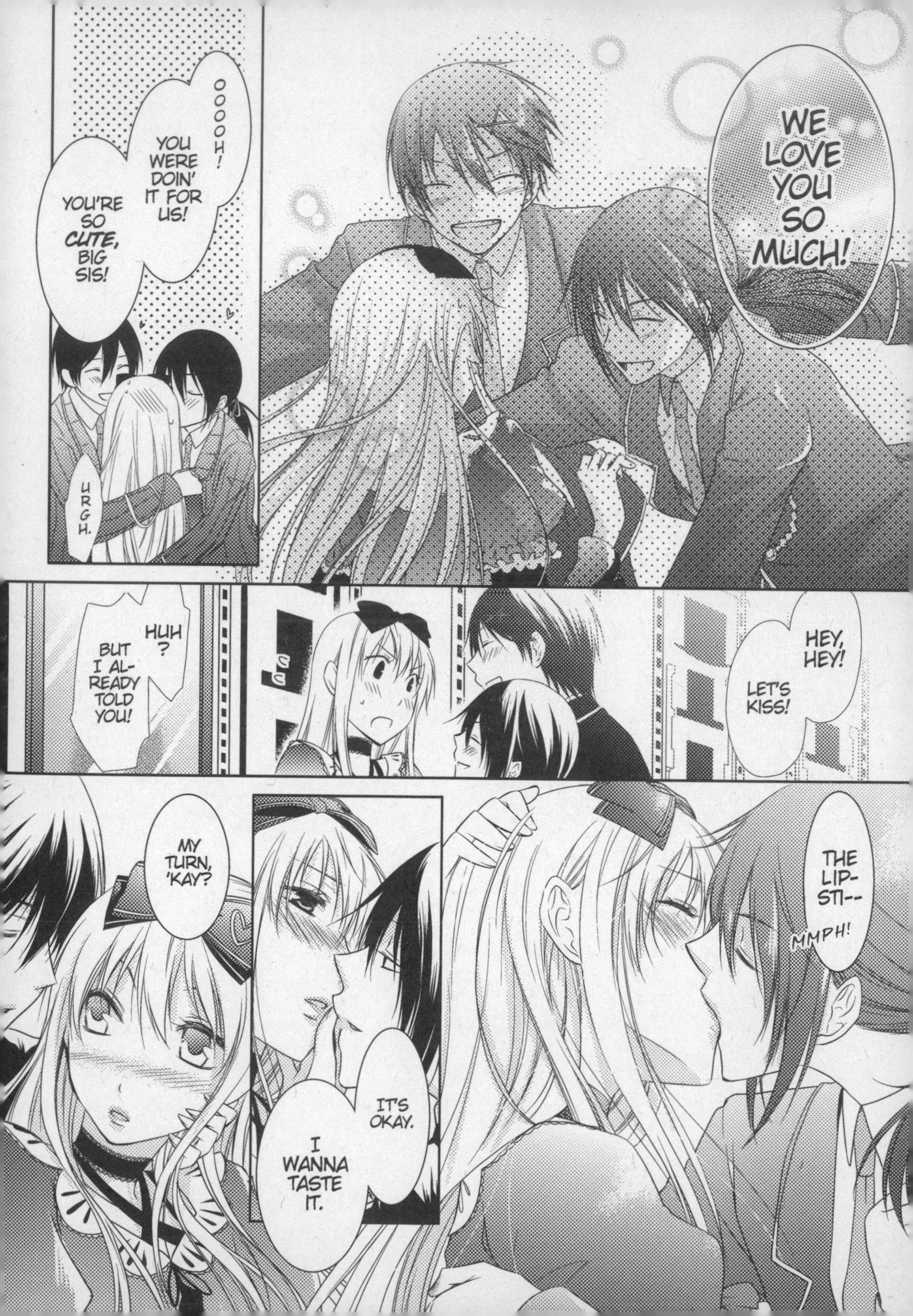
WE LOVE YOU SO MUCH!
OOOOH!
YOU WERE DOIN' IT FOR US!
YOU'RE SO *CUTE*, BIG SIS!
URGH.
HEY, HEY!
LET'S KISS!
HUH?
BUT I AL-READY TOLD YOU!
THE LIP-STI--
MMPH!
MY TURN, 'KAY?
IT'S OKAY.
I WANNA TASTE IT.

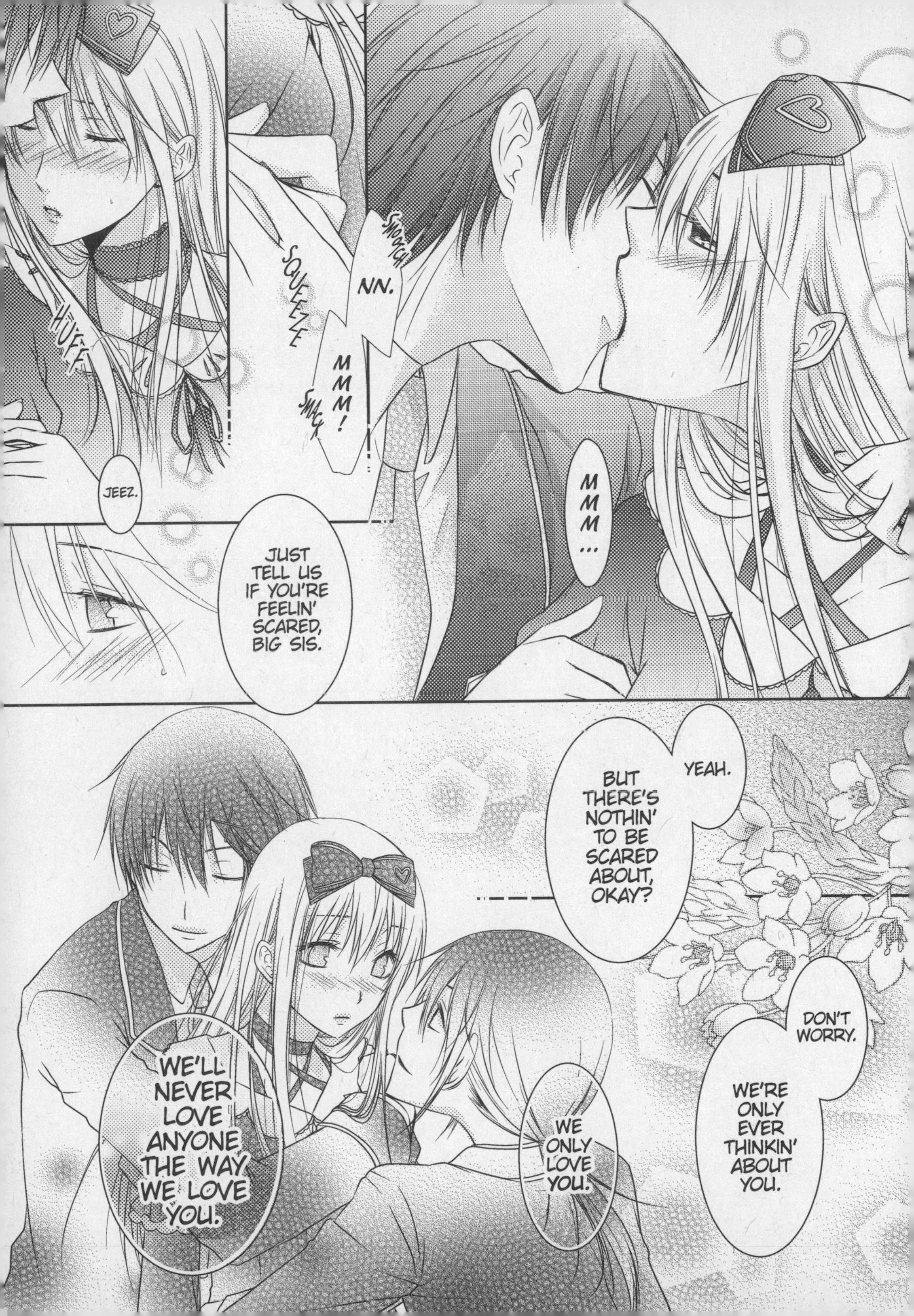
SMOOCH
NN.
MMM!
SMACK
MMM...
SQUEEZE
HUFF
JEEZ.
JUST TELL US IF YOU'RE FEELIN' SCARED, BIG SIS.
YEAH.
BUT THERE'S NOTHIN' TO BE SCARED ABOUT, OKAY?
DON'T WORRY.
WE'RE ONLY EVER THINKIN' ABOUT YOU.
WE ONLY LOVE YOU.
WE'LL NEVER LOVE ANYONE THE WAY WE LOVE YOU.

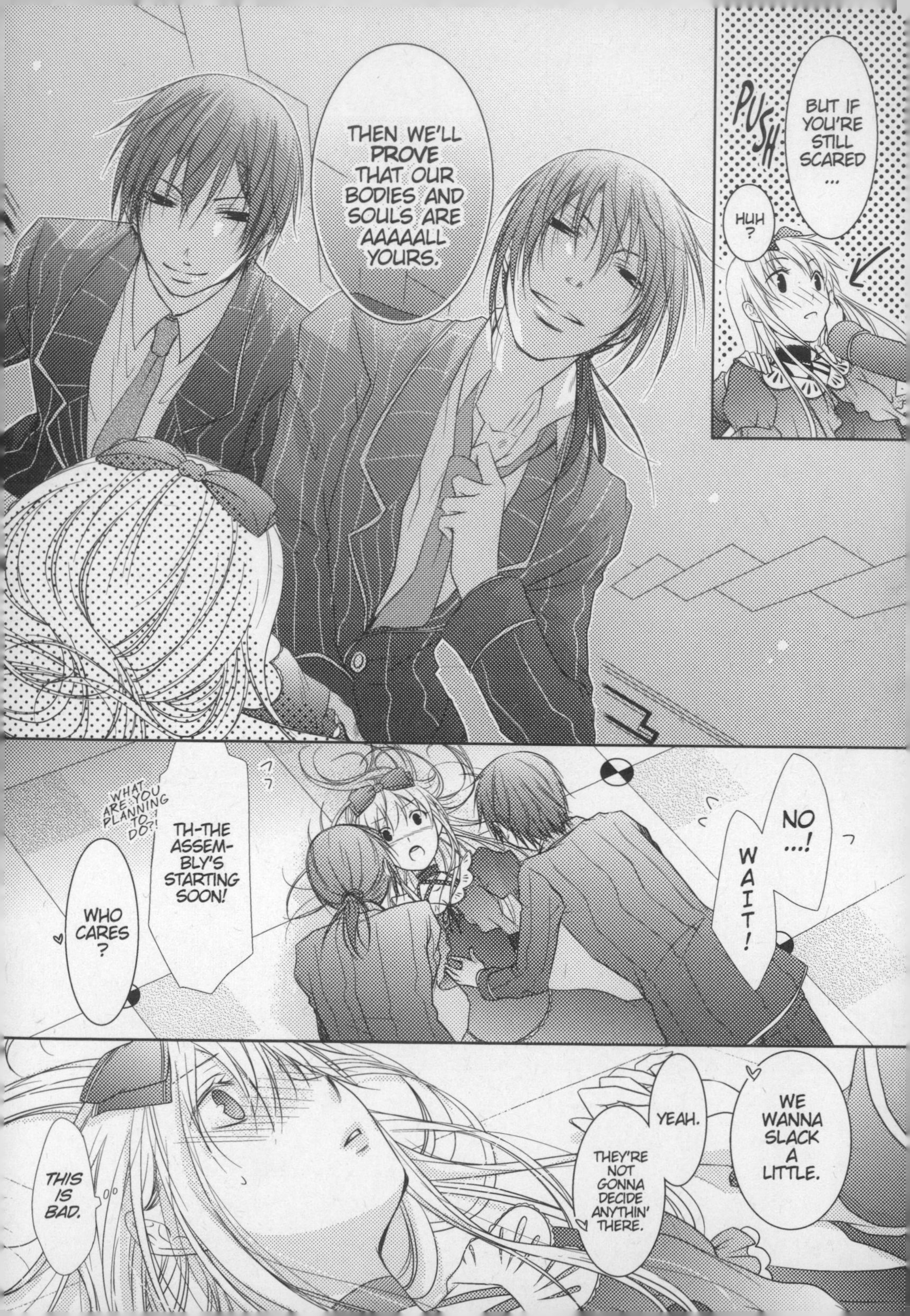
PUSH
BUT IF YOU'RE STILL SCARED...
HUH?
THEN WE'LL PROVE THAT OUR BODIES AND SOULS ARE AAAAALL YOURS.
NO...!
WAIT!
WHAT ARE YOU PLANNING TO DO?!
TH-THE ASSEM-BLY'S STARTING SOON!
WHO CARES?
WE WANNA SLACK A LITTLE.
YEAH.
THEY'RE NOT GONNA DECIDE ANYTHIN' THERE.
THIS IS BAD.

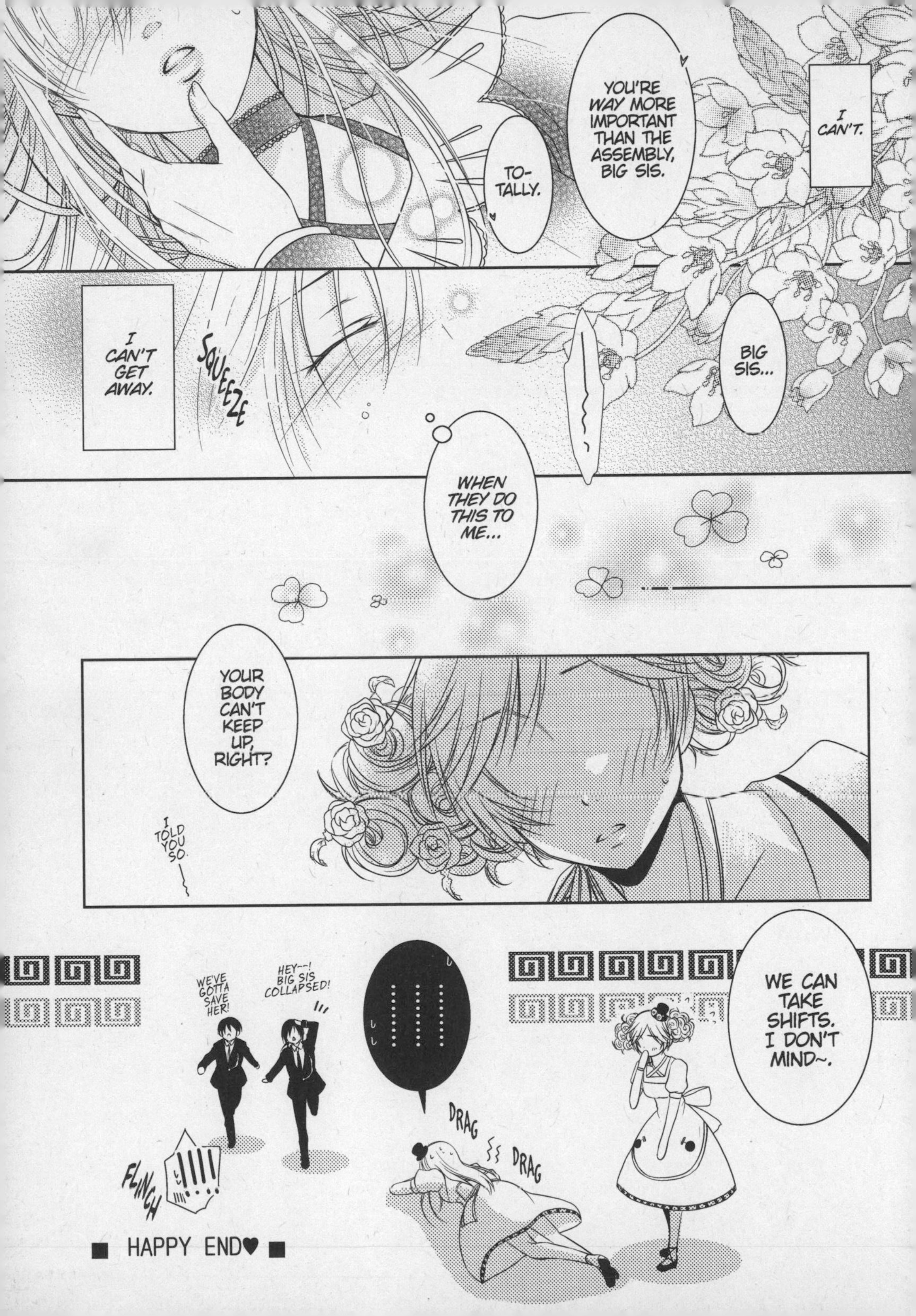
I CAN'T.
YOU'RE WAY MORE IMPORTANT THAN THE ASSEMBLY, BIG SIS.
TO-TALLY.
BIG SIS...
WHEN THEY DO THIS TO ME...
SQUEEZE
I CAN'T GET AWAY.
YOUR BODY CAN'T KEEP UP, RIGHT?
I TOLD YOU SO.
WE CAN TAKE SHIFTS. I DON'T MIND~.
DRAG
DRAG
HEY--! BIG SIS COLLAPSED!
WE'VE GOTTA SAVE HER!
FLINCH
!!!!
■ HAPPY END♥ ■

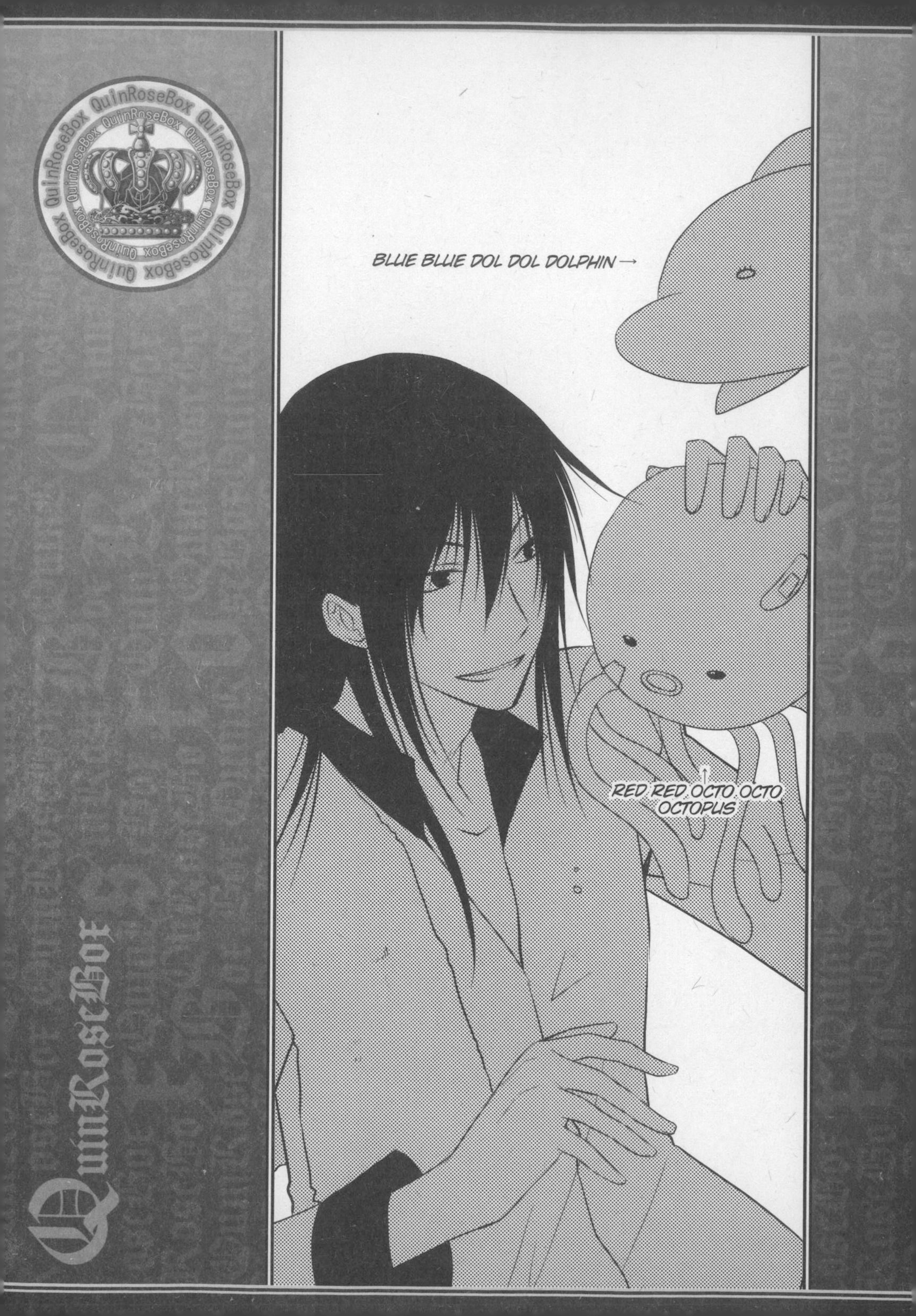
BLUE BLUE DOL DOL DOLPHIN →
↑
RED RED OCTO OCTO OCTOPUS

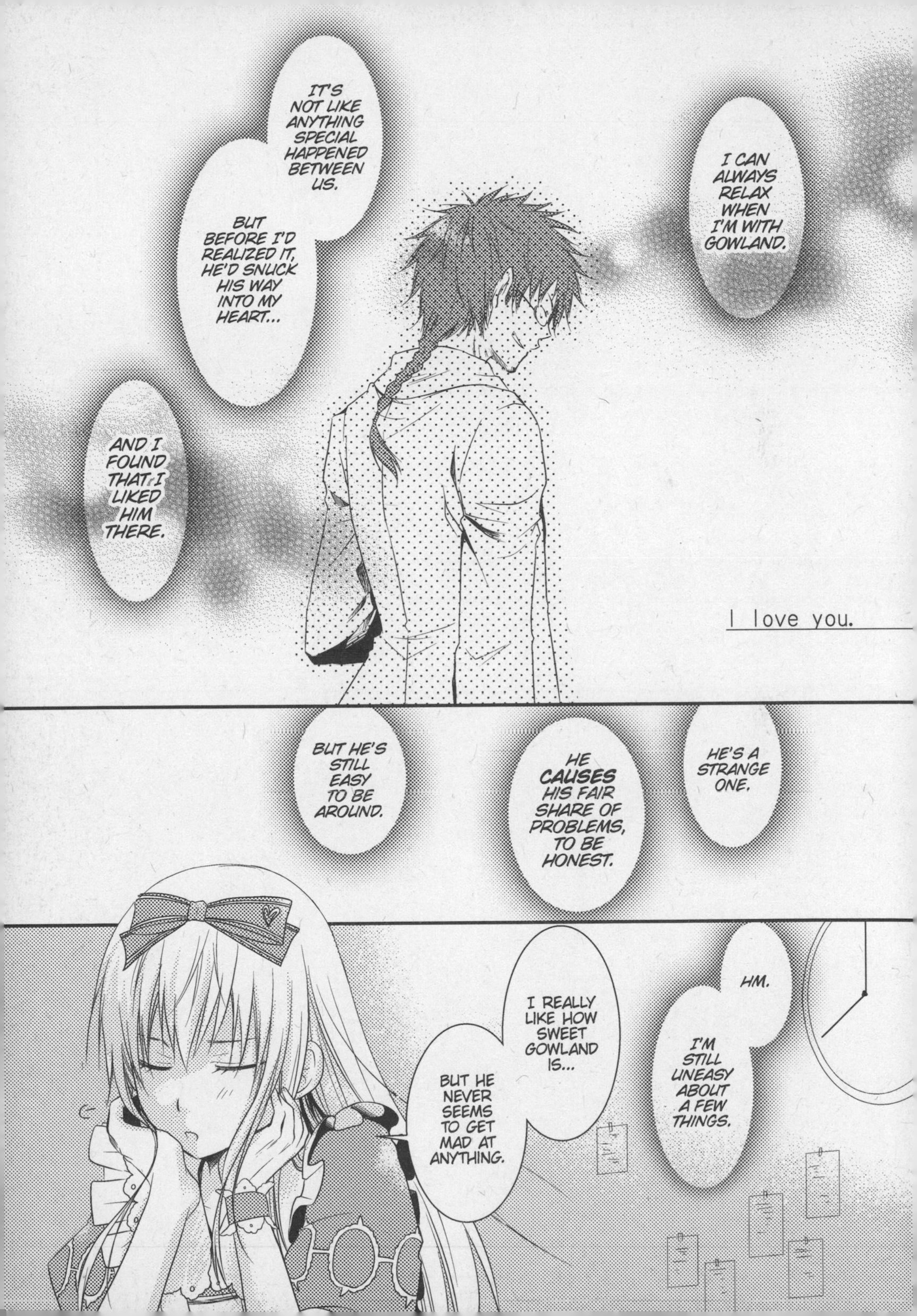
I CAN ALWAYS RELAX WHEN I'M WITH GOWLAND.
IT'S NOT LIKE ANYTHING SPECIAL HAPPENED BETWEEN US.
BUT BEFORE I'D REALIZED IT, HE'D SNUCK HIS WAY INTO MY HEART...
AND I FOUND THAT I LIKED HIM THERE.
I love you.
HE'S A STRANGE ONE.
HE CAUSES HIS FAIR SHARE OF PROBLEMS, TO BE HONEST.
BUT HE'S STILL EASY TO BE AROUND.
HM.
I'M STILL UNEASY ABOUT A FEW THINGS.
I REALLY LIKE HOW SWEET GOWLAND IS...
BUT HE NEVER SEEMS TO GET MAD AT ANYTHING.

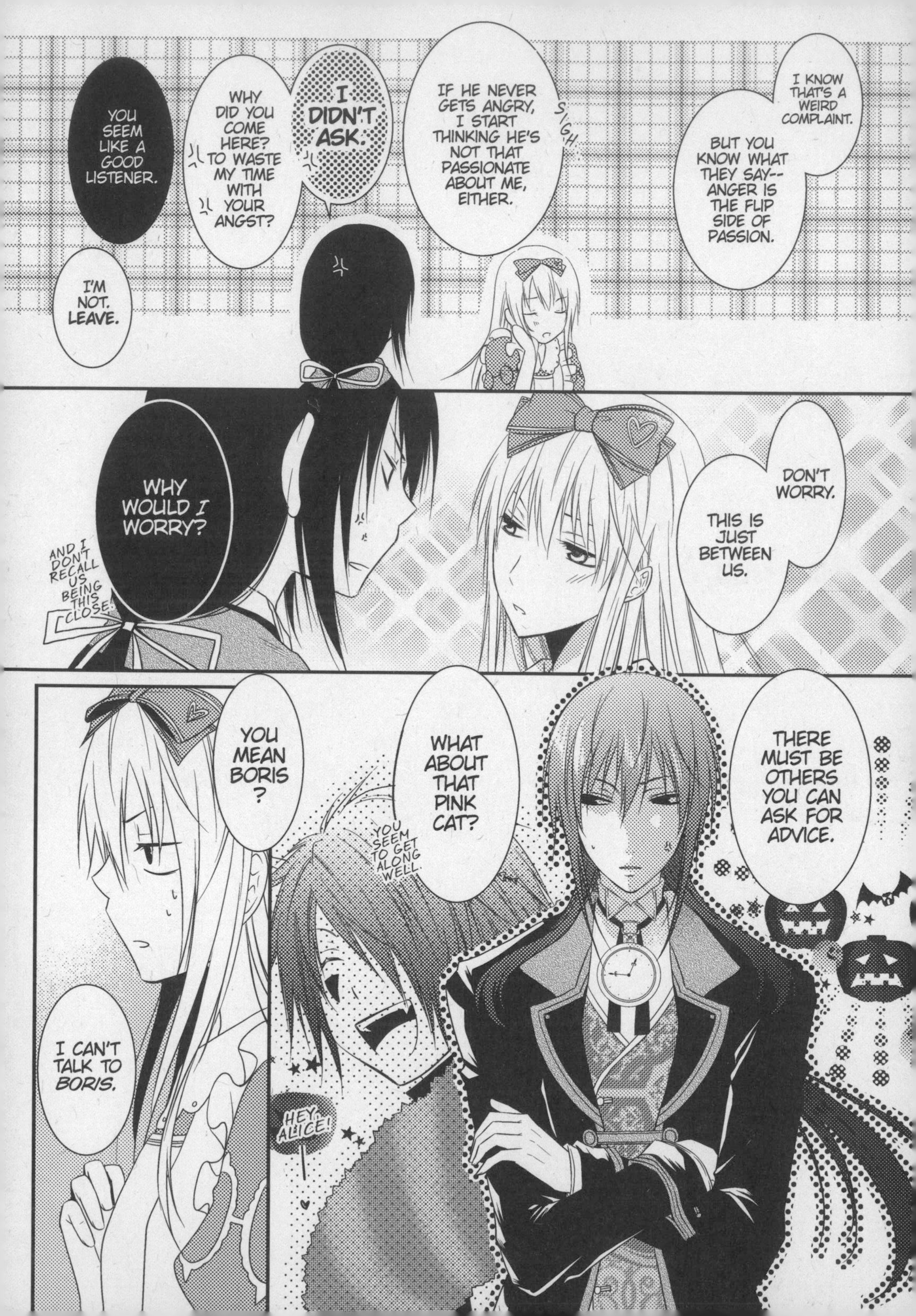
I KNOW THAT'S A WEIRD COMPLAINT.
BUT YOU KNOW WHAT THEY SAY-- ANGER IS THE FLIP SIDE OF PASSION.
SIGH
IF HE NEVER GETS ANGRY, I START THINKING HE'S NOT THAT PASSIONATE ABOUT ME, EITHER.
I DIDN'T ASK.
WHY DID YOU COME HERE? TO WASTE MY TIME WITH YOUR ANGST?
YOU SEEM LIKE A GOOD LISTENER.
I'M NOT. LEAVE.
DON'T WORRY.
THIS IS JUST BETWEEN US.
WHY WOULD I WORRY?
AND I DON'T RECALL US BEING THIS CLOSE!
THERE MUST BE OTHERS YOU CAN ASK FOR ADVICE.
WHAT ABOUT THAT PINK CAT?
YOU SEEM TO GET ALONG WELL.
YOU MEAN BORIS?
HEY, ALICE!
I CAN'T TALK TO BORIS.

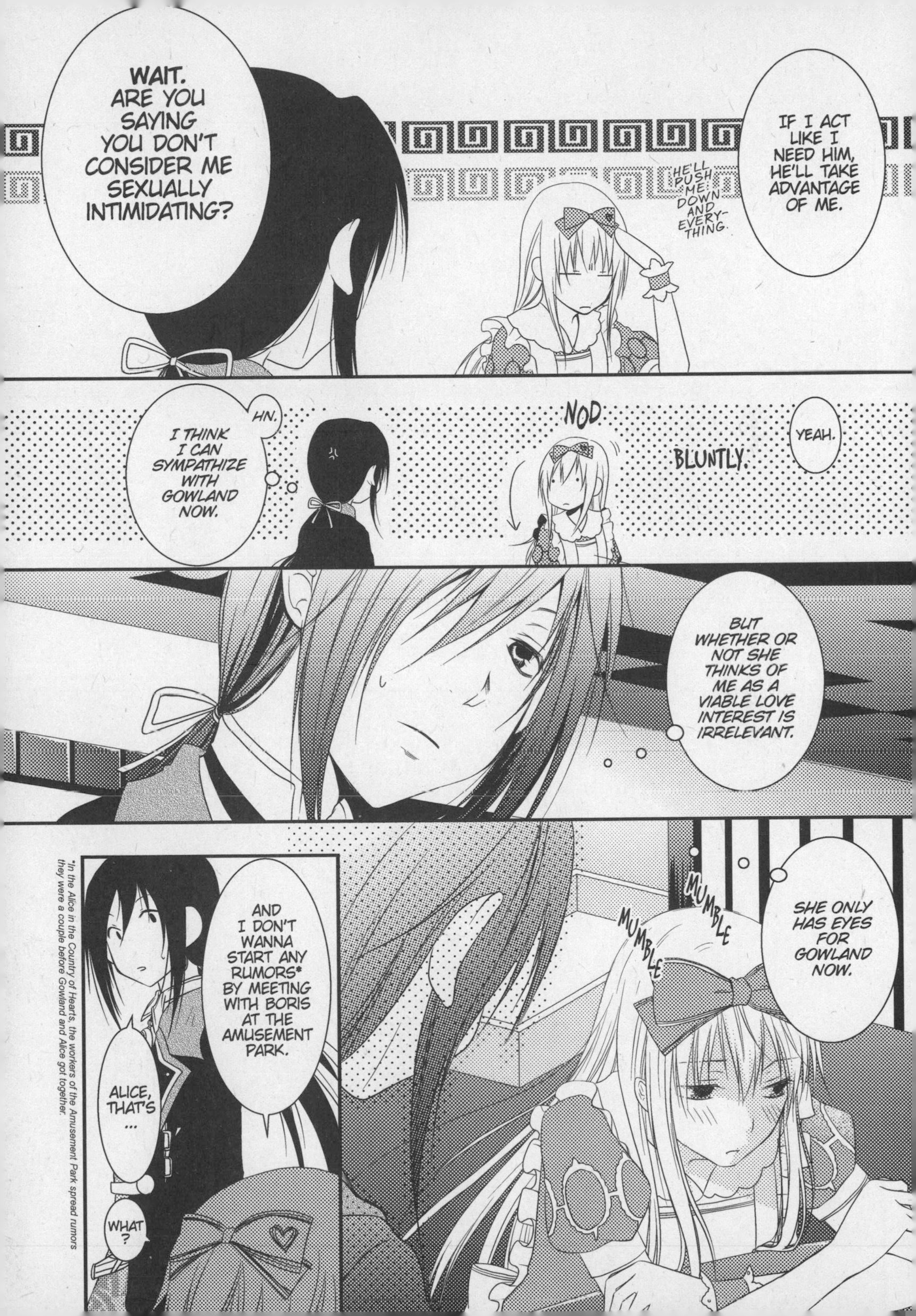
IF I ACT LIKE I NEED HIM, HE'LL TAKE ADVANTAGE OF ME.
HE'LL PUSH ME DOWN AND EVERY-THING.
WAIT. ARE YOU SAYING YOU DON'T CONSIDER ME SEXUALLY INTIMIDATING?
YEAH.
BLUNTLY.
NOD
HN.
I THINK I CAN SYMPATHIZE WITH GOWLAND NOW.
BUT WHETHER OR NOT SHE THINKS OF ME AS A VIABLE LOVE INTEREST IS IRRELEVANT.
SHE ONLY HAS EYES FOR GOWLAND NOW.
MUMBLE
MUMBLE
AND I DON'T WANNA START ANY RUMORS* BY MEETING WITH BORIS AT THE AMUSEMENT PARK.
ALICE, THAT'S ...
WHAT ?

*In the Alice in the Country of Hearts, the workers of the Amusement Park spread rumors they were a couple before Gowland and Alice got together.

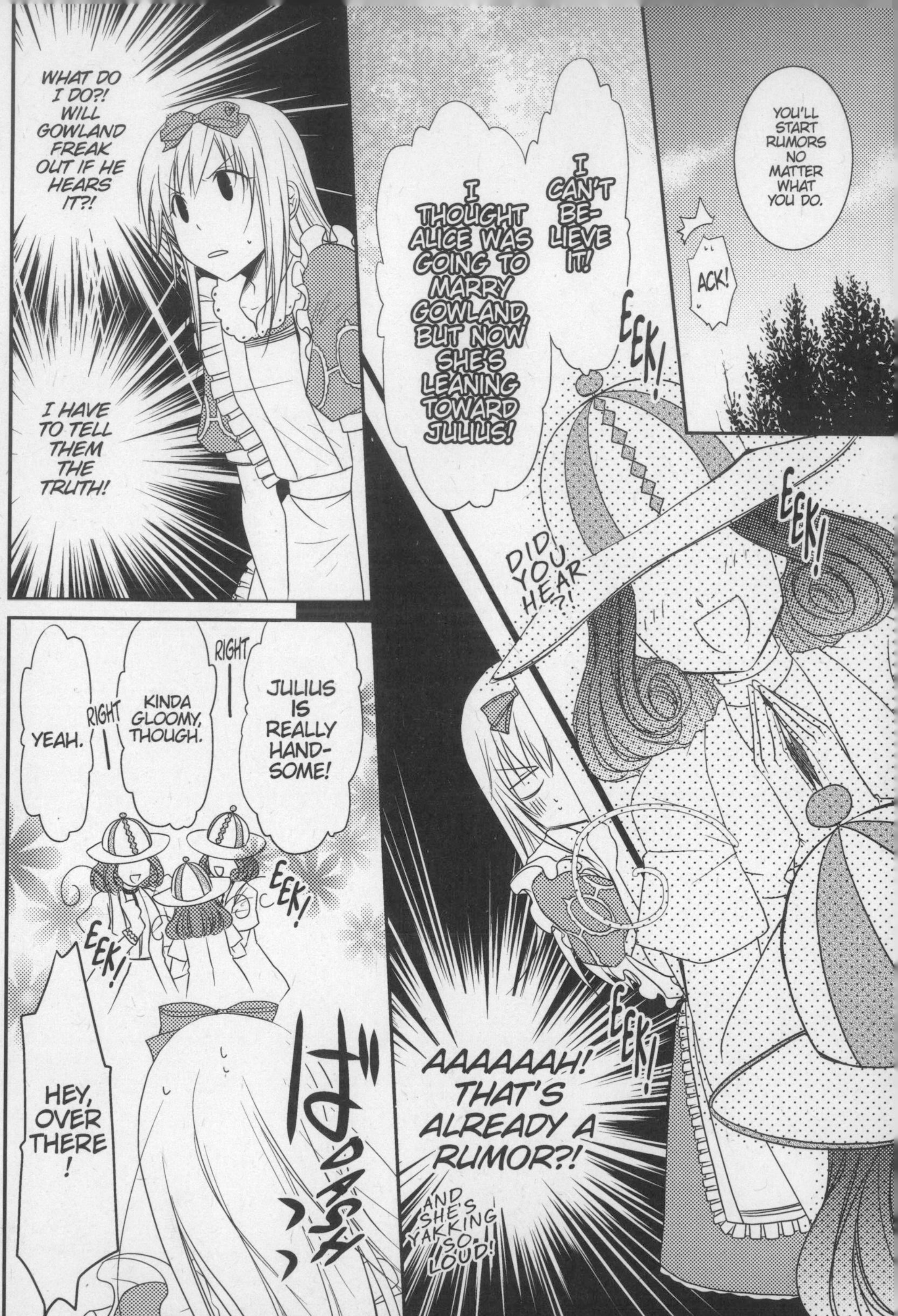
YOU'LL START RUMORS NO MATTER WHAT YOU DO.
ACK!
I CAN'T BE-LIEVE IT!
I THOUGHT ALICE WAS GOING TO MARRY GOWLAND, BUT NOW SHE'S LEANING TOWARD JULIUS!
EEK!
EEK!
DID YOU HEAR?!
EEK!
AAAAAAH! THAT'S ALREADY A RUMOR?!
AND SHE'S YAKKING SO LOUD!
WHAT DO I DO?! WILL GOWLAND FREAK OUT IF HE HEARS IT?!
I HAVE TO TELL THEM THE TRUTH!
JULIUS IS REALLY HAND-SOME!
RIGHT
KINDA GLOOMY, THOUGH.
RIGHT
YEAH.
EEK!
EEK!
HEY, OVER THERE!
DASH

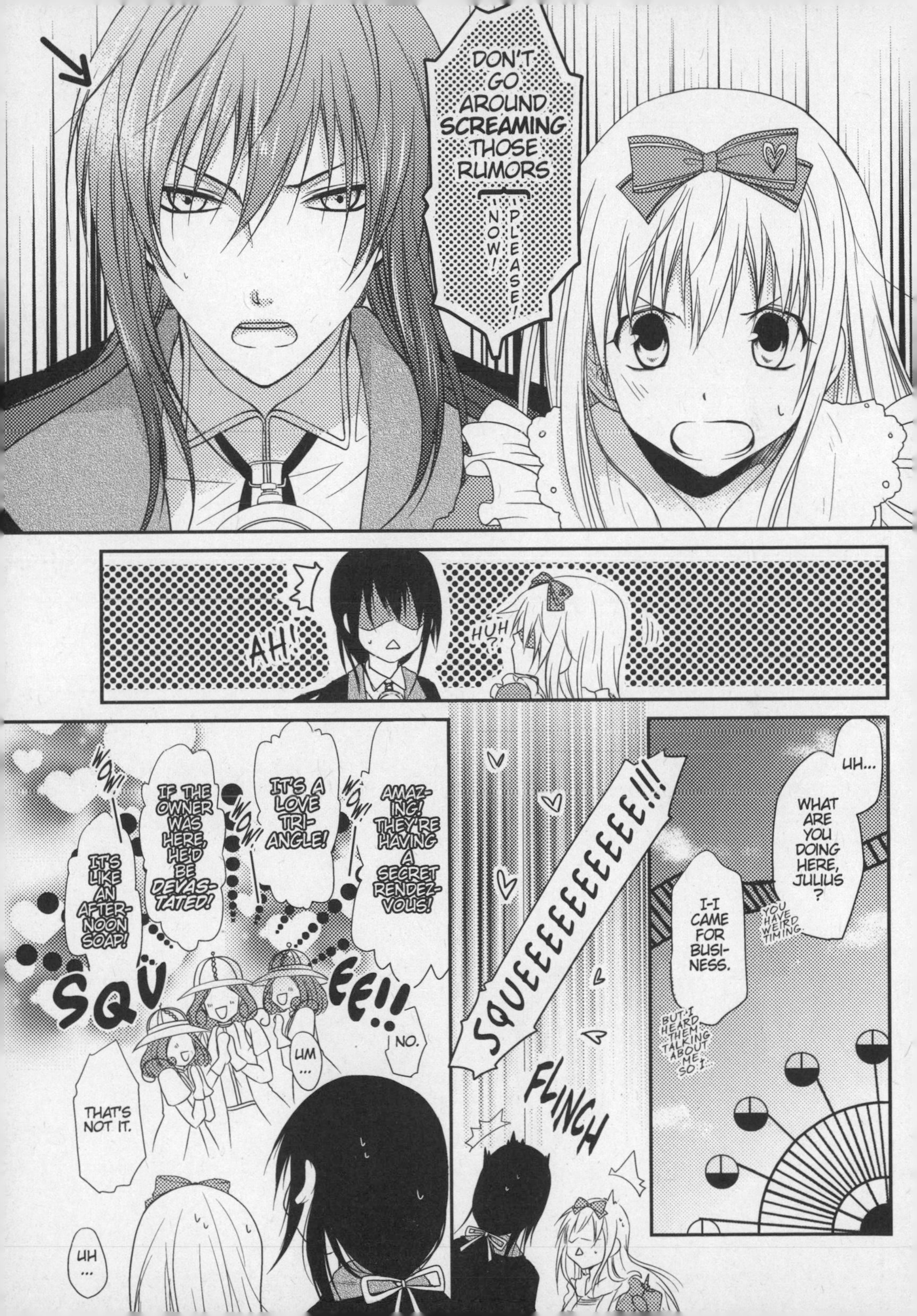
DON'T GO AROUND SCREAMING THOSE RUMORS —
PLEASE!
NOW!
HUH?
AH!
UH...
WHAT ARE YOU DOING HERE, JULIUS?
YOU HAVE WEIRD TIMING.
I-I CAME FOR BUSINESS.
BUT I HEARD THEM TALKING ABOUT ME, SO...
SQUEEEEEEEEEEEE!!!
FLINCH
AMAZING! THEY'RE HAVING A SECRET RENDEZVOUS!
WOW!
IT'S A LOVE TRIANGLE!
WOW!
IF THE OWNER WAS HERE, HE'D BE DEVASTATED!
WOW!
IT'S LIKE AN AFTERNOON SOAP!
SQUEE!!
NO.
UM...
THAT'S NOT IT.
UH...

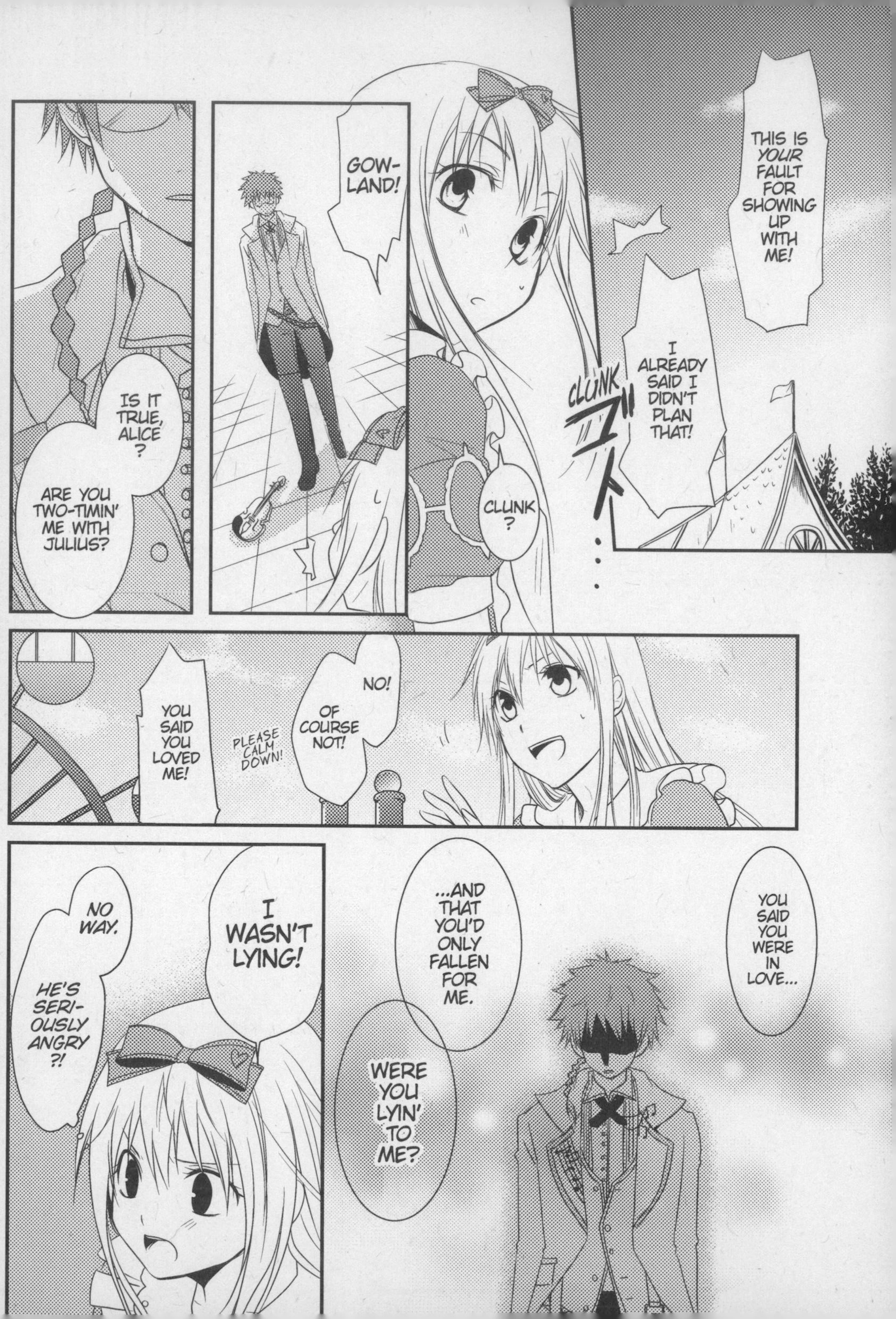
THIS IS YOUR FAULT FOR SHOWING UP WITH ME!
I ALREADY SAID I DIDN'T PLAN THAT!
CLUNK
...
CLUNK?
GOW-LAND!
IS IT TRUE, ALICE?
ARE YOU TWO-TIMIN' ME WITH JULIUS?
NO!
OF COURSE NOT!
PLEASE CALM DOWN!
YOU SAID YOU LOVED ME!
YOU SAID YOU WERE IN LOVE...
...AND THAT YOU'D ONLY FALLEN FOR ME.
WERE YOU LYIN' TO ME?
I WASN'T LYING!
NO WAY.
HE'S SERIOUSLY ANGRY?!

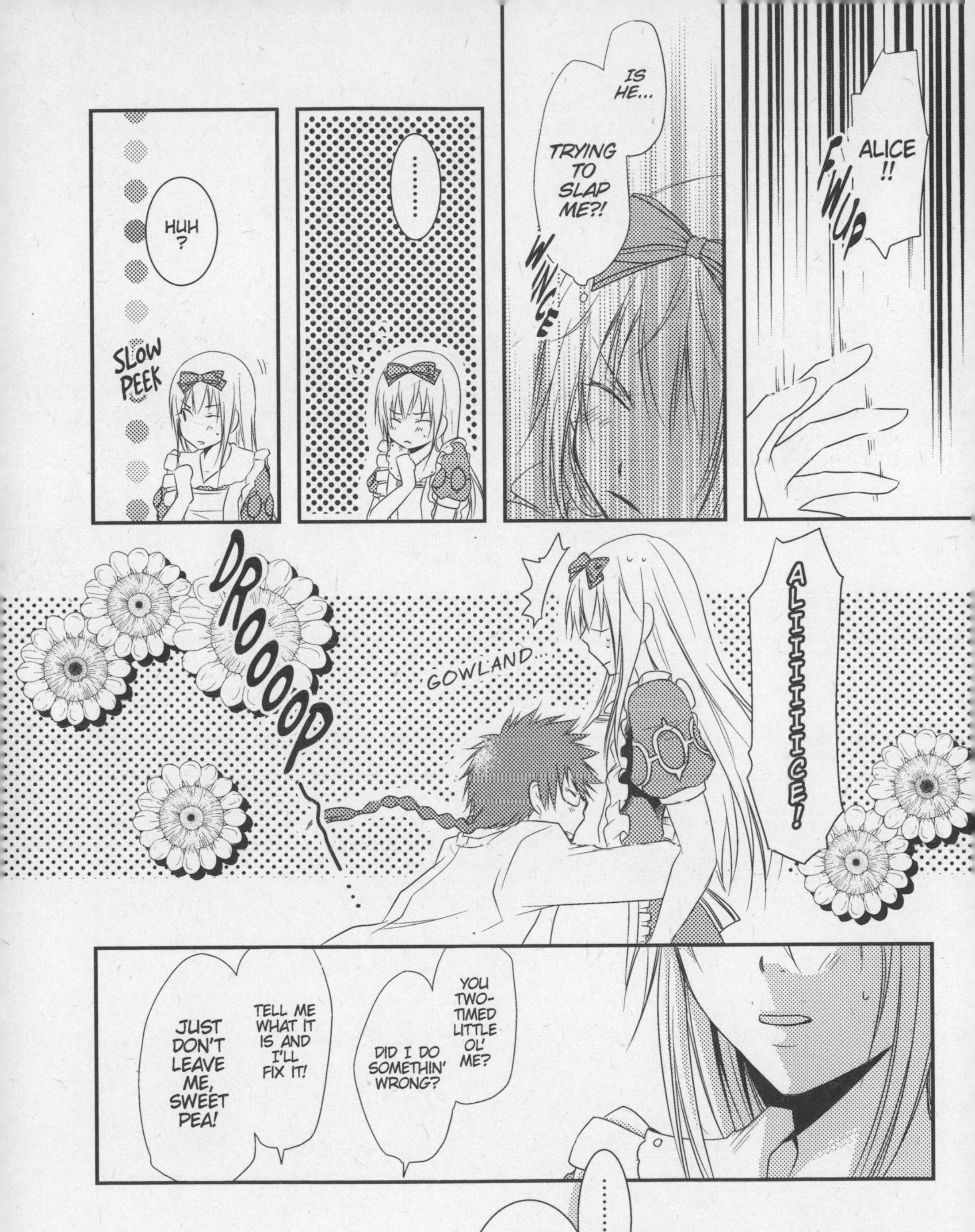
ALICE!!
FWUP
IS HE...
TRYING TO SLAP ME?!
WINCE
......
HUH?
SLOW PEEK
ALIIIIIIIICE!
DROOOOOP
GOWLAND...
YOU TWO-TIMED LITTLE OL' ME?
DID I DO SOMETHIN' WRONG?
TELL ME WHAT IT IS AND I'LL FIX IT!
JUST DON'T LEAVE ME, SWEET PEA!
......
DON'T BE RIDICULOUS.

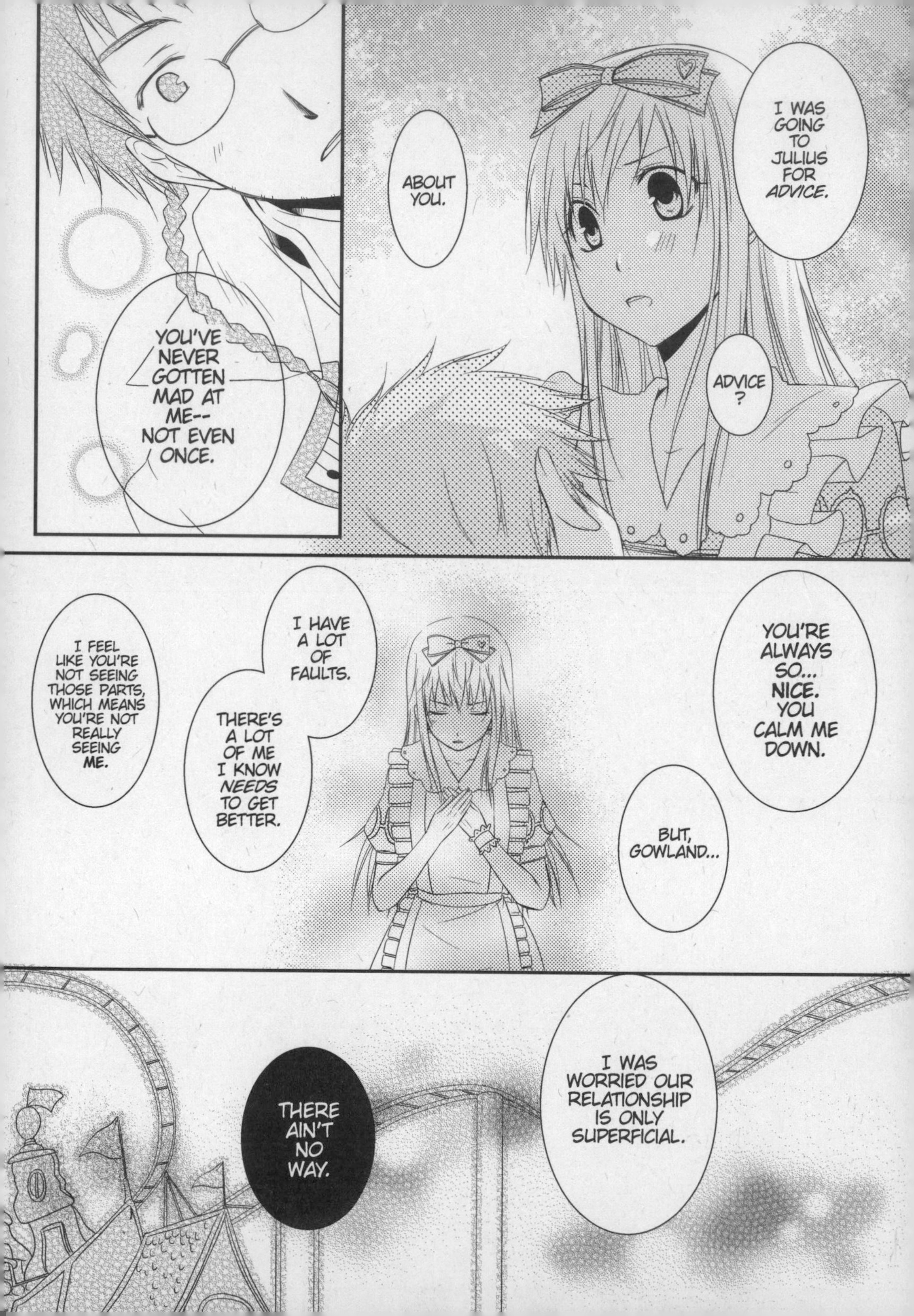
I WAS GOING TO JULIUS FOR *ADVICE.*
ABOUT YOU.
ADVICE?
YOU'VE NEVER GOTTEN MAD AT ME-- NOT EVEN ONCE.
YOU'RE ALWAYS SO... **NICE.** YOU CALM ME DOWN.
BUT, GOWLAND...
I HAVE A LOT OF FAULTS.
THERE'S A LOT OF ME I KNOW *NEEDS* TO GET BETTER.
I FEEL LIKE YOU'RE NOT SEEING THOSE PARTS, WHICH MEANS YOU'RE NOT REALLY SEEING **ME.**
I WAS WORRIED OUR RELATIONSHIP IS ONLY SUPERFICIAL.
THERE AIN'T NO WAY.

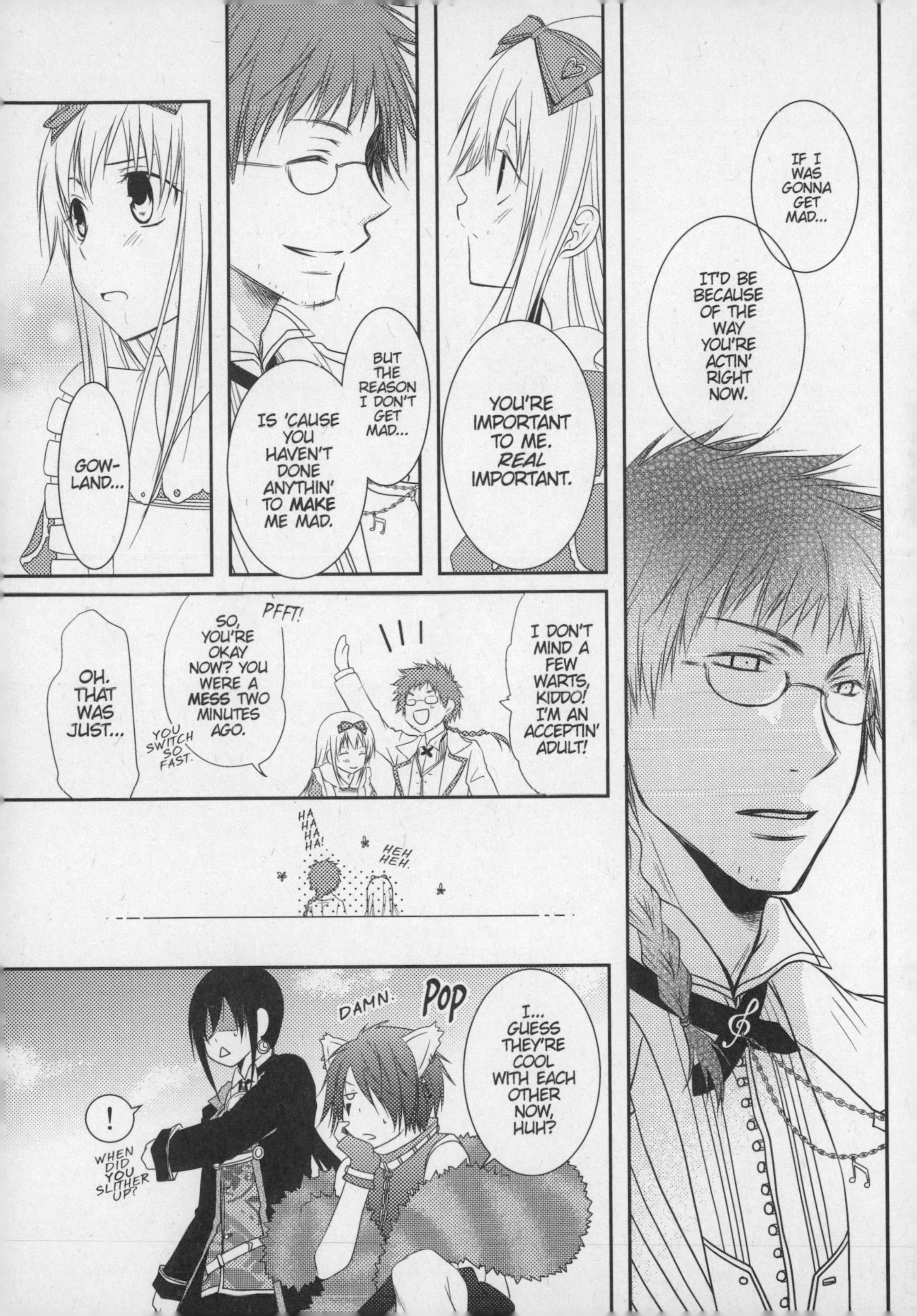
IF I WAS GONNA GET MAD...
IT'D BE BECAUSE OF THE WAY YOU'RE ACTIN' RIGHT NOW.
YOU'RE IMPORTANT TO ME. REAL IMPORTANT.
BUT THE REASON I DON'T GET MAD...
IS 'CAUSE YOU HAVEN'T DONE ANYTHIN' TO MAKE ME MAD.
GOW-LAND...
I DON'T MIND A FEW WARTS, KIDDO! I'M AN ACCEPTIN' ADULT!
PFFT!
SO, YOU'RE OKAY NOW? YOU WERE A MESS TWO MINUTES AGO.
YOU SWITCH SO FAST.
OH. THAT WAS JUST...
HA HA HA HA!
HEH HEH.
POP
I... GUESS THEY'RE COOL WITH EACH OTHER NOW, HUH?
DAMN.
!
WHEN DID YOU SLITHER UP?

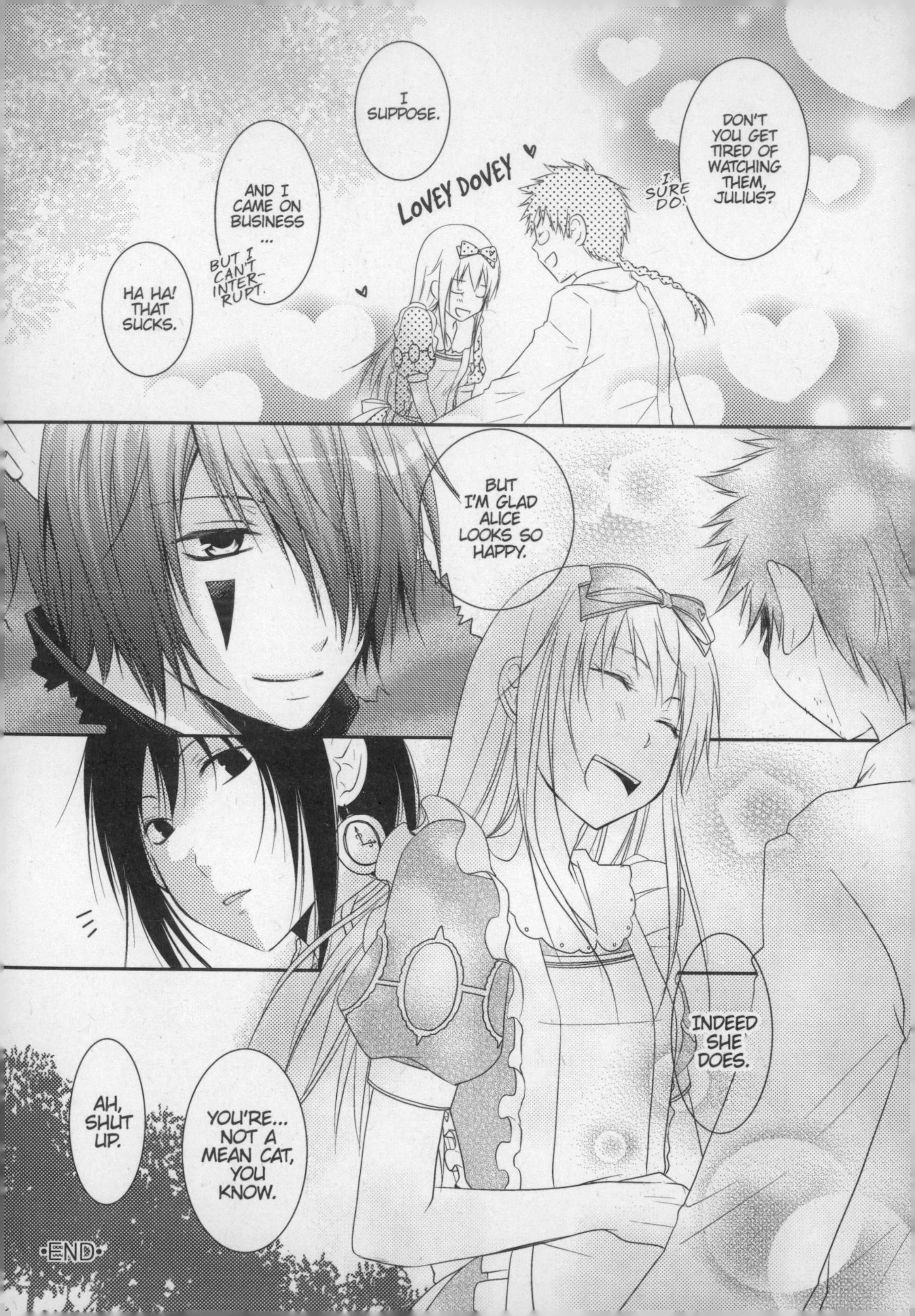
DON'T YOU GET TIRED OF WATCHING THEM, JULIUS?
I SURE DO!
LOVEY DOVEY
I SUPPOSE.
AND I CAME ON BUSINESS ...
BUT I CAN'T INTER-RUPT.
HA HA! THAT SUCKS.
BUT I'M GLAD ALICE LOOKS SO HAPPY.
INDEED SHE DOES.
YOU'RE... NOT A MEAN CAT, YOU KNOW.
AH, SHUT UP.
END

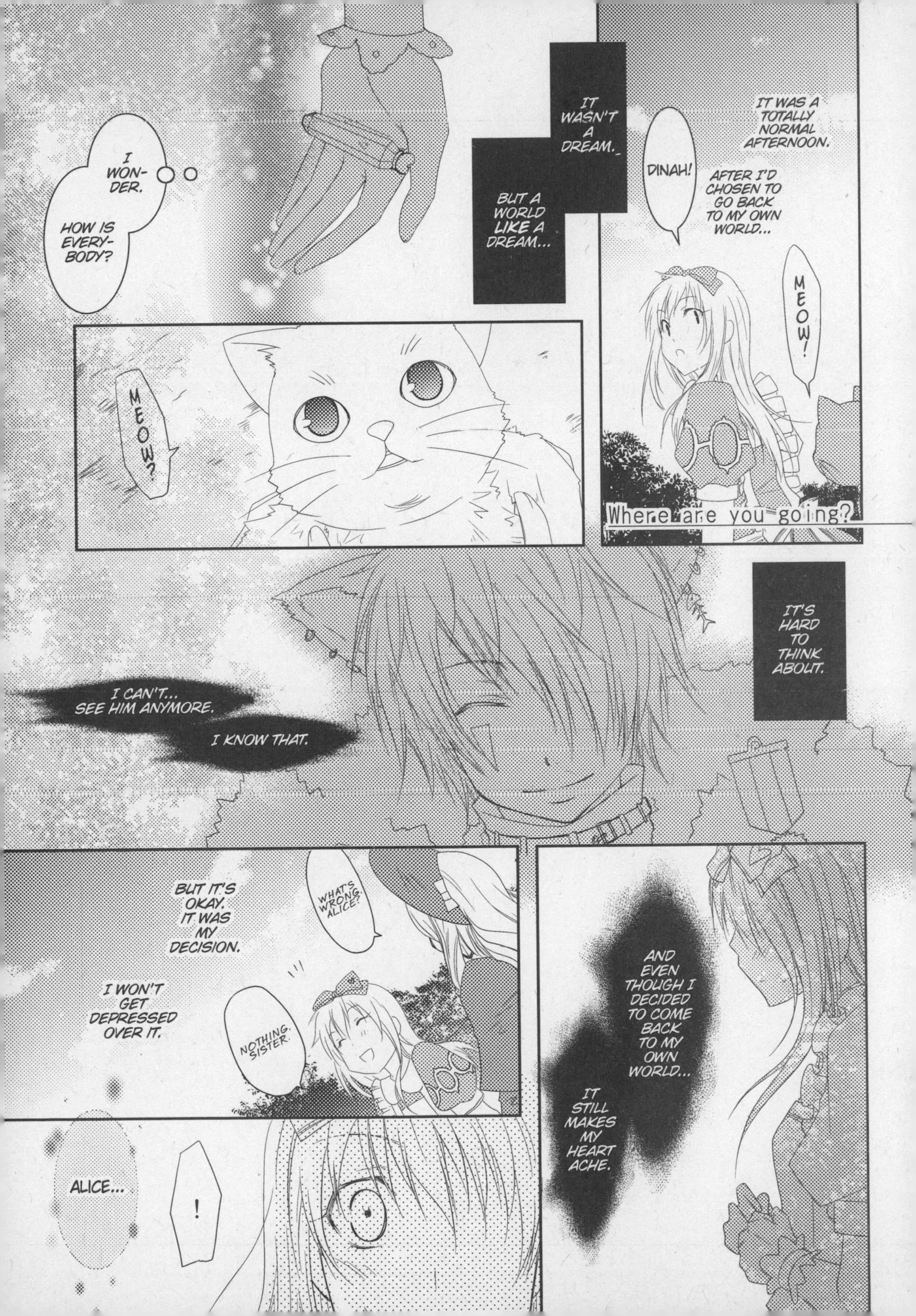
IT WAS A TOTALLY NORMAL AFTERNOON.
AFTER I'D CHOSEN TO GO BACK TO MY OWN WORLD...
DINAH!
MEOW!
Where are you going?
IT WASN'T A DREAM.
BUT A WORLD LIKE A DREAM...
I WONDER.
HOW IS EVERYBODY?
MEOW?
IT'S HARD TO THINK ABOUT.
I CAN'T... SEE HIM ANYMORE.
I KNOW THAT.
AND EVEN THOUGH I DECIDED TO COME BACK TO MY OWN WORLD...
IT STILL MAKES MY HEART ACHE.
BUT IT'S OKAY. IT WAS MY DECISION.
WHAT'S WRONG, ALICE?
I WON'T GET DEPRESSED OVER IT.
NOTHING, SISTER.
ALICE...
!

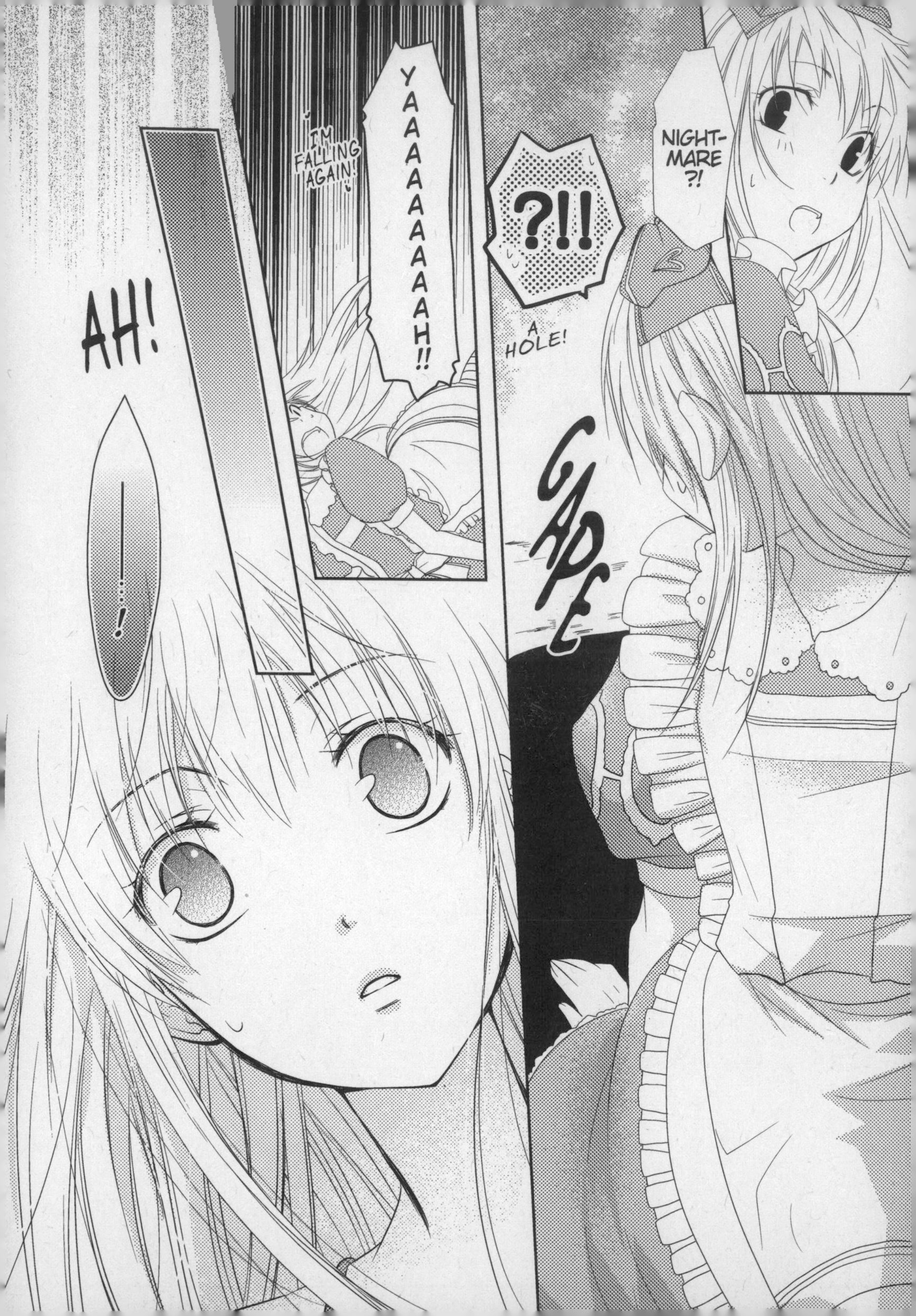
NIGHT-MARE ?!
?!!
A HOLE!
GAPE
YAAAAAAAAAH!!
I'M FALLING AGAIN!
AH!
......!

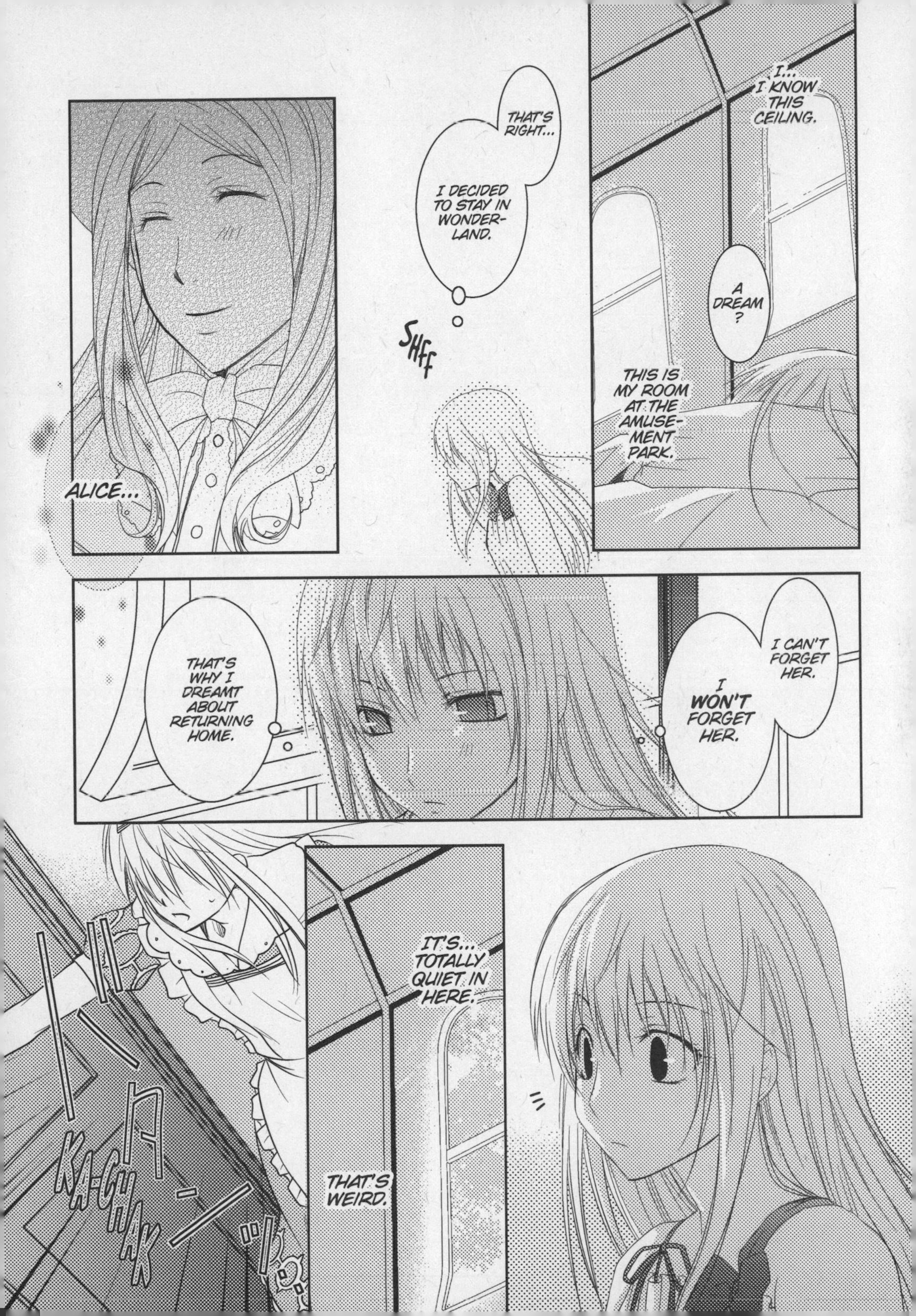
I... I KNOW THIS CEILING.
A DREAM?
THIS IS MY ROOM AT THE AMUSEMENT PARK.
THAT'S RIGHT...
I DECIDED TO STAY IN WONDERLAND.
SHFF
ALICE...
I CAN'T FORGET HER.
I WON'T FORGET HER.
THAT'S WHY I DREAMT ABOUT RETURNING HOME.
IT'S... TOTALLY QUIET IN HERE.
THAT'S WEIRD.
KA-CHAK

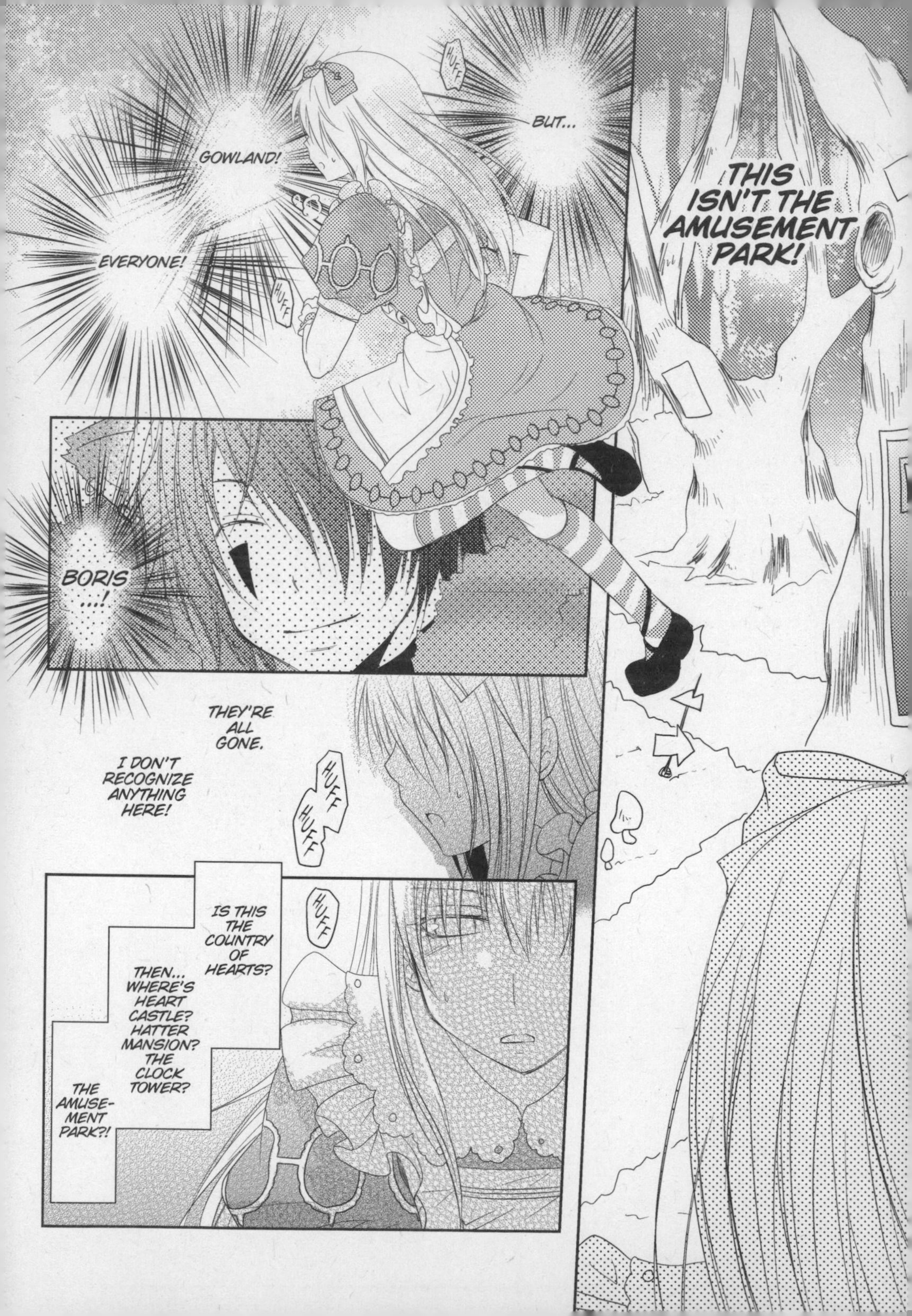
THIS ISN'T THE AMUSEMENT PARK!
HUFF
BUT...
GOWLAND!
EVERYONE!
HUFF
BORIS ...!
THEY'RE ALL GONE.
I DON'T RECOGNIZE ANYTHING HERE!
HUFF HUFF HUFF
HUFF
IS THIS THE COUNTRY OF HEARTS?
THEN... WHERE'S HEART CASTLE? HATTER MANSION? THE CLOCK TOWER?
THE AMUSE-MENT PARK?!

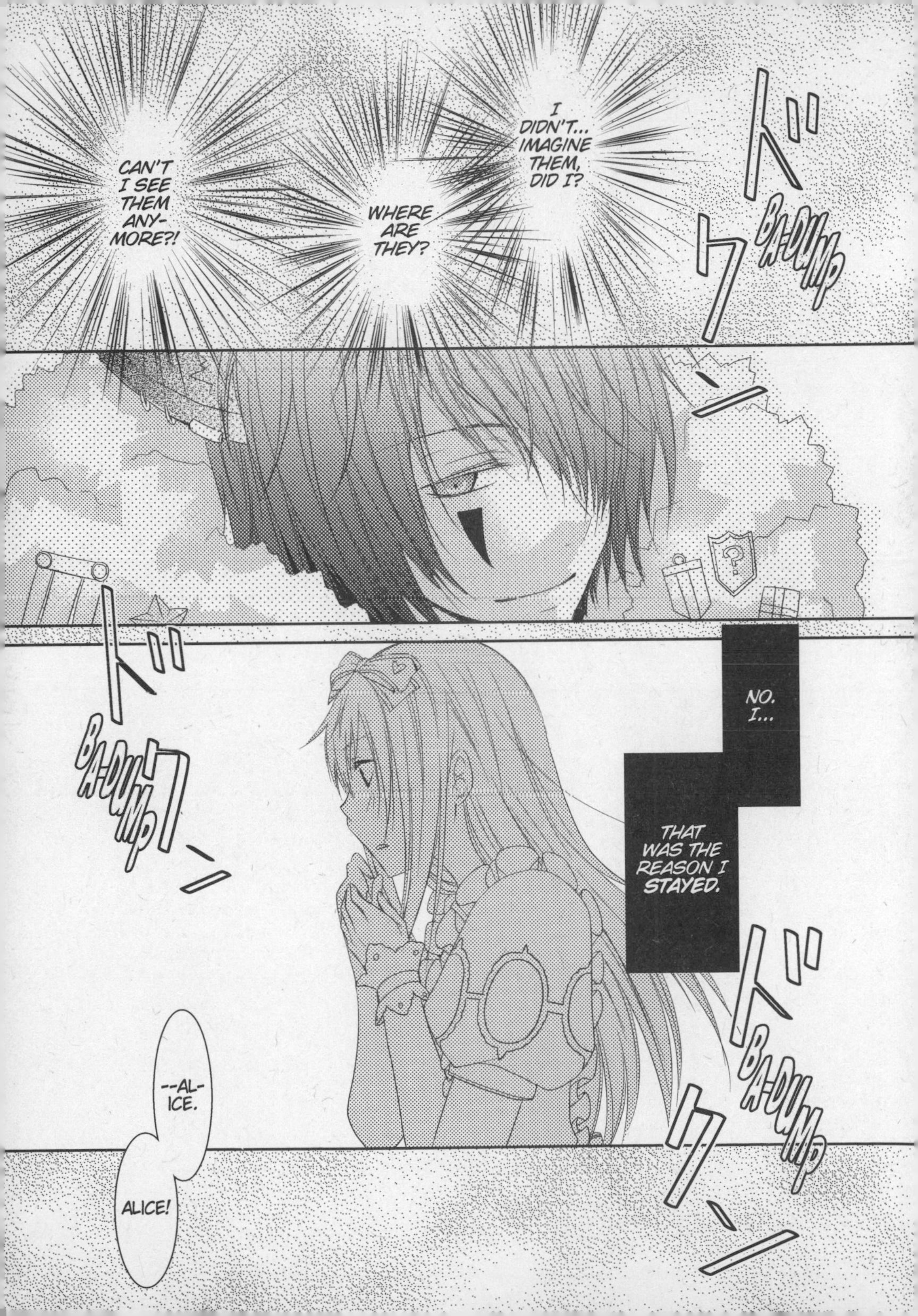
BA-DUMP
I DIDN'T... IMAGINE THEM, DID I?
WHERE ARE THEY?
CAN'T I SEE THEM ANYMORE?!
NO. I...
THAT WAS THE REASON I STAYED.
BA-DUMP
BA-DUMP
--AL-ICE.
ALICE!

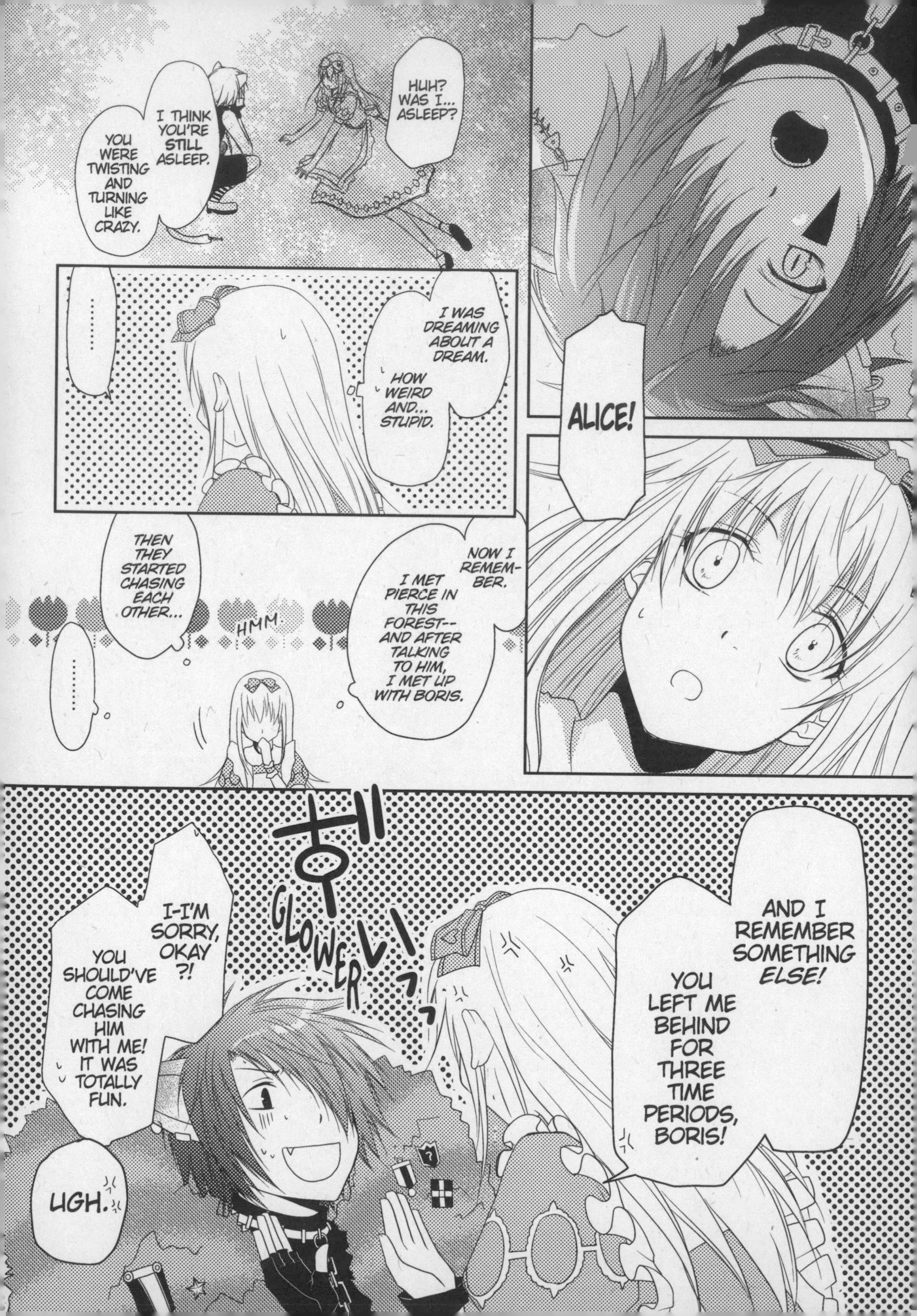

ALICE!
HUH? WAS I... ASLEEP?
I THINK YOU'RE STILL ASLEEP.
YOU WERE TWISTING AND TURNING LIKE CRAZY.
I WAS DREAMING ABOUT A DREAM.
HOW WEIRD AND... STUPID.
......
NOW I REMEMBER.
I MET PIERCE IN THIS FOREST--AND AFTER TALKING TO HIM, I MET UP WITH BORIS.
THEN THEY STARTED CHASING EACH OTHER...
HMM
......
AND I REMEMBER SOMETHING ELSE!
YOU LEFT ME BEHIND FOR THREE TIME PERIODS, BORIS!
GLOWER
I-I'M SORRY, OKAY?!
YOU SHOULD'VE COME CHASING HIM WITH ME! IT WAS TOTALLY FUN.
UGH.

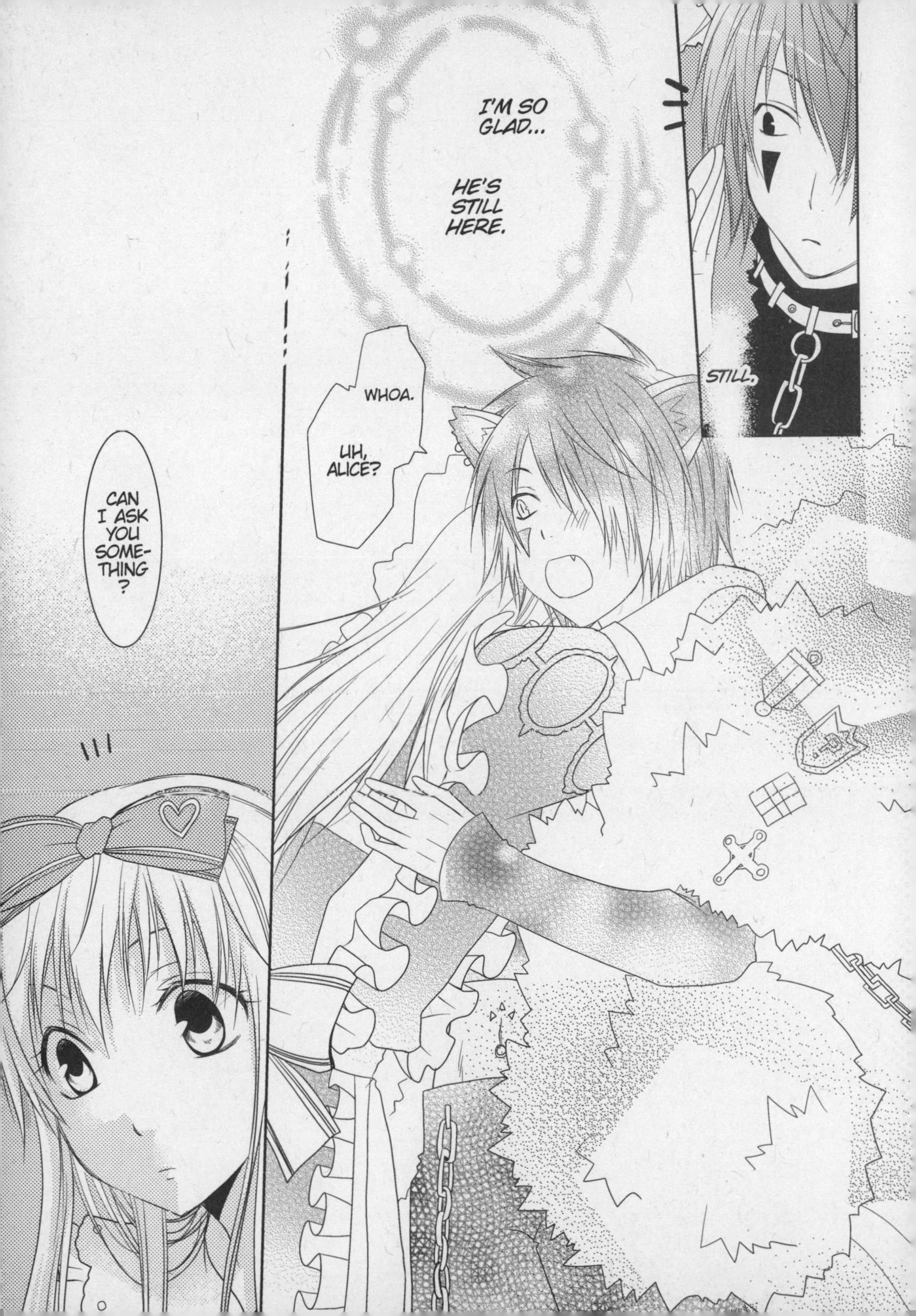
STILL.
I'M SO GLAD...
HE'S STILL HERE.
WHOA.
UH, ALICE?
CAN I ASK YOU SOMETHING?

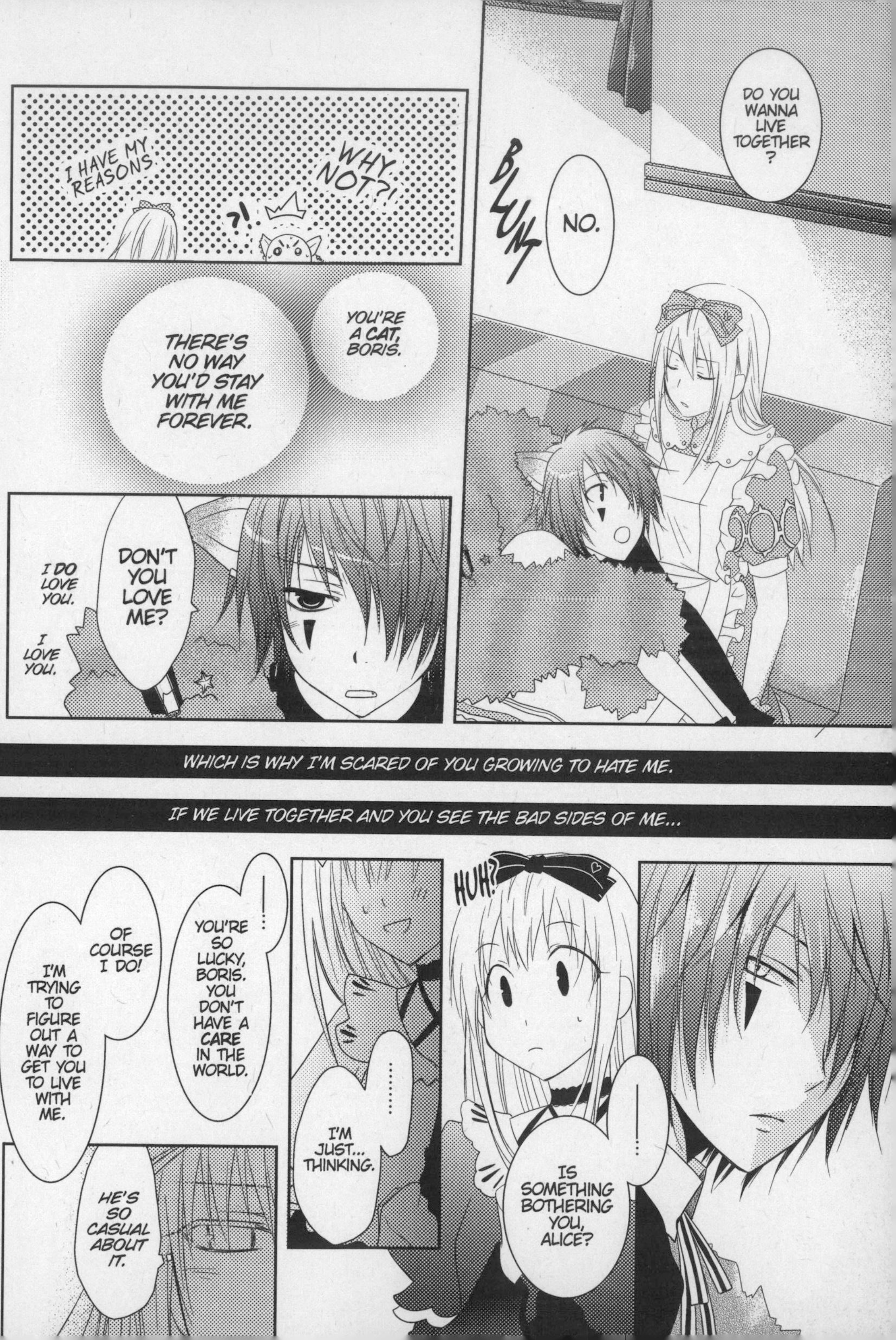
DO YOU WANNA LIVE TOGETHER?
BLUNT
NO.
WHY NOT?!
I HAVE MY REASONS.
?!
YOU'RE A CAT, BORIS.
THERE'S NO WAY YOU'D STAY WITH ME FOREVER.
DON'T YOU LOVE ME?
I DO LOVE YOU.
I LOVE YOU.
WHICH IS WHY I'M SCARED OF YOU GROWING TO HATE ME.
IF WE LIVE TOGETHER AND YOU SEE THE BAD SIDES OF ME...
HUH?
...
IS SOMETHING BOTHERING YOU, ALICE?
......
I'M JUST... THINKING.
...
YOU'RE SO LUCKY, BORIS. YOU DON'T HAVE A CARE IN THE WORLD.
OF COURSE I DO!
I'M TRYING TO FIGURE OUT A WAY TO GET YOU TO LIVE WITH ME.
HE'S SO CASUAL ABOUT IT.

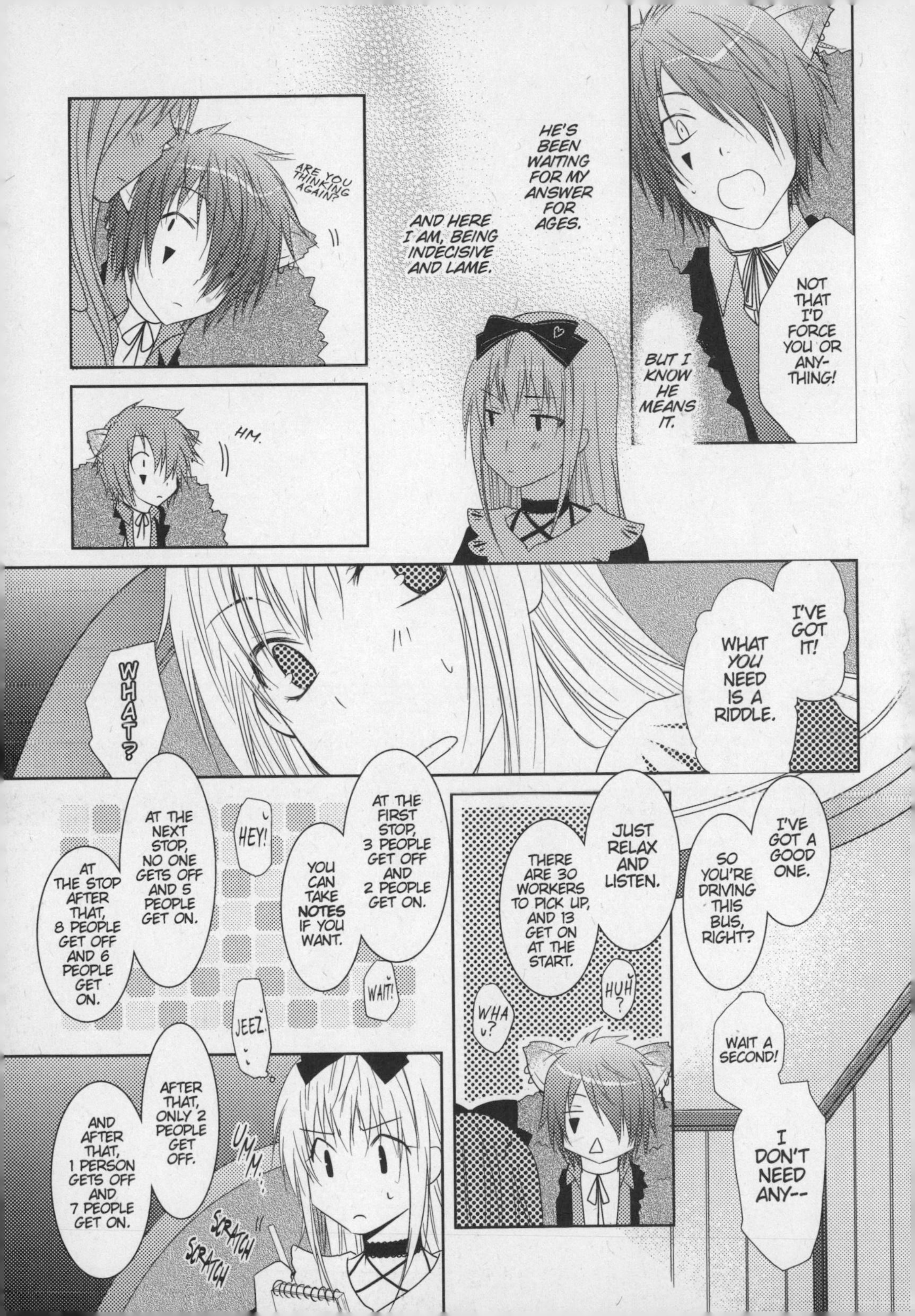
NOT THAT I'D FORCE YOU OR ANY-THING!
BUT I KNOW HE MEANS IT.
HE'S BEEN WAITING FOR MY ANSWER FOR AGES.
AND HERE I AM, BEING INDECISIVE AND LAME.
ARE YOU THINKING AGAIN?
HM.
I'VE GOT IT!
WHAT YOU NEED IS A RIDDLE.
WHAT?
I'VE GOT A GOOD ONE.
SO YOU'RE DRIVING THIS BUS, RIGHT?
JUST RELAX AND LISTEN.
THERE ARE 30 WORKERS TO PICK UP, AND 13 GET ON AT THE START.
HUH?
WHA?
WAIT A SECOND!
I DON'T NEED ANY--
AT THE FIRST STOP, 3 PEOPLE GET OFF AND 2 PEOPLE GET ON.
YOU CAN TAKE NOTES IF YOU WANT.
HEY!
AT THE NEXT STOP, NO ONE GETS OFF AND 5 PEOPLE GET ON.
AT THE STOP AFTER THAT, 8 PEOPLE GET OFF AND 6 PEOPLE GET ON.
WAIT!
JEEZ.
AFTER THAT, ONLY 2 PEOPLE GET OFF.
AND AFTER THAT, 1 PERSON GETS OFF AND 7 PEOPLE GET ON.
UMM...
SCRATCH
SCRATCH

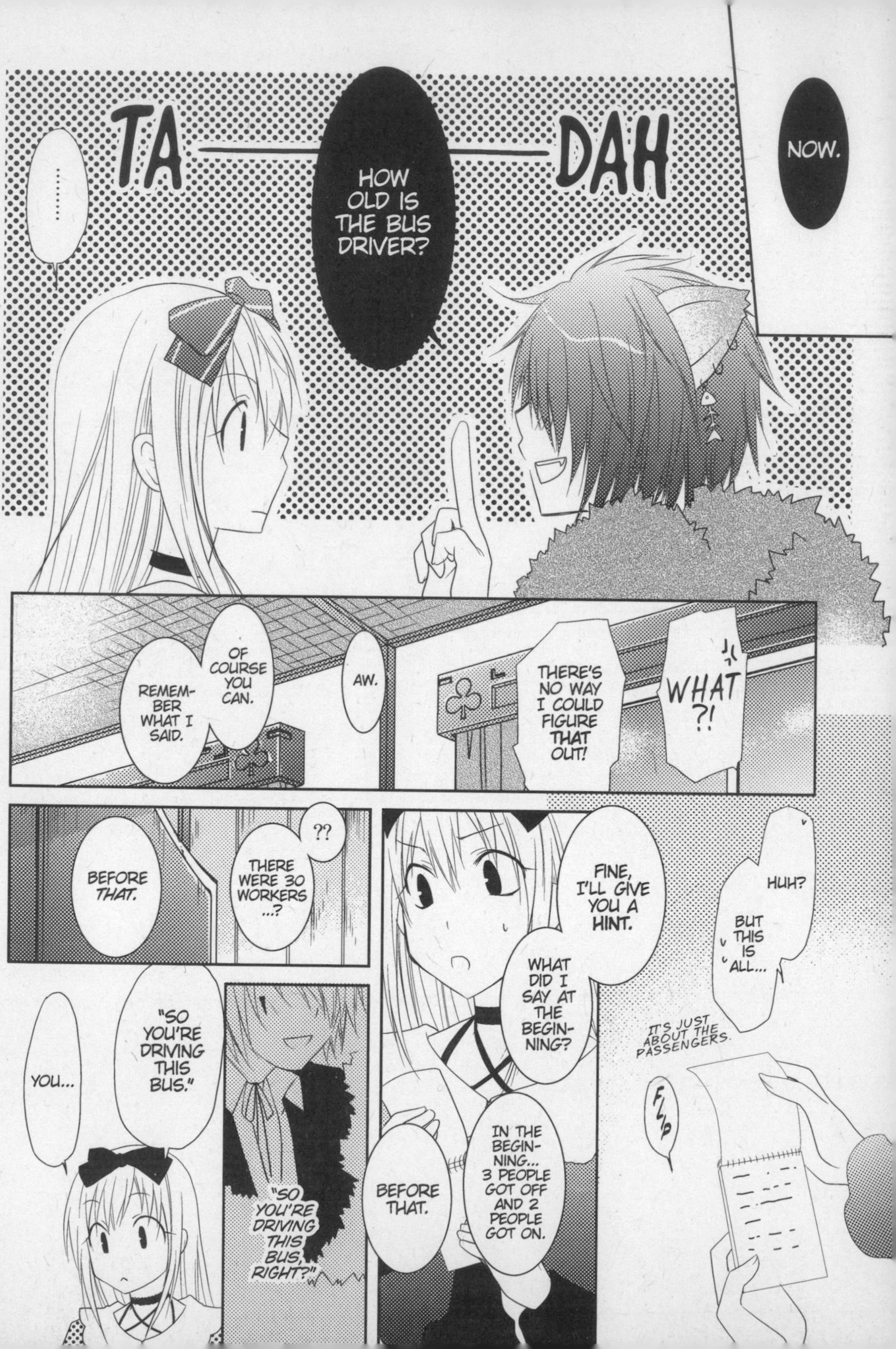
NOW.
TA——DAH
HOW OLD IS THE BUS DRIVER?
......
WHAT ?!
THERE'S NO WAY I COULD FIGURE THAT OUT!
AW.
OF COURSE YOU CAN.
REMEMBER WHAT I SAID.
HUH?
BUT THIS IS ALL...
IT'S JUST ABOUT THE PASSENGERS.
FLIP
FINE, I'LL GIVE YOU A HINT.
WHAT DID I SAY AT THE BEGINNING?
IN THE BEGINNING... 3 PEOPLE GOT OFF AND 2 PEOPLE GOT ON.
BEFORE THAT.
??
THERE WERE 30 WORKERS ...?
BEFORE THAT.
"SO YOU'RE DRIVING THIS BUS, RIGHT?"
"SO YOU'RE DRIVING THIS BUS."
YOU...

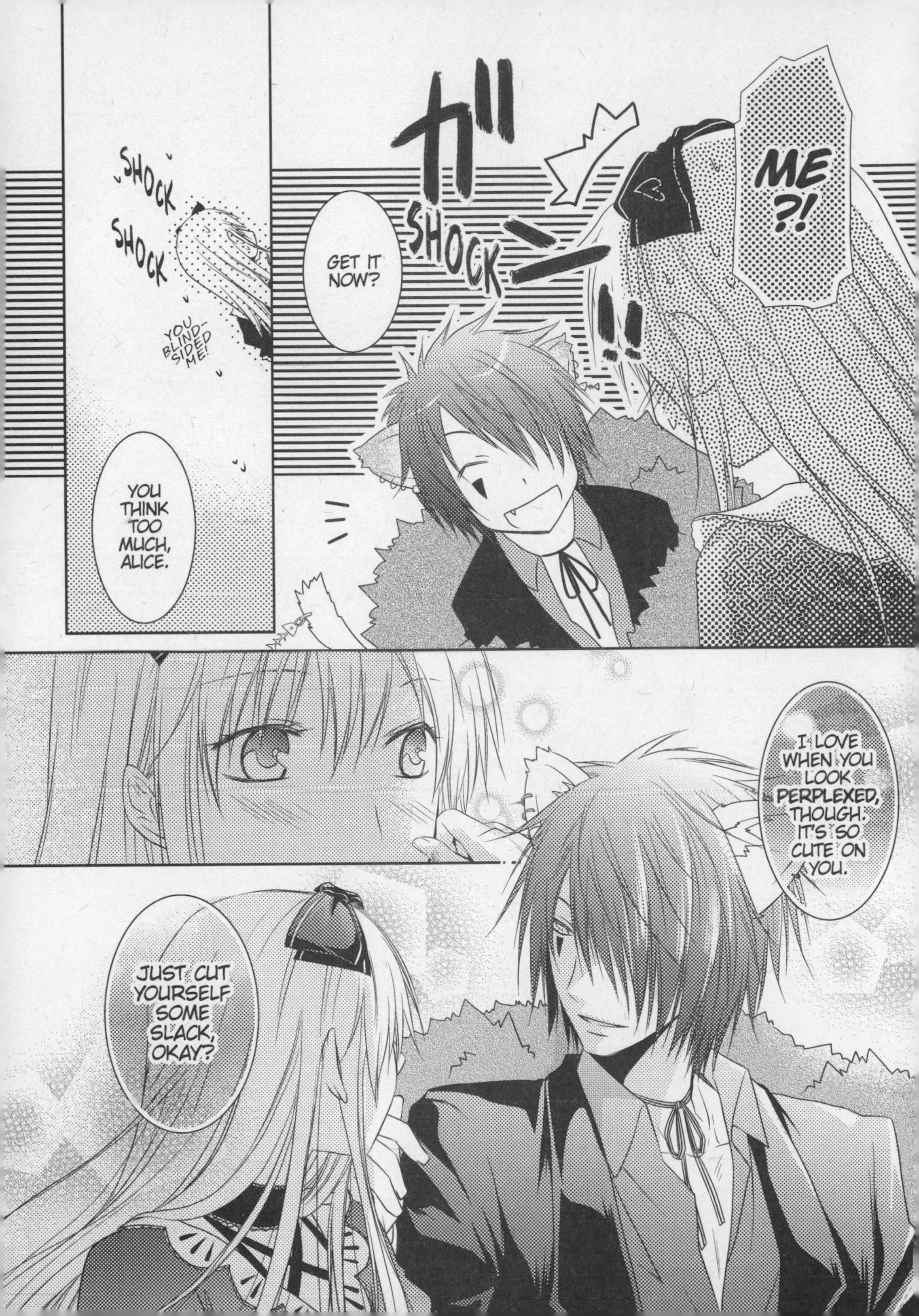
ME?!
ガ
SHOCK
GET IT NOW?
SHOCK
SHOCK
YOU BLINDSIDED ME!
YOU THINK TOO MUCH, ALICE.
I LOVE WHEN YOU LOOK PERPLEXED, THOUGH. IT'S SO CUTE ON YOU.
JUST CUT YOURSELF SOME SLACK, OKAY?

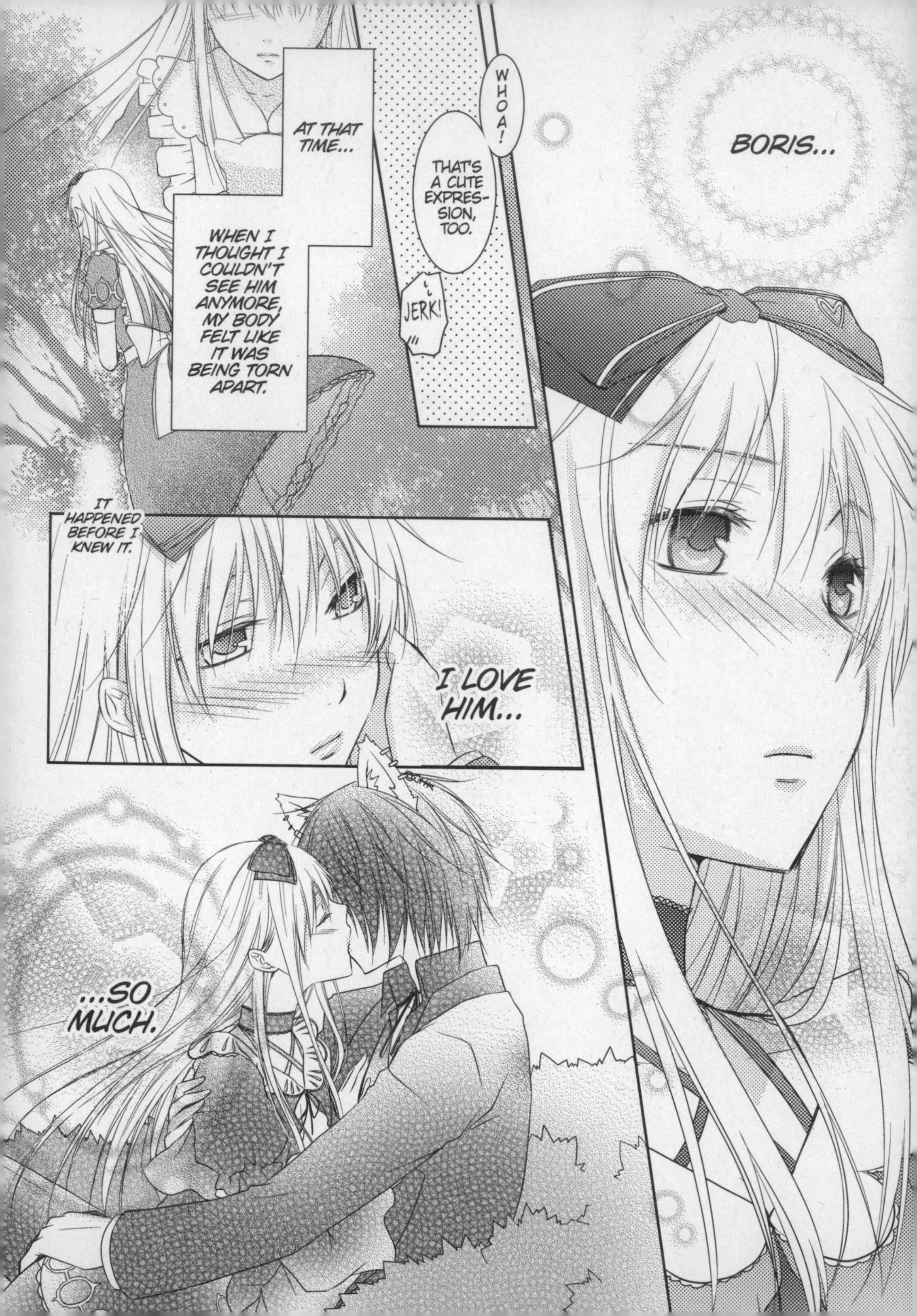
BORIS...
WHOA!
THAT'S A CUTE EXPRESSION, TOO.
JERK!
AT THAT TIME...
WHEN I THOUGHT I COULDN'T SEE HIM ANYMORE, MY BODY FELT LIKE IT WAS BEING TORN APART.
IT HAPPENED BEFORE I KNEW IT.
I LOVE HIM...
...SO MUCH.

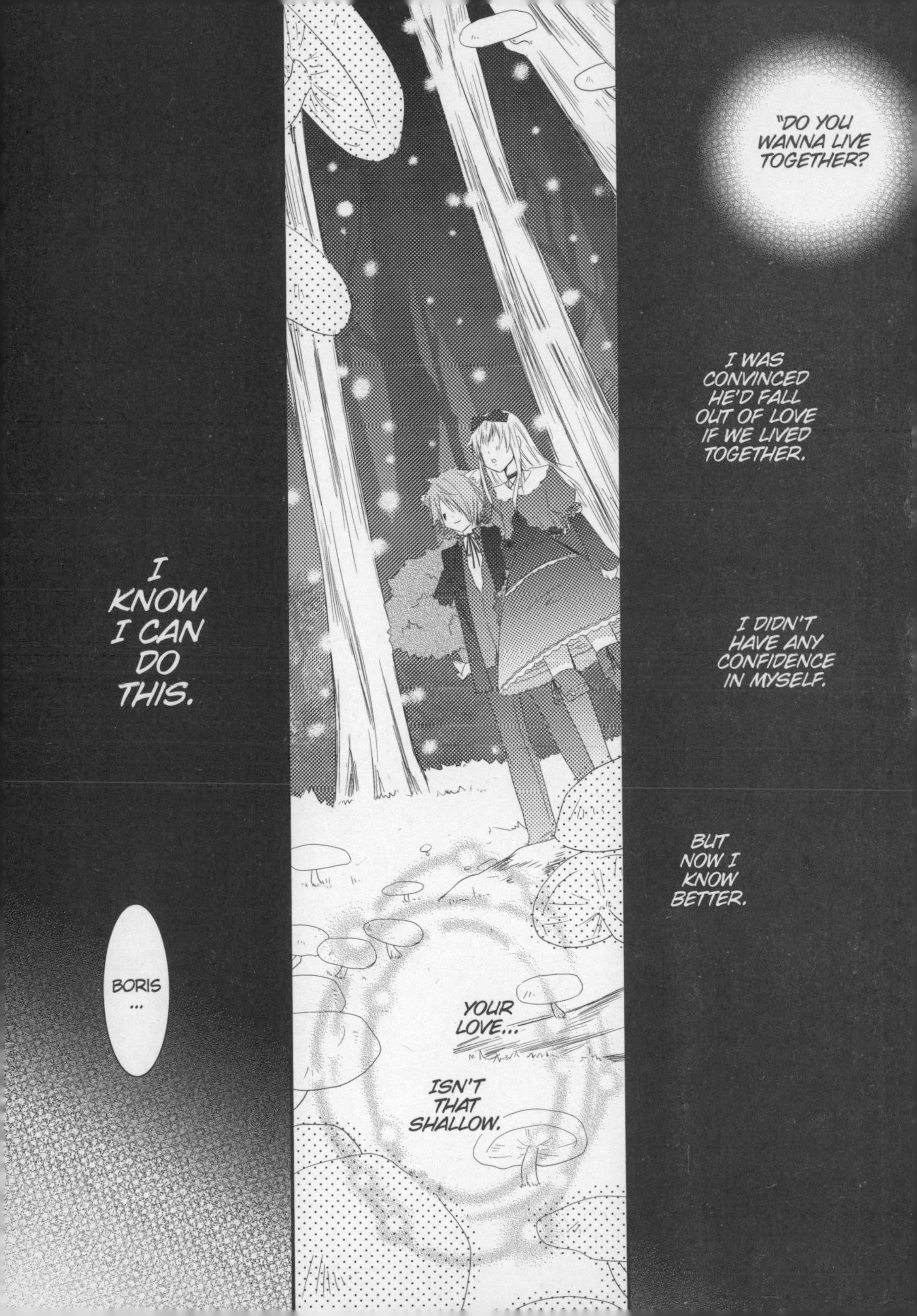
"DO YOU WANNA LIVE TOGETHER?
I WAS CONVINCED HE'D FALL OUT OF LOVE IF WE LIVED TOGETHER.
I DIDN'T HAVE ANY CONFIDENCE IN MYSELF.
BUT NOW I KNOW BETTER.
YOUR LOVE...
ISN'T THAT SHALLOW.
I KNOW I CAN DO THIS.
BORIS ...

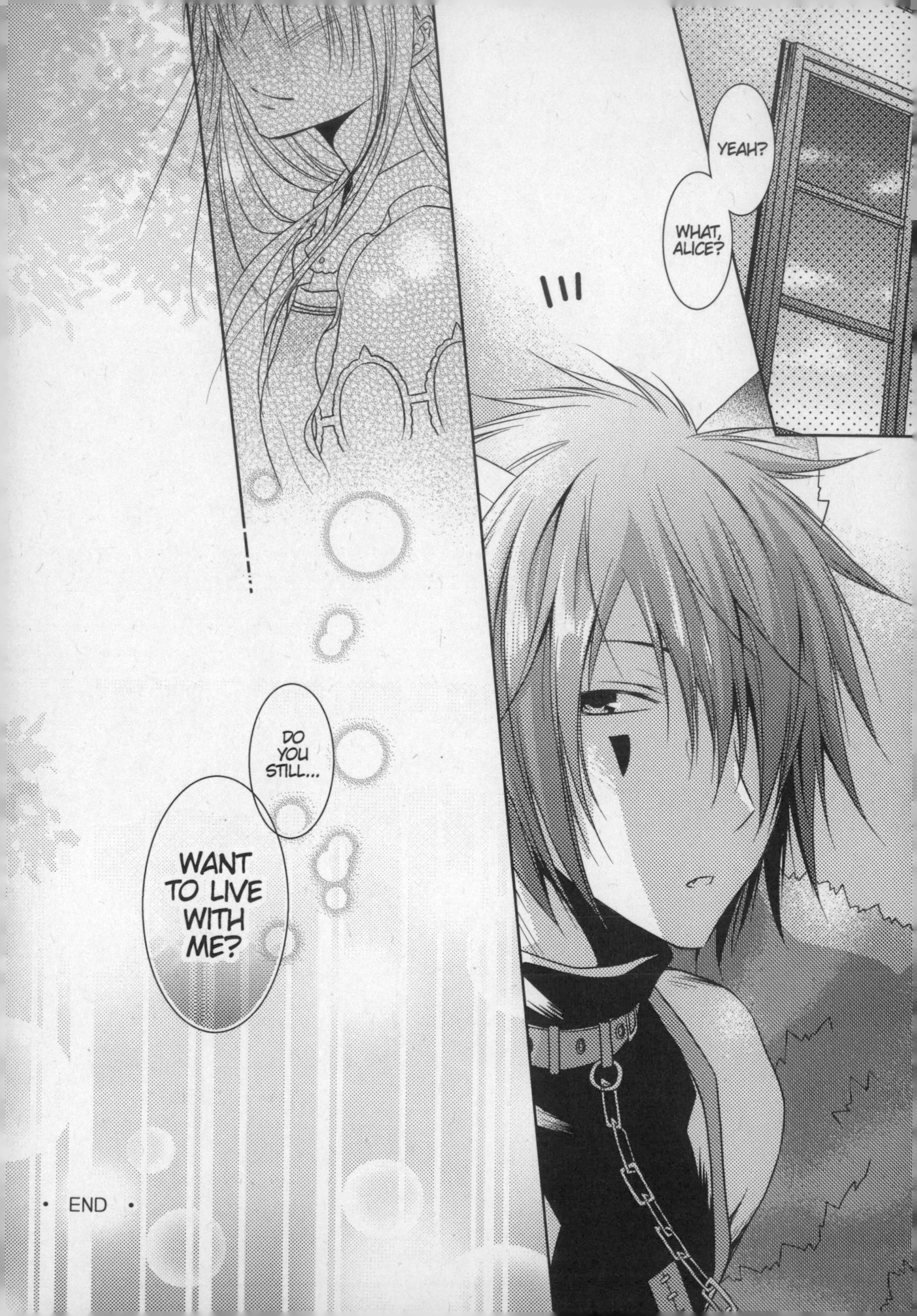
YEAH?
WHAT, ALICE?
DO YOU STILL...
WANT TO LIVE WITH ME?
• END •

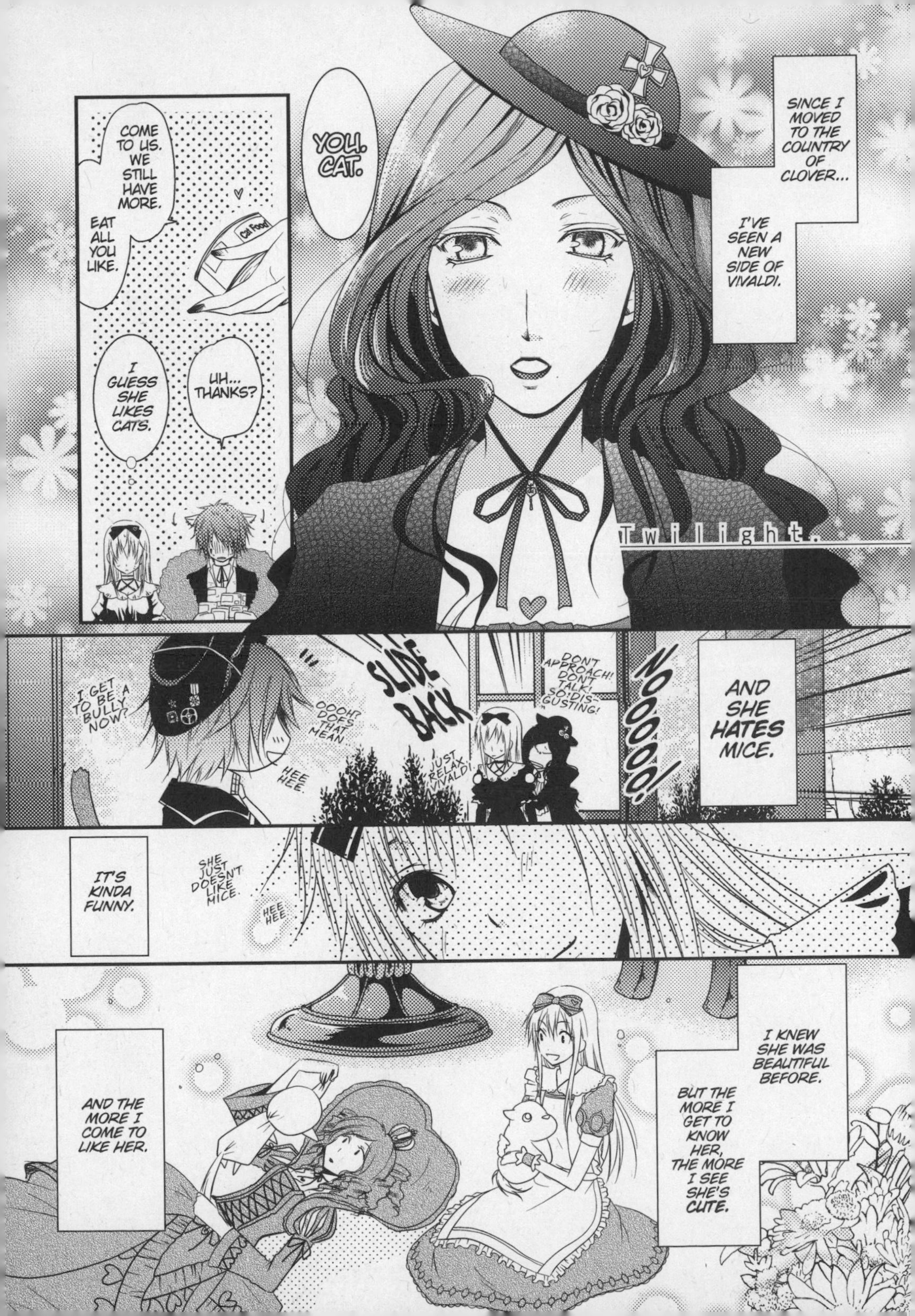
SINCE I MOVED TO THE COUNTRY OF CLOVER...
I'VE SEEN A NEW SIDE OF VIVALDI.
YOU. CAT.
Twilight.
COME TO US. WE STILL HAVE MORE.
EAT ALL YOU LIKE.
Cat Food
UH... THANKS?
I GUESS SHE LIKES CATS.
AND SHE HATES MICE.
NOOOOOO!
DON'T APPROACH! DON'T TALK! SO DIS-GUSTING!
JUST RELAX, VIVALDI.
SLIDE BACK
OOOH? DOES THAT MEAN
I GET TO BE A BULLY NOW?
HEE HEE.
SHE JUST DOESN'T LIKE MICE.
HEE HEE
IT'S KINDA FUNNY.
I KNEW SHE WAS BEAUTIFUL BEFORE.
BUT THE MORE I GET TO KNOW HER, THE MORE I SEE SHE'S CUTE.
AND THE MORE I COME TO LIKE HER.

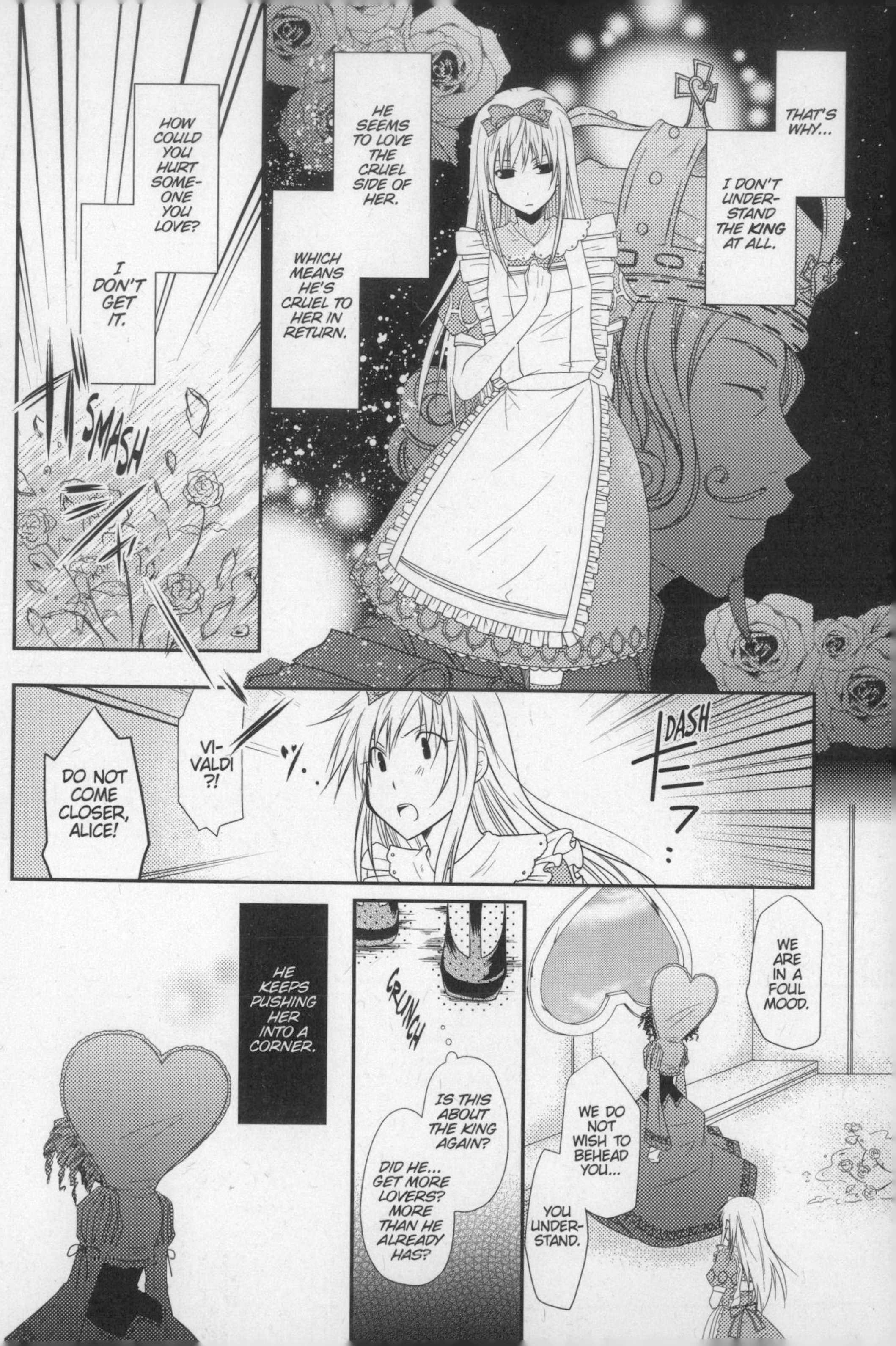
THAT'S WHY...
I DON'T UNDER-STAND THE KING AT ALL.
HE SEEMS TO LOVE THE CRUEL SIDE OF HER.
WHICH MEANS HE'S CRUEL TO HER IN RETURN.
HOW COULD YOU HURT SOME-ONE YOU LOVE?
I DON'T GET IT.
SMASH
DASH
VI-VALDI ?!
DO NOT COME CLOSER, ALICE!
WE ARE IN A FOUL MOOD.
WE DO NOT WISH TO BEHEAD YOU...
YOU UNDER-STAND.
IS THIS ABOUT THE KING AGAIN?
DID HE... GET MORE LOVERS? MORE THAN HE ALREADY HAS?
CRUNCH
HE KEEPS PUSHING HER INTO A CORNER.

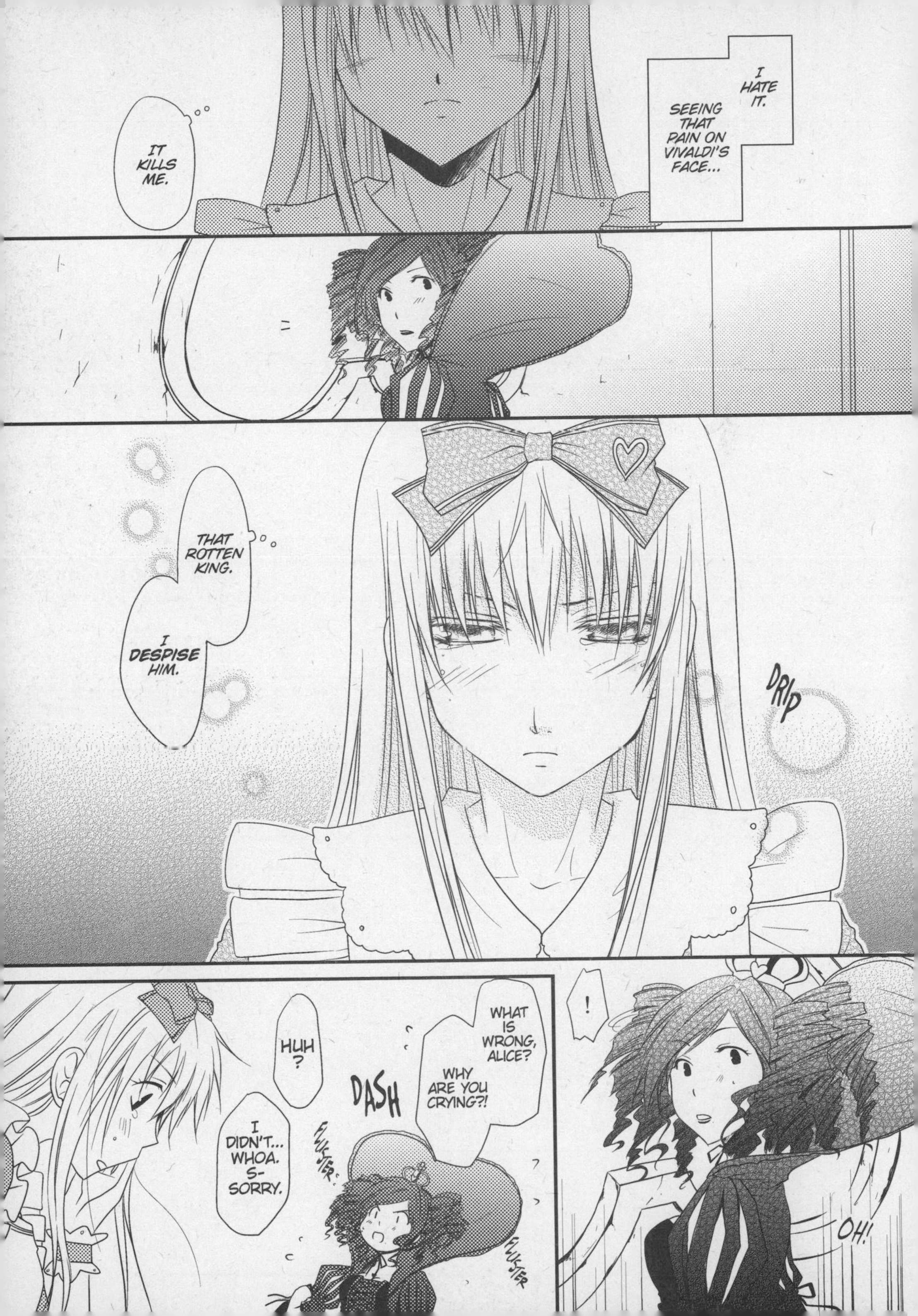
I HATE IT.
SEEING THAT PAIN ON VIVALDI'S FACE...
IT KILLS ME.
THAT ROTTEN KING.
I DESPISE HIM.
DRIP
!
OH!
WHAT IS WRONG, ALICE?
WHY ARE YOU CRYING?!
HUH?
DASH
I DIDN'T... WHOA. S-SORRY.
FLUSTER
FLUSTER

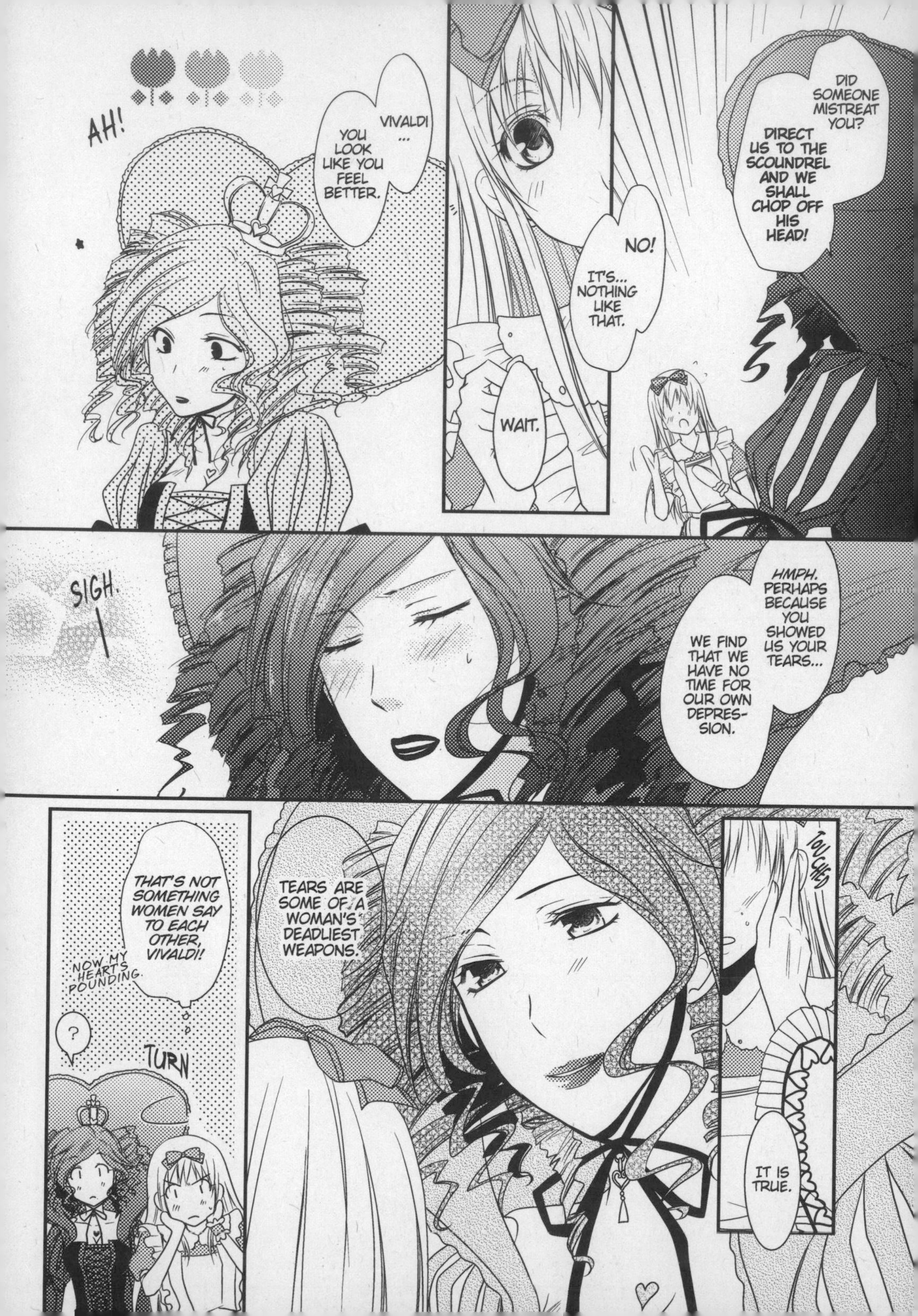
DID SOMEONE MISTREAT YOU? DIRECT US TO THE SCOUNDREL AND WE SHALL CHOP OFF HIS HEAD!
NO!
IT'S... NOTHING LIKE THAT.
WAIT.
AH!
VIVALDI ...
YOU LOOK LIKE YOU FEEL BETTER.
HMPH. PERHAPS BECAUSE YOU SHOWED US YOUR TEARS...
WE FIND THAT WE HAVE NO TIME FOR OUR OWN DEPRESSION.
SIGH.
TOUCHED
IT IS TRUE.
TEARS ARE SOME OF A WOMAN'S DEADLIEST WEAPONS.
THAT'S NOT SOMETHING WOMEN SAY TO EACH OTHER, VIVALDI!
NOW MY HEART'S POUNDING.
TURN
?

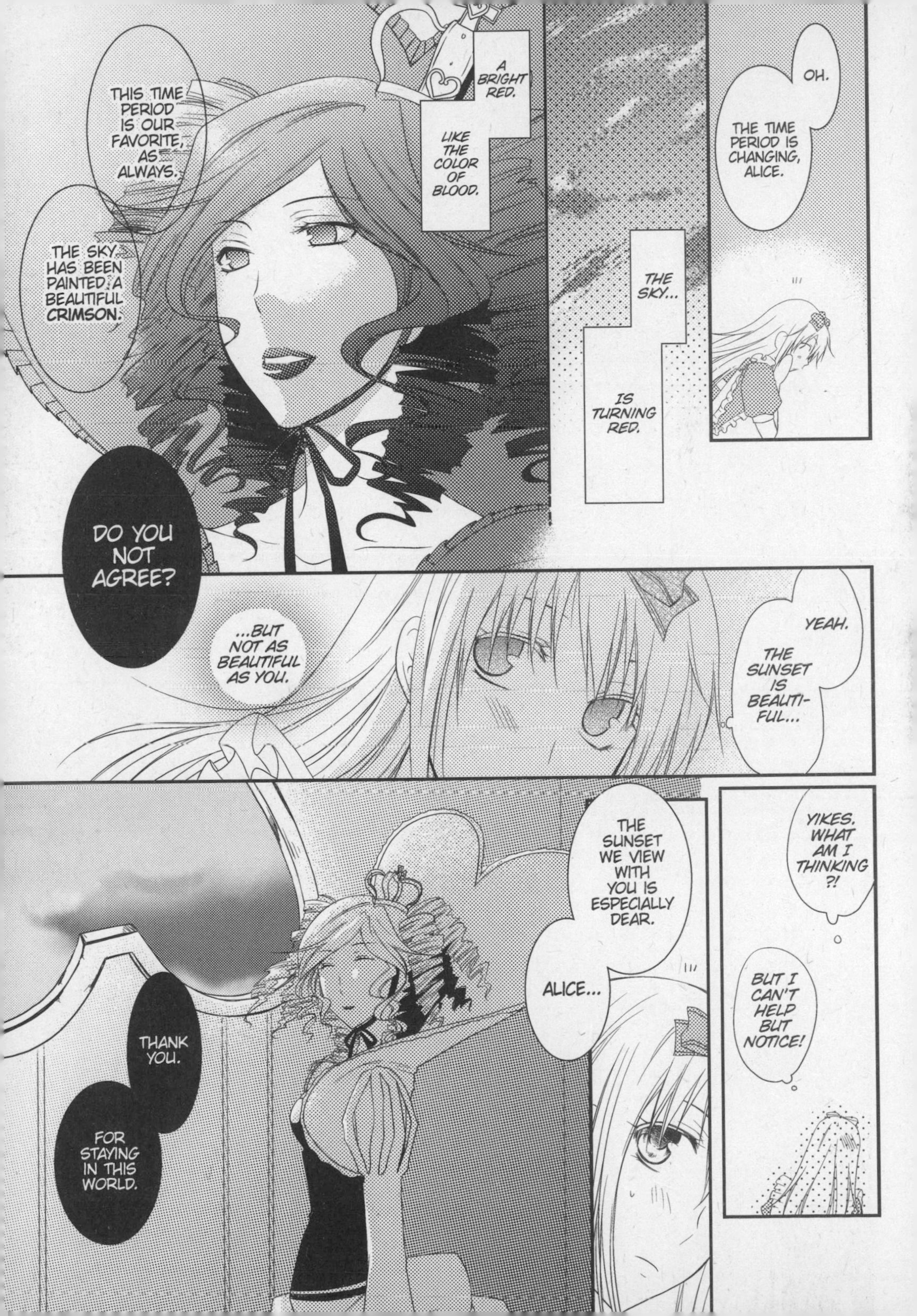
OH.
THE TIME PERIOD IS CHANGING, ALICE.
THE SKY...
IS TURNING RED.
A BRIGHT RED.
LIKE THE COLOR OF BLOOD.
THIS TIME PERIOD IS OUR FAVORITE, AS ALWAYS.
THE SKY HAS BEEN PAINTED A BEAUTIFUL CRIMSON.
DO YOU NOT AGREE?
YEAH.
THE SUNSET IS BEAUTI-FUL...
...BUT NOT AS BEAUTIFUL AS YOU.
YIKES. WHAT AM I THINKING?!
BUT I CAN'T HELP BUT NOTICE!
THE SUNSET WE VIEW WITH YOU IS ESPECIALLY DEAR.
ALICE...
THANK YOU.
FOR STAYING IN THIS WORLD.

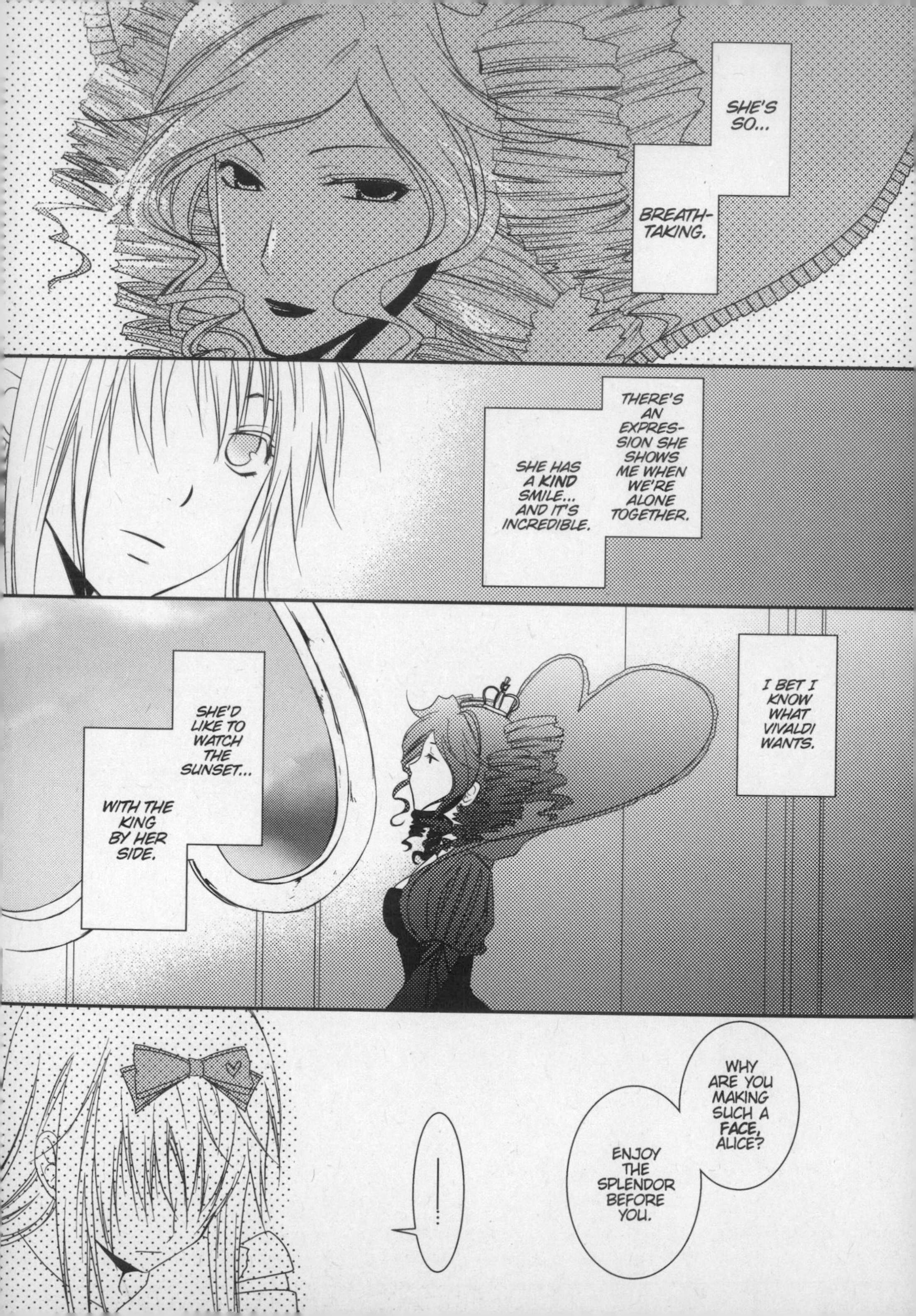
SHE'S SO...
BREATH-TAKING.
THERE'S AN EXPRES-SION SHE SHOWS ME WHEN WE'RE ALONE TOGETHER.
SHE HAS A **KIND** SMILE... AND IT'S INCREDIBLE.
I BET I KNOW WHAT VIVALDI WANTS.
SHE'D LIKE TO WATCH THE SUNSET...
WITH THE KING BY HER SIDE.
WHY ARE YOU MAKING SUCH A FACE, ALICE?
ENJOY THE SPLENDOR BEFORE YOU.
—!...

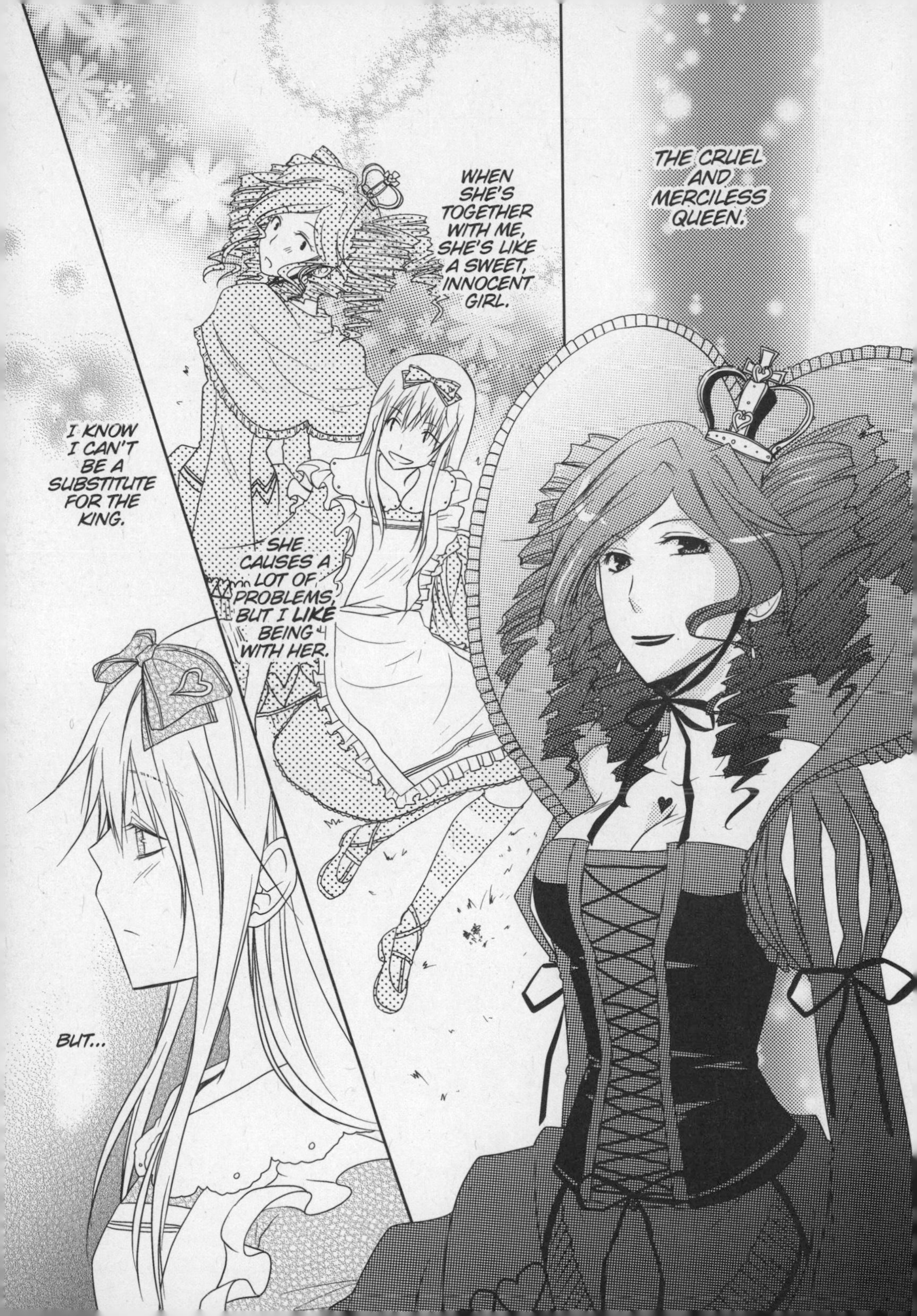
THE CRUEL AND MERCILESS QUEEN.
WHEN SHE'S TOGETHER WITH ME, SHE'S LIKE A SWEET, INNOCENT GIRL.
SHE CAUSES A LOT OF PROBLEMS, BUT I LIKE BEING WITH HER.
I KNOW I CAN'T BE A SUBSTITUTE FOR THE KING.
BUT...

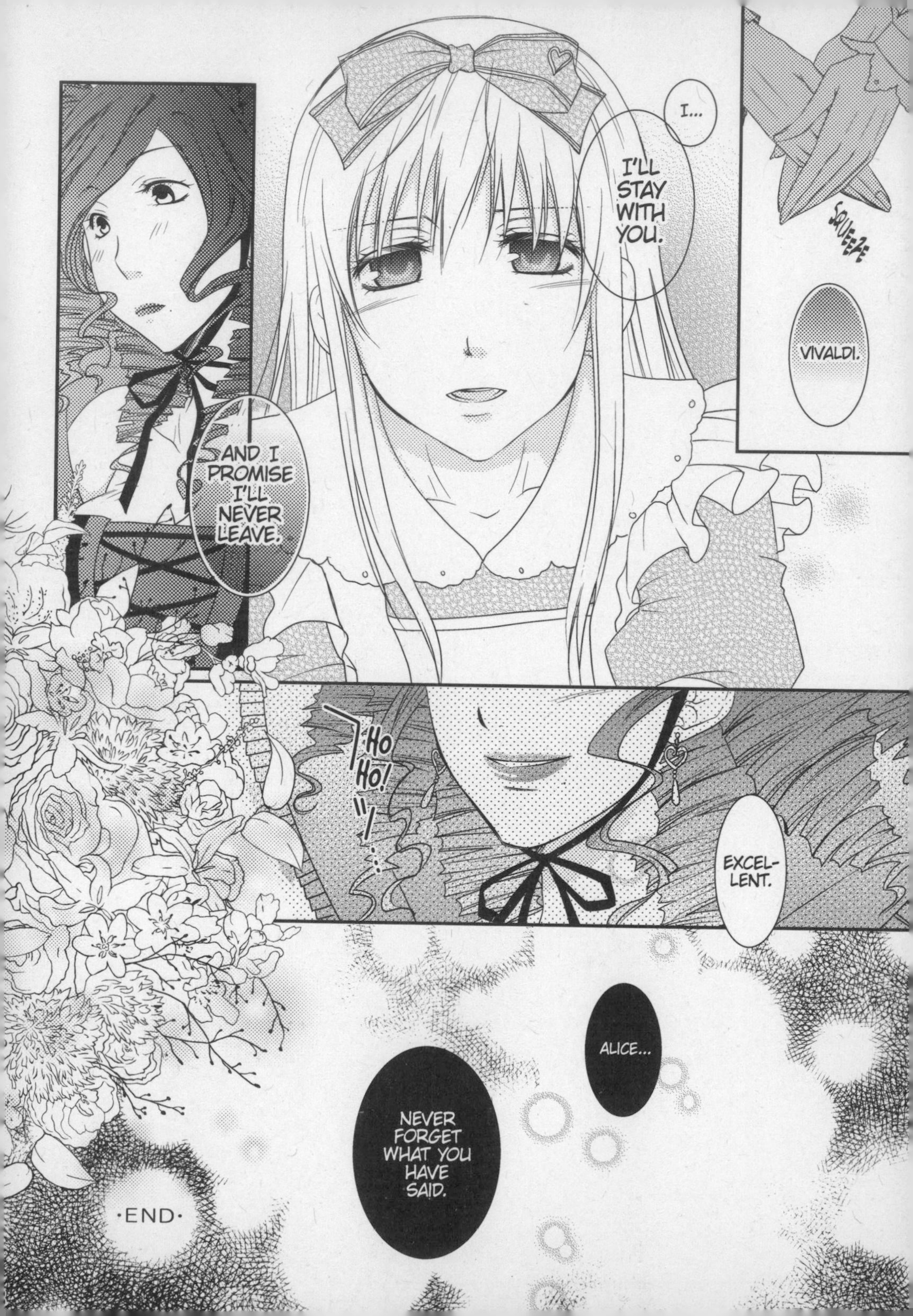
SQUEEZE
VIVALDI.
I...
I'LL STAY WITH YOU.
AND I PROMISE I'LL NEVER LEAVE.
HO HO!
EXCEL-LENT.
ALICE...
NEVER FORGET WHAT YOU HAVE SAID.
·END·

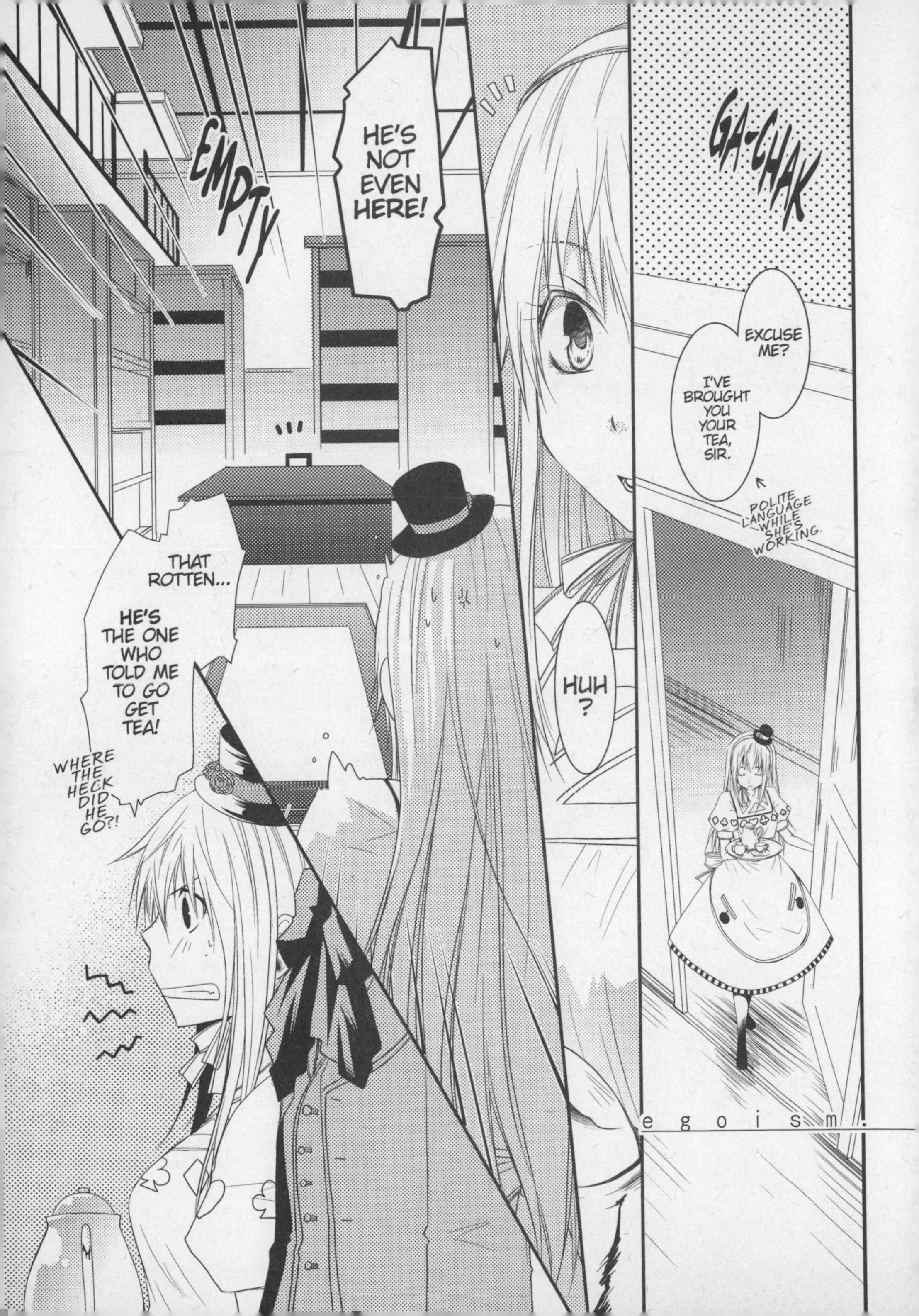
GA-CHAK
EXCUSE ME?
I'VE BROUGHT YOU YOUR TEA, SIR.
POLITE LANGUAGE WHILE SHE'S WORKING.
egoism.
HUH?
EMPTY
HE'S NOT EVEN HERE!
THAT ROTTEN...
HE'S THE ONE WHO TOLD ME TO GO GET TEA!
WHERE THE HECK DID HE GO?!

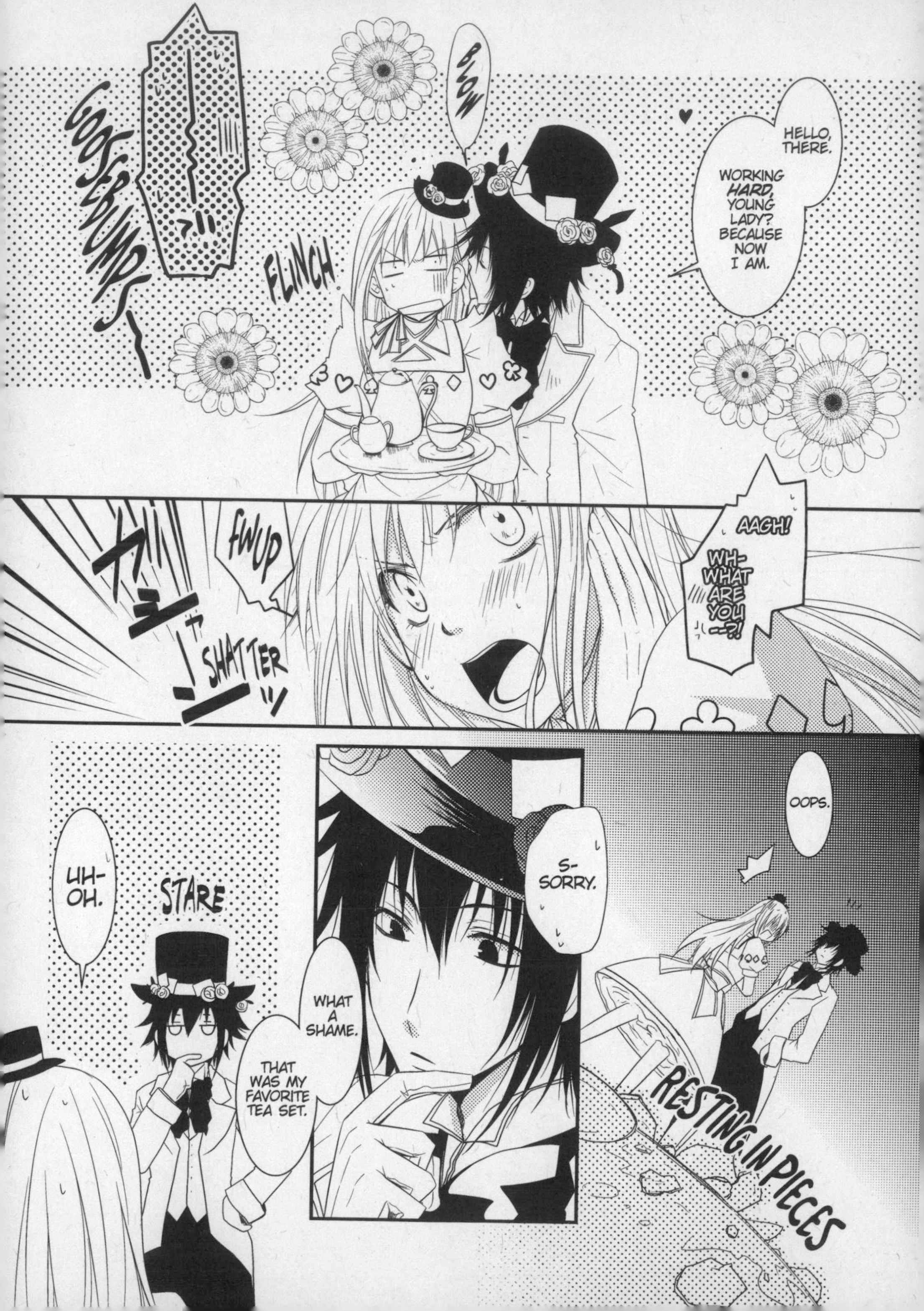
HELLO, THERE.
WORKING HARD, YOUNG LADY? BECAUSE NOW I AM.
BLOW
FLINCH
--?!
GOOSEBUMPS~
AAGH!
WH-WHAT ARE YOU --?!
FWUP
SHATTER
OOPS.
RESTING IN PIECES
S-SORRY.
WHAT A SHAME.
THAT WAS MY FAVORITE TEA SET.
UH-OH.
STARE

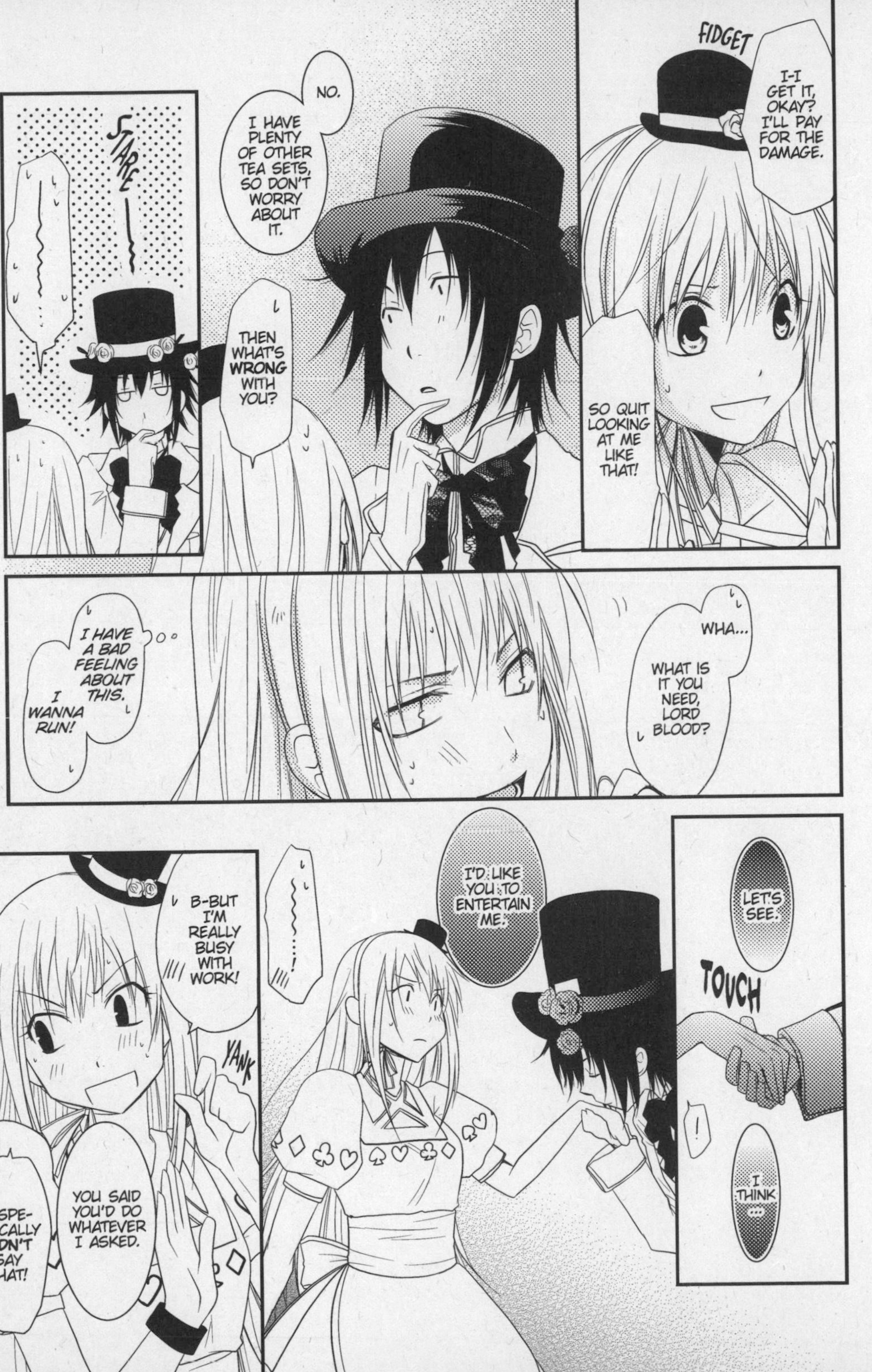
FIDGET
I-I GET IT, OKAY? I'LL PAY FOR THE DAMAGE.
SO QUIT LOOKING AT ME LIKE THAT!
NO.
I HAVE PLENTY OF OTHER TEA SETS, SO DON'T WORRY ABOUT IT.
THEN WHAT'S **WRONG** WITH YOU?
STARE
WHA...
WHAT IS IT YOU NEED, LORD BLOOD?
I HAVE A BAD FEELING ABOUT THIS. I WANNA RUN!
LET'S SEE.
TOUCH
!
I THINK...
I'D LIKE YOU TO ENTERTAIN ME.
B-BUT I'M REALLY BUSY WITH WORK!
YANK
YOU SAID YOU'D DO WHATEVER I ASKED.
I SPE-CIFICALLY **DIDN'T** SAY THAT!

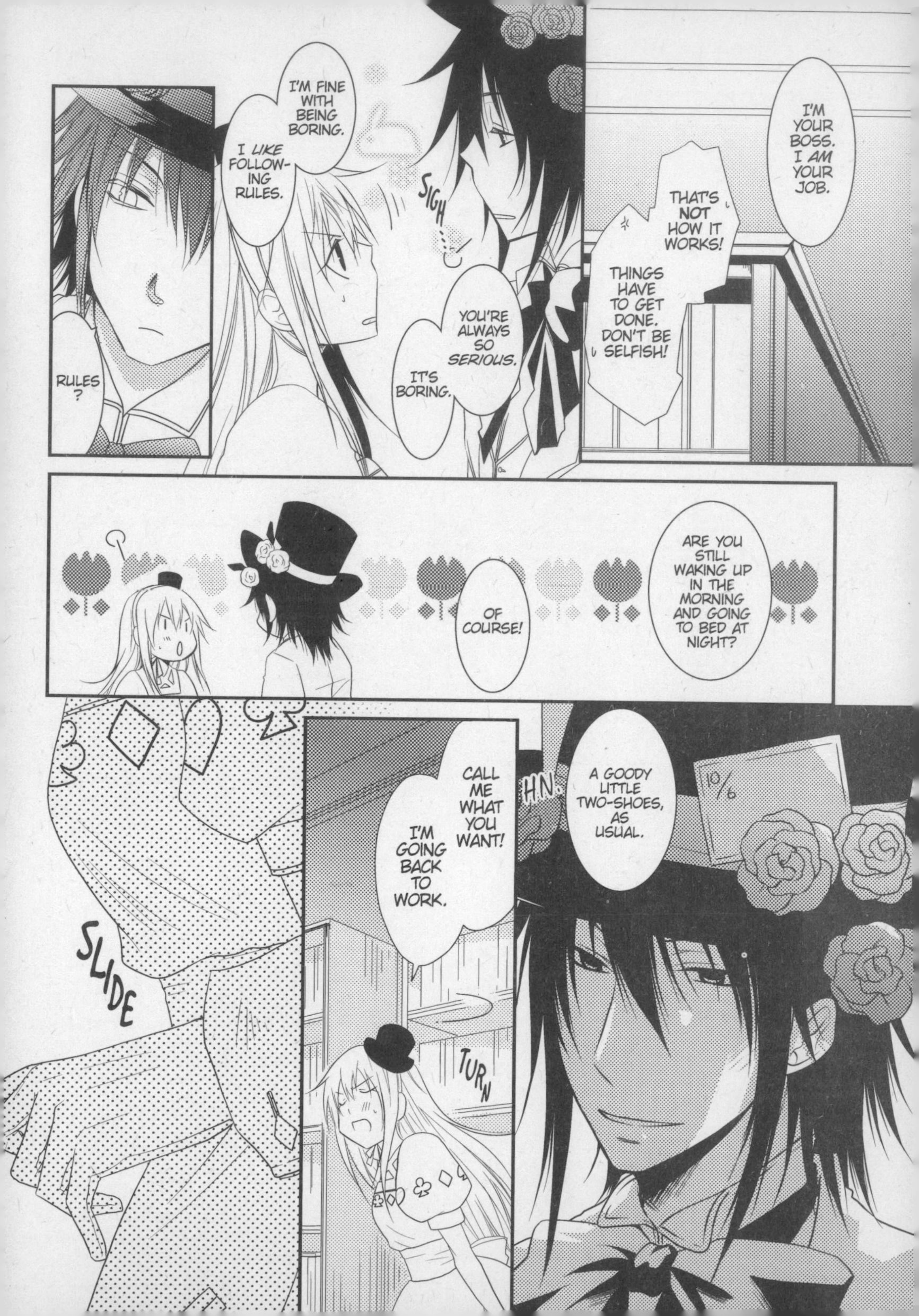
I'M YOUR BOSS. I *AM* YOUR JOB.
THAT'S NOT HOW IT WORKS!
THINGS HAVE TO GET DONE. DON'T BE SELFISH!
YOU'RE ALWAYS SO *SERIOUS.*
IT'S BORING.
SIGH
I'M FINE WITH BEING BORING.
I *LIKE* FOLLOWING RULES.
RULES?
ARE YOU STILL WAKING UP IN THE MORNING AND GOING TO BED AT NIGHT?
OF COURSE!
10/6
A GOODY LITTLE TWO-SHOES, AS USUAL.
HN.
CALL ME WHAT YOU WANT!
I'M GOING BACK TO WORK.
TURN
SLIDE

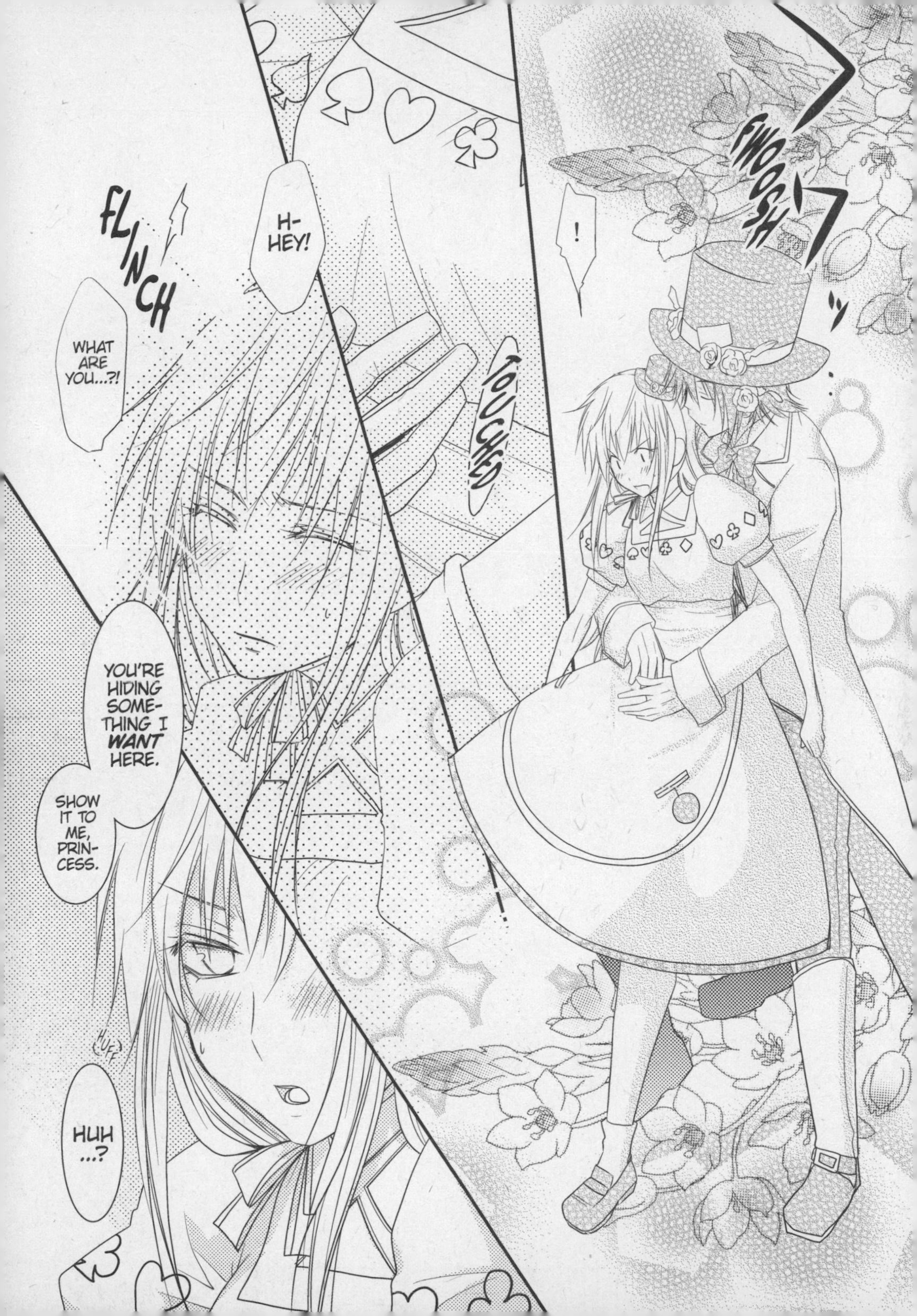
FWOOSH
!
ッ
TOUCHED
H-HEY!
FLINCH
WHAT ARE YOU...?!
YOU'RE HIDING SOMETHING I *WANT* HERE.
SHOW IT TO ME, PRINCESS.
HUFF
HUH ...?

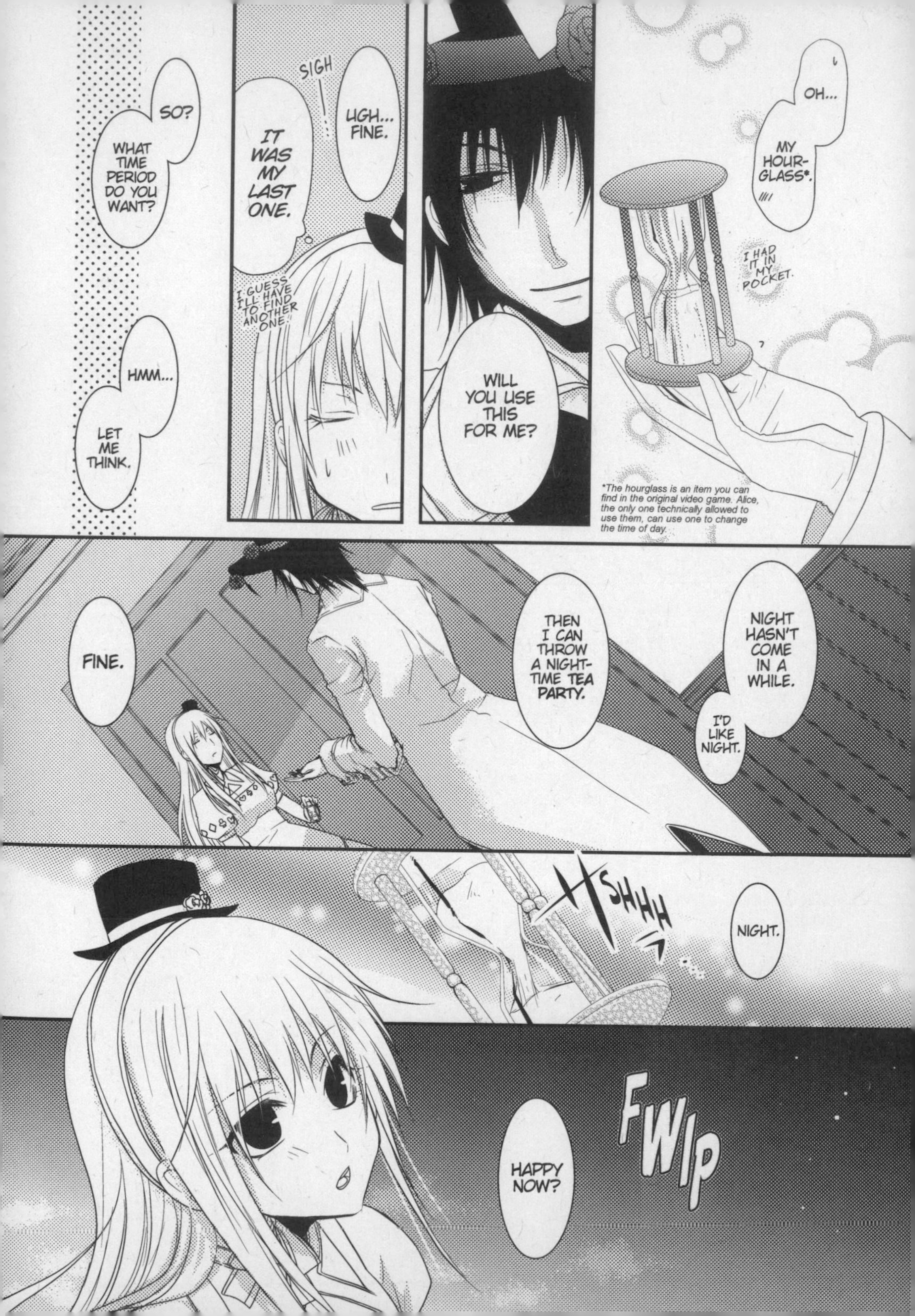
OH...
MY HOURGLASS*.
I HAD IT IN MY POCKET.
WILL YOU USE THIS FOR ME?
SIGH
UGH... FINE.
IT WAS MY LAST ONE.
I GUESS I'LL HAVE TO FIND ANOTHER ONE.
SO?
WHAT TIME PERIOD DO YOU WANT?
HMM...
LET ME THINK.
NIGHT HASN'T COME IN A WHILE.
I'D LIKE NIGHT.
THEN I CAN THROW A NIGHT-TIME TEA PARTY.
FINE.
NIGHT.
SHHH
FWIP
HAPPY NOW?
*The hourglass is an item you can find in the original video game. Alice, the only one technically allowed to use them, can use one to change the time of day.

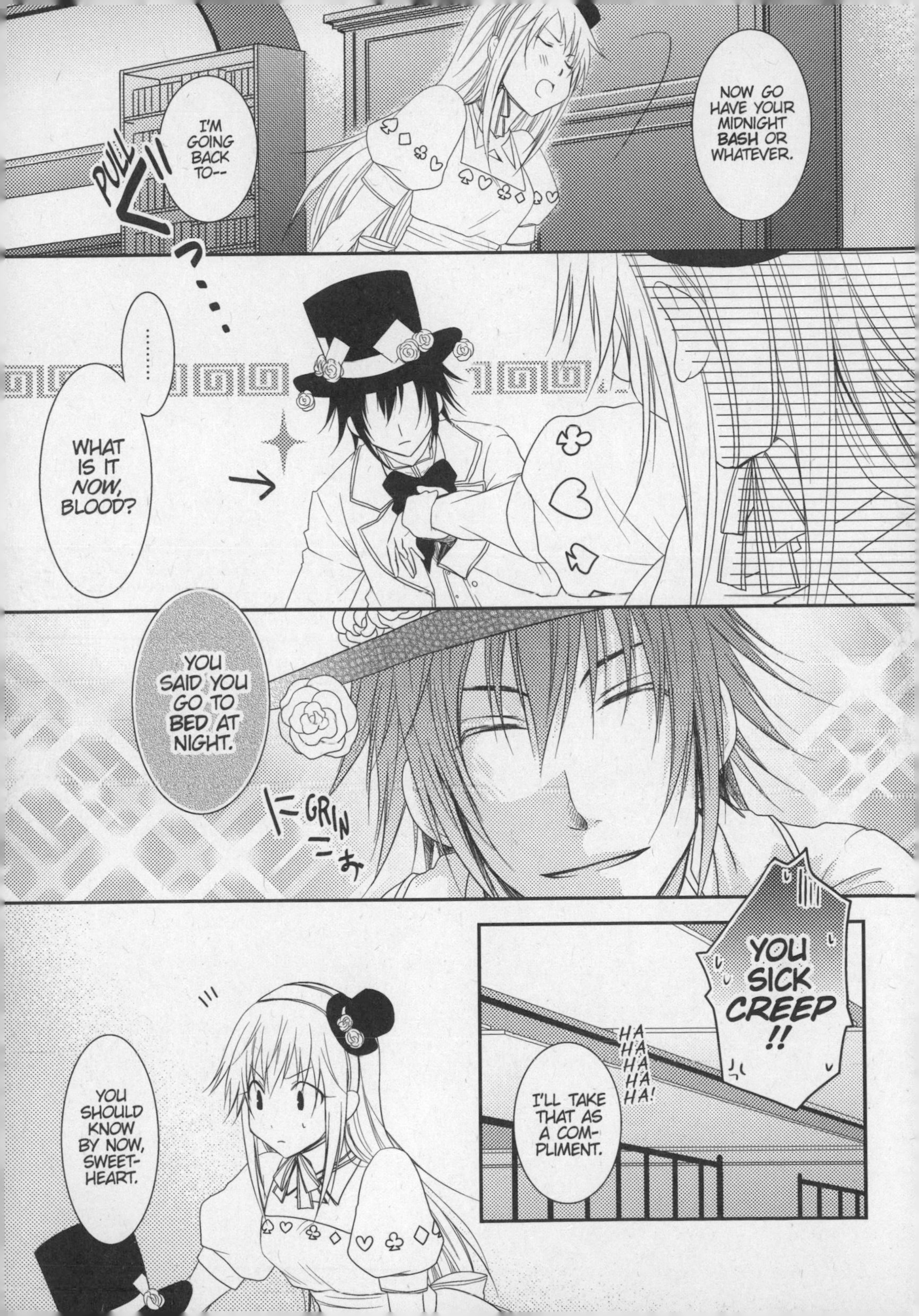
NOW GO HAVE YOUR MIDNIGHT BASH OR WHATEVER.
I'M GOING BACK TO--
PULL
...
......
WHAT IS IT NOW, BLOOD?
YOU SAID YOU GO TO BED AT NIGHT.
GRIN
YOU SICK CREEP!!
HAHAHAHAHA!
I'LL TAKE THAT AS A COM-PLIMENT.
YOU SHOULD KNOW BY NOW, SWEET-HEART.

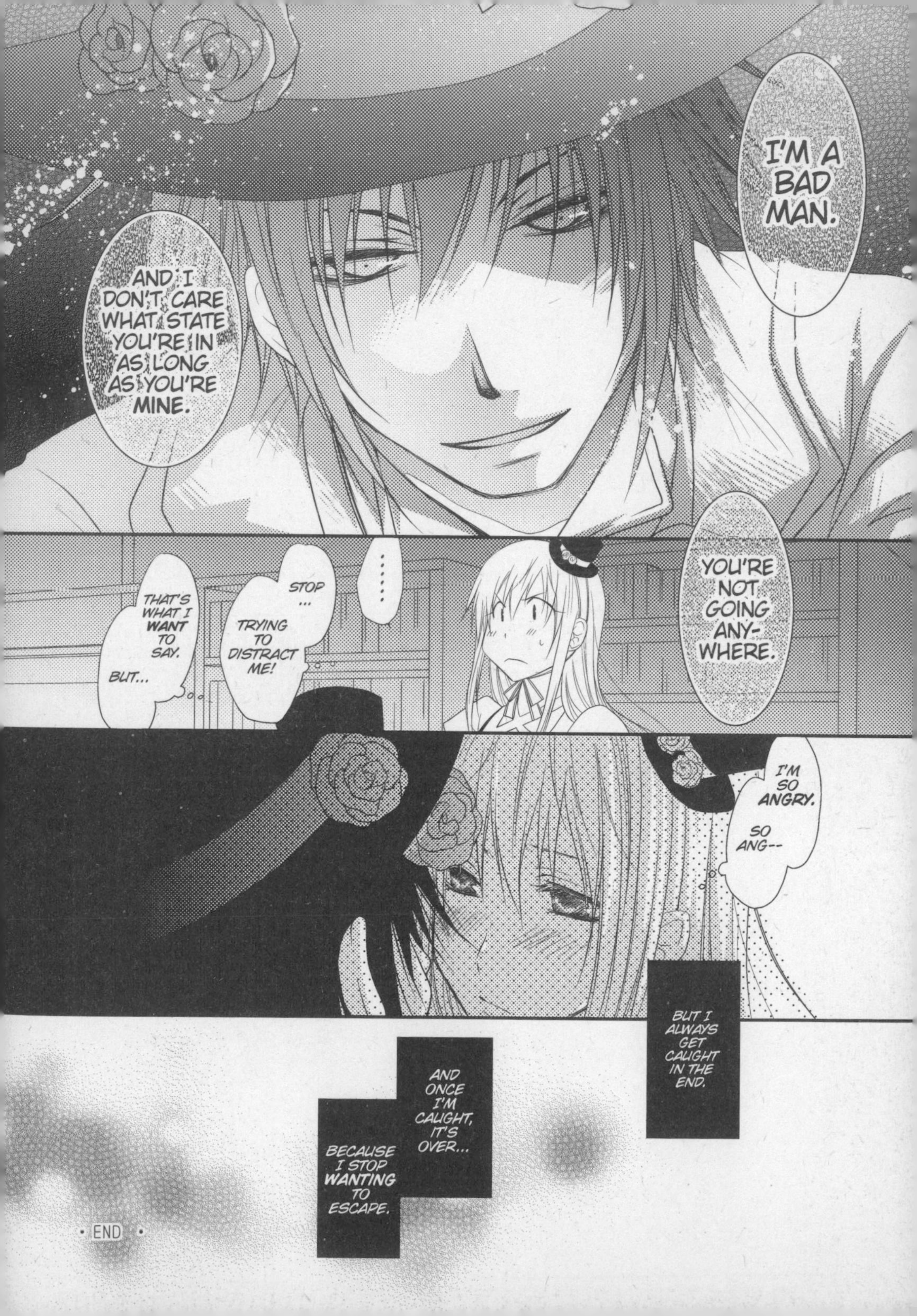
I'M A BAD MAN.
AND I DON'T CARE WHAT STATE YOU'RE IN AS LONG AS YOU'RE MINE.
YOU'RE NOT GOING ANY-WHERE.
......
STOP ... TRYING TO DISTRACT ME!
THAT'S WHAT I WANT TO SAY. BUT...
I'M SO ANGRY.
SO ANG--
BUT I ALWAYS GET CAUGHT IN THE END.
AND ONCE I'M CAUGHT, IT'S OVER...
BECAUSE I STOP WANTING TO ESCAPE.
• END •

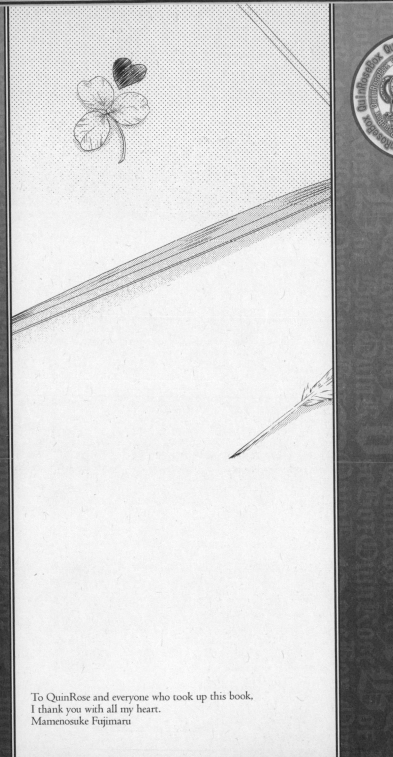

To QuinRose and everyone who took up this book,
I thank you with all my heart.
Mamenosuke Fujimaru

BLOODY TWINS - STAGE: 1 - POST-MORTEM

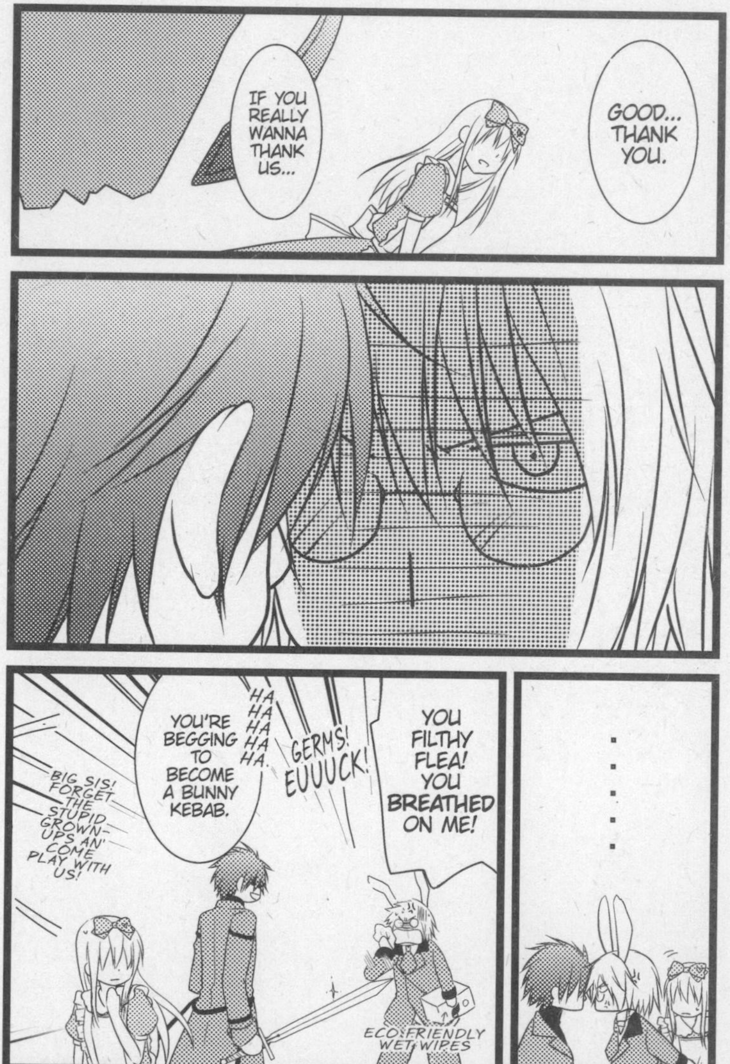
GOOD... THANK YOU.
IF YOU REALLY WANNA THANK US...
......
YOU FILTHY FLEA! YOU BREATHED ON ME!
GERMS! EUUUCK!
HA HA HA HA HA.
YOU'RE BEGGING TO BECOME A BUNNY KEBAB.
BIG SIS! FORGET THE STUPID GROWN-UPS AN' COME PLAY WITH US!
ECO-FRIENDLY WET WIPES

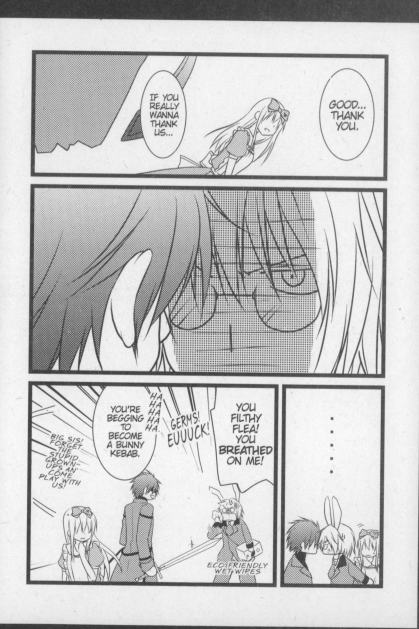

BLOODY TWINS - STAGE: 3 - POST-MORTEM

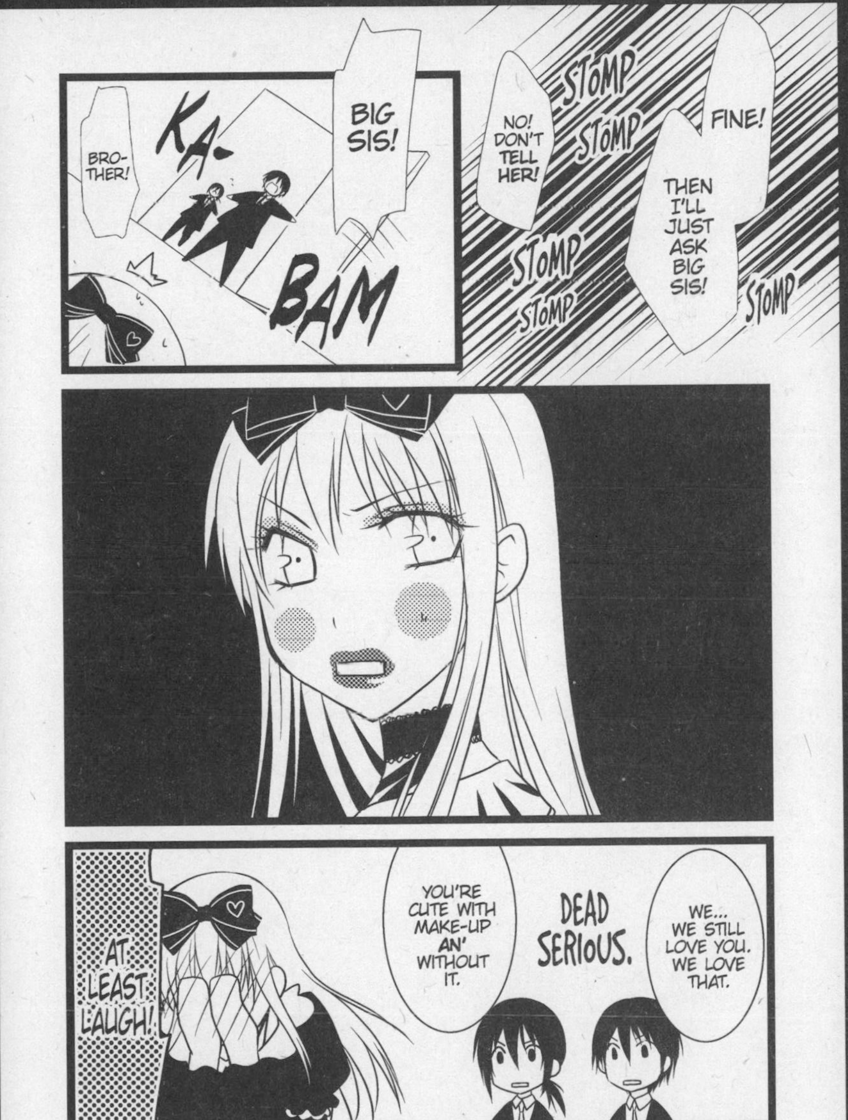
FINE!
STOMP
STOMP
NO! DON'T TELL HER!
THEN I'LL JUST ASK BIG SIS!
STOMP
STOMP
STOMP
BIG SIS!
KA-
BROTHER!
BAM
WE... WE STILL LOVE YOU. WE LOVE THAT.
DEAD SERIOUS.
YOU'RE CUTE WITH MAKE-UP AN' WITHOUT IT.
AT LEAST LAUGH!

Alice in the Country of Clover

FUN FACTS

In *Alice in the Country of Clover*, Alice decided to stay in Wonderland, but didn't fall in love with anyone. The basic plot was explained at the beginning of the book, but here are a few character details that you might (or might not) find interesting to know!

- **Pierce** is very stupid and afraid of cats. The reason he drinks coffee (he hates it cause its bitter) is to stay awake so that he won't get attacked by Boris while he's sleeping. Pierce is a part of the Hatter Family, but is currently running away from home since Blood said he couldn't drink any coffee. He's a "cleaner" and cleans up dead bodies (usually to send them over to enemies before they turn into clocks) and is considered dirty by everyone in *Clover*. Julius and Ace dislike him because he makes it difficult to retrieve the clocks...

- **Vivaldi** actually likes the King. It's not clear if it's in a true love kind of way, but she was forced to become the Queen of Hearts when she was young and take on a "role". At first, Vivaldi was a faceless, as was Blood. When Vivaldi took on a role, Blood decided to take on a role as well. The King seems really weak, but actually he has the guts to have lovers all the time and leave Vivaldi alone. That is one of the reasons she feels so frustrated all the time. Blood and Vivaldi are brother and sister, but no one except Alice knows this. They meet in a secret garden of roses as brother and sister periodically, but still go all out to kill each other.

- **Boris** connects doors, so actually he can go to the Amusement Park and such. He uses this as a way to misguide Alice sometimes. The doors only talk to people who are lost and if Alice opens the door, she will go to the place she wants to most.

- **Ace** is crazy in *Clover*. Since Julius is gone, he lets loose his pent up frustration against Alice and Gray. Gray is the one person who is stronger than him. When Gray was young, he was a very bad guy and really similar to Ace. While this isn't overt in this book, it may appear randomly throughout other volumes.

- **Peter** is a total germaphobe. This is common knowledge from the first game, but it helps to explain why he has a box of wet wipes in the omake strip.

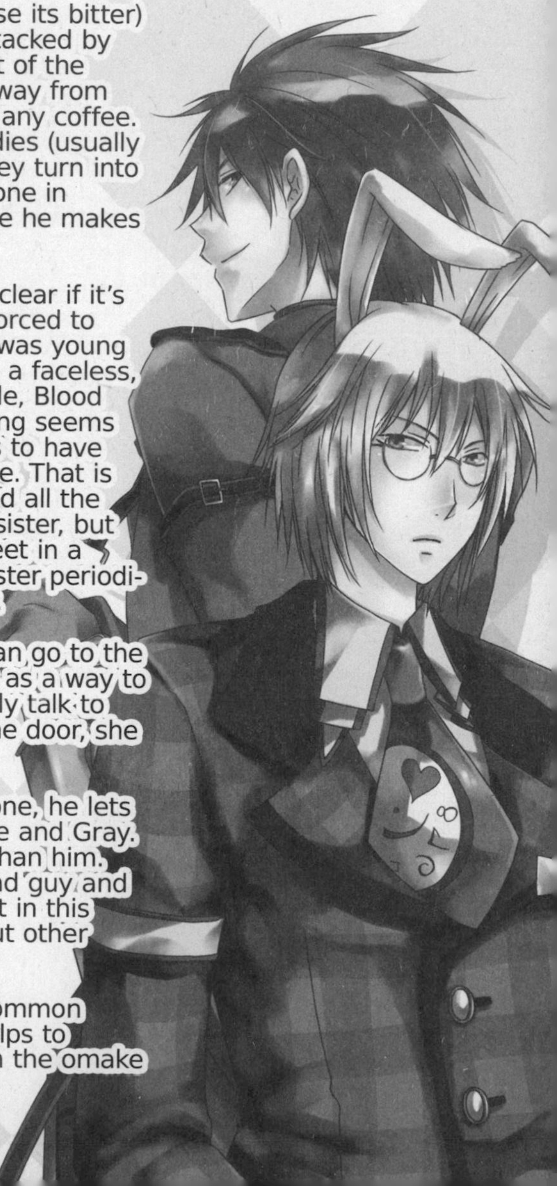

NEXT TIME...

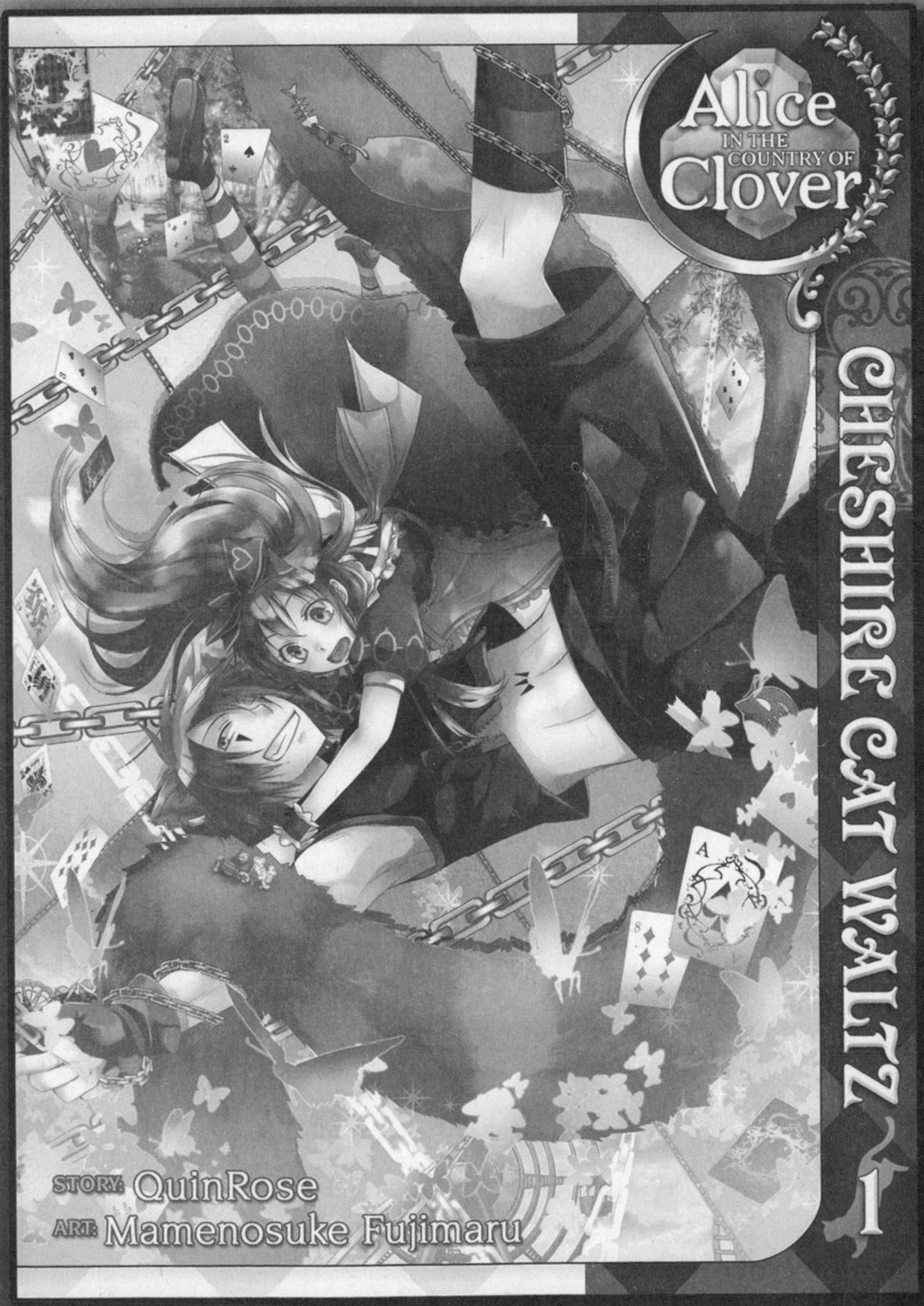
Alice
IN THE COUNTRY OF
Clover
CHESHIRE CAT WALTZ
1
STORY: QuinRose
ART: Mamenosuke Fujimaru

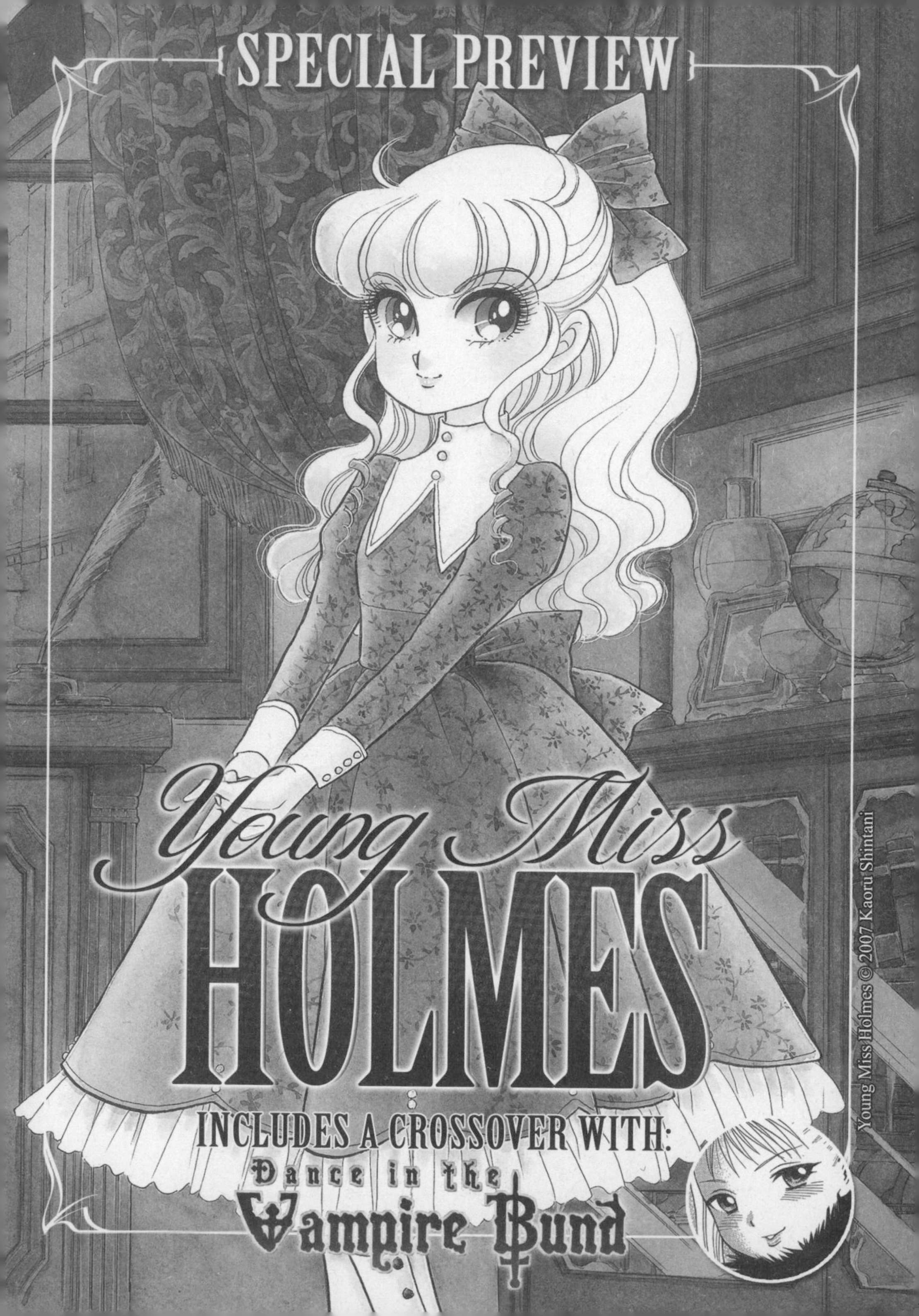
SPECIAL PREVIEW
Young Miss
HOLMES
INCLUDES A CROSSOVER WITH:
Dance in the
Vampire Bund
Young Miss Holmes © 2007 Kaoru Shintani

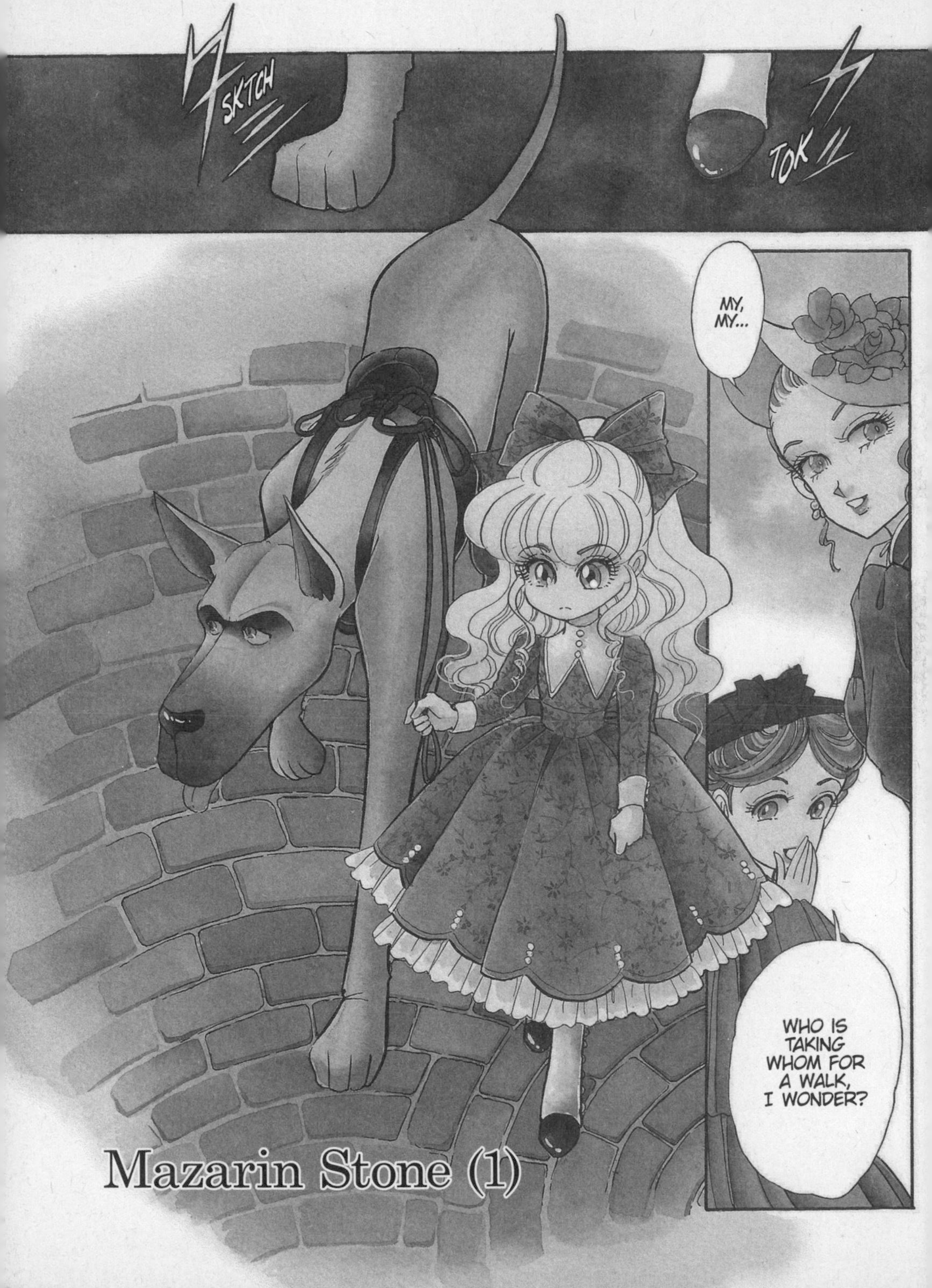
TOK
SKTCH
MY, MY...
WHO IS TAKING WHOM FOR A WALK, I WONDER?
Mazarin Stone (1)

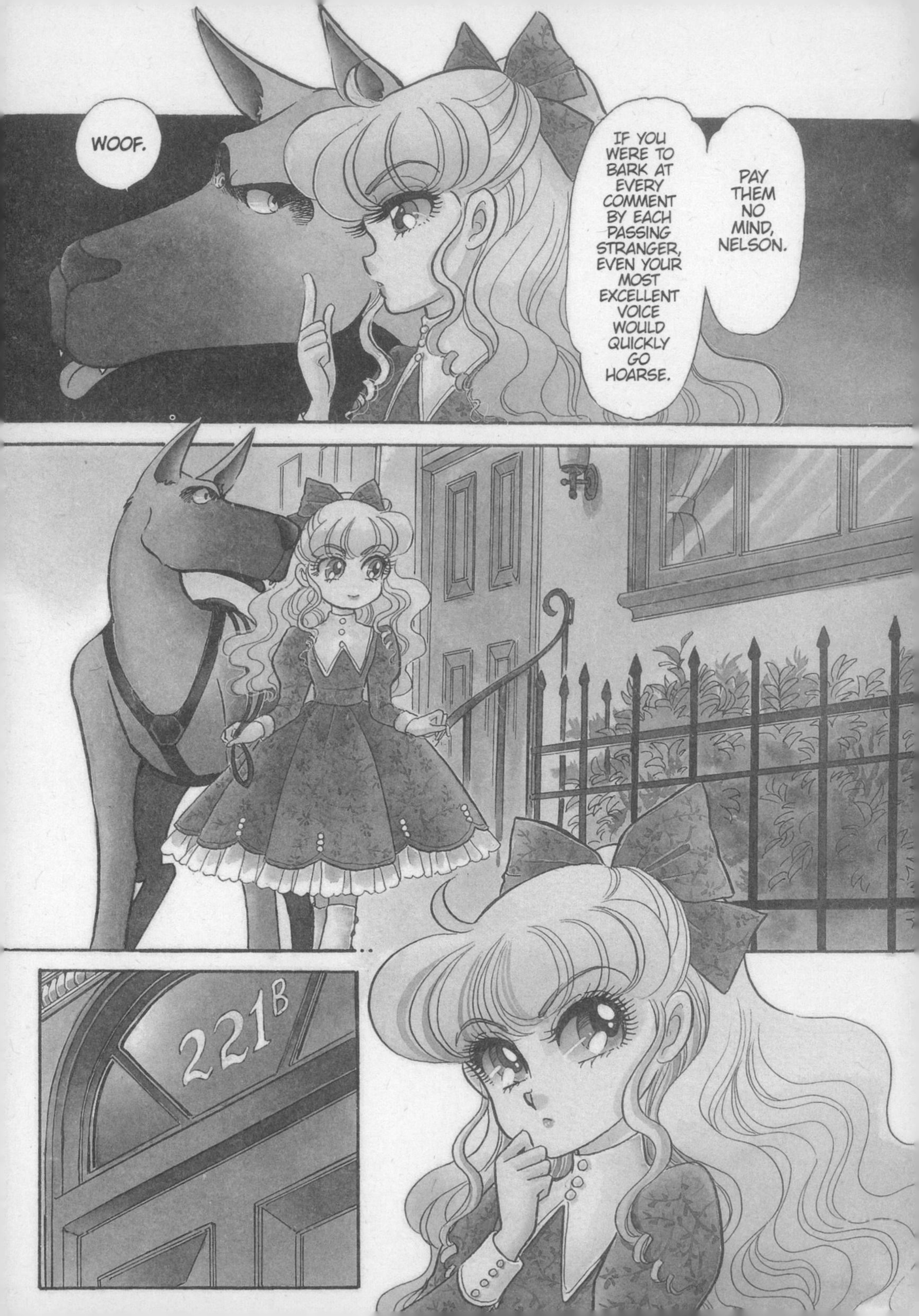
PAY THEM NO MIND, NELSON.
IF YOU WERE TO BARK AT EVERY COMMENT BY EACH PASSING STRANGER, EVEN YOUR MOST EXCELLENT VOICE WOULD QUICKLY GO HOARSE.
WOOF.
...
221B

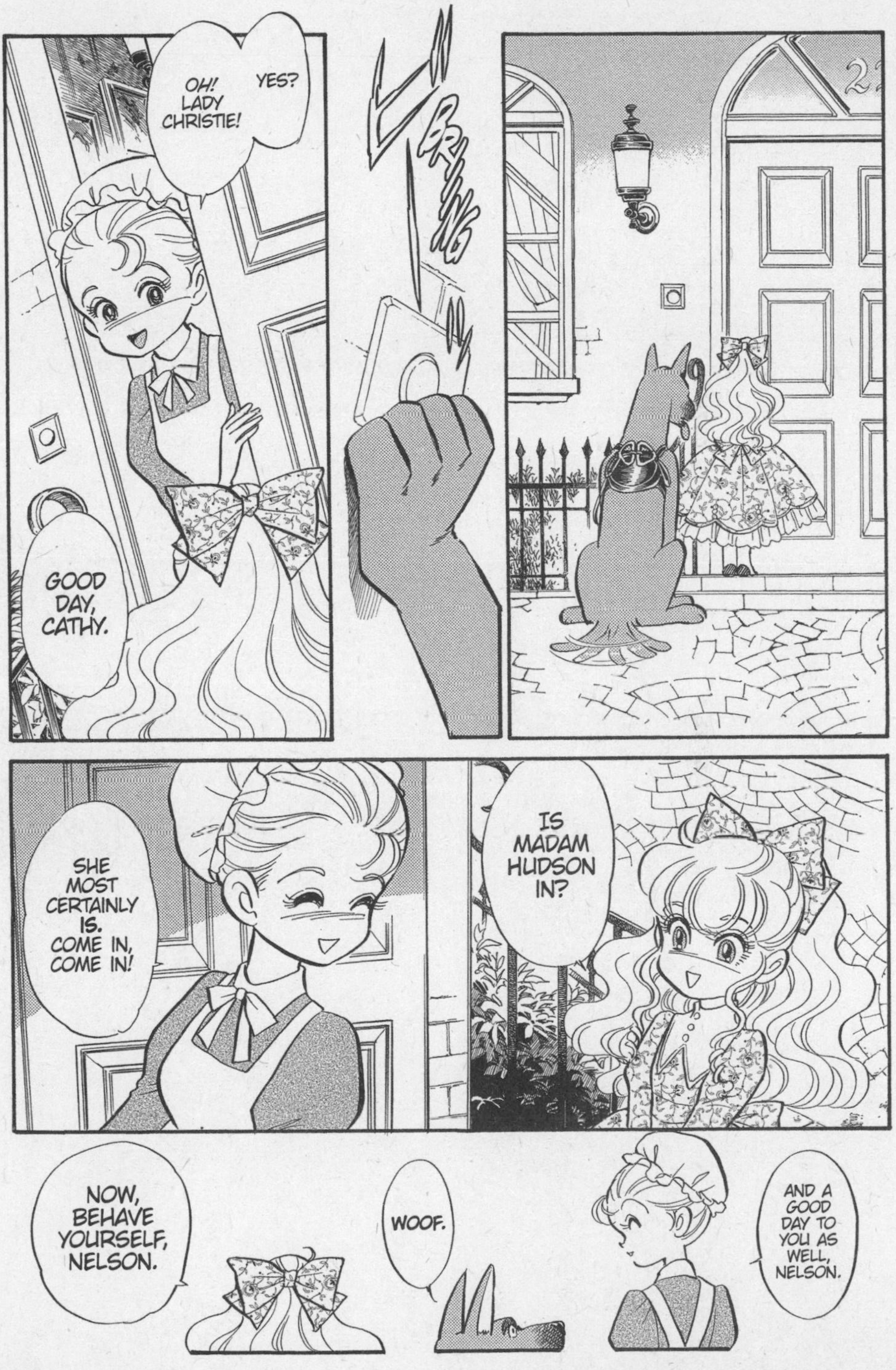
BRRING
YES?
OH! LADY CHRISTIE!
GOOD DAY, CATHY.
IS MADAM HUDSON IN?
SHE MOST CERTAINLY IS. COME IN, COME IN!
AND A GOOD DAY TO YOU AS WELL, NELSON.
WOOF.
NOW, BEHAVE YOURSELF, NELSON.

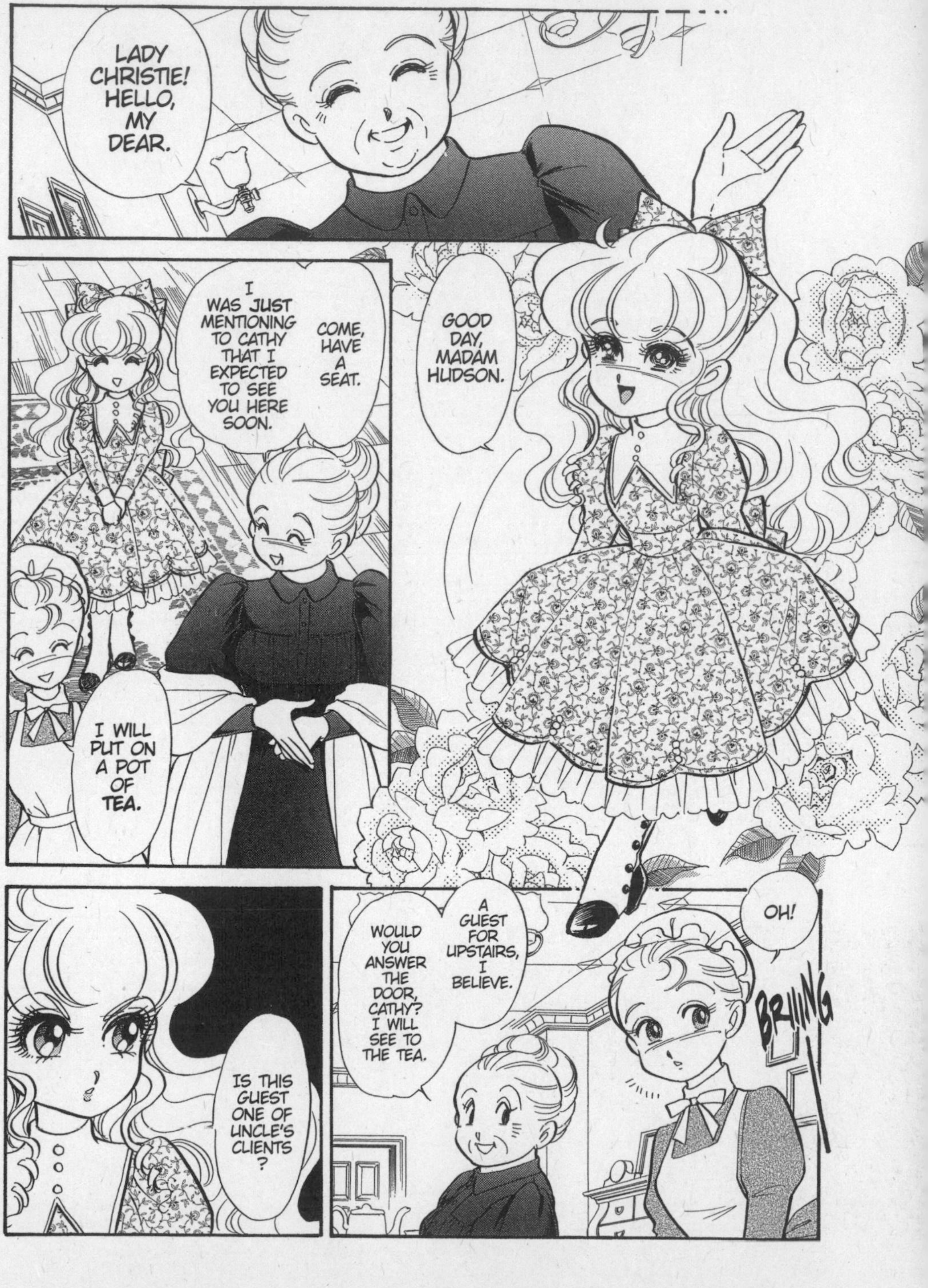
LADY CHRISTIE! HELLO, MY DEAR.
GOOD DAY, MADAM HUDSON.
I WAS JUST MENTIONING TO CATHY THAT I EXPECTED TO SEE YOU HERE SOON.
COME, HAVE A SEAT.
I WILL PUT ON A POT OF TEA.
OH!
BRIIING
A GUEST FOR UPSTAIRS, I BELIEVE.
WOULD YOU ANSWER THE DOOR, CATHY? I WILL SEE TO THE TEA.
IS THIS GUEST ONE OF UNCLE'S CLIENTS?

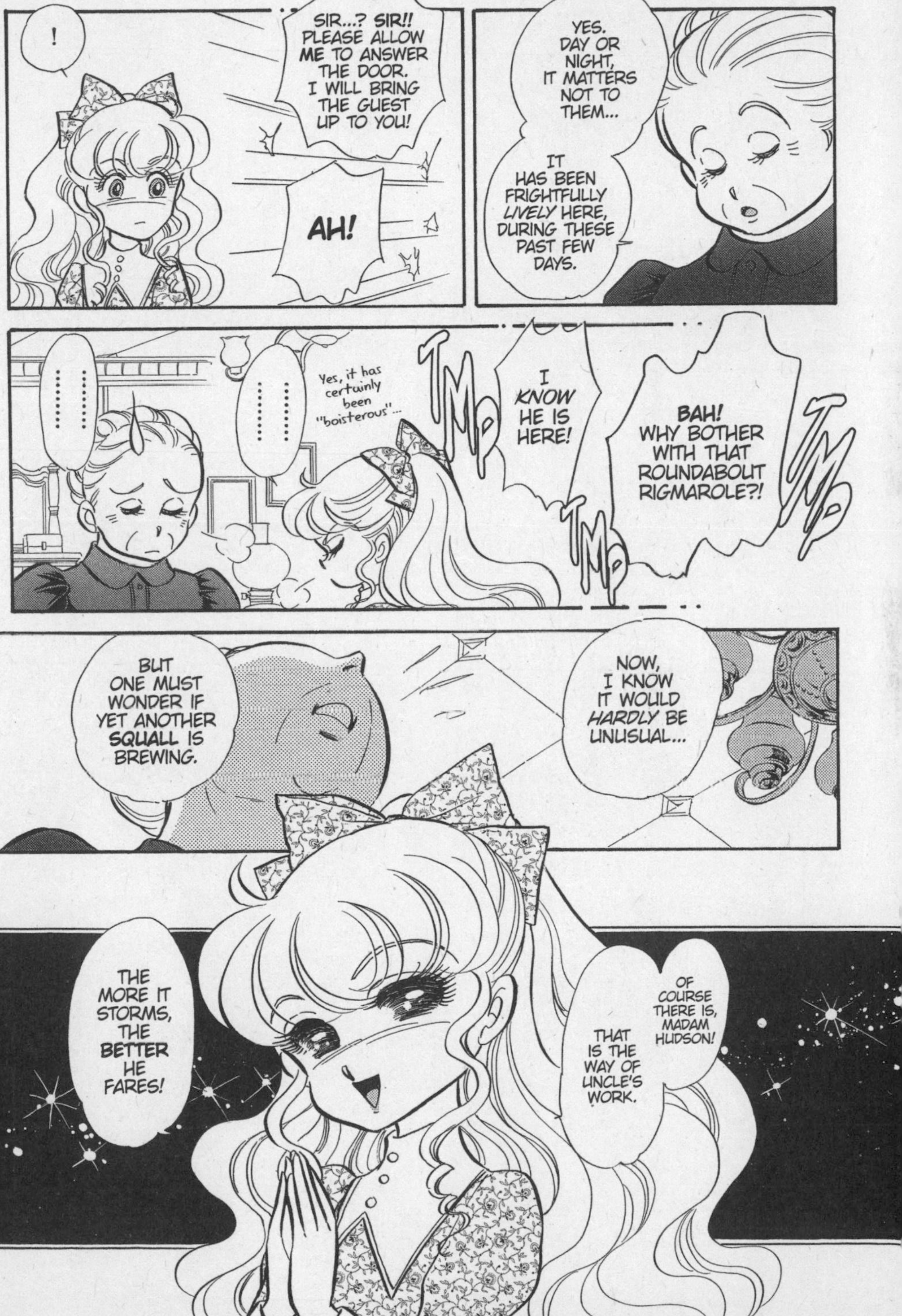
YES. DAY OR NIGHT, IT MATTERS NOT TO THEM...
IT HAS BEEN FRIGHTFULLY LIVELY HERE, DURING THESE PAST FEW DAYS.
SIR...? SIR!! PLEASE ALLOW ME TO ANSWER THE DOOR. I WILL BRING THE GUEST UP TO YOU!
AH!
!
BAH! WHY BOTHER WITH THAT ROUNDABOUT RIGMAROLE?!
TMP
TMP
I KNOW HE IS HERE!
TMP
Yes, it has certainly been "boisterous"...
......
......
NOW, I KNOW IT WOULD HARDLY BE UNUSUAL...
BUT ONE MUST WONDER IF YET ANOTHER SQUALL IS BREWING.
OF COURSE THERE IS, MADAM HUDSON!
THAT IS THE WAY OF UNCLE'S WORK.
THE MORE IT STORMS, THE BETTER HE FARES!

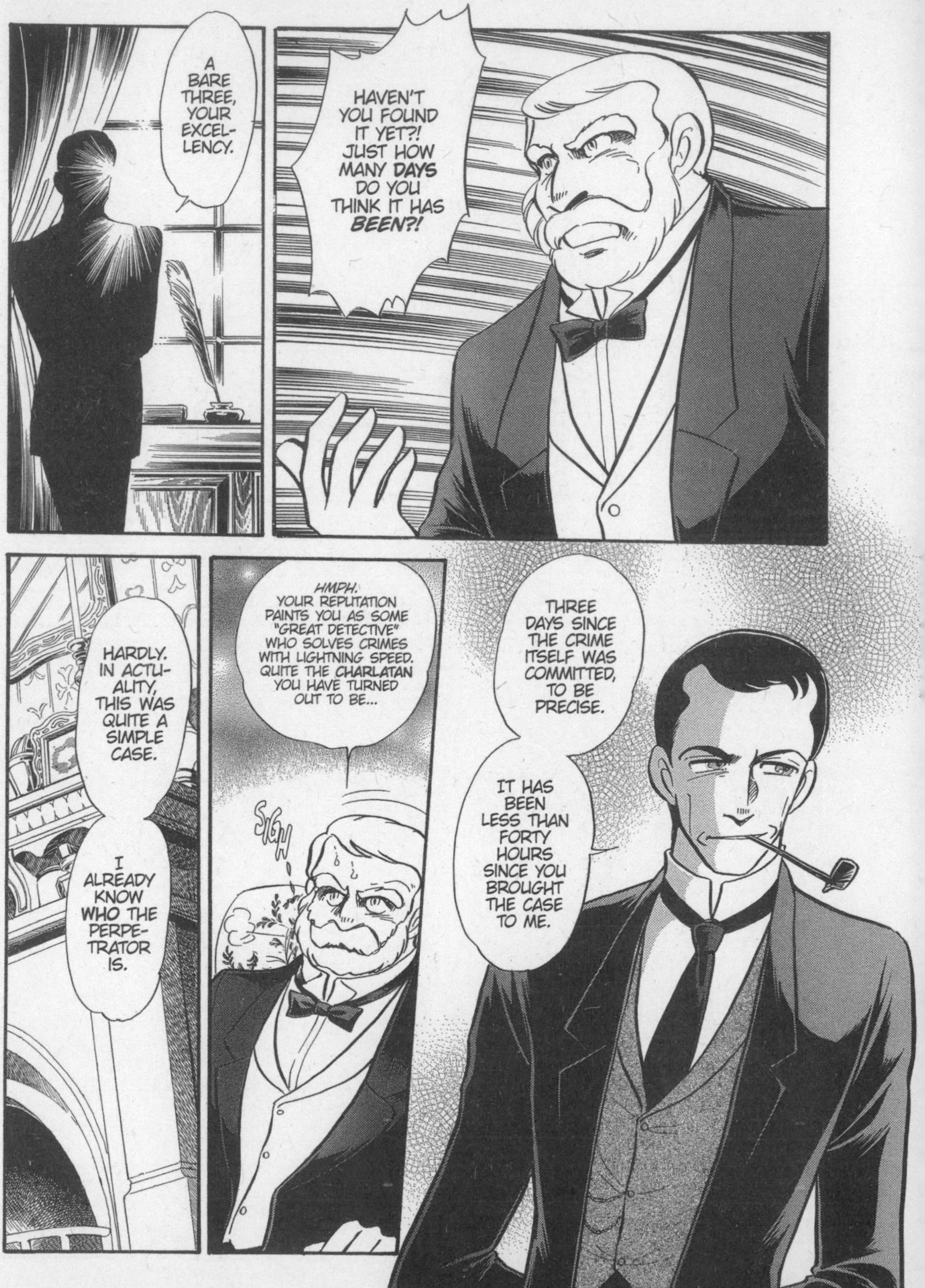
HAVEN'T YOU FOUND IT YET?! JUST HOW MANY **DAYS** DO YOU THINK IT HAS ***BEEN?!***
A BARE THREE, YOUR EXCELLENCY.
THREE DAYS SINCE THE CRIME ITSELF WAS COMMITTED, TO BE PRECISE.
IT HAS BEEN LESS THAN FORTY HOURS SINCE YOU BROUGHT THE CASE TO ME.
HMPH. YOUR REPUTATION PAINTS YOU AS SOME "GREAT DETECTIVE" WHO SOLVES CRIMES WITH LIGHTNING SPEED. QUITE THE CHARLATAN YOU HAVE TURNED OUT TO BE...
SIGH
HARDLY. IN ACTUALITY, THIS WAS QUITE A SIMPLE CASE.
I ALREADY KNOW **WHO** THE PERPETRATOR IS.

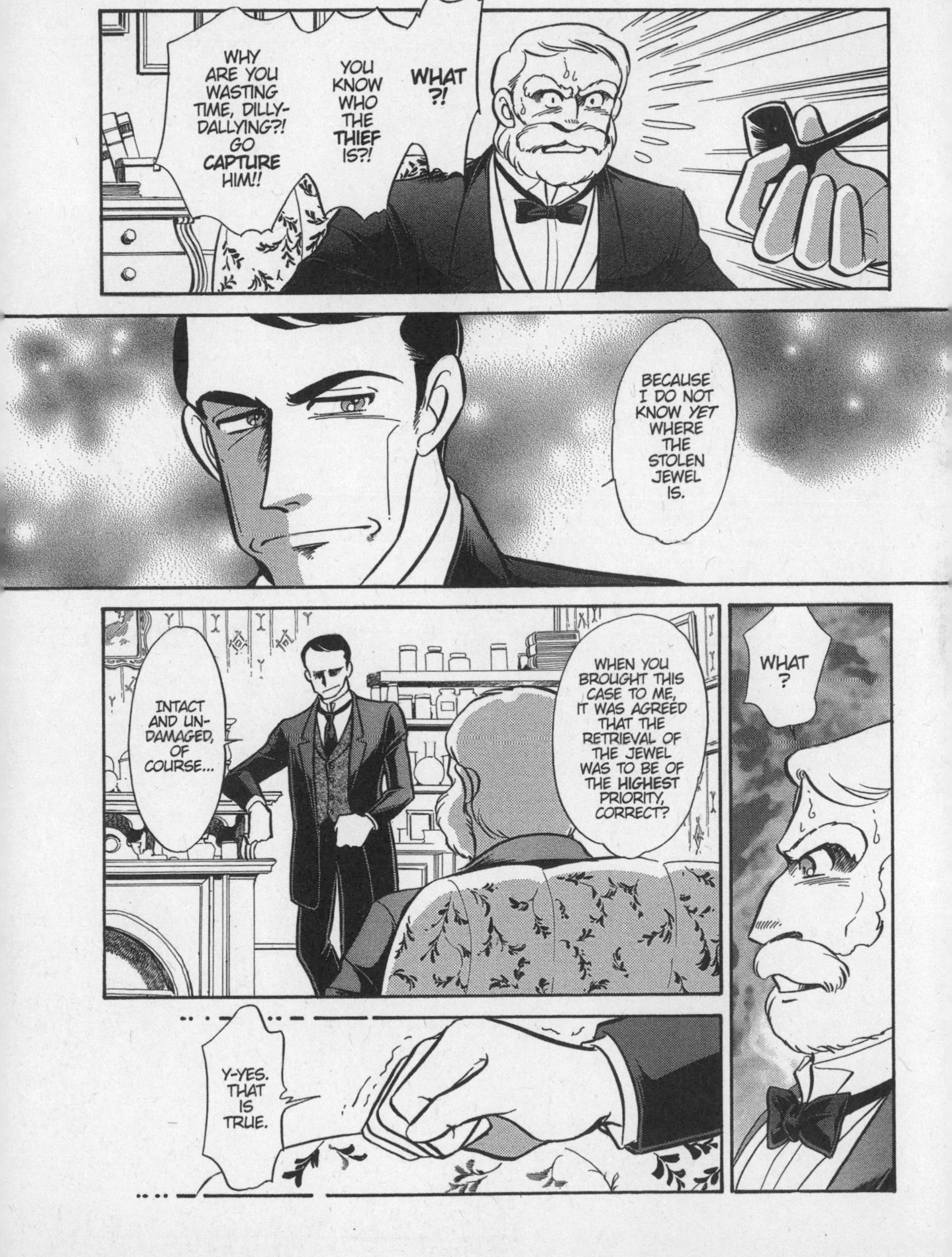
WHAT?!
YOU KNOW WHO THE THIEF IS?!
WHY ARE YOU WASTING TIME, DILLY-DALLYING?! GO CAPTURE HIM!!
BECAUSE I DO NOT KNOW *YET* WHERE THE STOLEN JEWEL IS.
WHAT?
WHEN YOU BROUGHT THIS CASE TO ME, IT WAS AGREED THAT THE RETRIEVAL OF THE JEWEL WAS TO BE OF THE HIGHEST PRIORITY, CORRECT?
INTACT AND UN-DAMAGED, OF COURSE...
Y-YES. THAT IS TRUE.

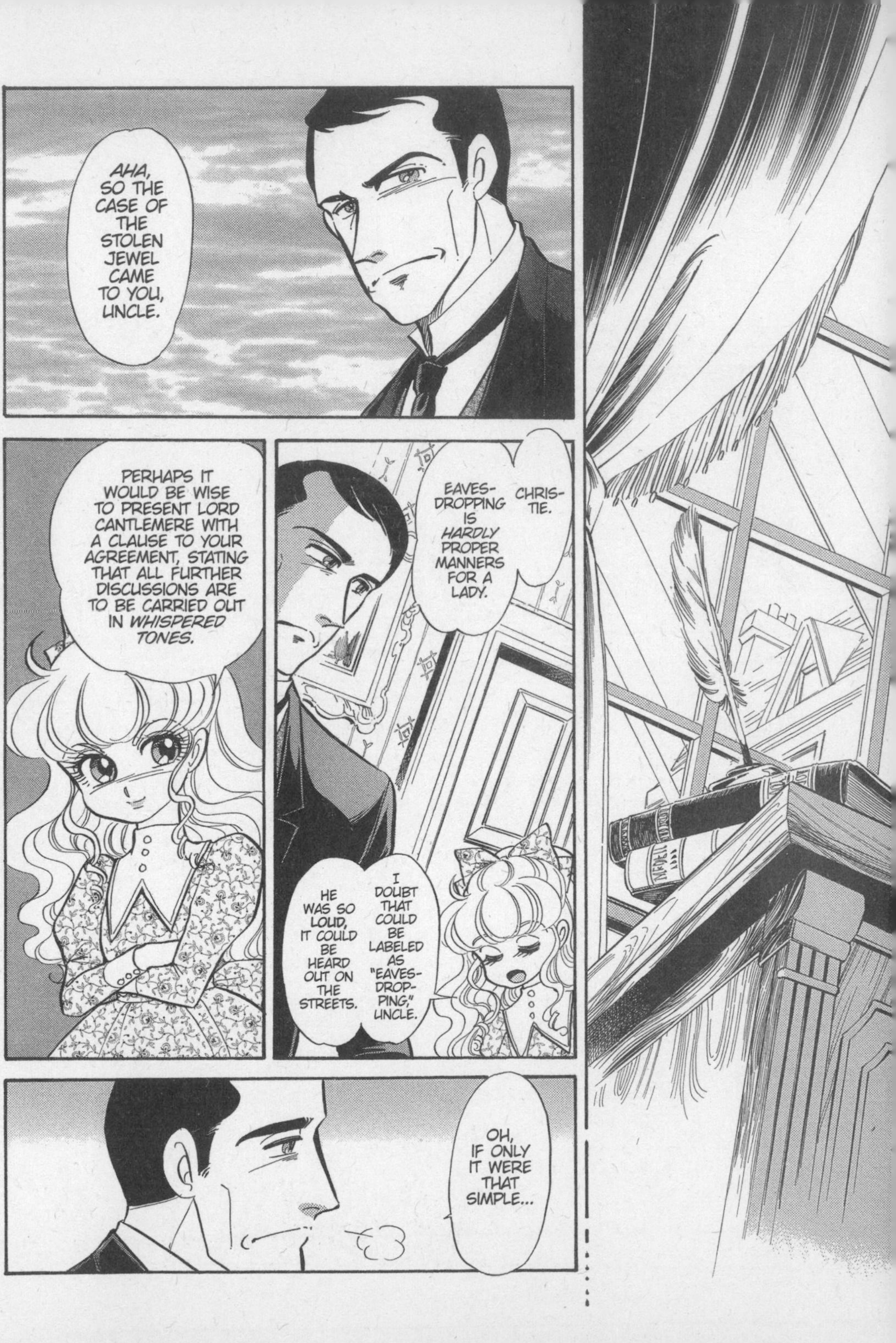
AHA, SO THE CASE OF THE STOLEN JEWEL CAME TO YOU, UNCLE.
CHRISTIE.
EAVESDROPPING IS *HARDLY* PROPER MANNERS FOR A LADY.
I DOUBT THAT COULD BE LABELED AS "EAVESDROPPING," UNCLE.
HE WAS SO LOUD, IT COULD BE HEARD OUT ON THE STREETS.
PERHAPS IT WOULD BE WISE TO PRESENT LORD CANTLEMERE WITH A CLAUSE TO YOUR AGREEMENT, STATING THAT ALL FURTHER DISCUSSIONS ARE TO BE CARRIED OUT IN *WHISPERED TONES.*
OH, IF ONLY IT WERE THAT SIMPLE...

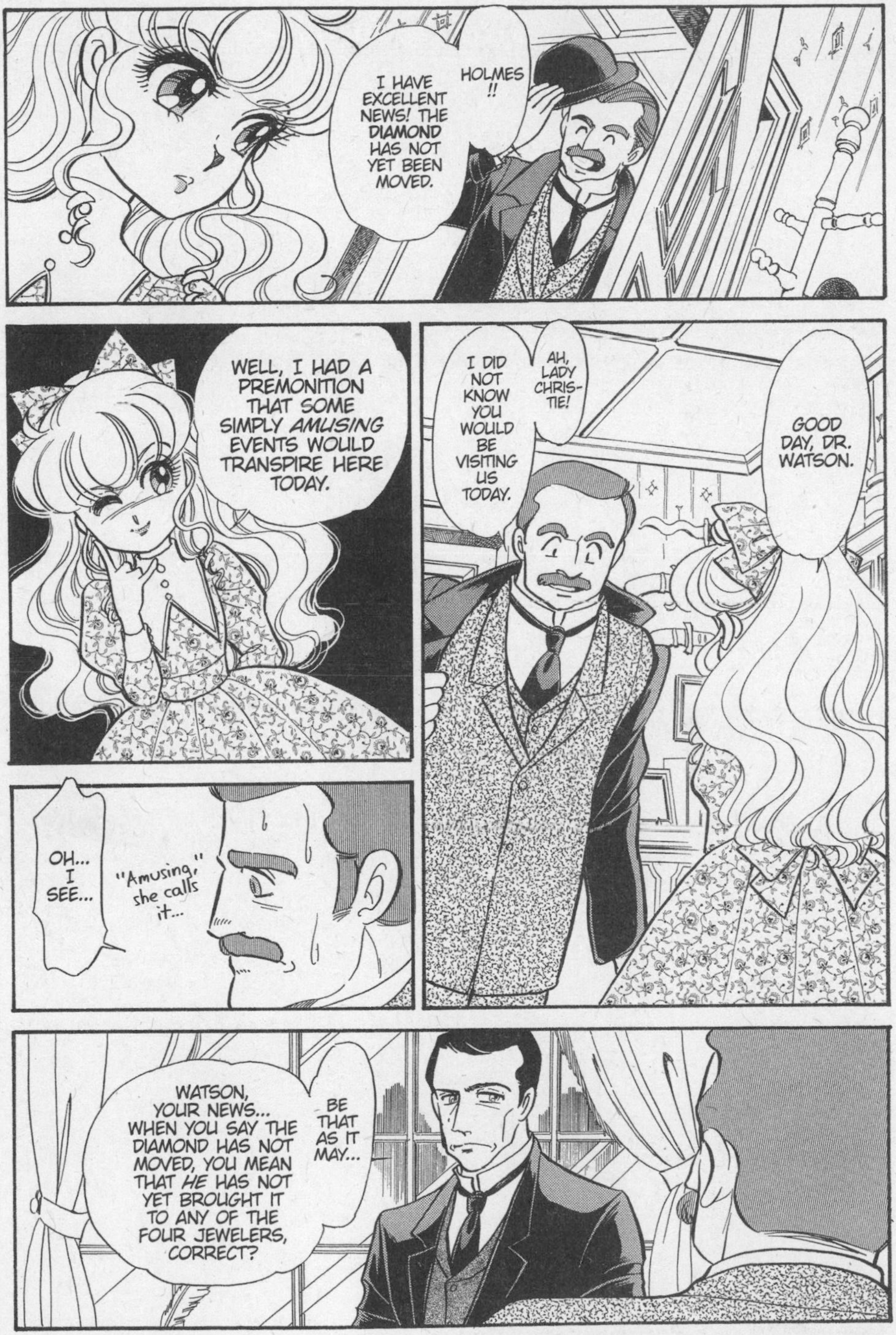
HOLMES !!
I HAVE EXCELLENT NEWS! THE DIAMOND HAS NOT YET BEEN MOVED.
GOOD DAY, DR. WATSON.
AH, LADY CHRISTIE!
I DID NOT KNOW YOU WOULD BE VISITING US TODAY.
WELL, I HAD A PREMONITION THAT SOME SIMPLY *AMUSING* EVENTS WOULD TRANSPIRE HERE TODAY.
OH... I SEE...
"Amusing," she calls it...
BE THAT AS IT MAY...
WATSON, YOUR NEWS... WHEN YOU SAY THE DIAMOND HAS NOT MOVED, YOU MEAN THAT *HE* HAS NOT YET BROUGHT IT TO ANY OF THE FOUR JEWELERS, CORRECT?

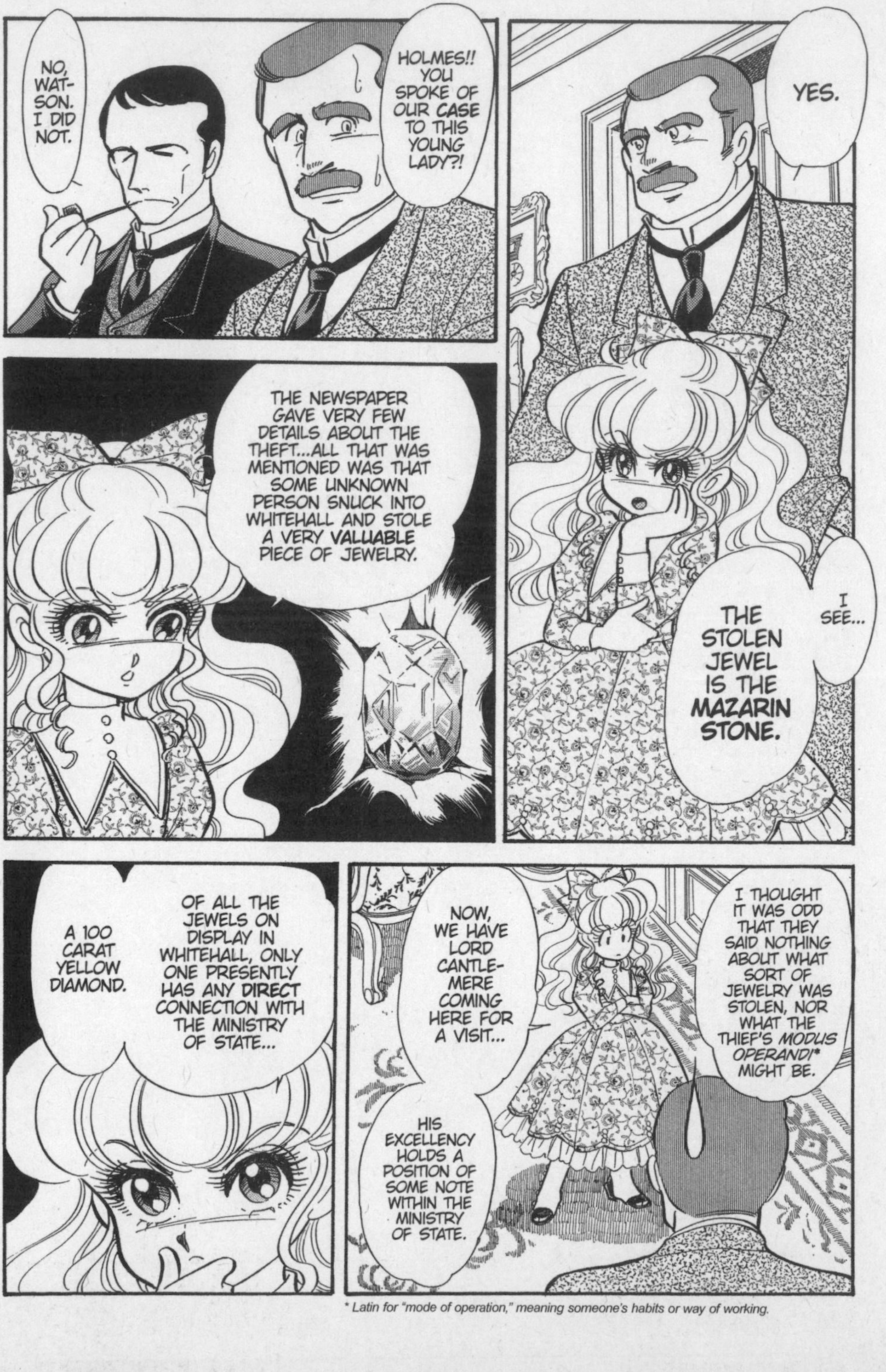
YES.
I SEE...
THE STOLEN JEWEL IS THE MAZARIN STONE.
HOLMES!! YOU SPOKE OF OUR CASE TO THIS YOUNG LADY?!
NO, WATSON. I DID NOT.
THE NEWSPAPER GAVE VERY FEW DETAILS ABOUT THE THEFT...ALL THAT WAS MENTIONED WAS THAT SOME UNKNOWN PERSON SNUCK INTO WHITEHALL AND STOLE A VERY VALUABLE PIECE OF JEWELRY.
I THOUGHT IT WAS ODD THAT THEY SAID NOTHING ABOUT WHAT SORT OF JEWELRY WAS STOLEN, NOR WHAT THE THIEF'S MODUS OPERANDI* MIGHT BE.
NOW, WE HAVE LORD CANTLEMERE COMING HERE FOR A VISIT...
HIS EXCELLENCY HOLDS A POSITION OF SOME NOTE WITHIN THE MINISTRY OF STATE.
OF ALL THE JEWELS ON DISPLAY IN WHITEHALL, ONLY ONE PRESENTLY HAS ANY DIRECT CONNECTION WITH THE MINISTRY OF STATE...
A 100 CARAT YELLOW DIAMOND.

** Latin for "mode of operation," meaning someone's habits or way of working.*

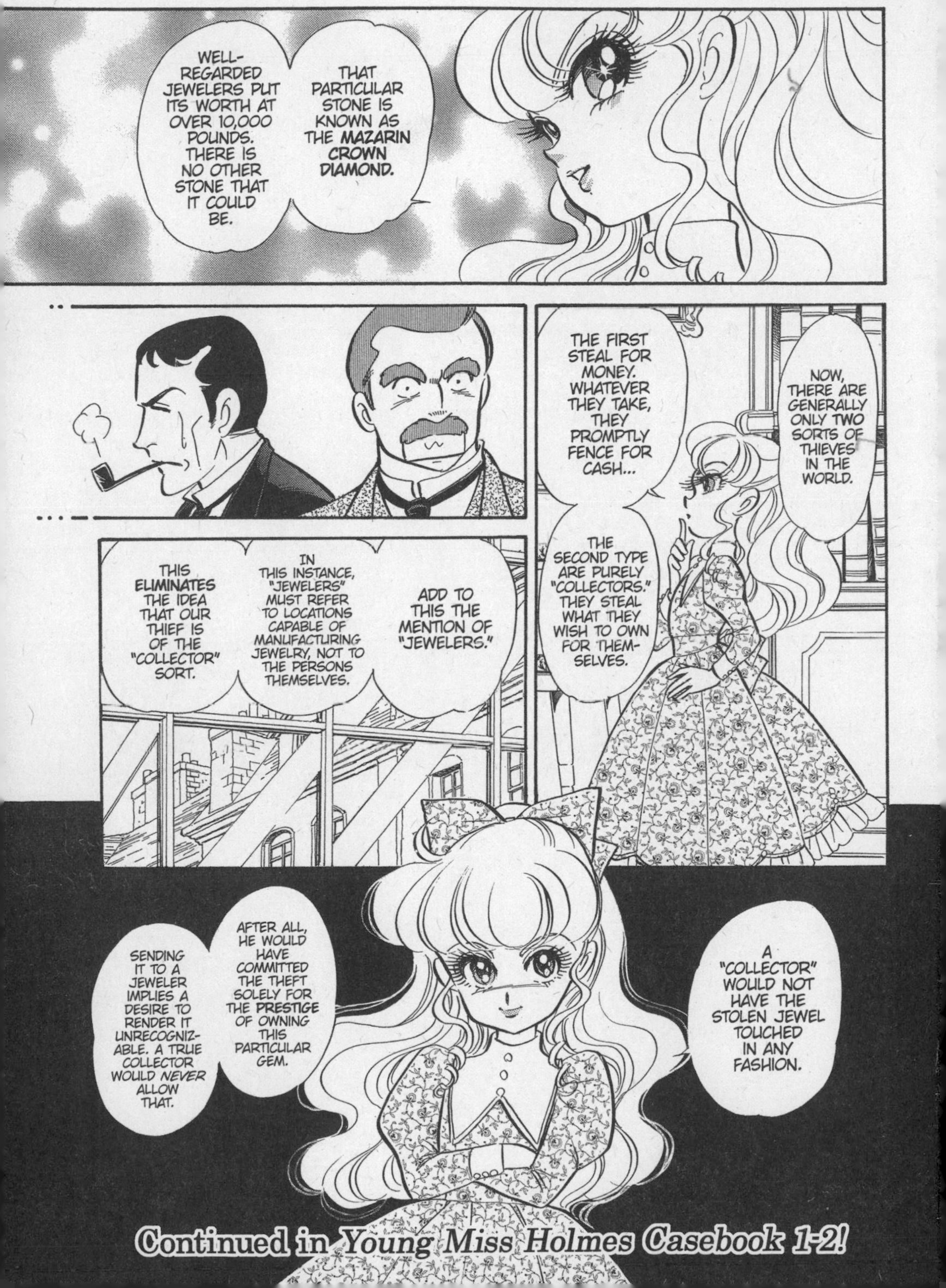
THAT PARTICULAR STONE IS KNOWN AS THE **MAZARIN CROWN DIAMOND.**
WELL-REGARDED JEWELERS PUT ITS WORTH AT OVER 10,000 POUNDS. THERE IS NO OTHER STONE THAT IT COULD BE.
NOW, THERE ARE GENERALLY ONLY TWO SORTS OF THIEVES IN THE WORLD.
THE FIRST STEAL FOR MONEY. WHATEVER THEY TAKE, THEY PROMPTLY FENCE FOR CASH...
THE SECOND TYPE ARE PURELY "COLLECTORS." THEY STEAL WHAT THEY WISH TO OWN FOR THEMSELVES.
ADD TO THIS THE MENTION OF "JEWELERS."
IN THIS INSTANCE, "JEWELERS" MUST REFER TO LOCATIONS CAPABLE OF MANUFACTURING JEWELRY, NOT TO THE PERSONS THEMSELVES.
THIS **ELIMINATES** THE IDEA THAT OUR THIEF IS OF THE "COLLECTOR" SORT.
A "COLLECTOR" WOULD NOT HAVE THE STOLEN JEWEL TOUCHED IN ANY FASHION.
AFTER ALL, HE WOULD HAVE COMMITTED THE THEFT SOLELY FOR THE **PRESTIGE** OF OWNING THIS PARTICULAR GEM.
SENDING IT TO A JEWELER IMPLIES A DESIRE TO RENDER IT UNRECOGNIZABLE. A TRUE COLLECTOR WOULD *NEVER* ALLOW THAT.
Continued in *Young Miss Holmes Casebook 1-2!*